SPACES MAPPED
and MONSTROUS

....

FILM AND CULTURE

FILM AND CULTURE

A series of Columbia University Press

Edited by John Belton

For a complete list of titles, see page 289.

SPACES MAPPED
and MONSTROUS

DIGITAL 3D CINEMA
AND VISUAL CULTURE

NICK JONES

Columbia University Press

New York

Columbia University Press
Publishers Since 1893
New York   Chichester, West Sussex
cup.columbia.edu
Copyright © 2020 Columbia University Press
All rights reserved

A complete CIP record is available from the Library of Congress.
ISBN 978-0-231-19422-8 (cloth : alk. paper)
ISBN 978-0-231-19423-5 (pbk. : alk. paper)
ISBN 978-0-231-55071-0 (e-book)

Columbia University Press books are printed on permanent
and durable acid-free paper.

Printed in the United States of America

Cover image: Courtesy of Photofest/Twentieth Century Fox Film Corporation
Cover design: Lisa Hamm

CONTENTS

ILLUSTRATIONS

ACKNOWLEDGMENTS

This book was made possible by a British Academy Early Career Fellowship awarded in 2015. I am enormously grateful to everyone at the academy for their support, in particular Jack Caswell and Alun Evans for their time and attention.

This project began in the Film Studies Department of Queen Mary University of London, where I received generous encouragement from colleagues, in particular Alasdair King, who was diligent in reading drafts of early chapters and providing invaluable suggestions, and Guy Westwell, who once told me that there might possibly be some mileage in my work on 3D, and that I should give the British Academy a punt. At Queen Mary, I would also like to single out the help offered by Lucy Bolton, Lisa Duffy, Adrian Garvey, Janet Harbord, Alice Pember, Anat Pick, Hollie Price, and Libby Saxton.

The book was finished three short years later in the Department of Theatre, Film, Television, and Interactive Media at the University of York, and I would like to thank my colleagues there for the support they offered, in particular David Barnett, Andrew Higson, Jenna Ng, and Duncan Petrie. Further afield, I am grateful to Phil Wickham and the staff at the Bill Douglas Cinema Museum at the University of Exeter, where a research stipend allowed me to handle a series of stereoscopes and stereocards, an experience valuable to this whole project but particularly chapter 8. Rod Bantjes, Esther Jacopin, Duncan Marshall, Lisa Purse, Miriam Ross, and Ben Woodiwiss also deserve my sincerest thanks. In its final stages, this book benefited greatly from the editorial support of Philip Leventhal at Columbia University Press and the perceptive, reasonable, and supportive comments by anonymous peer reviewers. As ever, errors remain my own.

Laura Mayne deserves special mention, because that's the least I can do after dragging her out in the cold and rain to see a 3D showing of *Aquaman*.

Fragments of this work overall appeared previously as part of the article "'There Never Really Is a Stereoscopic Image': A Closer Look at 3-D Media," in *New Review of Film and Television Studies* 13, no. 2 (2015): 170–88, published by Routledge (in particular portions of chapter 6). A slightly different version of parts of chapter 5 appeared as "Expanding the Esper: Virtualised Spaces of Surveillance in SF Film," in *Science Fiction Film and Television* 9, no. 1 (2016): 1–23, published by Liverpool University Press. My thanks to the editors for granting permission to reprint and expand upon this material here.

SPACES MAPPED and MONSTROUS

INTRODUCTION

This book is about contemporary 3D cinema and its place in visual culture. Exploring the production methodologies of digital 3D filmmaking and the optical peculiarities of its cinematic reception, I place the production and circulation of 3D cinema within a web of aesthetic, technological, and cultural contexts. In this way, I argue that stereoscopic mediation is central to our mappings and representations of space in the twenty-first century. 3D cinema may not be unanimously popular among audiences or critics, but it is firmly entrenched as an exhibition practice and is crucial to the workings of mainstream digital cinema. Even so, the scope of its connections to other technologies and media are often overlooked, as are the uniqueness and strangeness of its inherently distorting experience of space. In the pages that follow, I seek to redress these absences.

Digital film production and 3D cinema might not be entirely synonymous, but they do intersect and overlap in important ways. Both digital cinema and 3D cinema represent a spatialization of the form, a move toward the capture and delivery of totalized spaces rather than the single viewpoint of the photographic camera. Digital technology reads, or maps, space in a certain way, and then generates from these readings virtual recreations of space. We cannot truly understand digital 3D and account for its presence in today's cinematic landscape without addressing the linked development of immersive virtual reality systems, the digitization of all aspects of filmmaking, the rise of globe-spanning telecommunication networks, and the shifting nature of the screen in the new media landscape. Paying attention to these contexts situates digital 3D within a highly technologized set of practices, and so asserts its cutting-edge, computerized form of optics, and its relationships with those state, corporate, and military entities that rely on such optics.

Nevertheless, digital 3D simultaneously seems to run counter to the logics of quantification and simulation that are often thought to define digital media.[1] Rethinking the meaning and function of the screen, 3D cinema is an acutely haptic and embodied media form, an unusual optical illusion that destabilizes distinctions between the observed image and the lived-in space. As such, this is also a book about perception, subjectivity, and the material conditions of stereoscopic media observation. Producing perceptual spaces that are distorted and ephemeral, 3D reworks the way our sight functions in subtle but important ways. Like all stereoscopic media—from "stereo," meaning solid, and "scope," meaning sight—the reception of 3D cinema conjures a palpable perceptual strangeness, a strangeness that is too often either elided in favor of claims of binocular authenticity, or proffered as proof of the format's unworkability. Neither proposition is useful, and the evident distinctiveness of 3D cinema—a distinctiveness aggressively asserted by some films and concealed by others— must be faced head-on in any thorough analysis of both particular 3D films and the wider importance of 3D to digital visual culture more generally.

In the pages that follow, I will explore both digital 3D's rigorous mapping procedures and virtualized creation of simulated spaces as they manifest in its production processes and rhetorics of presentation, as well as the spatial distortions and optical illusions upon which digital 3D relies for its perception. Only by attending to digital 3D through both of these lenses—as a medium that creates spaces that are simultaneously mapped and monstrous—can we fully understand the manner in which space is produced and vision is organized in twenty-first century cinema. In either case, 3D represents a rethinking of how images work and what they are for, and does this to such an extent that, I contend, stereoscopic media are ultimately nonimagistic and so demand new tools for analysis that are not beholden to the existing, planarcentric tools of film analysis. *Spaces Mapped and Monstrous* will accordingly propose a variety of new ways for thinking about 3D's cultural importance and aesthetic particulars, as it not only excavates the history and prehistory of 3D cinema but also maps its technological conditions and distinctive visual attributes.[2]

THE DIGITAL 3D LANDSCAPE

Crucial to this project are theories of both digital cinema and of space. Digital 3D cinema—a term that names any 3D filmmaking and/or 3D projection that employs digital production pipelines and/or exhibition technologies—remains reliant on many preexisting cinematic conventions, including most obviously the traditional cinema screen (albeit a screen now silver-coated, frequently supersized, and in some cases curved).[3] Even so, it functions as part of a broader reconceptualization of screens, spaces, and images in the digital age, with the alignment of digital formats and 3D mediation making 3D into something like a privileged or presumptive modality of the digital.

In suggesting this, I take it that digital technologies conceive of space, vision, and experience in certain delineated ways, ways that 3D is helpful in propagating. Rather than consider digital technology simply as a facilitator for certain tasks or a neutral way of framing the world, it is necessary to admit that across its various manifestations and uses digital mediation forcibly reorganizes the world. This restructuring of space occurs as much in imagination as it does in material reality: our expectations around the makeup and meanings of space are affected by the tendencies for digital tools and process to work in certain ways, while in turn those tools and processes are shaped by our uses of them.[4] In this regard, as the reading and representation of corporeal space by virtual technologies marks a quantitative change in the extent of our abstract *knowledge* of space, so too these processes enact a qualitative change in how we *conceive* of space. Whether or not we use email or own a smartphone, we live in an environment in which digital systems monitor, direct, and (most pertinently) map our lives and actions. These systems may at present be accessed for the most part through the use of flat-screen technologies, but they depend on logics of virtual world simulation that are volumetric and stereoscopic.

3D cinema plays an essential role engendering, documenting, and highlighting this situation. It produces ephemeral three-dimensional environments that emphasize access, manipulability, and interactivity. It thus advertises and extends an already-existing stereoscopic imaginary, as its spaces both visualize and build upon other developments in the recording, rendering, and accessing of digital data. As a technology for the visualization and (re)production of space, digital 3D has important connections with other contemporary technologies, such as global positioning systems (GPS) and laser-based mapping devices; disembodied telecommunication and gaming systems; digital architectural practices and other forms of computer-aided design; proliferating mechanisms of networked surveillance; and augmented reality tools, among many others. Thinking digital 3D through and alongside these technologies places it in the lineage of what Paul Virilio calls "vision machines," and it also situates digital 3D firmly within the contemporary military-industrial-media-entertainment network outlined (albeit in different ways) by James Der Derian and Pasi Väliaho.[5] Indeed, 3D in many ways exemplifies the spatial logics described by those scholars: asserting that space can be instrumental-ized and reproduced as a highly navigable—yet disconcertingly immaterial—environment, digital 3D encapsulates prevailing methods for imagining and producing space in the twenty-first century.

But 3D media of various kinds have a history far beyond the digital era, and what follows is productively informed by scholarship on other 3D technolo-gies such as the nineteenth-century stereoscope and twentieth-century ana-log 3D cinema. These technologies, along with the content designed for them and the various scholarly evaluations of their workings and aesthetics, all help us learn more about stereoscopic visuality. Such a historical view, for instance, reveals aspects of stereoscopic media that have remained stable as it has moved from the nineteenth century to the twenty-first, from Grand Exhibitions and Victorian drawing rooms to the shopping mall and the multiplex. This view also brings to light the particular manner in which digital effects and contem-porary film production methods adapt or disregard historical properties of the 3D medium in ways that make digital 3D cinema distinct from earlier stereoscopic media forms.

This work is urgently called for. Despite the long history and perpetual pres-ence of stereoscopic media in one form or another, it is a method of visual organization little explored within film studies. Work undertaken prior to the digital turn provides valuable insights into the historical conditions and aes-thetic style of 1950s 3D, but in highlighting moments of "emergence," or direct address, and in stressing 3D's momentary, aberrant appearances in mainstream film history, this work can problematically privilege planar cinema as a more stable, lasting, and essentially *cinematic* media form with which 3D cannot suc-cessfully compete.[6] More recent accounts have welcomingly questioned how 3D cinema differs experientially, optically, and aesthetically from planar cin-ema, with the increasing prominence of digital 3D providing impetus to reas-sess and explore cinematic 3D more generally.[7] As Jihoon Kim describes, this fresh academic attention "seems long overdue if we consider [3D] not as a spe-cial effect in the fields of cinema and photography, but as a particular mode of viewing and imagery that has been pervasive throughout the history of mod-ern media technologies and across different forms and platforms."[8]

The expansion of digital 3D alongside the rise of media archaeology also seems apt. As Jussi Parikka outlines, media archaeology is "interested in exca-vating the past in order to understand the present and the future," seeking out a better recognition of "what the newness in 'new media' means."[9] This criti-cal lens thus rejects hype, even as it also ungrounds accepted narratives and teleologies. In the case of 3D, this involves avoiding pejorative statements around what cinema is or should be (2D or 3D?) and probing encrusted ortho-doxies regarding where 3D comes from and why it becomes culturally signifi-cant at certain times and forgotten at others. Jens Schröter has notably rejected any claims that 3D is marginal or peripheral to the visual culture of the mod-ern world by demonstrating its repeated importance since the 1850s.[10] With an eye on the digital era, Thomas Elsaesser has described 3D in relation to what he terms the "logics and genealogies of the image in the twenty-first century," arguing that its contemporary cinematic adoption functions within a wider context of digital technologies that are reshaping "our idea of what an image is and, in the process, changing our sense of spatial and temporal orientation and our embodied relation to data-rich simulated environments."[11]

If I similarly use media archaeological tools to explore the changing nature of the image in digital culture, then I do so with more of an emphasis upon the inherently paradoxical nature of stereoscopic media. While digital 3D com-bines, propagates, and disseminates dominant ideas of vision and space that all focus on abstraction, control, and surveillance, it also offers a unique form of visuality that is entrenched in the haptic, the proximate, and the distorted. However different these visual modes seem—the data-rich, mapped optics of computer vision on one hand, and the distorting, peculiar visuality of stereo-scopic media on the other—I propose that any reading of digital 3D cinema must appreciate how they are simultaneously present and account for the com-plex and intriguing ways in which they coexist.

TECHNIQUES OF THE STEREOSCOPIC OBSERVER

In stereoscopic media, represented content appears not to be situated upon a screen but to extend in front of and recede behind this screen. This requires a duplication of planar visual material. Two images—or, in the case of 3D *cin-ema*, two streams of moving images—are presented simultaneously, and the vision of the observer is manipulated such that each eye sees only one of these images (or image streams). This paired material contains minor differences evoking the divergent views one gains from the left and right eyes (thanks to human eyes being just over two inches apart). The fusion of these images by the viewer's perceptual system creates an impression of spatial depth. Hope-fully most readers have experienced some form of 3D media, although it has been suggested that between 3 and 15 percent of people are stereoblind or oth-erwise stereo-impaired.[12] Presently, 3D can be manufactured in a cinematic context either through the "native" capture of twinned image streams during production or through the use of digital visual effects tools in postproduction (called "conversion" in these pages, but sometimes also referred to as "post-conversion" or, more rarely, "dimensionalization").

Competing taste cultures circulate around 3D cinema. Most unhelpful among these is the tout court objection to 3D on the grounds that it is unnecessary, or fundamentally uncinematic. Perhaps this objection is nuanced with the grudging admission that 3D "works" in some cases, but only some: big-budget effects cinema, say, or in the hands of validated auteurs like Alfred Hitchcock, Martin Scorsese, or Werner Herzog (see chapter 1). In a separate but linked discourse, converted 3D might be attacked or dismissed as somehow "fake" in comparison with "genuine" (and thus more artistically validated) native 3D shooting (see chapter 5). However, this book will decisively not propagate criterions of value around 3D production methods, genres, or directors; it will not critically evaluate the worth of one 3D film over another; and it will certainly not proclaim the ways in which 3D *should* or *should not* be used by practitioners. I eschew such categorizations, qualitative appraisals, and stylistic declarations in order to facilitate an approach to 3D cinema that treats it holistically as a distinctive mode of representing space. We must avoid seeing 3D as an alternative to or a variation upon a more established, more critically acceptable planar cinema. To do this it is necessary to dismantle many presumptions around this exhibition format, with its far from unblemished critical reputation, problematic association with commercialism, and deeply complicated relationship with realism and verisimilitude. This will open up ,avenues for an understanding of 3D cinema as and for itself and allow us to better comprehend how it functions within the contemporary digital media landscape.

Such work demands a detailed consideration of 3D's distinct visuality, and in treating 3D as a unique optical experience I pick up and seek to extend Jonathan Crary's interpretation of stereoscopy. In *Techniques of the Observer: On Vision and Modernity in the Nineteenth Century* (1990), Crary investigates nineteenth-century visual technologies and discourses, and shows how these point to a shift in optical knowledge that produced a new and distinctly modern observer.[13] As his influential archaeology of media devices and debates indicates, knowledge was at this time reorganized and social practices radically altered by new forms of vision, forms that modified "the productive, cognitive, and desiring capacities of the human subject" in numerous ways (2–3). This subject, meanwhile, was itself "made adequate to a constellation of new events, forces, and institutions that together are loosely and perhaps tautologically definable as 'modernity'" (9). Crary considers the harnessing of stereopsis to be a crucial part of this reorganization of vision. Binocularity and stereopsis—the fusing of right and left eye views by the brain—became the focus of scientific study in the 1830s, their key principles disseminated to the broader social sphere in the 1850s through the popularization of the stereoscope (a process I describe in more detail in chapter 1). This device provided users with a three-dimensional impression from two-dimensional source material. The aesthetic traits of the stereoscope—its highly subjective and embodied visuality—helped to shatter ideas of an objectively observed external world (127). Apart from the somewhat notable exception of photography, Crary proposes that the stereoscope is "the most significant form of visual imagery in the nineteenth century," as it signifies a shift from geometrical optics (associated with the camera obscura, perspective, and photography) to a subjective kind of physiological optics dependent on the vagaries and perceptual instabilities of embodied vision (116).

Crary's insights around this device, and in particular his concise description of stereoscopic media as essentially nonimagistic, will be expanded upon in what follows. His work, along with that of a range of other media scholars, will help me contextualize and think through not only stereoscopic technologies but also the unique aesthetic of stereoscopic media. So while I assert the importance of 3D to digital visual culture, this is not to relegate the longer history of 3D to irrelevance. 3D media have consistent properties, the meanings of which nonetheless shift in a digital age. After all, as Crary himself proposes, an even more profound "transformation in the nature of visuality" than that which occurred in the 1830s might well be underway today as a result of new digital technologies that relocate vision "to a plane severed from a human observer" and recode it as abstract data (1). In the decades since Crary's writing, this seems to have been borne out, and I focus on this theme of digital transformation in chapters 2, 3, 4, and 5.

Crary's model of an epistemological fissure in techniques of observation has been disputed. He admits that "familiar modes of 'seeing' will persist and coexist uneasily" with newer forms (2), but such words underplay the apparent faltering of physiological optics (as represented by the stereoscope) in contrast to the ongoing vitality of planar, geometrical optics. Stereoscopic media have moved in and out of public consciousness for more than a century and a half, 3D cinema in particular seeming on the surface to appear and disappear in "waves" from the 1940s onward. If the marshalling of stereoscopic visuality hailed a new visual regime, then why has the place of stereoscopic media on the public stage been so erratic? If the stereoscope became unpopular thanks to the rise of photography as Crary suggests, then how is this reconcilable with his claim that the former was emblematic of a newly dominant form of vision (133)? A solution lies in considering the media landscape as varied and multi-faceted—as Schröter argues, multiple forms of "optics" can be copresent at any time, with stereoscopy's physiological optics existing alongside and in dialogue with geometric optics in both entertainment and operational contexts (such as scientific and military imaging).[14] In the words of Rod Bantjes, there "cannot have been a crisis of the observer in the 1840s because neither the eighteenth century nor the late nineteenth century was organized as a coherent and distinct episteme in the way that Crary suggests," and the same is no doubt true today.[15]

Nonetheless, Crary's point that particular periods have their own historically constituted modes of observation, and specifically that we can understand these by interrogating optical technologies and their functioning, is well taken. His concept of the observer, for all its difficulties, helps us read visual technologies as something other than methods to improve mimetic representation—as artistic problem-solving[16]—or as the result of sustained corporate sponsorship and the commodification of attention—as ways of organizing the "attention economy"—even if these themes also have their place in critical analysis.[17] For Crary, "what determines vision at any given historical moment is not some deep structure, economic base, or world view, but rather the functioning of a collective assemblage of disparate parts on a single social surface" (6). Throughout this book, I similarly propose that an analysis of digital 3D might be a useful way of discussing the contemporary shape of this wider assemblage, as well as the contours of its concurrent social surface.

Digital 3D cinema may be just one aspect of contemporary representation and its emerging and dominant technologies, but it reveals many converging approaches to vision in the twenty-first century, particularly what forms of space are created and presupposed by certain forms of seeing (and vice versa). Indeed, the distinctive way of recording and re-presenting space found in any given media technology reveals important ideas around space, technology, and media in any given historical moment, ideas often rendered invisible through normalization (see chapter 2). As the philosopher and sociologist of spatiality Henri Lefebvre argues, space, for all its seeming neutrality, is always a production of some sort, a production that encapsulates and propagates assumptions around what space is for and how it can be used.[18] And if the social relations and power dynamics of space might be rendered invisible through cultural ubiquity, so too the visual depiction of space is always imbued with social meaning and structures of power both assumed and asserted. As productions of (visual) space, then, mainstream media need to be explored for how they conceive of space and what they consider space to be for. This work can then extend to consider those wider changes in our imagination of space that have occurred in recent decades, of which digital 3D is a trace, catalyst, and emblem.

Digital 3D cinema, then, is not only a particular kind of "optics" but produces very particular spaces and spatial experiences, and these are highly unlike those of 2D cinema. For Akira Mizuta Lippit, 3D differs from 2D to such an extent that they are effectively antitheses of one another: the former is not only a "voluminous supercinema," but a "form of anti-cinema."[19] Though such a claim may be disputed given the close alignment of 2D and 3D in the twenty-first-century cinematic landscape (Lippit writes in the late 1990s), it helpfully asserts the radical difference of 3D. And if 3D *is* so different, then this difference is spatial; not merely the addition of plenitude in the form of another dimension, but a deeper, more unstable, less easily articulated alternative kind of space that is nonetheless folded within planar cinematic language.

Further to this comparison with 2D cinema, 3D also diverges in powerful ways from everyday vision. The neutral documentation of material reality by any medium is of course an impossibility, and any proposal to the contrary is a fallacy built on idea(l)s of verisimilitude and technological determinism (the vaunted capacity for the latest style or technology to do a better job at documenting "reality" than previous styles and technologies). 3D is just as likely as other cinematic technologies to prompt such statements: it has been described as a cinematic revolution in the same vein as the application of synchronized sound in the late 1920s or the comprehensive take-up of color film stock in the mid-twentieth century—in other words, as yet another milestone on the road to a fully mimetic cinema. This fits a pattern whereby technological innovations are sold through the invocation of greater realism, even if the attention paid to the generation of this realism paradoxically turns it into a form of spectacle.[20] In the case of 3D, arguments are often made that, since human vision is binocular, stereoscopic cinema more accurately reflects real-life perceptual conditions than does planar cinema, providing "simply a more realistic, more natural approximation of how we experience life."[21] However, stereoscopic 3D offers viewers nothing like real-life perception, and it is exactly the divergences between the two which endow stereoscopic visuality with its peculiar aesthetic.

André Bazin comes to this realization across two pieces on mid-century 3D cinema. In 1952, the beginning of the boom in US analogue 3D film production, this prominent film theorist proposed that 3D might offer a step toward a "total cinema" that entirely recreates reality; yet in an article published just the following year he has somewhat changed his mind, asserting that objects represented stereoscopically exist in a "ghastly or impalpable state," appearing within an "unreal, unapproachable world."[22] While the embodied vision we experience when interacting with material space does rely upon binocular cues, 3D stimulates these in a very different manner than everyday spatial perception. A viewer of stereoscopic cinema perceives purely *optical* stimuli as relational and volumetric, as both optical *and spatial*. This results in the creation of an unreal, supraoptical environment. For this reason, stereoscopic content has both a palpable materiality as well as a palpable immateriality, the former related to its seeming affinity with everyday binocular spatial perception, the latter to its felt illusionistic quality. Viewers perceive space, but this space is constructed from images alone, even if it supersedes these images. This illusionism, a just-tangible kind of visual strangeness, is the result of the abnormal perceptual work performed by the viewer. While some planar cinema may be thought to invoke these ideas (particularly films involving special photographic or digital effects), this is a far cry from stereoscopy media's production of phantasmagorical, distorted, subjective, and ephemeral spaces. Instead of taking this perceptual monstrousness as evidence that 3D is not a viable or appropriate method of cinematic representation, this book will investigate not only 3D's connections with digital technologies of mapping and quantification, but also the "ghastly, unapproachable world" that it creates.

OVERVIEW

This book is divided into three parts: 1) "Contexts," 2) "Mapped Spaces," and 3) "Monstrous Spaces." The first part covers theoretical terrain crucial to the project. Chapter 1 outlines the history of stereoscopic media, from the nineteenth-century stereoscope to the 3D films of the twentieth century and beyond. In the process, I describe how stereoscopy has been approached by scholars and critics, highlighting how existing accounts of 3D cinema often position it as an alternative to or augmentation of a more fundamental, more acceptable planar cinema. Chapter 2 then broadens this theoretical landscape, introducing Erwin Panofsky's concept of the "symbolic form" and other accounts of perspectival art, reading these alongside explorations of digital cinema by the likes of Sean Cubitt and David Rodowick. This work stresses the links between perspective, capitalism, strategies of spatial control, and digital 3D.

Part 2, "Mapped Spaces," introduces film analysis and focuses in particular upon the production techniques of contemporary 3D cinema and how these influence the aesthetics, address, and themes of 3D films.[23] The three chapters here interpret digital 3D as a kind of operational media that relies upon visual nominalism, and they explore a range of other technologies that function in similar ways. Like perspectival art, the spaces of digital 3D abstract subjective optical experience to create a rationalized, homogenous space that is Euclidean in nature. In privileging this aspect of 3D, this part of the book effectively agrees with Rosalind Krauss that "stereographic space is perspectival space raised to a higher power."[24]

Chapter 3 explores the extraction of form from matter that occurs in this amplification and proposes that simulation is a key conceptual framework for interpreting 3D space. In this context, *Avatar* (2009) is shown to present a mise en abyme of stereoscopic technology and matterless reality, keenly demonstrating the links between 3D's immaterial spatial productions and the simulationist logic of military planning. Chapter 4 looks at immersion and 3D, indicating how digital 3D cinema is part of a broader effort to provide audiences and computer users perceptual access to the imagined spaces of digital networks. Operating alongside technologies like augmented reality (AR) and virtual reality (VR), 3D cinema envisions the world as a volumetric dataspace, an interpretation revealed by scenes of holographic displays across various 3D films. Chapter 5 then connects digital 3D production tools to contemporary practices of surveillance, interpreting the mapping and virtualization of space undertaken by 3D conversion as innately surveillant in nature.

Yet this is not the entire story. Even though digital 3D is undergirded by mathematical logics, this stereoscopic visuality is very different from perspectival geometry and the monocular, stable visual field that perspective creates. 3D is not planar cinema, nor is it the embodied vision of psychophysiological space.[25] As a third category of perceptual experience, the uniqueness of stereoscopic media necessitates a deeper understanding of what exactly makes them unique and how this manifests within specific textual examples. I here label the space produced by 3D cinema "monstrous" because it reorganizes the expected optical situations of both planar cinema and everyday perception.[26] So while the logic of perspective was embedded in the foundations of part 2, the concept of anamorphosis haunts part 3. Like anamorphosis—a form of perspectival rendering that nonetheless radically unsettles the spatial representations and visual presumptions of perspective—3D visuality may rely in its *production* on processes of mapping, abstraction, and surveillance, but its *reception* reconfigures these in a manner that can defamiliarize the act of cinematic spectatorship and visual observation in general. As will be shown, the distorting traits of stereoscopic media have been remarked upon since the creation of the stereoscope and remain vitally important in understanding the optical conditions of 3D cinema. Accordingly, the three chapters in this part of the book turn to theoretical accounts of stereoscopic visuality taken from a range of contexts, and use these to explore how these might apply digital 3D cinema.

Chapter 6 examines how 3D media defamiliarize the screen, relying as they do upon a latent continuum of perceptual space in front of and behind this screen. I demonstrate the presence—and strangeness—of this continuum through an exploration of depth-racking (a visual effect that realigns space in odd and unique ways) and artifacts like lens flare (which coagulate the potential space of 3D while still retaining aesthetics associated with planar capture and exhibition). Chapter 7 then uses critical work on the stereoscope's haptic qualities to think through the ways in which 3D offers significantly distorted spaces. I compare *Goodbye to Language* (2014) and *Clash of the Titans* (2010) to reveal the range and effects of these distortions, and how stereoscopic space is a malleable, creative construct. Finally, chapter 8 investigates what is usually considered a defect of 3D—namely, its tendency toward miniaturization—and connects this with simultaneous and linked sensations of closeness or intimacy. Description of the stereoscopic scalar play in various films gives way to an extended analysis of *Love* (2015), a film that acutely investigates erotic, cinematic, and stereoscopic intimacy.

This journey through the last several years of digital 3D filmmaking—a journey that begins with a quarter-billion-dollar effects film trumpeting the cutting-edge technology of 3D and its key place within a corporatized and militarized media culture and ends with a small and sexually explicit melodrama highlighting the limits and melancholic nostalgia of 3D's intimate aesthetics—will show how digital 3D is a medium of measurement, simulation, mapping, and surveillance, while it is also a medium that relies upon illusionistic, embodied, intimate, and above all distorted and distorting sensations of space and vision. Instead of understanding these potentially alternative models of digital 3D content as mutually exclusive aesthetic or formal modes that compete with one another, the conclusion of this book reiterates the argument made throughout that the mapped and the monstrous are inevitably copresent.[27]

Such a co-constitutive interpretation of 3D poses critical challenges, requiring us to appreciate vision not as a sequential series of optical approaches through history but as an evolving palimpsest of different perceptual modes.[28] To consider digital 3D as either an emblem of the rigorously ordering logics of digital image processing, or as an ephemeral, embodied, and slippery form of haptic visuality, would each on their own be insufficient. It is necessary instead to see 3D as being both at the same time. Like a set of twinned stereoscopic pairs, it is only by looking at each of these perspectives on contemporary 3D simultaneously, with one eye on each as it were, that we will be able to discern in depth its cultural importance and unique aesthetic traits.

PART 1

CONTEXTS

D igital 3D is positioned by studio marketing depart-
ments, trade publications, and technological commentary as an innovative, cutting-edge, future-oriented
mode of exhibition. The purpose of the first two chapters of *Spaces
Mapped and Monstrous* is to plug 3D cinema back into several contexts
that can be marginalized in such a procedure. As I argue, in order to
understand this commercial cinema exhibition format it is necessary
to interrogate the longer history of 3D, and the relationship of 3D visuality to histories of planar visuality and contemporary digital media.
This contextualization usefully expands the critical frames of reference
for digital 3D beyond the current historical moment and the specific
medium of cinema.

To aid its function as a key part of the economy of technological
advancement that defines blockbuster cinema, digital 3D works to extri-
cate itself from a longer history of stereoscopic media. Chapter 1 returns
to this history in order to reveal that stereoscopic media have always
existed in an uneasy relation with more dominant, planar media, and
also how 3D cinema has always been capable of the kind of unusual
effects that will be discussed in part 3 of this book. Similarly, examining
the relationship of stereoscopic media to other forms of visualization,
past and present, is helpful in articulating the specific place of 3D cinema
in today's visual culture. Chapter 2 accordingly considers 3D's relationship to planar art and digital media, doing so to indicate the extent to
which contemporary 3D cinema is a key part of digital visual culture.

1

HISTORY

· ·

The Long View of 3D Film and Theory

I ndustrial presences frequently downplay or elide the existence, prominence, and popularity of stereoscopic media prior to the twenty-first century, framing (digital) 3D as pioneering and cutting-edge in order to excite audiences and justify ticket surcharges. Although retro or arcane technologies and media might have extensive (and potentially profitable) after-lives, 3D's present use is predicated on a presumption that it is as advanced as the latest smartphone or a new software update. Despite the fact that stereoscopic media have existed in some form or another since the 1830s, any disclosure of this lineage dangerously infers that 3D cinema "went away" and has now "returned," a trajectory that can easily suggest failure, or at least a lack of freshness.

This industrial emphasis on digital 3D's future-orientation has been challenged by those who aim to "uncover" the longer history of 3D and so often debunk aspirational assertions around the format's current use. For instance, Anthony Lane, Mark Kermode, and Thomas Doherty all use 3D's long history to discredit its claims of newness.[1] This longer history incriminates the medium—they find in this lineage films of low critical repute like *Bwana Devil* (1952), *The Stewardesses* (1969), and *Jaws 3-D* (1983), which they variously argue to be emblematic of their respective 3D "waves" (in the early 1950s, early 1970s, and mid-1980s), brief swells of empty spectacle and cynically commercial novelty that crested and then seemingly vanished. For these writers, the apparently transitory adoption of 3D in the mainstream at these earlier moments justifies the medium's critical denigration and broad dismissal. This dismissal is undergirded by a presumption that, since 3D did not install itself as a de facto part of filmmaking at any time in the twentieth century, whatever aesthetic effects it may offer are supplementary to cinema's essential workings. This is to implicitly read 3D through André Bazin's influential idea of "total cinema," and to find it wanting.[2] That is, if 3D was required for cinema's narrative or representational operations, then it would have been gratefully received and widely adopted at the earliest technological opportunity. Yet, unlike new techniques for exhibition such as synchronized sound and color photography, 3D projection has taken well over a hundred years to become standard industry practice, and even now it is often thought to face an at best uncertain future.[3] For many, 3D occupies a place outside the teleological narrative of cinema technology; as Akira Mizuta Lippit puts it, the "history of 3D cinema is remarkable for its ahistoricity," erupting as it does in "amnesiac stutters and lapses," being always "at once past and still to come."[4]

It is vital to counter this amnesia, addressing the long but submerged pervasiveness of 3D and challenging presumptions that it only appears fleetingly and failingly. Part of media culture for nearly two hundred years, the standard model of commercial boom periods and isolated waves of adoption is only half the story and highlights those moments when 3D filmmaking asserted itself within public consciousness while downplaying or ignoring 3D's proven persistent presence beyond them.[5] Such exclusions denounce 3D as commercial trend and industrial fad and so close down analysis outside of these limited parameters. The widespread adoption of digital 3D cinema following 2010 forces a reconsideration of this "ahistorical" history.

This chapter will accordingly provide a brief overview of stereoscopic media's centuries-long existence. Initially, I will explore the first apparatus of stereoscopic exhibition, the stereoscope. Various theories regarding stereoscopic perception will be introduced here, to be picked up and interrogated more comprehensively in later chapters. Following this, I will outline in some detail the manner in which film studies has historically dealt with 3D cinema and will combine this overview with a brief summary of 3D filmmaking in the 1950s, the period upon which much of this scholarship focuses. I will concentrate on readings that consider 3D as a momentary and disruptive interruption, a brief special effect that does not successfully cohere with its surrounding text. Constructing a dichotomous model in which 3D's very "3D-ness" seems to prevent it from being used in the service of narrative cinema, this work can be helpful, but it also threatens to limit our understanding of the distinctive aesthetics and spatial productions of stereoscopic cinema.[6]

The chapter then ends with a discussion of how this schismatic earlier work continues to influence scholarly thinking around digital 3D.

THE STEREOSCOPE
· ·

Investigations into stereoscopy were part of a broader interest in subjective vision in the 1820s and 1830s. As human physiology and anatomy came under greater scrutiny in the nineteenth century, the doubled nature of human sight and the ways this was reconciled into a coherent visual field could not be ignored or treated as trivial curiosity. The stereoscope mobilized and focused arising debates regarding the perception of space through binocular vision. As Nicholas Wade describes, the apparatus "opened a completely novel area of endeavour for visual scientists—stereoscopic depth perception—and this has proved to be one of the most enduring topics of empirical and theoretical enquiry in vision."[7] Yet even though the stereoscope provided radical new optical experiences and helped uncover the workings of binocular physiology in an enormously influential manner, it did not provide unanimously accepted concrete truths.[8] Furthermore, in its movement into the commercial sector, the very meanings the device and its spatial depictions carried underwent a profound change.

The principles of binocularity upon which stereoscopic media rely were described by Sir Charles Wheatstone in an 1838 paper to the Royal Society in London (based on earlier research from 1832). An English scientist also intensely interested in electronics and acoustics, Wheatstone's investigations into optics led him to design and build the mirror stereoscope, a device that split vision using angled mirrors, presenting different images to the left and right eyes. As made clear by Wheatstone's extensive account of this device in his *Scientific Papers* (1879), his primary purpose was to investigate the physiology of optical perception. He suggested that this project was prompted at least in part by his attempts to discover why pictorial representations of nearby solid objects were not "faithful representations"—that is, why such images always somehow lacked realism.[9] Placing an object a few inches from one's face and covering each eye in turn revealed that the left and right eyes discern proximate objects slightly differently: the left eye has a fuller view of the left-hand side of the object than the right eye, and vice versa. These dissimilarities exist only in space and cannot be replicated in a single image upon a plane; as a result, a painted representation cannot "be confounded with the solid object."[10] Wheatstone's mirror stereoscope aggressively divided an observer's vision, using mirrored planes to angle the view of each eye away from the other; these bisected viewing angles then met pairs of abstracted artistic renderings of nearby objects, their differences mimicking the differences between left- and right-eye views. The simple shapes—cubes, lines, patterned circles—allowed the user to clearly discern the resulting generation of depth cues. Two paired, split images of one square inside another square with lines connecting the corner of each shape to the other became, when observed through the mirrored apparatus, a shape: a single receding box into which the user seemed to be peering. Two flat pictures appeared to become a deep space.

Wheatstone thus demonstrated that our own cognitive operations provide information about depth and shape through the perceptual convergence of the slightly divergent visual material received by each eye. This phenomenon of binocular disparity operates only at relatively close distances, since the further away an object, the less disparity between the views of it that are seen by each eye. In this way Wheatstone showed that monocular, pictorial representations of close-by subjects necessarily lack the dimensions that would otherwise be associated with them. Far from merely academic, Wheatstone's work seemed to challenge accepted ideas about how human beings perceive the world. The stereoscope divulged the inescapable subjectivity of vision, in the process undermining previous models built on the presumption of perceptual stability. The stereoscope user was presented with a world already "fragmented into *two* nonidentical models" from which they reconstituted dimensions that were not initially apparent.[11] Tricking our perceptual equipment in this way underlines how we are not passive receivers of sense data, and shows that vision and cognitive activity interpret and assemble the world we experience.

For Crary, this makes the stereoscope a different kind of optics to the camera obscura and other planar representational media. Divorcing the act of observation from the reference point of the objective world, the mirror stereoscope eradicated "'the point of view' around which, for several centuries, meanings had been assigned reciprocally to an observer and the object of his or her vision."[12] If we could be made to see a single, dimensional shape from the stimuli of two radically divorced and manipulated sightlines, then how else might our sight be misleading us? An "instrument for phenomenological interrogation and the study of the vagaries of vision,"[13] Wheatstone's mirror stereoscope literally dismantled binocular sight in order to question its operation, thus exposing "the strange and epistemologically dubious way that we *construct* the real in 'natural vision.'"[14]

Wheatstone would claim that his discoveries around binocular dissimilarity and our perception of depth were entirely new insights, although some of his contemporaries suggested otherwise.[15] In either case, the operationalization of this work signifies an important shift in thinking around perception. The mirror stereoscope was certainly the first technical demonstration of the phenomenon under discussion—and, crucially, it was a device designed specifically for technical demonstration, with its large size and logistical intricacy clearly making it a piece of laboratory equipment. This was entirely in keeping with Wheatstone's intentions and his scientific exploration of "the indeterminate nature of vision itself," an exploration that need not produce an appealing, accessible, or portable way of exhibiting stereoscopic content.[16] However, several years after Wheatstone's initial experiments, Scottish physicist Sir David Brewster designed a more popular version of the stereoscope using angled lenses or prisms to keep the left and right eye views separate (unlike Wheatstone's mirrors). These semilenses also magnified the images, allowing Brewster's stereoscope to be smaller and thus portable—Brewster's stereoscope effectively mimicked a pair of binoculars, a quality also shared by Oliver Wendell Holmes's even more user-friendly 1861 version of the device.[17] This portability aided commercial uptake of the stereoscope from mid-century onward.[18]

Like Wheatstone, Brewster was a fellow of the Royal Society and a keen inventor, but he was far more active in the public promotion of his work. He did this in particular through saleable contraptions: his early invention of the kaleidoscope proved enormously popular throughout Europe, although a delay in patenting prevented him from directly profiting from this success.[19] In the case of the stereoscope, what for Wheatstone was an exploratory apparatus for testing how vision works became in the hands of Brewster and other entrepreneurs something of a parlor toy, an appealing sensory diversion combining the intense visuality of the kaleidoscope with a realist paradigm of hyperaccurate pictorial representation. Hand-held stereoscopes of the sort that Brewster developed (but were themselves made by Parisian Jules Duboscq) were presented at the Great Exhibition of 1851 in London, and it was here that Queen Victoria's impressed reaction led to the mass commercial success of the apparatus, with close to a quarter of a million stereoscopes sold in Paris and London following her glowing commendation.[20] This popularity continued throughout the nineteenth century and into the early twentieth, stereoscopes capturing the collective imagination and being widely purchased and discussed both in Europe and the United States.[21]

Key to the stereoscope's success at this time was the invention of photography, particularly the development in the 1850s of the wet-plate collodion process, which produced replicable, detailed photographic images. So, while the "conceptual structure and the historical circumstances" of the stereoscope's invention were quite separate to the development of photography, once available photography nonetheless became the preferred mode of producing the stereoscopic pairs with which hand-held stereoscopes were easily loaded.[22] Photographic content had the capacity to be more detailed and more straightforwardly aligned than the geometric drawings and daguerreotypes that Wheatstone had used in his original mirror-based stereoscope. Moreover, the content itself could be mass-produced. Successful stereo pairs could be printed hundreds or thousands of times and sold to consumers who had also purchased what were, by the 1860s, affordable and compact stereoscopes.

As Laura Burd Schiavo has noted, this fundamentally changed the nature of the stereoscope itself. Through its wide dissemination, the apparatus began circulating within a cultural discourse quite alien to Wheatstone's empiricist ideas of perception:

> Photographers, retailers, and those in the optical trades not only promoted a vernacular form, the "parlor stereoscope," but also advanced a more positivist theory of vision that both relied upon and further reinforced the assumption that the subjects of sight were stable and that observation of those subjects led to accurate judgements. The masterful visual encounter attributed to the three-dimensional stereoscopic view, then, was not due to the medium's structure, but was rather the result of the inscription the instrument underwent as it became a consumer good.[23]

Photography and commodification shifted the meaning of stereoscopic media, pulling them toward a realist paradigm that seemed to negate much of Wheatstone's original thinking and writing. For Wheatstone, not only did the stereoscope's visual trickery hint at the "insufficiency of the eye," it emphasized "the active role of the viewing subject, and correspondingly a far more unstable being-in-the-world" than had previously been widely acknowledged.[24] By extreme contrast, makers of handheld stereoscopes increasingly argued that the addition of binocular depth cues to photographic images provided a replication of reality that was more enhanced, more convincing, and, above all, more accurate than that of photography alone.[25] In the words of Jib Fowles, stereography "offered a new canon for truth," one that Americans and other national populations readily purchased in bulk.[26]

The touted realism of stereoscopic media allowed people to immerse themselves in impressive or exotic sites without leaving their homes. For John Plunkett, this helped create a more mobile concept of the self in the nineteenth century, in which the individual extended "beyond the local, corporeal limits of the body" and became embedded in national and global contexts in a "televisual" manner.[27] Connected to this, Fowles suggests that the stereoscope worked as a standardizing tool in line with broader industrialized processes, operating "on the visible world as yet another resource," converting this world into segmented, packaged units for consumption.[28] Imbricated in a capitalist nexus of empire, media, and product, stereocards helped European and US citizens of the late nineteenth century feel like they were at the center of the globalizing machinery in which they were inevitably enmeshed. As Leon Gurevitch argues, the views featured on stereocards were "both industrialized visual commodities in their own right and spectacular representations deployed in the promotion of the vast array of industrial commodities, spaces, processes, and people emerging at the time."[29] Dimensional views of machinery, factories, and colonial outposts all employed the supposed realism of the stereoview in order to sell the very idea and permanence of these phenomena, while also tying the media device itself into this global nexus of trade, control, and display.

Despite such enormous uptake and cultural gravitas, the stereoscope fell out of public favor in the early twentieth century, with large-scale production and purchase all but stopping by the 1920s. As a result, and regardless of the fact that it was bought in massive numbers and used in various contexts for many decades, the stereoscope became all but forgotten within popular memory. This has severely impacted its critical standing. For instance, in his history of nineteenth-century photography Alan Thomas takes the position that the stereoscope was a parlor toy. Although having "large implications for the future of photography," he claims it ended up a mere trifle:

> Stereoscopy enjoyed a vogue for a decade or so, bringing the wonders of the world into the home in the manner of a glossy travel magazine. At the height of its success the London Stereoscopic Company offered for sale a stock of more than 100,000 slides of different views. But the fashion waned gradually, its influence and place in nineteenth-century society largely unregistered before its eclipse by the moving picture of the 1890s.[30]

By commenting that the stereoscope's place in sociocultural life went "unregistered," limiting the dates of its uptake to a single, precinematic decade, and devoting only a short passage to its discussion, Thomas, like many other commentators, makes his assertion of irrelevance somewhat self-fulfilling.[31]

Despite descriptions of its eclipse by other media like photography and cinema, stereoscopic media far from disappeared with the waning of the stereoscope. The introduction of the View-Master at the 1939 World's Fair in New York inaugurated this plastic, stereoscope-like device's fifty-year dissemination, initially as a method of education used in military contexts and then more comprehensively as a children's toy and popular marketing prop for tourist sites and major film releases.[32] Elsewhere, stereoscopic techniques were used in reconnaissance missions during World War II, and in classrooms stereoscopic apparatuses persisted as educational tools, with polarized stereoscopic systems bleeding into other areas of children's culture such as 3D comics.[33] The Stereo Realist slide camera—a 35 mm device made by the David White Company—was popular between the late 1940s and 1970s and highlights how stereoscopic photography had not been entirely superseded by the monocular snapshot.[34] In the 1980s, video games alighted upon 3D, with 1982's Vectrex and 1988's Sega-Scope3D offering numerous games in the format through spinning-disc and liquid-crystal shutter technology.[35] If Nintendo's Virtual Boy, released in 1995, had a relatively brief shelf life (possibly due to its monochromatic visual field), the same has not been true of Nintendo's 3DS handheld console, released in 2010, which uses an autostereoscopic parallax barrier LCD screen to provide players with a 3D gaming experience without glasses. Stereoscopic visuality has also, in the computer display age, become a fundamental aspect of virtual reality interfaces, interfaces that in many ways resemble stereoscopes (see chapter 4).[36] All of this indicates the extent to which, while the stereoscope itself may have gradually left public consciousness across the early decades of the twentieth century, stereoscopic media in general certainly did not.[37]

The most culturally visible use of stereoscopic 3D in the twentieth century was to be found in cinema. Especially pronounced in the early 1950s and early 1980s in the US market, 3D cinema is far from restricted to these times and places. While cinema has long been established as a planar, 2D medium, the extensive list of inventions and patents throughout the second half of the nineteenth century that worked toward stereoscopic moving image projection reveal how this planarity was far from inevitable.[38] Attempts to create stereoscope-like devices that could cycle through numerous cards in a series (and so give the impression of movement along with tangible depth), as well as efforts to project both still and moving 3D scenes, all testify to the imagined possibility and uses of 3D filmmaking. For instance, as early as 1861, engineer Coleman Sellers built a peep show operated by paddle wheel for displaying a series of stereoscopic photographs in an attempt to produce the impression of movement in three dimensions.[39] Meanwhile, a book published in 1868 on optical phenomena and related devices describes a combination of a stereoscope and phenakistoscope—resulting in the quick successive viewing of stereo scenes in a protocinematic manner.[40] These and numerous other endeavors to create and popularize stereoscopic cinema of one sort or another may not have led to this medium of exhibition being widely adopted, but they must serve as a reminder that monocular moving images were not (and are not) the stable, unquestioned telos of film exhibition.

SPECTACLE AND EMERGENCE IN THE 1950s

Nonetheless, in the long history of moving-image–based entertainment media, 2D content has been much more widely produced, disseminated, and discussed than 3D content. 3D media also seems to come and go in waves, which implies that it is unable to secure a more lasting cultural position. This makes it easy to argue, firstly, that 2D and 3D media have essential affinities that allow their coexistence within broader domains (including photography and cinema), but, secondly, that despite this copresence and conceptual resemblance 2D media are usually better at whatever task of representation is being undertaken, leading to their consistency and longevity over and above 3D alternatives. The stereoscope may have used photographic material and been immensely successful, but it disappeared from public and private life while photography in its planar guise remained a crucial medium of representation throughout the twentieth century and beyond. 3D cinema may have been sporadically popular between the 1950s and the present day, but its periods of prominence might be considered mere representational blips in comparison to the unfailing presence of planar films before, during, and after moments of widespread 3D cinema exhibition.

This is the starting premise of a great deal of film theory that has explored 3D. Much of this theory equates 3D with 2D by using tools and frameworks associated with the latter to understand the former. Yet this marks 3D as distinctive above all in its ultimate failure as a mode of representation, categorizing the medium as not-quite-2D, and so not-quite-film, and so (often) not-quite-worthy of sustained critical attention.

As we will see, much of this work focuses on US stereoscopic filmmaking in the 1950s and so downplays the prior existence of 3D cinema, which has a longer and more varied history than many narrow historical periodizations suggest. Early patents for stereo cinema in the 1890s and 1900s were actualized in 1915 by a screening in New York of stereoscopic material shot by Edwin S. Porter and William E. Waddell, while 1922 saw the wider and more notable release of the first feature-length 3D film—the now-lost *The Power of Love*—as well as a series of stereoscopic shorts called *Plastigrams*.[41] These were followed in 1935 by an Academy Award–nominated short called *Audioscopiks*, the success of which prompted *New Audioscopiks* in 1938 and *Third Dimension Murder* in 1941, all of which were rereleased in the early 1950s—at which point Bazin would comment that they were "adroitly directed" with "intense and irresistible" depth effects.[42] Abel Gance produced 3D segments for his totemic biopic *Napoleon* (1927), but chose not to include them in the final cut for fear they would prove "too overwhelming" and so overshadow the rest of the work.[43] Meanwhile, the Lumière brothers reshot their iconic *L'Arrivée d'un Train à La Ciotat* (1896) stereoscopically; although this may have been undertaken as early as 1903, evidence for this date is superficial, and it was only assuredly presented in 1935, screened not in a basement café to a paying audience but to the French Academy of Science.[44] An experimental stereoscopic film by Edwin Land in 1935 led to his hiring by car manufacturer Chrysler, and his promotional 3D animation of an automobile for the 1939 World's Fair in New York drew great crowds.[45] 3D shorts filmed in London and 3D animated shorts by Canadian artist Norman McLaren were screened to some acclaim at the Festival of Britain in 1951,[46] and in Moscow autostereoscopic (glasses-free) 3D cinemas were constructed in 1940 and 1947, showing films such as *Robinson Crusoe* (1946) as well as travelogues and scientific instructional films.[47]

This complex, detailed history is trivialized in accounts of stereoscopic cinema that take the 1950s as their starting point. Even so, it is certainly true that at this time the visibility of 3D cinema significantly increased thanks to mainstream dissemination, popular discussion, and film-studio backing. The popularization of television was impacting cinema attendance, while the ongoing divestiture by major film studios of their cinema chains (a result of a landmark 1948 antitrust case that ruled against the studios and sought to dismantle aggressive vertical integration) further threatened Hollywood's previously assured income streams.[48] Against this background, studios pursued technologies that would revivify a struggling industry and recapture a consumer base that seemed happy to source their media content elsewhere.

The aggressive expansion of 3D cinema in this climate may have been inevitable, but was kick-started in 1952 thanks to the enormous financial success of the low-budget independent exploitation release *Bwana Devil*. Major studio

Warner Bros. quickly hired Natural Vision, the company that made the film, for a two-picture deal. Natural Vision only had one 3D camera and could not meet the sudden demand for content, so other studios quickly devised their own competing systems.[49] Key texts produced in *Bwana Devil*'s wake include Warner Bros.'s *House of Wax* (1953), the MGM musical *Kiss Me Kate* (1953), Universal Studios' *Creature from the Black Lagoon* (1954), and Alfred Hitchcock's *Dial M for Murder* (1954), also for Warner Bros. For all the radical differences between these five films—which are, respectively, campy safari adventure, gothic period horror, colorful Shakespearean metamusical, po-faced creature-feature adventure, and taut claustrophobic thriller—critical writing overwhelmingly groups them together in a single "wave" of 3D content, a wave that is seen to crest and disappear entirely before the end of 1954.

This momentary adoption of 3D is often contrasted with other insistently marketed technologies of the time, such as stereo sound, widescreen, and single-strip color processes. Like 3D, these were spectacular enticements for the cinematic experience over and above alternatives (and, like 3D, none were brand-new inventions). Unlike 3D, their aesthetic effects would all become established elements of filmmaking practice. So, while not every film automatically uses dynamically spatialized sound, a widescreen frame, and color cinematography, these have all to varying extents been overwhelmingly prevalent aspects of cinema since the 1960s. The same cannot be claimed of 3D subsequent to its mid-twentieth-century period of visibility.

Partly as a result of this manifest impermanence, scholarship regarding 3D in the 1950s proceeds from the position that it is not only a novelty, but a novelty in the most negative sense of the word: a transitory and decorative feature overwhelmingly linked to commerce rather than creativity. And this reading applies both to the history of film—in which 3D cinema itself is seen as an occasional and unhelpful disruption of planar norms—as well as the use of 3D within particular film texts themselves, in which ostentatious 3D "effects" unsettle otherwise standardized film practice. The style of 3D films therefore echoes 3D's alleged place in film culture generally: in either case, 3D is found to be incompatible with established ideas of narrative cinema and is denigrated as an unwelcome intrusion.

On a textual level, incompatibility appears to arise from the shared intentions of 2D and 3D, intentions that are nonetheless understood as somehow discordant. Both 3D and 2D cinema have their own methods for representing space, but the procedures of the former can be interpreted as unnecessary, given the successes of the latter. For instance, unapologetic advocate of 3D media Ray Zone describes how attempts to create stereoscopic cinema in the

1890s and 1900s may have been thwarted by the sense of depth that moving images could provide even in their monoscopic presentation:

> Camera movement on the z-axis in conventional cinema, even though not actually stereoscopic, has traditionally conveyed a sense of depth—an enveloping of the spectator in projected imagery moving on the screen. These two-dimensional cinematographic techniques were so effective in conveying a feeling of depth that, to some extent, the need to create a genuine stereoscopic cinema may have been diminished.[50]

And, indeed, this is not just a property of camera movement, but the movement of contents of the frame itself, which generates depth sensations in ways immobile photography does not. In short, the Lumières' train need not be presented in 3D, since in its planar version the movement of the train toward the viewer already provides a clear idea of depth. Zone points to the commentary of film theorist Nöel Burch, who offhandedly dismisses 3D during a discussion of illusionism and film's prehistory in other technologies (a dismissal that offers Burch the chance to slyly taunt models of cinema that are based upon a teleology of realism):

> From Daguerre's Diorama to Edison's project of the Kinetophonograph, each of the technologies that positivist historiography sees as a series of advances converging on the Cinema, was intended by its technicians and perceived by its publicists as one more step towards the Recreation of Reality, towards the realisation of a perfect illusion of the perceptual world. . . . I believe it was this aspiration to three-dimensionality that was satisfied by the blossoming of the institutional Mode of Representation [IMR] from around 1910, and that the latter continues to satisfy us more than all the ephemeral re-appearances of red-and-green or polarising spectacles, raster screens, etc.[51]

Burch's IMR consists of standardized practices of composition, editing, sound design, and lighting, all of which work to create the impression of a legible three-dimensional space. As a model of narrative cinematic representation, Burch's IMR has been somewhat superseded by the work of David Bordwell, Kristin Thompson, and Janet Staiger and their enormously influential codification of "classical continuity."[52] In either case, the production of spatial coherence through the careful management of filmic language serves an illusionistic purpose, convincing viewers of the reality of the spaces, people, and actions they are observing within the film text. As Burch plainly states, the systematic organization of planar images paradoxically seems to fulfil the medium's "aspiration to three-dimensionality" more successfully than the more pronounced binocular impressions of 3D. Since mainstream narrative cinema privileges economy, 3D faces a seemingly inherent structural problem: it is not *necessary*. For Burch, stereoscopic cinema is defined not only by its required prostheses—the polarized glasses mass audiences must wear to observe most stereoscopic content—but also by its "ephemerality." Perhaps he is pointing to 3D's tendency to come and go over time as a form of cinematic exhibition, but this word also hints at the kind of unstable, psychogenic representation of space found in stereoscopic media and that certainly seems at odds with the institutional mode of representation and its emphasis on concreteness, boundedness, and perspective order.

Jens Schröter similarly places 3D and planar film grammar in competition, awarding the latter an uncomplicated victory. His book *3D: History, Theory, and Aesthetics of the Transplane Image* works hard to argue that 3D content (or what he terms "transplane images") is distinct from any alternative modes of representation. Like myself, Schröter draws upon Jonathan Crary to argue for the importance of stereoscopic technology within the histories of optics and spatial representation. Yet, despite his methodology, Schröter gives 3D cinema short shrift. Including detailed chapters on photo sculpture, Lippman photography, and holography, he explains the relative absence of 3D in both cinema history and his study in two brief footnotes:

> Since space in the movies is already constituted narratively . . . , the additional stereoscopic information on space [in 3D cinema] is superfluous (apart from occasional thrusts in the increase of spectacularity). Apart from the diverse technical difficulties, this may be why stereoscopy did not succeed in the movies . . .[53]
>
> Films—and especially those that (largely) follow the "Hollywood mode of narration"—live from a coherent narrative that constructs a coherent space as well. Additional information on space is not necessary—quite irrespective of the technological and receptive problems of the stereoscopic (or even holographic) cinema.[54]

Although he insists elsewhere that transplane images are important and far-reaching methods for the operationalization of space, in relation to cinema

Schröter sketches a competition between the continuity narrative style (or "Hollywood mode of narration") and 3D representation, with the former being coherent and the latter capable of only of "thrusting spectacularity."

This is how 3D cinema has been framed by a range of other scholars. Philip Sandifer, for instance, argues that 3D cinema can never overcome its fundamentally "demonstrative" nature and so can never properly immerse spectators.[55] In planar cinema, as in perspectival planar art in general, the screen contains and delineates the space being represented, and even if it acts as an imaginative window, the separation of this space from the viewer's space is absolute (66–67). In 3D, however, the separation breaks down, and objects in the film world can seem to "co-exist" with the spectator in the space of the theater: "The objects in a 3-D film always exist not only in relation to diegetic space but also in relation to the actual viewer and the theater in which the film is being watched. Rather than being immersive, 3-D film is profoundly bound up in an act of spectatorship whereby the theater, instead of disappearing, is even more conspicuously visible" (69).

This connection with the physical site of exhibition is only heightened by the cinemacentric way in which the industry deploys the technology. That is, 3D is explicitly employed to emphasize the importance of the screening environment of the cinema as opposed to that of the home, whether the latter offered its own competing novelty of TV channels (1950s), home entertainment systems (1980s), or internet piracy and film streaming (2000s). Sandifer suggests that 3D functions in such periods—and, indeed, in general—"in the form of an event": a media technology to be looked *at* (71).

In addition to the macro effect of stressing the site of the cinema both as social space and exhibition environment, 3D performs a similar effect at the micro level, highlighting its own presence within film texts at certain key points. For Sandifer, these moments—in which objects ostentatiously move off the screen and into the space of the theater—have come to define accepted articulations of 3D's use, value, and (especially) limitations. He describes a sequence that takes place halfway through *House of Wax*, in which a paddle-baller in Victorian New York advertises a wax museum, as indicative. In this scene, the paddleballer engages with passers-by and encourages them to visit the museum; he also engages with the viewers of the film, knocking the ball at—and, in 3D, *through*—the screen, telling us to close our mouths lest the projectile hit our tonsils. "Careful sir, keep your head down or I'll tap you on the chin," he warns with a slightly off-putting straight face. Obviously, *House of Wax* is here playing up its mode of exhibition, and it is unlikely that the on-screen performer would be offering this kind of playful direct address were the film not seeking to highlight its apparent ability to enter the space of the theater through 3D exhibition. As such, this moment can be seen as an extraneous, "dropped-in crowd-pleaser"—and while Sandifer proposes that it connects thematically with the film's broader concerns around art and commerce and the intermingling of violent shock with popular entertainment, he still considers it to be evidence of an "aesthetic of spectatorship and astonishment" that typifies 3D, an aesthetic that "fits poorly with the traditional conventions of narrative cinema" (71–72). In this statement, Sandifer evokes Tom Gunning's influential "cinema of attractions" model of early cinema, in which the spectator is acknowledged and their attention unashamedly solicited in the manner of vaudeville.[56] Added to this narrative/spectacle friction are challenges around 3D composition and editing that, for Sandifer, prove ultimately insurmountable. As a result, 3D is prevented from being as satisfying as so-called "normal" cinema and even denied the possibility of operating comfortably alongside it.[57]

By way of summary, Sandifer suggests that stereoscopic cinema has a particular form of cinematic grammar: a "grammar of allure, based not on narrative or story, and certainly not on immersive realism," for 3D does not create "a compelling narrative experience," but, rather, at best, a "compelling spectacle."[58] Planar cinema and associated systems of continuity editing are contrasted with 3D cinema and its alluring grammar; the former is considered standard practice, historically authenticated, and artistically meaningful, qualities denied to the latter. This dichotomous model is echoed by William Paul across his own two essays on stereoscopy, "The Aesthetics of Emergence" from 1993 and "Breaking the Fourth Wall" from 2004.[59] Paul may offer a more sympathetic assessment of 3D cinema, but he equally considers 3D to so diverge from planar aesthetics that the two are again incompatible. As with Sandifer's focus on the paddleballer, both of Paul's essays are concerned with moments in which the 3D film enters the space of exhibition, an effect industrially termed "negative parallax" (since the twinned left and right eye images must overlap in an inverted fashion) but also known as "emergence," or, in reference to the theatrical convention, "breaking the fourth wall." The aforementioned scene from *House of Wax* is an overt example of this, as the paddleball emerges from the screen and the paddleballer himself clearly breaks the fourth wall by addressing the audience. Paul points out the industrial factors contributing to the use of this effect—namely, the need for 3D to provide clear spectatorial pleasures to justify the technological expenditure it demanded of studios and cinema owners, costs passed on to cinemagoers in the form of higher ticket prices or a further charge for 3D glasses. Yet, beyond this economic rationale, Paul asks whether such sequences can ever be truly warranted, since they appear to be present solely for their own sake or the sake of technological display and do not serve narrative purposes. "Can the story be the star while the audience is being startled?" he asks, deciding ultimately that, no, it cannot.[60] Again, story and spectacle are contrasted, the former being the provenance of correct Hollywood practice, the latter becoming an unwelcome intrusion, and one synonymous with 3D exhibition.

Linking 3D with direct address puts it at an automatic disadvantage. As Alexander Galloway describes, explicitly pointing to the existence of the viewer is a culturally sidelined, even ostracized, practice:

> Addressing the viewer is a very special mode of representation that is reserved for special occasions. It appears in debased forms like pornography, or folk forms like the home video, or marginalized political forms like Brechtian theater, or forms of ideological interpellation like the nightly news. Direct address is always treated in a special way. Narrative forms, which are still dominant in many media, almost entirely prohibit it.[61]

Direct address, including the kind found in *House of Wax*, as well similar moments from other 3D films in which knives, hands, or other objects move toward the spectator in an ostentatious fashion, is effectively uncinematic. Classical Hollywood's emphasis on coherent story worlds and the willing suspension of disbelief implicitly includes direct address through negation— however the classical style works, what it precisely does *not* do is turn to the camera and wave hello in the fashion of the early cinema of attractions. So when the screen of the film, normally "invisible" through viewing conventions, becomes "visible" through its address and violation, the otherwise dominant workings of narrative continuity are usurped, and the film as a narrative text suffers.

Galloway may refer to Brechtian drama, ideological interpellation, and home video, but the primary form of cinema with which 1950s 3D was associated was exploitation (which might be considered close to pornography, thanks to its appeal to base pleasures and its embrace of amateurish production values). This "sensationalist and lurid" cinema already had a tendency to challenge conventional style,[62] offering what Scott Higgins describes as "greater diegetic latitude" in its appeals to spectators less averse to the presence of "disruptive gimmickry" and direct textual confrontation.[63] The "decorum, proportion, formal harmony, respect for tradition, self-effacing craftsmanship, and cool control of the perceiver's response" that Bordwell describes as crucial to classical narrative cinema were all radically deemphasized in exploitation films.[64] 3D exploitation cinema, from the exotic travelogue of *Bwana Devil* to the creature-feature thrills of *Creature from the Black Lagoon*, could use confrontational stereoscopic aesthetics in tandem with a sensationalism inherent in the genre that already implicitly acknowledged the viewer and encouraged a playful relationship with the film text. Indeed, 3D could add to and underline this playful relationship.[65]

This link with exploitation cinema speaks to what has historically been perceived as 3D's own marginal place within film culture. As Paul states, 3D is an "institutionalized aberration" that is "born of the mainstream cinema, yet must always be cast aside by it."[66] This explains why the technology is employed so briefly, and always apparently with commercial imperatives foregrounded. 3D in the 1950s was only mainstream for a year or so, while the subsequent adoption of 3D by popular cinema in the 1980s—consisting of films like *Friday the 13th Part III* (1982), *Amityville 3D* (1983), and *Jaws 3-D*—was equally short-lived. The predominance of horror sequels at that later moment highlights 3D's usefulness as a brief novelty employed to draw attention to otherwise stale product, as in a similar way does the use of the format for the (wildly profitable) soft-core pornographic feature *The Stewardesses* in 1969.[67]

That said, much as 3D breaks through the screen, it also occasionally breaks through into the critically accepted mainstream. While Hitchcock was apparently unimpressed with his own work on the 1954 adaptation of the popular Frederick Knott play *Dial M for Murder*, the film has garnered attention for what is seen as its relatively restrained use of 3D effects. Much of it takes place on a single set, and the film is shot in such a way as to exaggerate this theatrical staging. Moreover, shots are frequently composed with a barrier of furniture, bottles, or general domestic bric-a-brac between viewer and characters. In 3D exhibitions this generates layered depth planes, placing the actors at some remove from the perceived screen, creating a palpable gulf between characters and audience. Both Sandifer and Sheldon Hall suggest that this deliberate framing highlights the film's claustrophobic setting and generic credentials in useful ways, ways that moreover keep with Hitchcock's preexisting auteur signature.[68]

Furthermore, the film features only two moments of excessive negative parallax. Crucially, these occur in the context of significant narrative developments. In the first, Margot (Grace Kelly) is being strangled in her apartment, and her hand reaches toward and as though through the screen, seemingly appealing to the viewer for help. Later, a vital clue concerning her attempted murder—a key—is brandished in a close-up that brings it into negative parallax space. For Paul, these moments of emergence demonstrate how 3D can be used in ways that both fit with but also challenge the conventional grammar of classical film style. As Margot's hand reaches out of the screen, it "reiterates the unbridgeable gulf that separates our space from that of the film image because we know we cannot reach back"; as a result, "our status as passive viewers is forcefully reinscribed at a moment that effectively makes us complicit in the attempted murder."[69] Meanwhile, for Hall, the emergence of the key gives this prop "greater physical 'presence' and dramatic force" than it would otherwise attain, justifying the use of 3D effects in this moment.[70]

Unlike other 3D films of this period then, emergence is used in *Dial M for Murder* to pull the viewer *into* the diegesis and the story. This is in sharp contrast to the recoiling spectators imagined by *House of Wax*'s paddleballer. Yet, paradoxically, this more restrained and supposedly more effective use of 3D is perceived by scholars to be evidence once again of the format's incompatibility with narrative cinema—in order to make it work, one must use 3D sparingly and in a manner that does not run counter to the accepted operations of classical continuity style. As Sandifer puts it, *Dial M for Murder*'s success as a 3D film "is largely because it declines to make much use of its 3-D technology."[71] It is the camera's positioning that constructs Margot's reaching as a reaching toward the spectator; it is a dolly-in that pushes the key into the spectator's space. In each case, the fourth wall is not being broken as overtly as it is in *House of Wax*, *Kiss Me Kate*, or exploitation films like *Bwana Devil*. Overall, then, scholars suggest to varying degrees that *Dial M for Murder* is a relatively successful 3D experience thanks to Hitchcock's methodical application of depth effects, the avowed restraint in emergence and the subdued dimensionality in general—to the point that the film is seen to succeed almost in spite of its method of shooting.[72]

Across this broad history of film theory, it is clear that 3D—as incarnated in Hollywood films of the early 1950s—is overwhelmingly perceived as a stylistic irregularity, one motivated by commercial concerns and seemingly at odds with accepted workings of film style. Stereoscopic effects are considered somewhat separate from or surplus to the true meaning of a text and the stylistic systems at work within it. In their own ways, Burch, Schröter, Paul, and Sandifer all describe a schism between classical filmmaking and 3D, meaning the latter is doomed to remain a gimmick within both film studies and review discourse.[73] (Hitchcock's work in the format is validated through his use of it counter to expectations—namely, expectations that the format always pushes out at the viewer and in this way shocks and even threatens them). 3D is unwarranted and superfluous to the needs of narrative cinema, making it not just an aberration, but an unhelpful, unnecessary, and awkward one.

Given the parameters laid down by both scholarship and cultural discourses around 3D cinema, such a conclusion is inevitable and seems generally reasonable. Having equated 3D with moments of aggressive emergence, these are then sought out in film texts as proof of their overwhelming presence; in the process, other aspects of 3D exhibition (such as deep space, the creation of volume, or the impression of immateriality) are downplayed or potentially ignored entirely. Those disruptive moments of emergence that have been identified then themselves recapitulate 3D's own place in film history as an unwanted and ostentatious incursion of crass technological novelty into a 2D exhibition landscape that does not demand or deserve such novelties. The impropriety of this incursion is underscored by the lasting adoption of other aesthetic developments that apparently better serve the realist paradigm of narrative cinema and function more productively alongside classical continuity practices. Hollywood's deployment of technological spectacle to freshen up narrative entertainment is a resounding success when it comes to adding synchronized sound, enriching the image with a range of colors, or expanding the screen into a horizontally enveloping rectangle, but is a rare failure when it comes to the adoption of 3D exhibition. Forever the paddleballer, in the eyes of mainstream film studies 3D is always an unwanted, almost inexplicable, inevitably brief intrusion.

NOVELTY, REDUNDANCY, AND AUTEURISM IN DIGITAL 3D

These theoretical models must be updated. While it is true that 3D cinema never exactly disappeared at any point in the twentieth century, it has recently proliferated in cinemas and other selected contexts in a more concerted manner than ever before. Ubiquitous since the release of *Avatar* at the end of 2009 is the digital 3D blockbuster, with a majority of mainstream, high-profile studio films (especially those featuring extensive and elaborate CGI spectacle) being distributed in both 3D and 2D. Some may argue that, in the decade since *Avatar*'s release, 3D has collapsed under the weight of critical and commercial apathy and will shortly disappear from the mainstream landscape, but the persistent production and release of 3D films belies this.[74] The merits of the format may continue to be debated, but cinemas have overwhelmingly switched to digital projection, and both multiplexes and art-house cinemas exhibit 3D films regularly. Between them, the major Hollywood studios release between twenty and forty films in 3D in Western markets per year, and these and more are produced and released around the world, with mainstream Chinese film exhibitors notably embracing 3D (along with IMAX projection and forms of sensorially enhanced cinema like 4DX). The predominance of 3D in the current era indicates that, in the terms set by the above scholars, some kind of negotiation has been successfully achieved, with stereoscopic effects more productively integrated into the continuity systems of narrative cinema than at prior historical moments.[75]

Even so, digital 3D cinema is often viewed through the same rubric of novelty and commercialism that defined discussion of earlier periods of the format. John Belton, for instance, emphasizes how digital 3D provides a "novelty phase" for digital cinema. Evoking in form and content that which it supersedes (analog production and projection), Belton suggests that digital cinema deploys 3D to visibly justify a widespread rollout of digital projection. Though it has been successful in this regard, he concludes that 3D will "never become a norm" and describes familiar dichotomies: "If 3D is to be 3D, it must necessarily exploit the phenomenon of emergence, *violating* the segregation of spaces that lies at the core of the experience of classical cinema."[76] More sympathetically, Scott Higgins explores the capacity of twenty-first-century 3D films to offer a "restrained"—and therefore more "sustainable"—3D aesthetic than earlier releases could provide.[77] Rather than focus on emergence, Higgins recognizes the wider range of effects of which 3D is capable, and he proposes some films that that "map out some expressive terrain for [today's] 3D by displacing the opposition between protrusion and screen space with a continuum of dimensional volume before and behind the frame."[78]

One of his key case studies, the stop-motion animated feature *Coraline* (2009), is also discussed by David Bordwell, and for these and other scholars the distortions and miniaturizations of stereoscopic visuality actually aid that film's aesthetic project and its narrative developments.[79] In Higgins's words, emergence effects are downplayed, "temper[ed] and limit[ed] both in duration and space," and Stephen Prince explicitly links the "conservative" depth budget (the scale of stereoscopic space presented both in positive and negative parallax) to the film's successful integration of 3D with the "compositional and editing strategies of planar cinema."[80] Again, the assumption remains that for 3D to work within narrative cinema it needs to somehow downplay its more radical or visible tendencies, tendencies that, it is implied, would otherwise overdefine and overwhelm. 3D's novelty is once more both its appeal and its undoing, creating a mode of spectatorship that cannot be normalized to conventional viewing practices and subsequently diffused into the broader environment of visual entertainment media.

Productions that are deemed aesthetically valuable like *Coraline* are important precisely because they seem to work predominantly with the depth behind the screen rather than with protrusion in front. Moreover, this recessive depth is often seen to be capable of, and even as tending toward, a kind symbiotic relationship with other systems of expressive visual representation, such as color and composition. For instance, Higgins describes how in *Hugo* (2011) director Martin Scorsese modulates the 3D "*in tandem with* [the] other highly dynamic visual parameters of the contemporary auteur, including lighting, lens choice, cutting rate, speed of motion, and color grading."[81] Successful depth apparently sets out to compliment a broader array of cinematic stylistics in ways that might be holistically satisfying, but that also render these 3D effects potentially redundant. So, even as Higgins makes the provocative and well-taken suggestion that in the present moment of digital 3D, "popular films struggle with the very definition of cinematic space," he nonetheless indicates that 3D is something of an optional extra within a wider tool kit, a tool kit most visible, or most interesting, in the hands of a master craftsperson.[82] This may reflect the description of 3D in some industrial discourse, but, in making 3D subtly elective, this interpretation also makes it potentially surplus to requirements. While its use can be creatively rewarding and can increase an audience's sense of immersion, stereoscopic depth is simultaneously rendered hypothetically redundant.[83]

This redundancy is best tackled by auteurs—or, at least, that is the implication made by many commentators. Hitchcock and Scorsese, and to an extent Selick and James Cameron, are positioned as creative presences able to tame the novelties and disruptions of the format. Meanwhile, although few 3D films may win their directors Academy Awards, the cinematographers of *Avatar* (Mauro Fiore) and *Hugo* (Robert Richardson) *have* received Oscars for their work on these films, as have the cinematographers of the Ang Lee–directed *Life of Pi* (2012, Claudio Miranda) and the Alfonso Cuarón–directed *Gravity* (2013, Emmanuel Lubezki).[84] In all cases, these are films in which the director has been foregrounded in industrial discourse as an artistic presence able to meet the aesthetic challenge of 3D.[85] This operates as a kind of proof that, in Chuck Tryon's words, digital 3D is not an industrial gimmick being discourteously foisted upon viewers and filmmakers, but an "artistic revolution" that can be "used imaginatively by creative and innovative directors."[86] This dynamic extends beyond mainstream narrative cinema: documentary films like *Cave of Forgotten Dreams* (2010) and *Pina* (2011) and avant-garde experiments like *Goodbye to Language* (2014) were marketed in ways that foregrounded their respective notable directors Werner Herzog, Wim Wenders, and Jean-Luc Godard.

Scholarly work must be wary of uncritically recapitulating these taste cultures and their endorsement of only select texts. The 3D canon is wider than auteur films and exploitation cinema, and this terrain needs exploring for the format to be properly understood. 3D is more than a narrowly industrial and/or auteuristic practice, able only to work as (at best) a productive augmentation of other cinematographic properties, or (at worst) a spectacular and occasional textual disruption. In this vein, Miriam Ross has articulated an alternative way of reading 3D based on haptic visuality and optical illusions, focusing on the changed place of the spectator in relation to 3D content.[87] A 2013 article by Thomas Elsaesser on the logics and genealogies of the image in the twenty-first century, meanwhile, usefully questions many orthodoxies around 3D's industrial position and aesthetic affordances in order to update our understanding of the history of cinema in general.[88] This work testifies to the extent that digital 3D can and should prompt the development of new conceptual tools, since investigating and assessing it using frameworks offered in relation to 1950s or 1980s contexts and practices can fail to fully account for digital 3D's uses, effects, and industrial position. Applying such earlier models to current digital 3D releases equates these historical periods and their technologies in problematic ways. Doing so also risks, in Ariel Rogers's words, "ignoring the nuances of this recent instance of upheaval," nuances that arise from contemporary 3D's enmeshing in broader digital culture and experience.[89]

Equally, 3D is done a serious disservice if analyzed using planar tools and methodologies. Such work falls prey to what Schröter (referencing the "logocentrism" of Jacques Derrida) calls "planocentrism": a privileging of the plane or image surface.[90] For Schröter, this tendency has led to the neglect of transplane or stereoscopic media in histories of art and optics, since these cannot be easily subsumed into planar (or planocentric) models of analysis. (It is telling, then, that even he engages in planocentric discourse when discussing cinema, as we have seen). Planocentrism affects studies of 3D in that such studies overwhelmingly proceed from presumptions and theories that have been developed through analysis of the workings of a planar narrative cinema. This automatically closes off any full-fledged exploration of 3D aesthetics on their own terms. Moments of excessive emergence are drawn attention to for several reasons: they were often highlighted by Hollywood studios in marketing materials and posited by this discourse as key textual pleasures;[91] they clearly diverge from the normal organization of screen space and modes of address found in continuity cinema; and they offer the most visible evidence of 3D even when the film text under discussion is not being exhibited in this fashion.[92] On this last point, Paul playfully states that if, while skipping through TV channels, you "come across a film from the early fifties where they keep throwing things at the camera, you've probably discovered one of the 46 feature movies that were released in 3-D between 1952 and 1955"—a comment revealing how emergence is visible even when it does not stereoscopically emerge.[93] It is thus far more straightforward—and, in an era prior to the relatively easy access to 3D content provided by Blu-ray discs and 3D-enabled televisions, logistically simpler—to discuss the light-hearted paddleballer of *House of Wax* or Margot's desperately reaching hand in *Dial M for Murder* than it is to explore the recessive depth of the former's gothic New York streets or the latter's layered recessive depth planes, not to mention more complex aspects of 3D such as visual distortion and sensations of pronounced immateriality (aspects that are entirely absent in 2D presentations).

Moreover, the dichotomous model of positive and negative parallax, of emergence and recession, itself greatly undervalues the extent to which stereoscopic space is rounded, volumetric, and potentially enveloping. Paddleballers aside, spectators may not be obviously aware of exactly when objects, shapes, and characters are protruding from the screen and, indeed, will likely not have a concrete idea of where the screen itself actually is (see chapter 6). As Ross makes clear, the screen perceptually disappears in the "spatial continuum" produced by 3D.[94] As such, the very categorizations of emergence and recession are problematic, since that from which content might be thought to conceptually emerge or recede is rendered immaterial, perceptually unlocatable. What is needed, then, are increasingly detailed and nuanced methodologies that respond to the particular technological, industrial, and aesthetic contexts of contemporary 3D production. The development of these is the focus of the remainder of this book.

• • •

In this chapter I have sought to uncover the history of stereoscopic media and dominant discourses around it, placing particular emphasis upon sceptical interpretations of 3D cinema's content and workings. I have highlighted how stereoscopic presentation is frequently perceived to be both a fundamental divergence from normalized cinematic convention, and a sort of special effect that is surplus to the spatial coherence demanded by narrative cinema. Stereoscopic exhibition provides perceptual spatial impressions that are often considered *additional* to that which a given media form (photography, cinema) would likely provide anyway. Attempts by filmmakers to carve out a place for these effects in and of themselves prove counterproductive—as in *House of Wax*'s ostentatious, apparently distracting paddleballer and his direct-to-camera antics. Yet this is not the only way to see 3D. Indeed, in a short piece on *House of Wax* written at the time of its release, Bazin fails to even mention the infamous paddleball. For him, this is "a film in full stereoscope relief which for the first time makes the ultimate worth of the third dimension perceptible," and, while no "revolutionary masterwork," integrates its 3D effects in a fundamental and vital fashion.[95] He describes the film's 3D as working to refresh the novelty of cinema, connecting stereoscopy to the shocks and excitements of the earliest film screenings in the 1890s, even if he also doubts that the third dimension will become "an absolute or habitual norm."[96]

Bazin is no proselytizer, then, but he is alert to 3D's holistic difference *as difference*, rather than as addition or incursion. More enthusiastic is another iconic figure, Soviet director and theorist Sergei Eisenstein, who felt that 3D was an enveloping and piercing aesthetic force.[97] Writing in the late 1940s—nearly one hundred years after the Great Exhibition of 1851 and the first popular adoption of stereoscopic viewing devices, but before the concerted wave of 3D film production in Hollywood in the early 1950s—Eisenstein considered 3D to have enormous potential and was eager to apply 3D to his own filmmaking. "We should not be afraid of the coming era," he urged. "We should prepare our consciousness for the coming of new themes which, multiplied by the potentialities of new techniques, will demand a new aesthetics for skilfully realizing these new themes in the new, breath-taking works of the future."[98] Eisenstein's death in 1948 prevented him from contributing to such works, but his words hint at the kind of alternative scholarly and cultural reception 3D cinema might have elicited. Rather than an additional filmmaking tool, shackled (unhelpfully) to continuity systems, it might be interpreted as a radically different mode of cinematic address with its own aesthetics, themes, and spectatorial effects.

Words like Eisenstein's seem in hindsight to be at best naïve after a twentieth century of only occasional 3D adoption in cinematic contexts, but perhaps, in the twenty-first century, a new era has arrived, albeit an era helmed by a globally hegemonic, capitalistic cinema of the sort that would horrify the Soviet director. In this moment, 3D is both ascendant and strangely submerged: as much as stereoscopic cinema is marketed as a different, spectacular experience over and above standard planar cinema (and is priced for audiences accordingly), it nonetheless shares traits with this 2D alternative. Any cinema screen showing stereoscopic films probably also shows nonstereoscopic content some of the time, and the vast majority of mainstream films released in 3D are also released nonstereoscopically, audiences free—depending on their preferences and the availability of screening times—to choose between the two. As a result, these releases carefully negotiate competing aesthetic and formal requirements: on the one hand they must provide noteworthy 3D spectacle, and on the other they must be successful, effective entertainments when not exhibited stereoscopically, a negotiation I have explored in some detail elsewhere.[99] This dualism has haunted cinematic 3D since at least the 1950s, when audiences allegedly flocked to planar screenings of *Dial M for Murder* but stayed away from the 3D version.[100]

Approaching 3D as a format of exhibition that modifies content destined to be more widely viewed in 2D (in both cinematic and home entertainment contexts) unquestionably hinders the development of a 3D aesthetic that stands as and for itself, as well as any analysis of this aesthetic. In the case of emergence, a large body of film theory condemns 3D's outright evocation of (one of) its key features, considering it at best uninteresting and at worst offensive. Thinking of 3D as anathema to mainstream film style somehow both admits to the distinctiveness of the format even as it divests 3D of serious scholarly value by labeling it unsuccessful. This potentially limits our understanding of the contemporary cinematic landscape and its productive relationship with wider technologies and representational strategies. 3D is capable of generating an intriguing range of spaces, shapes, and dimensions (in the case of positive parallax and impressions of volume and shape) that are only now beginning to be understood. As Elsaesser asserts, the aesthetic possibilities of digital 3D "are by no means limited to telling a silly story, suitable only for kids hungry for superheroes, action toys, or sci-fi fantasies."[101] To make such an assumption—even though it may be logical given that the majority of mainstream 3D releases do fall into such broadly defined categories—is to disregard the wider changes to vision and space that 3D engenders and is itself evidence of. As such, I will assert through the following chapters that 3D cinema offers a distinctive aesthetic that needs to be explored on its own terms, and that this aesthetic is predicated on a virtual production of space the properties of which we urgently need to comprehend.

2

VISUALIZATION

· ·

From Perspective to Digital 3D

3D films may require a screen to deliver their content, but their mode of representation radically changes the nature of this screen. If 3D cinema offers ocular, technological, and aesthetic dissimilarity both from images more generally and (2D) cinema specifically, then how do we begin to explore these divergences? Perhaps ironically, the best way to counter planocentrism when analyzing 3D is to begin by paying considerable attention to this plane. Only by carefully defining the histories, dimensions, and workings of the planar image is it possible to assess how stereoscopic media adapt, transform, or disregard the plane or screen. In so doing, this chapter takes what may seem a detour away from contemporary digital 3D cinema, looking closely at the history and wider contexts of imagistic, planar mediation.

In order to think through these changes, the concept of the symbolic form proves useful. Symbolic forms, while closely associated with perspective and the art historian Erwin Panofsky, are actually applicable in a much broader range of contexts.[1] A symbolic form is not only a way of describing a culturally and historically important method of interpreting the world, but also identifies this method as predefining and limiting the scope of world-knowledge. In the context of the symbolic form, we can only discover that which fits the parameters and underlying assumptions of said form. Applying this to digital 3D is therefore fruitful in two ways. First, it places this medium of exhibition within longer art historical discourse, specifically putting it into dialogue with the perspective, the logics of which, as I will show, digital 3D recapitulates and intriguingly extends. Second, as a critical framework, symbolic forms help to position 3D as characteristic of the workings, presumptions, and ideologies of the technoaesthetic terrain of the digital and allow us to explore how this wider terrain produces space in a particular fashion. It may be too much to claim that digital 3D is a (or even the) symbolic form of twenty-first-century media culture; but, equally, to marginalize digital 3D as an irrelevant novelty overlooks its fertile alignments with a range of other technologies and spatial representations in a computer screen–filled world.

A discussion of symbolic forms will thus take up the first section of this chapter. Perspective not only preorders the represented environments of art and the material environments of architecture but also influences the deep structure of ideas around space in the Western world, ideas that treat space as abstract, neutral, and objective in order to turn it into distributable units. After exploring these themes, I will expand on the meanings of the term "digital cinema," sketching how film theory has investigated the aesthetic and ontological properties of digital media and has done so with consistent emphasis on abstraction and the rendering of the image as a unit-based grid of measurement. The work of David Rodowick, Philip Rosen, and Sean Cubitt will be of particular use here, as their theories of the digital establish how concepts of the image and indexicality undergo profound changes under current technological conditions. Finally, after this excursus away from explicit discussion of stereoscopic media, the chapter's final section will connect these planar and digital concerns to digital 3D.

ABSTRACTING SPACE TO PLANE: PERSPECTIVE

In perspectival art, geometric rules and consistent compositional codes are used to make the medium of the work perceptually disappear, turning a planar surface into a perceptual window onto a spatially extensive world. Perspective presumes that human vision consists of an expanding pyramid with the eye at its tip, and that a painting can mimic an intersection or slice of this pyramid, fooling the viewer into thinking their vision is extending into a deep space when actually it is falling upon a flat surface decorated with appropriate color, shape, and shade.[2] While commonly considered a painting tool "invented" or "discovered" in fifteenth-century Italy, art historian Erwin Panofsky sketches a longer and more encompassing history. He describes how ancient Greek art employed aspects of perspectival systems, but argues that these generated "aggregate" rather than "systematic" spaces as a result of their haphazard application of perspectival frameworks. They lacked the rigorousness that would in the Renaissance come to define perspective; as a result, they produced "unmodern" views of space.[3] After faltering experiments with perspectival rendering throughout Byzantine and Romanesque art, what we would recognize as the "modern" view of space associated with regimented perspectival rules was developed by artist Filippo Brunelleschi and architect Leon Battista Alberti in the 1400s. Brunelleschi's paintings of the Florentine Baptistry and his method of displaying them in direct comparison to the physical building itself asserted the seeming capacity of linear perspective to exactly replicate visual and spatial experience, while Alberti's 1435 treatise *On Painting* was the most concerted written explanation of this method of organizing planar visual material.

Alberti begins *On Painting* with the plea that his text be approached as the work of an artist, not a mathematician. Such a proviso is necessary given the extensive diagrams and algorithms in his pages that describe how to geometrically measure the intersection of objects in the world with the visual field. These calculations track the "rays" of human vision that were presumed to shoot out in perfectly straight lines from the center of the eye, encountering objects on their way and sending impressions of these back to the observer. To paint realistically, an artist was required to establish and record the quantified spatial relations in the same fashion as these rays; the more successfully a painter could transmute the appearance of reality through this mathematical lens, the better a painter they were.[4] There are three crucial assumptions at work here: first, that the world has a natural geometric order; second, that human perception is sensible to this geometry; and, third, that this geometry should be recapitulated in artistic renderings of this world for purposes of both believability and beauty. To appear in a perspectival work of art, the precise location, shape, and volume of an object must be ascertained, such that the work of art itself functions as much as a record of these attributes as it does a representation of the object within a meaningful artistic composition.

Something of a "philosopher's stone of art," perspective offered a systematic method "to conjure up a measurable, precise illusion of the world," and to do so on command.[5] It thus ensured the "objectification of the subjective:" everything from subject position to physiology, and even history, myth, and religion were all deemphasized in favor of a standard mode of seeing that was endlessly repeatable.[6] Yet even if, as an aesthetic stratagem, perspective is a perceptually convincing mirror of reality, it is necessary to consider why its particular interpretation of sight and space seem so convincing in the first place. This will then allow us to appreciate what is distinctive about 3D visuality, which in many ways updates perspectival approaches.

The association of perspective with concepts like accuracy, fidelity, and objectivity are central to this tool's designation as a symbolic form. It was Panofsky's *Perspective as Symbolic Form* that influentially made this connection in 1927, taking the idea from his contemporary, the German philosopher Ernst Cassirer. Cassirer is usually downplayed in discussion of Panofsky's work, but he deserves closer consideration. In the four volumes of *The Philosophy of Symbolic Forms* (written across the 1920s), Cassirer describes how these forms separate us from preconscious beings, and how they influence our thinking in deep-seated, often invisible ways.[7] This is a Kantian understanding of consciousness, emphasizing not a preexisting empirical world that is "mirrored" by our perception, but rather the perceptive application of forms to intuit and categorize experience and knowledge.[8] Using the examples of language, myth, science, art, and religion, Cassirer explores how human culture seeks to transform "the passive world of mere *impressions*, in which the human spirit seems at first imprisoned, into a world that is pure *expression* of the human spirit" through the application of structural systems to the sense data of the external world.[9] For Cassirer, no matter how "given" any perception would seem to be, it has nonetheless passed through an organizing filter that dictates how we recognize it and what we do with it. What seems merely "is" is in fact "made," "conditioned and determined by some primary meaning-giving function."[10] As systems of knowledge, symbolic forms continually adapt and update, and each symbolic form remains relatively rigid and distinct from others. For example, even though they may have in antiquity grown out of the same impetus as myth-making, the sciences cannot see the world as myth, and this is what makes them separate symbolic forms—that is, what defines them *as the sciences*.[11] While his work is concerned with unpacking and revealing the workings of these various symbolic forms, Cassirer suggests that this will never provide us access to a clear, unprocessed perception of reality. To achieve this, we would need to process the world like truly premythical, prelinguistic, pretheoretical organisms, who do not have the filtering lenses of symbolic forms: "Only then, to use a metaphor, could we compare with certainty the genuine and original metal of reality to the subsequent minting that it underwent in thought."[12] For human beings, the world is always in some ways mediated, since it is precisely this act of mediation—the interpretation and organization of sense data according to culturally inherited models—that makes us human.

We can see from this brief overview why Cassirer's model interested Panofsky, who himself sought to account for the development of perspective by paying particular attention to its appeal for artists and their audiences as a kind of worldview. Cassirer is clear that artists do not "merely trace the contours of things," but produce a new world, a "world-discovery," according to a preexisting structural system.[13] As a structural system, perspective is highly visible (it is, as will be shown, enormously influential in visual culture) but it also relies upon a presumption of invisibility—the crucial mark of a symbolic form. This therefore disguises or at least normalizes its conjoining of a geometric, mathematical interpretation of space with an artistic, nominally subjective one, and the linked assertion that this marriage results in a window on the world, a clear-eyed "looking through" in the literal translation of the Latin *perspicere*. Perspective's rigorous codification by Brunelleschi and Alberti and its widespread adoption in the Renaissance is testament to the perceived accuracy of the specific conception of the world it offered: one of Euclidean, infinitely extended space, populated by specifically positioned objects whose dimensions and relations could be exactly measured.[14]

In proposing that perspective is a symbolic form, Panofsky argues for its radical influence as a method for turning impressions of the world into expressions of systematic meaning, placing it on a par with other forms such as science and myth. Through this crucial maneuver Panofsky is stating that the particular form of "realism" engendered by and through perspective is as prominent and as forceful as these other ways of interpreting the world.[15] Indeed, the power of perspective lies not so much in its ability to capture visual truth as in its concealed reordering of perception itself. The willingness of observers to take perspectival images as unproblematically accurate representations (not only of the world but also of the way that they themselves see the world) speaks to broader reconceptualizations of the world as a preexistent Euclidean site of neutral, abstract coordinates. In line with Cartesian dualism, perspective splits the autonomous observer from their observed landscape, which is therefore placed at a distance from them. The eye of the observer becomes a mastering, God's-eye gaze upon a fixed scene, and "the entire process of perception [becomes] reduced to a mathematical form."[16]

This is quite different to the embedded, phenomenological conception of lived visual experience that Panofsky terms "psychophysiological space"—our subjective impression of surroundings that includes the periphery curvatures of vision, our own movements and micromovements, and the fused but competing twinned perceptions of binocular vision. Art historian Robert Hughes argues against understanding perspective as a transparent, accurate image of the world precisely because of these aspects of psychophysiological perception. He accordingly highlights the fluctuations of embodied viewing:

Look at an object: your eye is never still. It flickers, involuntarily restless, from side to side. Nor is your head still in relation to the object; every moment brings a fractional shift in its position, which results in a miniscule difference of aspect. The more you move, the bigger the shifts and differences become. If asked to, the brain can isolate a given view, frozen in time; but its experience of the world outside the eye is more like a mosaic than a perspective setup, a mosaic of multiple relationships, none of them (as far as vision is concerned) wholly fixed. Any sight is a sum of different glimpses. And so reality includes the painter's efforts to perceive it. Both the viewer and the view are part of the same field. Reality, in short, is interaction.[17]

Perspective generalizes certain aspects of vision and does away with others entirely, eradicating this sense of interaction. In order to "guarantee a fully rational—that is, infinite, unchanging and homogenous—space," it abstracts from "our actual subjective optical impression" and turns psychophysiological space into mathematical space.[18] This mathematical space is then perceptible by a mathematical being: a human with an immobile, monoscopic, and mastering eye engineered to sense distance and space by compositing the coordinates detected through multiple "rays" of cyclopean vision. Artistic credibility is assessed through visual accuracy and geolocational consistency, and meaningfulness is communicated through symbolic ordering rather than impressionistic visual interpretation.

The "discovery" of perspective did not by itself transform psychophysiological space into mathematical space. As Henri Lefebvre describes, artists of the fifteenth century could employ perspective so convincingly and effectively in both theory and practice because such a space already "lay before them" in their daily lives.[19] Italy at this time had been restructured by the changing relationship between the rural and the urban, and the increasing expenditure on architecture that resulted from surplus production and rise of merchant capitalism. Buildings, streets, and squares stressed their presence as visual constructions and as part of an emerging urban semiotics. Perspective responded to changes in spatial practice that emphasized linear visibility and the importance of sight lines, the use of building facades as markers of power and influence, and the intensifying readability of an increasingly commerce-oriented urban space.[20] Perspective and the buildings, public squares, and towns it was at this time most often used to depict must be seen in synthesis, as linked and mutually reinforcing occurrences in the history of space and dominant perceptions and imaginations around space. For Panofsky, the representation of geometrically systematic space is something "which modernity demands and realizes," this systematic space being a concrete expression of broader Renaissance thinking around epistemology, philosophy, and commerce.[21]

From the sixteenth century onward, the application of geometric space to physical, lived space allowed not only sight lines, linear projection, and geometric harmony to become key to the development of buildings and cities, but also the creation of what Lefebvre calls abstract space—a schematic and capitalistic conception of space-as-void. Seemingly neutral but in actuality ideologically loaded, within abstract space capital accumulation and exchange seem the only reasonable actions.[22] In a linked fashion, John Berger describes European oil painting since the Renaissance as a history of property accumulation and its proud depiction. Although such images purported to be, per Albertian perspective, "an imaginary window open onto the world," Berger argues in *Ways of Seeing* (1972) that a better model for them is "a safe let into the wall, a safe in which the visible has been deposited."[23] In either case, what seems neutral through abstraction—whether space or image—is actually tightly managed and controlled through this very same process of abstraction.

The Cartesian grid and infinite Euclidean space of perspective have since become, in Sean Cubitt's words, "unfelt norms of practice."[24] They not only pass "below the threshold of consciousness" but become automatic ways of seeing the world and of judging the realism of representations, even though they are predicated on a geometry that can be perceived as quite different from embodied vision.[25] This abstraction of space is willed into being by a system of commodity exchange and a nexus of social, imaginative, technological, and creative practices that all buy into its claims to dominance.

Were it not for perspective, the mechanization and globalization of the nineteenth and twentieth centuries would not have taken place: "neither homogeneity of space nor uniformity of nature, and science and technology as now conceived" would exist at all, as William Ivins argues.[26] The conceptual space of accumulation upon which the world market relies is a perspectival space, and therefore both perspective and capital need and propagate one another.[27] For instance, as a tool that schematizes space, perspective literally allows for the invention of schematics. Buildings could not only be represented with an objective, mathematical eye; they could be envisioned in this manner as well. It is hardly inconsequential that Brunelleschi was both a painter and an architect, his greatest achievement being the dome of the Cathedral of Santa Maria del Fiore in Florence.[28] The largest brick dome in history, this was realized through the employment of perspectival previsualization, which allowed Brunelleschi to create a building inaugurating "architectural neoplasticism," in which volume is made arbitrary and buildings attain a kind of weightlessness.[29] Objects and machinery could be previsualized in useful ways too, resulting in improved efficiency in design and production. As Samuel Edgerton describes, "Linear perspective drawing to scale made it possible to conceive, improve, and modify the most complicated machinery without having to waste time and money building and testing expensive three-dimensional models."[30]

The reductions enabled by schematics and this kind of schematic visuality are not only dimensional but social and spiritual. Lefebvre in particular argues that by instating planar representations of space as truthful, objective renditions of the world, we have abandoned the physical, embodied space in which we live and allowed ourselves to be dominated by plans and planners, instruments and instrumentalism.[31] As the psychophysiological is devalued in favor of the mathematical, the restless mosaic of embodied vision that Hughes describes—and the interaction it demands between subject and surroundings—is replaced by a rigid schematic, and a distanced observer. And if we believe that we can only read space productively if we reduce it to geometry, then we will not be able to conceive of uses for space that escape the explicit or implicit demands for productivity that come along with such abstraction.

FROM MUMMIFICATION TO INFORMATION: THEORIES OF DIGITAL MEDIA

This remains true for representations of space that are photographic. Perspective does not disappear with the rise of photographic spatial representation; photography might be considered a medium of the fleeting and the contingent, but as a method of producing images that were seemingly precise replications of visual space, perspective is its natural precursor. Photography creates multiple identical copies of (viewed) spaces through the application of a consistent, repeatable, algorithmic procedure, and most camera lenses are manufactured to produce an effectively perspectival space if used in the expected manner.[32] Lev Manovich goes so far as to suggest that photography automated perspectival images to an even greater extent than painters' previous reliance on mathematics and physical perspective machines.[33] Meanwhile, in his study of Panofsky's work, Hubert Damisch describes how the twentieth century is without doubt "much more massively 'informed' by the perspective paradigm, *thanks to photography, film, and now video,* than was the fifteenth century."[34] An image-saturated culture, especially one whose images are informed by

Renaissance art and produced through technological means that mimic its dictates, is necessarily a perspective-saturated one.[35]

For all this, however, the indexicality of analog photography seemed to supersede the mathematical view of space upon which it was built, and it is only with the ascent of digital images that the schematic, geometric qualities of perspective have been placed back on the agenda. This speaks to a fundamental theoretical schism between analog capture and digital representation, one which—due to the specifically digital nature of digital 3D—deserves attention here. This schism has been discussed at some length in film theory, especially in the late 1990s and early 2000s, a time in which the adoption of digital methods for the capture, manipulation, distribution, and exhibition of film and other moving-image media became inescapable. In what follows, I use this theoretical work in order to discuss the particular traits of digital media and establish the relationship of the digital to stereoscopic 3D.

Around the turn of the millennium, Sean Cubitt and Lev Manovich influentially described digital media as an inherently spatial media form, in contrast to the temporality of analog film.[36] This interpretation was echoed by David Rodowick, who in *The Virtual Life of Film* (2007) argued that the installation of digital technologies within the cinematic landscape moves film from a temporal art of representation to an atemporal and even nonrepresentational art form.[37] His argument is predicated on a Bazinian understanding of the photographic image as an indexical impression of a historical moment in space-time. The moving film image, consisting of numerous photographic sources animated through projection, augments this inherent connection with a specific event. Film allows us to view the world unseen and in doing so encourages phenomenological recognition of our own existence in the world and the conditions of this existence. Cinema may literally *screen* us from the world it visualizes, but it assures us that this world was once present, that the moment we are screened from *happened* at some prior point in historical time.[38] As an analogical art, film gives us a passing and passed moment that can be re-viewed but from which we are inherently, paradoxically separated in time and space.[39] This is its fundamental power, and it is a power that Rodowick, among others, believes is lost in the digital era. Rather than offer us an isomorphic, temporally deep connection with the past and with time itself, digital capture turns light into code, recording not existence but mathematically ordered sets of information.

Yet, for all that digital media differs from photographic media, this change is hard to pin down, since digital media work hard to evoke their analog predecessors. For Rodowick, the "felt change" that occurs in "our phenome-nological relationship" with film images—an ontological shifting of gears that is difficult to discern and define—is "uncanny and unsettling" precisely because the default models of form and function for these digital media seem to closely resemble those which came before.[40] Generally speaking, digitally captured content often strives to closely resemble the way in which the same content would appear had it been captured cinematographically. Meanwhile, digitally generated visual effects strive for what Stephen Prince has influen-tially called "perceptual realism"—a sense that they are anchored within the spatiotemporal environments into which they are digitally inserted.[41] So, while digital production methods do certainly change the horizon of possi-bilities for filmmakers and impact upon the aesthetic of their films, the kinds of shots and sequences, screens and images that they produce can be consid-ered broadly familiar to photochemical cinephotography. This resemblance functions to reassure spectators—even in the midst of heavily marketed tech-nologies such as CGI, IMAX, and 3D itself—that the fundamentals of film experience remain recognizable and consistent. Relatively stable for almost a hundred years, the dominant mode of mainstream cinematic entertainment remains a roughly two-hour narrative consisting of multiple edited shots that articulate a comprehensible world and unfolding actions within it.

This effectively disguises the changes that have occurred through the growth of digital image capture and dissemination. As Rodowick proposes, cinema quietly becomes a simulation of what it once was: "Our audiovisual culture is currently a digital culture, but with a cinematic look."[42] To use the suggestive description of Thomas Elsaesser and Malte Hagener, even though "everything has changed (underneath)"—that is, cinema has moved "from photographic to graphic film, from representation to presentation"—nonetheless through digital cinema's visual familiarity we are assured "everything will stay the same (on the surface)."[43] Moreover, digital tools have not suddenly, abruptly swept away that which came before. Just as cinema itself was not "born" in any par-ticular place on any particular date but rather emerged as a holistic category only gradually (and indeed only in hindsight), so too digital media has been (and is being) culturally and industrially installed in a piecemeal, disjointed fashion—it did not emerge fully formed and instantly relegate to irrelevance all that came before. Digital processes have rather been slowly grafted onto their predecessors (and continue to be), meaning that digital cinema resem-bles and fulfills many of the same functions as predigital cinema. Contem-porary digital filmmaking still relies on shot compositions, editing structures, storytelling strategies, and even viewing procedures (such as theatrical exhibition) that are far from novel to the twenty-first century. The production and release of any given film may be heavily reliant on digital technology, but for the most part films still fit a generalized aesthetic mold that was established before such technologies were employed.[44]

The submerged changes that take place in the digital age so foundationally reorient this medium's operations that the persistent surface resemblance to analog forms can be interpreted as duplicitous. If one considers digital capture to evacuate the defining feature of moving-image photography, and thus of cinema as it has been made and discussed for a century, then it seems impossible to take at face value that things are much the same as ever. Rodowick's account of film's changing ontology in the digital era is accordingly infused with nostalgia for what has been lost. This is perhaps not surprising, since he was writing at a moment during which the digital's relationship to prior, physical, or indexical media was still highly contested, and the potential "death of cinema" touted in the late 1990s was still fresh in the memory. So, for all that Rodowick alights on the possibilities and particulars of the digital—understanding it as part of an evolving landscape in which the use, reception, and meaning of audiovisual narrative media is never stable—his book constructs its arrival as a loss of analog connection, of phenomenological investment, of a kind of film culture that may have once seemed permanent but is now revealed as a fleeting historical moment in which film worked in certain ways and meant certain things.

Central to what is lost for Rodowick is a connection between (photographic and photochemical) film and the world—digital technology seems too abstract to provide the kinds of useful world reflection that he and others associate with celluloid. Meanwhile, William Mitchell describes the difference between analog and digital in terms of calculation—while the former offers smooth traces or impressions, the latter offers step-based gradations. Subtle flow is replaced on a molecular level by cellular logic and pixilation, as pictures become "a two-dimensional array of integers (the *raster grid*) [that] can be stored in computer memory, transmitted electronically, and interpreted by various devices to produce displays and printed images."[45] In the hands of digital sensors and computer software, what the camera lens "sees" becomes a series of flexible, compatible, binary data sets: as Cubitt describes, information "has to be converted into numbers in order to be taken over into digital storage," and such quantifying operations always involve the selection of certain details and the discarding of others.[46] The screen is interpreted as a grid, color values are manipulated, and to save computerized storage space and meet streaming demands data is compressed in ways that seek to be minimally noticeable to viewers (lower levels of resolution for portions of the image that contain unchanging block colors, for instance). The information actually stored in digital media—binary code, numeric color designation, Euclidean coordination—is its core content, rather than any indexical trace of space-time past. Those images and sounds that digital media produce must then be especially rendered for the human observer from this source information. In Mark Hansen's description, "The digital image is not really an "image" at all: far from being a correlate of the imaginary domain of sense experience, it designates the "objective" circulation of digital data . . . emancipated from any constraining correlation with human perceptual ratios."[47] In Cubitt's words, "Digital media do not refer. They communicate."[48] Not a window on a temporal, past moment, screens are now interactive devices for accessing recorded, regimented data.

For all these writers, the malleability of digital images detaches them from the connection to the past that seemed to define analog media. While not all of this work—and certainly not the considerable amount of scholarship concerning the digital in the subsequent decades—puts this in starkly black-and-white terms and condemns the digital as incapable of ethical, emotional, or even aesthetic investment, nonetheless it is crucial to note the general agreement that digital images are in some sense ahistorical.[49] Thanks to the separation of input and output, instead of the Bazinian death mask of photographic cinema we are given a computed rendering of abstracted information regarding the constitution of light at a given moment. In the process of digitized capture, "the uniform image becomes an assemblage of discrete and modular parts subject to numerical processing and manipulation."[50] No longer called on to evoke the past and the passing of time, cinema in the digital age is used to sort and organize real-time information.

We might therefore see the digital as defined less by a particular aesthetic than by a social function—namely, the managing of data in the present tense. As Cubitt proposes in his more recent media archaeological study *The Practice of Light* (2014), the deep structure of digital image capture joins up with the "database economy" that is ascendant in the twenty-first century.[51] This economy relies upon quantified, numerically organized visual data and pixelated relations of equivalence. The gridded raster display of digital media profoundly echoes these conditions, converting time into a searchable and malleable spatial representation.[52] Philip Rosen's earlier study of digital media similarly emphasizes not indexicality, but three contrasting "ideals" of digital imagery: "(1) the *practically infinite manipulability* of digital images; (2) *convergence* among diverse image media; and (3) *interactivity*."[53] As "ideals," these traits may not be unique to the digital but operate as organizing principles and expectations, speaking to the apparent technical strengths of digital images and their broadly defined cultural expectations and uses.[54]

These scholars may have been writing for the most part at a time when digital media still had some possible sense of novelty, but their interpretations still apply to today's digital entertainment output. Their work indicates the extent to which the *image* as a concept is undergoing intense change in the digital era. Put overly simplistically, this change is from mummification to information, from representation to simulation, from the temporal to the spatial. This is not to claim that every analog image should be cherished as an indexical trace of past time, nor that every digital image must be scrutinized as a spatial rendering in the present tense. Rather, the "ideal" of the digital involves a spatial dimension that privileges not time passing but a flexible, interactive present. Sensors within digital cameras capture algorithmic information sets that must be processed to be visually presented to their user. More than this, such data sets are recorded and interpreted as spatial—they not only exist in and as a planar pixel spreadsheet in which each unit is tagged with a color value, but can include exact, measured, cartographic information about distance and shape in ways that could only be hypothesized in relation to analogue media. Digital technology allows and even encourages a spatialization of the image in which measured data around depth and positioning form the fundamental structure from which the represented world is built, or which are otherwise made available.

In this, digital media clearly take up the baton of perspectival imaging, continuing to propagate the idea that the correct quantification of space creates objective renderings that are superior to subjective impressions. This hardly troubles perspective's earlier installation at the heart of visual culture of a scientific mode of looking and is demonstrated particularly acutely in computer graphics. If perspective describes an atomistic, mapped world that is useful to commodity capitalism—since it allows objects to be plotted, moved, and exchanged against a background of abstract space—then this is similarly the world conjured by computer-generated images. As Mitchell describes, although the alliance Alberti established between painting and science may have been unsettled by photography, "with computer graphics it was born again," since algorithms to produce perspectival renderings were key to the development of computerized virtual worlds in the second half of the twentieth century.[55] Moreover, the light rays that Alberti describes emanating from the eye and rebounding back with exact distant measurements find technological expression in digital scanning techniques like LIDAR, with modes of military, medical, scientific, and entertainment imaging actively scanning and measuring the world, rather than providing a photographic embalming of it.[56] Computer graphics thus digitize perspective, both because graphics present their produced images in a perspectivally organized fashion, and because they are predicated on space that is mathematically coordinated rather than psychophysiologically perceived.

So, while the very nature of *images* and our relationship to them might be shifting in the digital era, it is vital to note how the *spaces* generated through digital 3D production practices remain on the whole heavily reliant upon the kind of Cartesian cartographic coordination associated with perspective and its organization of visual material. The detachment of input from output and the status of the pixelated image as a recorder of *information* rather than temporal presence enable this image to become a vehicle of recorded and even real-time spatial data, not just an illusionistic surface with all its potential ambiguities.[57] Digital media therefore quite literally, but very complexly, deepen the logic of perspective.

DIGITAL 3D AS SYMBOLIC FORM

What does all this have to do with 3D cinema? Images, as shown, are not what they once were. With the advent of the digital, the image changed "underneath," even though its surface appearance remains generally familiar. As Rodowick in particular puts it, digital technologies and computational processes have altered what were considered, in the photographic era, the norms of the image, fuelling "powerful countercurrents that reconfigure these norms, shifting the function of screens and challenging spectators to reconsider the very concept of the image."[58] What Rodowick in 2007 termed "countercurrents" might today better be thought of as the dominant currents (or perhaps riptides) of technosocial change in the twenty-first century. Digital 3D cinema is a key part of these. Even with its long history (outlined in the previous chapter), 3D cinema represents a highly visible site of the changes to the image engendered by the digital turn. Today, digital technologies alter the way 3D is produced, manipulated, and received; how they do this points to the smooth interlocking of digital processes, stereoscopic media, and spatialized, simulative renderings.

As I will show in more detail in part 2, the digital image is, at least potentially, always 3D, thanks to its data-rich, informational ontology. This, again, makes it quite different from analog media. A defining quality of the photo-chemical, as we have seen, is the sense that a moment in time has been captured; or, in Bazin's famous formulation, that change has been mummified.[59] Whatever decisions around lens choice, film stock, angle, and composition made at the time of analog capture are "baked in," intrinsic to the image. The expanded opportunities for alteration that digital images offer, by contrast, are key not only to their constitution, use by commercial entertainment industries, and cultural function, but are also fundamental in the creation of stereoscopic media. Analog equipment in the twentieth century was more than capable of capturing and exhibiting matched stereoscopic pairs, but errors in the capture stage were all but impossible to fix. 3D demands not only the screening of twinned images, but also their exactly calibrated alignment: the two image-streams must harmonize geometrically (the frames of each must match perfectly) as well as cinematographically (colorization, shutter speed, and light levels must be identical) and temporally (they must be timed exactly with one another to prevent any temporal offset). As such, all possible variables (lens shape, light levels, image quality, color tone, film speed, and so on) need to be matched across the two cameras of a stereoscopic rig, which is to say these variables must be measurable and repeatable. Beyond the capture stage, successful 3D exhibition similarly demands the perfect alignment of multiple projectors and/or reels of film. Since all of these are difficult to achieve with celluloid, image misalignment was common during analog projection, resulting in increased possibilities for "fatigue, eyestrain, discomfort, poor image quality, double vision," or even the loss of stereoscopic depth entirely.[60] Stephen Prince concludes as a result that the "medium of celluloid was inherently unsuitable as a technology for inducing stereoscopy."[61]

Digital image capture is not only more capable of dealing in exact attributes, but, as we have seen, is specifically predicated on this capacity: to "become manageable by computers, the world must become *information*, that is, quantifiable or numerically manipulable."[62] So, while analog 3D was problematic, the informational and manipulable nature of the digital image, by contrast, allows contemporary 3D films to align image pairs with mathematical precision, aiding both 3D film production and exhibition.[63] This is not a condemnation of analog 3D (nor a celebration of its digital incarnation), but a verifiable fact of industrial practice. In Leon Gurevitch's words, "Digital technology has finally allowed the combination of cinematic and stereoscopic spectacle as a viable economic form."[64] If celluloid film was "too unruly, too irregular in its taking and in its projecting" to become synonymous with 3D content,[65] then the capacity for digital tools to manipulate images at the capturing and editing stages and so bring them into carefully ruled, regularized alignment is crucial to the success of 3D media in the present moment.[66]

Further to this, computer-generated images find an appropriate home in 3D exhibition, which allows their Euclidean dimensionality to be effectively retained. Indeed, digital 3D's evocation of simulated spaces is perhaps most obvious and pronounced in the computer-generated effects that large-scale 3D films use to create their environments. Major Hollywood 3D productions like *Alice in Wonderland* (2010), *TRON: Legacy* (2010), *John Carter* (2012), and many others all make explicit the links between 3D and digital special effects—and contemporary 3D *as* a digital special effect—simply but powerfully through the visual abundance of and narrative reliance upon CGI environments. *Gravity* (2013), a film critically applauded for both its realism and its use of 3D, is for significant portions of its running time entirely computer animated, save for the faces of the two key actors. Even *The Great Gatsby* (2013), a drama set in Depression-era New York City, and *Life of Pi* (2013), a sentimental fable about a shipwrecked young boy, deploy pervasive digital special effects (including extensive environment creation) alongside 3D exhibition in a manner that underscores the fundamental correspondence between CGI and stereoscopy, a correspondence also accentuated by the overwhelming 3D availability of digitally animated feature films since 2010 (and even the conversion of earlier CG animated features).

In all these cases, the manufacture of CG environments and objects, like digital media more generally, has relied on the recording of space and time as strictly geometrical and analytical datasets, with these datasets then being used to create a simulated rendering of space. Stereoscopy can then function as a value of this simulated rendering, asserting the totality of the simulated space. While planar computer-generated images demand the reduction of computer-mapped geometry to two dimensions for the purposes of representation, stereoscopic exhibition retains the three-dimensional volumes with which digital environments are themselves manufactured in the virtual world of the computer. The temporality and unruly indexicality of analog cinema is replaced by mapped spaces that are endlessly visualizable. As a result, we can consider every piece of digital 3D, and most obviously postconverted digital 3D, as a computer-generated special effect of sorts—a geometrically coordinated, volumetrically mapped entity. This digital virtualization of reality is perspectivally organized, built from perspective rather than having had perspective applied to it.[67] Crucially, in the realm of computer graphics, such spaces are produced inevitably, whether they are presented on a planar screen or as a stereoscopic illusion.

This symbiosis is by no means just a happy accident. Indeed, the connections between digital and 3D media are such that Elsaesser (briefly) proposes that digital 3D might be a kind of contemporary symbolic form in the Panofskian sense. Elsaesser takes critics of 3D to task for considering it a method of "enhanced realism within Renaissance space," an approach that, as he says, can only lead to disappointment and accusations of failure.[68] He argues that 3D not only encompasses the concerns and rhetorics of the digital, but also displaces the concerns and rhetorics associated with perspective and thus installs itself as a new regime. Replacing perspective, digital 3D is for Elsaesser associated not with mathematical vision but with a kind of overwhelming media experience and a delocated, unshackled subject position (240). 3D is to be understood less as a special effect than an effort to naturalize a new "technologically produced spatial vision," a form of vision of which 3D is itself a significant example (221). Echoing the argument made in the previous chapter that 3D should not be seen as a system of spatial representation that might somehow recapitulate (and thus compete with) classical continuity practices, Elsaesser asserts that digital 3D works to "reset" our ideas around media and space in the current computerized milieu of multiple data screens and endlessly hyperlinked images and text, changing "our sense of spatial and temporal orientation and our embodied relation to data-rich simulated environments" (221).

Elsaesser's account will be taken up in further detail in what follows; however, his proposal that digital 3D replaces perspective is problematic. Calling digital 3D a symbolic form runs the risk firstly of suggesting that it has supplanted perspective in a holistic and integral fashion, and secondly that it commands the kind of cultural pervasiveness associated with perspectival art. Neither suggestion is quite accurate. Elsaesser argues that contemporary 3D extends the registers of "post-Euclidean space" and so increases a spectator's range of "conceptual responses" (240). This may be true, but even in the context of such new visual paradigms it is vital to stress the consistent logics that are in play in the move from planar, perspectival, geometric systems of spatial knowledge to digital 3D production and exhibition. Like computer graphics, 3D is a kind of intensification of perspective rules; in Rosalind Krauss's words, it is "stereographic space is perspectival space raised to a higher power."[69] Meanwhile, any claims around digital 3D's cultural importance as a mode of vision must be tempered by the awareness that planar media culture continues to proliferate in the digital age—screens both large and small, public and private, remain in many cases 2D.[70]

So, perhaps paradoxically, thinking of digital 3D as a kind of symbolic form points both to its links with perspectival rules, as well as to its distinctive qualities in the contemporary media environment. Simultaneously historical and novel, at once built from 2D images and entirely escaping imagistic logics in its reception, digital 3D's place in visual culture is privileged in a double sense: not only indicative, but also somehow exclusive. 3D media sum up many of the ideals of the digital, even as they also stand apart from the rest of digital media thanks to their highly distinctive visuality.

As we have seen, it is not necessary to presume sequential, discrete moments of optical organization; rather, vision and attention might better be understood as palimpsestic and multiple. If this is the case, then the value of approaching digital 3D as a symbolic form lies not in labeling the dominant, domineering visual organization of our age, but in unpicking the specific "world discoveries" that digital 3D presupposes. That is, if digital 3D is described as a symbolic form, then this prompts us to discover how this technology prestructures the spaces and experiences it provides.

• • •

Symbolic forms are dominant modes of interpreting the world that assert truthfulness even as they are selective about what they represent and highly prescribed in how they present it. Cassirer's model aims to cure us of the one-sidedness that symbolic forms themselves work to disseminate, reminding us of their structural operations and predetermined criteria of inclusion and exclusion. So, while physicists "come to believe in the literal existence of atoms, biologists of genes, economists of interests," interpreting science and economics as symbolic forms reveals atoms, genes, and economic structures to be "mere stratagems of the human intellect, sketches of a reality that forever outstrips in richness and magnitude the resources of any single representational framework."[71] Yet these stratagems become unseen, unconsidered conventions. The enormous influence of perspective upon ideas of art, realism, and visual culture is revealed through its apparent invisibility, which is to say its still-persisting evocation of accuracy, fidelity, and objectivity, and how it is generally taken as "equivalent to natural vision."[72] Nonetheless, perspective's depictions of visual and spatial experience are not automatically "superior" to any concurrently existing alternatives. As Martin Kemp explains, perspective is little more than a convention, albeit a convention "remorselessly promulgated by the societal, political, and economic forces which oversaw its birth. We have no reason for assuming that it is inherently better than the modes of representation adopted by other civilizations, whether we mean 'better' artistically or with respect to efficacy in depicting what we think we see."[73] The concept of space that perspective relies upon and disseminates is precisely a *concept*, one bound up with historical changes in both thinking about the place of human-kind in the universe and the social organization of societies and nations, which in the Renaissance were increasingly reliant on standardized practices of measurement and trade.

Therefore, the usefulness in applying the symbolic form concept to 3D lies less in claiming that digital 3D has replaced perspective, or that 3D is an ines-capable, monolithic optical mode. Certainly, we can claim that 3D is currently prevalent, influential, and popular to varying degrees, but this is not neces-sarily to also suggest that 3D media are all-encompassing and that other media are not available. Digital 3D has not supplanted perspectival art as the domi-nant visual mode in a now-globalized Western image culture; cinema and other visual media do not seem to be inherently and inexorably moving toward an ascendant stereoscopic mode of address. Nonetheless, 3D cinema *does* encapsulate many of the dominant and emerging logics that structure media, technology, and spatial knowledge at the present digital moment, logics that (as we will see in forthcoming chapters) also undergird the virtual spaces of operational military simulations, computer games, totalized surveillance appa-ratuses, and augmented reality media. As a result, thinking about digital 3D cinema in terms of symbolic forms begins to prise open the deep structure of the worlds that digital 3D presumes and propagates, revealing this medium's status as a visual technology that (like perspective, but in subtly different ways) prestructures knowledge and expectations around space, representation and action, and that is connected to a wider array of twenty-first-century visual culture.

3D media are "world discoveries" produced in accordance with an evolv-ing but structurally distinct system for the expression of perception, a system tied to broader sociocultural conditions. Just as it is useful to understand atoms as productions of the sciences rather than neutral objects in and of themselves, it is helpful for theorists of visual culture to understand digital 3D (and planar media, for that matter) as productions of particular technologies. Both perspec-tive and stereoscopic media are world-mediations that not only structure the world but preordain what we can and cannot perceive when applying this structure to the world in the first place. What kind of world this is will be the subject of part 2 of this book.

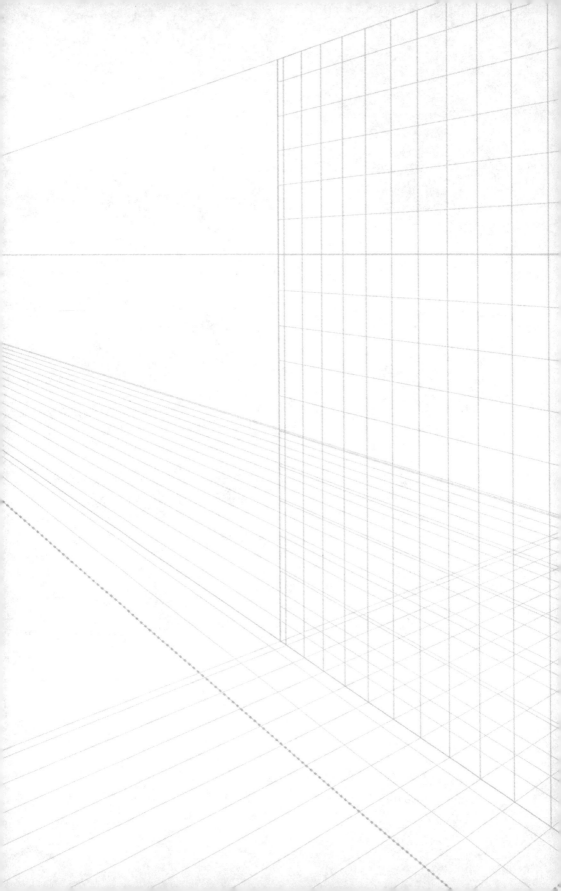

PART 2

MAPPED SPACES

The following three chapters concern the mapped spaces of digital 3D. They reveal how tools of 3D visualization productively connect with and also extend the reach, uses, and utility of cinematic computer-generated imagery and digital film production pipelines. They also demonstrate the way in which digital 3D simulates, virtualizes, and instrumentalizes the world and its contents in ways that join up with a variety of other digital technologies. My central claim throughout this part of the book is that digital 3D must be seen as a method for producing space, one dictated by ideas of accuracy, control, and operationalization, as well as influenced by and imbricated within a long-standing conception of space as neutral, abstract, and reproducible. These features, I argue, are embodied both within the production methods that create contemporary 3D, and the way the format is employed in the narrative and visual economies of specific films. That is, the plots and mise-en-scènes of the films I analyze in these chapters not only trace shifting ideas about screens, screened spaces, and our relationship to them, but these films themselves, through their 3D production methodologies, also propagate ideas around visualization and spatial representation that are shared by a range of other industries including digital projection, previsualization, volumetric mapping techniques, and laser scanning technologies. 3D is thus best seen as part of a broader change in visuality, one that is bound up with commercial, industrial, and military processes rather than confined to moving-image enter-tainment media.

My focus in what follows upon simulation and the technological mapping of space builds upon the analysis of digital media and sym-bolic forms undertaken previously. Rodowick argues that representa-tions have an isomorphic, analogical relationship to that which they represent, while the digital, by contrast, is an atemporal, manipulable media form; as a result, the digital can never be *representational*, only *simulative*.[1] Moreover, this simulative function encodes at a deeper level the algebraic workings and mathematical rationalizations of Euclidean cartography, which structures Western image-making more generally through the widespread adoption of perspectival techniques. As Rodowick states, "The goal of both digital capture and synthesis is to constitute a space that is mathematically definable and manipula-ble."[2] This emphasis on space is telling, and considering Rodowick's words alongside digital 3D can lead us to propose that the digital's definition of realism is not an indexical link to the past but the simu-lation of space as Cartesian cube. That is, although digital 3D enacts a spatialization of the image, digital 3D space is not space itself but image-as-space, an aggregation and visualization of spatial data points.

By connecting artifacts of popular cinema to other visual systems both within and beyond the sphere of entertainment media, I hope to show how digital 3D relies upon ideas of quantified simulation, immersive spatial generation, and surveillant visuality. Chapter 3 explores the operationalized 3D spaces of *Avatar* (2009), a key digital 3D film that unsurprisingly crystallizes the medium's capacity to record data and apparently disregard materiality. Chapter 4 further discusses the informational space of 3D, describing how the format aligns with virtual reality (VR) and augmented reality (AR) technol-ogies, and how films like *Iron Man 3* (2013) and *Insurgent* (2015) visu-alize the eradication of screen-based interfaces. Finally, chapter 5 dis-cusses digital 3D conversion alongside surveillance practices, tracing their tight interrelationship with reference to *RoboCop* (2014). In each case, I alight upon particular films as evidence of the importance of 3D not only to entertainment media but also military and industrial agents, an affinity revealed both in the way these films are made and in their depictions of technology and stereoscopic rendering. This is not solely a symptomatic relationship—the films to which I refer do not just trace existing technologies and technological imaginaries, but actively propagate and celebrate them. This is thanks to the links between digital 3D cinema and those other industrial contexts that will be described. Embedded within newly digitized industrial practices, CGI, the science-fiction genre, and the volumetric virtualization of space, digital 3D cinema embodies a future-oriented conception of cinema and space, describing a technologically deterministic vision of what media and the simulation of reality are for, a vision shared by broader technocultural forces. The films examined in this section reveal this with particular clarity, as they perform for global mass audiences the uses and pleasures of 3D technologies.

3

SIMULATION

· ·

Dematerializing and Enframing

F or all the pervasiveness of stereoscopic media across a range of contexts in the nineteenth and twentieth centuries, 1952's unlikely exploitation hit *Bwana Devil* represented the popularization of a marginal technology, a popularization that worked to instantly bring that technology into the mainstream (albeit, as we have seen, somewhat briefly). But if the dramatic uptake of analogue 3D cinema exhibition in the United States in the early 1950s was prompted by the unexpectedly enormous financial success of an independent, low-budgeted film, the widespread diffusion of digital 3D was driven by an enormously costly Hollywood production designed to be a flagship vehicle for the format. In the twenty-first century, industrial actors threw considerable weight behind the medium, with the creative personnel and studio backers of 2009's *Avatar*—at the time the most expensive film ever made and assertively hyped as a 3D event—placing concordant pressure upon exhibitors to acquire the necessary technology for its stereoscopic presentation.[1] *Avatar* aggressively sought to bring digital 3D (and with it digital projection systems) into a large number of cinemas not previously capable of exhibiting this format, in the process advertising not just the aesthetic potential of the medium to audiences but also its financial potential to exhibitors and studios.

Avatar was not the first narrative feature film to do this work. *The Polar Express* (2004), *Chicken Little* (2005), and *Beowulf* (2007) were all important precursors, and while all represent major financial investments that sought to advertise the stereoscopic medium, none of these earlier digital 3D films matched *Avatar*'s global commercial appeal, nor came close to its quarter-billion-dollar production budget or its near-$2.8bn global box office. These preceding films also did not place quite the same narrative and thematic emphasis on the digital simulation and navigation of space. Upon release, *Avatar*'s visuals drew a degree of critical praise (even if its plotting and characterisation did not),[2] and subsequently its 3D effects, depth composition strategies, and negotiation of empire, animation, and stereoscopy have all been the subject of significant scholarly attention.[3] Something of a critical and commercial standard-bearer for digital 3D, *Avatar* argues forcefully for the value and importance of simulated environments in the digital age and includes stereoscopy as a fundamental part of such environments. Its production methods of motion-capture suits and abstract filming stages, alongside its narrative of colonial mapping and disembodied presence and its aesthetic of ethereal holographic wonder, encapsulate many prevailing ideas of the successful deployment of digital 3D today. As much as it is aesthetically pleasing, this deployment is also outlined by the film as intensely operational.

In this chapter, I use *Avatar* to specifically explore ideas of digital simulation, with simulation here understood as a replication of space (following its careful mapping) that is put to functional use. I investigate simulation both as a feature *within* the text (stereoscopic simulative technologies and practices represented within the fictional diegesis) and as a feature *of* the text (digital 3D animation as itself a simulation). I focus in particular on *Avatar*'s depiction of the expected uses of simulation in the near future, and, by extension, how such simulations function in our own present day. *Avatar* may be set in 2154, but its diegetic and production technologies speak very clearly to today's virtual productions of space and their uses. As I show with the help of the work of Martin Heidegger and Jordan Crandall, the use of 3D "operational media" by on-screen characters, and the treatment of the world by these characters as a standing reserve of potential energy, is echoed in the film's own stereoscopic ontology.[4] Notwithstanding the ideological work performed by the narrative regarding ecological awareness and spiritual harmony, the film's broad aesthetic as well as particular elements of its mise-en-scène reveal the extent to which digital 3D is currently employed as a medium for future-oriented spatial mapping, visual recording, and imperial domination. Firmly embedded within military-industrial frameworks, the simulations provided by digital 3D allow and propagate nominalist mapping, action at a distance, and a highly regimented, Cartesian visual field, and this process is performed both within and by the film. Such a simulationist aesthetic is predicated on 3D's capacity to separate form from matter, and it is to this that I initially turn.

FORM DIVORCED FROM MATTER

. . . .

Jonathan Crary has argued that the nineteenth-century stereoscope unsettled the kind of disembodied and abstracted vision that was associated with the camera obscura and planar representation.[5] However, this is not a consistent reading of the device at its commercial height, and the stereoscope's depth effects can in fact be understood as useful simulations or reproductions of real space, which allowed stereoscopic media to be put to work within Victorian visual culture in a very precise, commodity-oriented manner. In the words of John Plunkett, the stereoscope was culturally appealing for the way it played to "a deep-seated western desire to erode the gap between the viewing subject and non-local object," an erosion the device seemed to achieve to a greater extent than photography.[6] As shown in chapter 1, while the laboratory use of the apparatus revealed that the visual perception of depth and space was something of a fiction generated by an observer, in popular culture it could seemingly demonstrate the opposite: the infallibility of the eye, and the eye's ability to even usurp and do duty for other senses.

A key proponent of this objectifying view of the stereoscope was US physician and writer Oliver Wendell Holmes, who saw the stereoscope as a way of making everything *even more* visible by turning the sense of touch itself into visual information. In his 1859 article "The Stereoscope and the Stereograph," Holmes praises those technological developments that allow the visual presence of something to remain, and remain fixed, after the thing itself has gone. He is enthusiastic about the Daguerreotype, a photographic process in which a sheet of silver captures a latent image, and that he calls a *"mirror with a memory."*[7] His excitement for the stereoscope is even more effusive. He considers it not just an amusing entertainment, but—when conjoined with photography—a radical step forward in mimetic realism. For Holmes, a stereoscope is not only "an instrument which makes surfaces look solid," but one capable of producing "an appearance of reality which cheats the senses with its seeming truth" (74). In the stereoscope, as he puts it, "by means of two different views of an object, the mind, as it were *feels round it* and gets an idea of its solidity," allowing the eyes to "clasp" the object as might hands or fingers (75). By displacing what we might think of as a haptic, embodied sense of material reality from the physical act of touch and moving it into the visual act of recognition, Holmes positions the stereoscope as a supreme technology for recording presence and existence. Just as thought becomes intelligible through its rendering as the written word, for Holmes form becomes more useful and productive through its abstraction from physical presence (80). In such a model, realism is less about believable or authentic presentation (although these remain vital) than it is about substituting the real with its simulated double.

This simulative paradigm allows Holmes to go further than just claiming stereoscopic photographs offer accurate or truthful reproductions of the world. He proposes they can in fact entirely and satisfactorily *replace* the world. As he states, albeit with some irony,

> *Form is henceforth divorced from matter.* In fact, matter as a visible object is of no great use any longer, except as the mould on which form is shaped. Give us a few negatives of a thing worth seeing, taken from different points of view, and this is all we want of it. Pull it down or burn it up, if you please.... Matter in large masses must always be fixed and dear; form is cheap and transportable. We have got the fruit of creation now, and need not trouble ourselves with the core. Every conceivable object of Nature and Art will soon scale off its surface for us. (80–81)

Earlier in this same essay Holmes discusses the inventions of railroad travel, commercial electrical telegraphy, and chloroform: all changed life in unimaginable ways in the nineteenth century but nonetheless quickly became standard aspects of travel, communication, and medicine, respectively. As such, he implies that stereoscopic media will become as fundamental and as useful as these other inventions. Thanks to the stereoscope, forms will not only circulate in a frictionless manner; they will supplant the existence of that concrete matter that informs and engenders them, rendering such material structures redundant.

Stereoscopes were not the first time that space had been simulated, but they simulated it in a manner that gratified Victorian desires for scientifically exacting replication and personalized, commodified use.[8] Jib Fowles accordingly connects the "new canon for truth" the stereoscope seemed to offer with the industrial context of nineteenth-century colonial powers. Just as natural resources were being transformed into economic goods on a mass scale, so too the stereoscope "operated on the visible world as yet another resource, converted it into manipulable units, and cultivated a profitable market for those units."[9] The stereoscope rendered everything "touchable" or haptically comprehensible to the privileged Western gaze, a gaze that was still at the center of knowledge and that now also displaced physical contact as a source of object-knowledge. Stereocards recorded the wonders of the world (explicitly labelling them as such) and brought these inside the borders of Western nations and even within the Victorian subject's own living room. Caught by such a "virtual grasp," "every spectacle became a specimen,"[10] and the observable was rendered "yet another standardized commodity, like bricks."[11] As this comparison indicates, the usefulness of the stereocard lay in both reproducibility and standardization. A single view could be sold many times over in many different territories. It could also enter a circuit of exchange alongside other views that were understood in the same way. Cards included carefully formulated information about the sight and site presented, classifying it and inserting it into a stable, preexisting system of knowledge, leaving the user in no doubt as to the meaning and significance of that which was visualized. Moreover, no matter how immense the sight recorded (say, the Sphinx, or the Brooklyn Bridge), the user was ultimately in control: the representation "did not tower over them; they towered over it."[12]

If the resource produced in this manner was immaterial rather than material, this was the very source of its value. Tom Gunning illustrates how Holmes's historical description above speaks to the way in which photography (and by extension the stereoscopic media Holmes was directly discussing) functioned to dematerialize commodity culture in expedient and profitable ways. Focusing in particular on the body, Gunning suggests that the visual culture of photographic reproduction in the nineteenth century should thus be understood

> not simply as the latest stage in realistic representation but also as part of a new system of exchange which could radically transform traditional beliefs in solidity and unique identity. Such fixed ideas could disintegrate in the solvents circulating through the modern networks of exchange and transportation. The body itself appeared to be abolished, rendered immaterial, through the phantasmagoria of both still and motion photography. This transformation of the physical did not occur through the sublimation of an ethereal idealism. The body, rather, became a transportable image fully adaptable to the systems of circulation and mobility that modernity demanded.[13]

What was true of the body was also true of space, which similarly became immaterial and subsumed into networks of visual exchange. The surface dimensions of a thing or an area need only be captured stereoscopically for their material form to become unnecessary, even expendable. As such, the purported realism of stereoscopic media need not be construed as an alternative kind of visuality (one offering an *embodied* experience of subjective space), but rather as a way of adding a kind of bonus dimension to undisturbed Cartesian, geometrical, *optical* experience. As in photography, the reproduction of not-present material in the stereoscope offered a way to take ownership of that which was being reproduced; the better the reproduction, the more effective the ownership, and the stereoscope seemed to offer marked "improvement" in its inclusion of depth and sensuous realism.[14] If this was a celebrated result of stereoscopic media in the nineteenth century, then this is no less true today.

PANDORAN PERCEPTION

The extraction of form from matter, far from ending with the close of the nineteenth century or the demise of the stereoscope's cultural standing, remains a sought-after goal of entertainment and other media and has reached something of a pinnacle in electronic and digital media and their simulations of space.[15] The image- and screen-saturated cultures of the twentieth and twenty-first centuries seem to work toward a mediated epistemology in which form is everpresent, and matter is a secondary consideration (if considered at all).[16] Digital 3D is an essential part of this tendency to privilege form at the expense of matter. Nondigital, non-3D cinema and photography may in many ways equally remove matter from the equation, but in digital 3D we witness an extension and extrapolation of this removal. Planar cinema abstracts matter through the use of an illusionistic screen *surface*; 3D intensifies this through its production of virtual volumetric *spaces* that are equally matterless. Furthermore, just as digital cinema can circulate globally thanks to wired connectivity—films downloaded to theaters and viewers rather than shipped to them or purchased in shops—so too digital 3D asserts contemporary technology's capacity to render space itself immaterial and transmittable as digital code through the network. In these ways, the digitally created content of contemporary 3D cinema updates the stereoscope's concern with the extraction of form from matter: going further than Holmes dreamed, the sources of the stereoscope's tangible spaces might not be burned up or torn down once their spatial dimensions have been captured, since these sources need not physically exist in the first place.

This can be seen through analysis of *Avatar*, a science fiction action-adventure film that revels in the digitally created space of Pandora and narrates the importance of technology in accessing and appreciating this space. The film's 3D CGI operates at the self-declared vanguard of a technological revolution reorganizing space as something virtual and simulated, operationalized and dominated. The plot concerns Jake Sully (Sam Worthington), a marine who in the near future travels to alien planet Pandora as part of a scientific expedition led by Dr. Grace Augustine (Sigourney Weaver).[17] Jake's twin brother was originally assigned to the mission but has been killed in a random mugging; Jake now acts as a willing, if bewildered, replacement. An unemployed, wheelchair-bound military veteran of an unspecified terrestrial conflict, Jake himself has no formal scientific training, but the similarity of his genetic signature allows his consciousness to be uploaded into the "avatar" of his dead sibling—a clone of the humanoid natives of Pandora, the Na'vi. Through his avatar, Jake meets a Na'vi tribe and becomes indoctrinated into their way of life (which resembles an idealized version of Native American cultural practices) and even falls in love with Neytiri (Zoe Saldana), a warrior in the tribe and the chief's daughter. Further conflict is introduced through the presence and actions of the Resources Development Administration (RDA), the rapacious corporation underwriting the considerate, environmentally conscious, and kind-hearted knowledge-gathering enterprise of Augustine and her peers. Led by the weasely Parker Selfridge (Giovanni Ribisi) and contemptuous of the natives, RDA is on Pandora solely to extract the hypervaluable mineral ore unobtanium, and eventually Jake chooses to defend the natives against this company's escalating colonial violence.

If *Avatar*'s narrative is deeply concerned with materiality, space, and exploration, then its 3D aesthetic in many ways underscores these concerns. The digital effects from which Pandora is constructed are simultaneously verisimilitudinous and spectacular, reflecting the enormous research and development operation that went into the creation of this on-screen ecology. The 3D constructs a volumetric world that surrounds and envelops: as Ellen Grabiner commends, "The viewer is pulled into the cinematic world and can thus imagine that she could move around in this fantasy space."[18] Although this might stress the perceptual realism of Pandora, this is a realism that relies upon immateriality, rather than concreteness.

Many scenes set in the planet's jungle are filmed with a roving, exploratory camera, a (virtual) camera not limited by the material constraints of objects and space. Although digitally rendered, these shots have been shaped by on-set camera operators, even if the conditions of this capture strain at existing definitions of camera and set. Performed on a sparsely decorated, blue-coated soundstage, the film's actors wore motion-capture (mocap) suits and head-mounted cameras to record facial expressions (with the data captured during this process then used to create and move simulated Na'vi bodies within CGI terrain), while their actions were simultaneously captured using a "SimulCam," a handheld camera providing its operator with a low-resolution image of the virtual environment that will be fully rendered in postproduction.[19] Rather than the camera operator being shown Sam Worthington in a black skinsuit and ungainly headgear on a blue floor, the camera's display shows a rudimentary version of Worthington's Na'vi form within a virtual rendering of not-physically-present objects (alien trees, branches, and other structures). These virtual elements can then be responded to by the operator as if they were physically present, or they can be consciously ignored, the camera moving through them knowingly and purposefully for aesthetic effect. These on-set decisions are then open to further manipulation—whatever movement is performed by the SimulCam operator can be altered in postproduction, as can the makeup of the virtual terrain through which the SimulCam moved.

As Jenna Ng describes, the SimulCam (or "swing camera," as she calls it) "is about the real time production *of its own reality*," placing its operator not in relation to the indexical but in relation to "the virtual camera's software-generated reality."[20] The SimulCam technique encourages the camera operator on the soundstage to respond to foliage and virtual obstructions in a manner that makes itself felt in the final film, but in ways that emphasize, rather than lessen, our impression of the landscape's immateriality. The virtual camera drifts into clusters of leaves and skirts branches, and these enter negative parallax and slip perceptibly *around* us as the camera moves. The use of these emergent elements simultaneously asserts the volumetric nature of this environment—its extension beyond and around that which is visible in any given shot—and challenges, if not entirely undermines, its materiality. Immersion is achieved through a visual approach that equally eradicates the concrete existence of that in which we are immersed. Negative parallax, far from simplistically rupturing the film's world, instead activates complicated impressions of tangible virtuality.

This technique asserts the immateriality of both Pandora and the camera itself in this kind of digital cinema. In his article on the film, William Brown refers to this as an aesthetic of "gaseous perception," an idea he takes from Gilles Deleuze's writing on Dziga Vertov. Such a perception can "pass through solid objects as if they were of the same consistency as thin air" and is opposed to a more standardized kind of "solid perception" in which we cannot see around or through objects.[21] A posthuman form of cinematic perception, for Brown the gaseous aesthetic of CGI virtual camera cinema decenters the characters of the drama and the embodied human experience of space in favor of a worldview that understands all matter to be equal—and equally immaterial. Thus, it is precisely the simulated (rather than representational) nature of space in *Avatar* and 3D digital effects cinema more generally that enables this kind of posthuman space. When onscreen elements that have been digitally rendered in a perceptually realistic fashion emerge into negative parallax space, or when they seemingly slip through the camera itself as though both were ethereal substances (as indeed they effectively are), this gaseous perception is at its most pronounced. The 3D cinematography constructs what Miriam Ross terms a "hyper-haptic" experience of "tactile visual fields": elements from the film world seem to manifest as part of our physical space, but are clearly *not* physical as, in negative parallax, they slip through the borders of the frame.[22] For her, the added sense of presence provided by 3D is somewhat countered by the impression of *im*materiality that comes with the knowledge that what one witnesses is an optical illusion with no weight or matter to it. Brown, meanwhile, suggests that such moments are evidence of a new kind of cinematic thinking that "enworlds" characters and viewers in the dynamic flux of existence.[23] Both *Avatar* and the industrial-commercial discourses that surround the film make every effort to assert both the beauty and the usefulness of the separation of form from matter that is the predicate for such enworlding. Indeed, some claim that *Avatar* offers the "next step" in the dematerialization of cinema, deploying a "production process, aesthetic and narrative that [all] explore alternatives to tangible matter."[24]

Significantly, intangibility also forms an integral part of the world philosophy and religion of the Pandoran characters. This transcendence of corporeal concerns is channeled through a kind of digital metaphysics. Appealing to contemporary technocultural discourse, the Na'vi are depicted as being able to "download" memories and "upload" their consciousness into their environment through glowing fibre-optic-like parts of their anatomy. Pandora may in the narrative of the film be a material environment rather than a literal virtual cyberspace, but the planet's connectivity is nonetheless discussed in terms highly suggestive of a digital virtuality: described by one character as like a human brain, it is equally evocative of networked computing, its ecology consisting of nodes that each offer almost infinite connections to other nodes, creating a rhizomatic, holistic, and literally globalized space in which any and every event is "felt" by the planet in its entirety. Jake's navigation of this world using an "avatar" is further suggestive of these virtual dimensions, and his eventual shrugging off of his human form in the final scene speaks to longstanding dreams of digital disembodiment.[25] Sylvie Magerstädt suggests that Pandora thus represents the next step in technological development, a move toward the biocomputing and implicit ecoharmony of "a more liberated, organic, global information network that no longer has a need for heavy machinery."[26] Organicism is here opposed to human technics, with the former adopting traits of immateriality as a contrast to the latter's stubborn, even damagingly material, nature.

The film thus aligns itself with the Na'vi and their plight by superseding the materiality of film exhibition—namely, the screen. Through its 3D presentation and SimulCam shooting, *Avatar* provides an experience of virtuality that appears unbounded, embracing the digital transcendence of the Na'vi. The depiction of Pandora solely through digital effects, the enhancement of the intangible but assertive presence of these effects through stereoscopic exhibition, and the use of emergent but ethereal elements all turn this world into a virtual terrain in which material concerns are abandoned in favor of digital spiritualism. This is a twenty-first-century update of Holmes's comments on the stereoscope, as matter is dematerialized and form is circulated easily and efficaciously for the benefit of all. The dematerialization offered by the Pandoran perception of the film's digital stereoscopic effects is advantageous, and the conclusion of the narrative is upbeat and even utopian precisely because Jake leaves behind his overtly corporeal being, uploading his consciousness entirely and irreversibly into his avatar.

ENFRAMING AND OPERATIONAL MEDIA

Yet this emphasis upon virtuality and immateriality should not blind us to the material foundations of the film—indeed, it is very literal material concerns that provide the bedrock of the plotting. Jake, the other members of the scientific expedition, and the privatized military force accompanying them are only on Pandora because of the planet's deposits of the mineral ore unobtainium. The richest seam lies beneath the home of the Na'vi, allowing the film to stage a battle not only between the alien race and the human invaders but between two ways of life: one materialist and plundering, the other transcendentalist and ecoempathic. But this ideological dichotomy is not clear-cut, and, as I will now show, the film's stereoscopic ontology propagates the kind of worldview that it otherwise urgently critiques.

As Melanie Chan has pointed out, the central conflict of *Avatar* can be productively read through Heidegger's essay "The Question Concerning Technology," originally published in 1954.[27] In it, Heidegger describes how technology is the result of a particular kind of metaphysics, one that has harmfully accelerated in the twentieth century. While technology once harnessed energy through harmonious encounters with natural forces, it has now shifted toward energy's violent capture. Machines like windmills work in delicate congruence with the flows of energy that they tap, for instance, whereas fossil fuel economies harvest energy for later deployment in a manner that disrupts natural flows. Modern machines thus operate according to a "productionist metaphysics": they treat the world as a standing reserve of potential power that can be extracted and stored, meaning that the natural environment, and human beings themselves, become always-on-call resources.[28] As we have seen, stereoscopic media can be seen to propagate this metaphysics, with Holmes and Fowles each showing how the stereoscope allows surface to be scaled off the world, these abstracted shapes and spaces becoming transportable and transposable like any other commodity.

This effectively develops the procedure of perspective, in particular its visual nominalism. As Lev Manovich describes, visual nominalism is a way of dividing up the world and its contents and making these more amenable to enframing. The "use of vision to capture the identity of individual objects by recording distances and shapes," nominalism has become increasingly automated through history.[29] Physical nets and grids placed over the field of vision to assist in perspectival painting are precursors of later electronic and digital devices that record or interpret object information using means both visual and nonvisual (e.g., sensor technologies that use parts of the electromagnetic spectrum to which human perception is not sensitive). While focused around planar representations of three-dimensional space, visual nominalism names any procedure whereby the visual field is rendered a collection of discrete items, each one inherently loaded up, as it were, with data about its position, size, and (in moving images) trajectories of movement. Radar is indicative, with its interpretation of the world as an abstract void filled only with precision-targeted elements of potential interest:

> All [radar] sees and all it shows are the positions of objects, 3-D coordinates of points in space, points which correspond to submarines, aircrafts, birds, or missiles. Color, texture, even shape are disregarded. . . . Here, the function of visual nominalism, which perspectival image [sic] performed along with many other functions, is isolated and abstracted. Radar image serves a single function—but it performs it more efficiently than any previous perspectival technique or technology.[30]

The geometric sight of visual nominalism need not be as elementally pared down as a radar screen, with its dots of color and its singular emphasis on relative positioning. As Manovich describes, the wealth of data that radar provided led directly to the development of more nuanced displays for the depiction of this data in the 1960s, 1970s, and 1980s, including most of the "key principles and technologies of the modern human-computer interface—interactive control, algorithms for 3-D wireframe graphics, [and] bit-mapped graphics."[31]

Visual nominalism is thus vital to digital media devices, none more so than those devices that explicitly assist in navigation, since these reinterpret space as a schematic and provide spatial data as an augmentation layered onto or within their represented images. Jordan Crandall refers to these sorts of enframing technologies as "operational media." Identifying visible objects, calculating distances, and offering other forms of seemingly useful enrichment through pop-ups and floating monitors, operational media can be recognized by a display's placement of "calculations and computer graphical overlays on screen-based representations of events, or [the presence of] luminous portable information scrims that hover between viewer and world."[32] Perceptible reality is presented through a filter that not only nominalizes its contents, but also overtly tags and usefully sorts these contents. As Crandall makes clear, while the groundwork for operational media were laid "in the 1940s WWII wartime sciences of operations research, game theory, and cybernetics," they are currently used in civilian, military, and policing contexts and even function as part of the "contemporary regime of spectacle"; they will be familiar to anyone who has played a computer game since the early 1990s or used an augmented reality system in the twenty-first century.[33]

This kind of graphical image can be seen throughout *Avatar*. From the control booths in the main operations center of the corporate base to the tablet-like screens used by the scientists, as well as the large viewscreen in the briefing room, there are a wealth of schematic, data-rich interfaces in the film's mise-en-scène that re-present the world as a nominalist simulation (figs. 3.1, 3.2, and 3.3). These are all 3D, any traditionally screen-based interface rendered here as a volumetric virtual illusion. The characters then view these without glasses, hinting at the diffusion of virtualized hologrammatic displays beyond today's perceived restrictions. Even screens glimpsed in the background are perceptible as three-dimensional, their content volumetrically emerging and receding from the apparent screen surface. So, while *Avatar*'s use of digital 3D

3.1, 3.2, AND 3.3 [opposite] A sample of the various 3D interfaces used throughout *Avatar* (2009).

may be most overt when depicting Pandora's jungles and mountains, its future-oriented mise-en-scène and staggering array of digital interfaces all offer their own kind of stereoscopic spectacle.

These dimensional screens or pseudoscreens—which are used by all the human characters without fail—display navigational and other data regarding Pandora, assisting in wayfinding and monitoring environmental threats. They often show a simulated rendering of the surrounding terrain tagged with numbers and overlain with diagrams and technical jargon, all of it floating in the operator's field of vision at various depths. Such displays might be considered merely evidence of the film's future setting: as Schröter states, uncountable science fiction films since at least *Star Wars* (1977) have used "(fictitious) transplane images" to represent "the futuricity of the future."[34] This is to an extent the case here, although, crucially, these displays are precisely not "fictitious" in the way that they were in earlier planar cinema (or as they are in planar presentations of *Avatar*): in stereoscopic screenings, these holograms are represented to the viewer in the same manner as on-screen characters perceive them—that is, as volumetric and dimensional datascapes.[35] In this way, the film propagates its own mode of exhibition, advertising the near-future presence of ubiquitous 3D media and digital simulation.

More than fulfilling the functions of technoprophecy and visual spectacle, though, these interfaces bolster the film's ideological dichotomy between the enframing RDA and the spiritual ecology of the Na'vi. Operational mediation reads the external environment not only as a source of exact information—of distance, speed, temperature, material composition, and so on—but also as the site of ever-present potential threat: overseeing surroundings and interpreting their contents protects the media user against the intrusion of the unexpected or unwelcome. Operational media thus manage contingency by subscribing to a simulative logic that plots likely outcomes based on the application of algorithmic calculations to recorded data. In this, they are fundamentally militaristic. The rendering of the lived world as transmissible information that is visible, even controllable, at a distance is necessary for the execution of contemporary warfare. Discussing how important distanced mediation is to military strategy, Friedrich Kittler points to Holmes's words on divorcing form from matter, which propose that once form has been extracted matter becomes expendable ("pull it down or burn it up, if you please"), and he argues that the reference Holmes makes to wanton demolition is telling, an indication that pure information collection begets a purity of destructive potential.[36]

It is not surprising, then, that operational media are associated with the technologically advanced RDA. These media assist these corporate presences in harvesting mineral deposits to use as a powerful fuel (Earth, it seems, has run dry of energy sources) and support their treatment of Pandora as hostile mining terrain with numerous unwanted obstacles—a standing reserve of scientifically demarcated objects-for-extraction. As such, the simulative production of operational, immaterial space not only protects (in a military context), but also standardizes (in a consumerist context): making space safer by making it more predictable, simulation is simultaneously driven by an acquisitive gaze that measures and identifies for the purposes of classification and replication.[37]

This is very different from how the Na'vi treat their surroundings. Repeatedly described as living in a harmonious balance with nature, the Na'vi take only what they need from their jungle environs. They use other animals to fly rather than technological machines and rely on bioluminescence to light their way at night rather than manufactured torches (whether flaming or electronic). While the RDA seek to visualize and target, the Na'vi way of seeing is quite different: in a briefly glimpsed language lesson Jake learns that "I see you" in Na'vi translates as something like a spiritual acknowledgement of copresence rather than a blunt visual surveying, and, in the finale, human computational instrumentation is rendered redundant thanks to atmospheric interference, giving the Na'vi and their unmediated perception a tactical advantage.[38] This structuring opposition is also indicated through the respective architectural spaces of these groups: while the human characters have concreted over a portion of the jungle and produced hermetically sealed, rectilinear chambers for habitation alongside an enormous unobtanium refinery, the Na'vi's domestic and civilian architecture consists solely of the natural spaces and foliage of Pandora itself, dwelt in with minimal alteration.

As the film goes on, the inherent violence of human enframing comes to the fore, and the essential beauty, compassion, and general rightness of the Na'vi approach seems the only reasonable site of audience sympathy. In this way *Avatar* sees itself as providing a kind of "alternative" ecology to materialist pursuits, giving the protagonist (and viewer) access to the more fulfilling, meaningful, and mystical way of being in the world associated with the Na'vi.[39] For Chan, the film dramatizes Heidegger's ideas in ways that allow it to critique the technological "enframing" procedure so closely associated with RDA, a critique that can even mobilize real-world political action—as in the case of protests regarding the Belo Monte hydroelectric dam in Brazil, which Cameron framed as threatening an existing Pandora here on planet Earth.[40] As such, Chan subscribes to Heidegger's optimistic but complex conceit that art might be able to "'free' things from their captivity in the matrix of instrumental dealings associated with the industrialism spawned by productionist metaphysics."[41] By contrast, I argue that *Avatar*'s narratively constructed dichotomy of worldviews marginalizes or even actively conceals the film's own alignment with operational mediation and nominalist-enabled strategies of enframing.

For all the ideological differences between the corporate human characters and the native inhabitants of Pandora, the two are connected by their mutual employment of electronically pulsating 3D visualizations. In the case of the former these visualizations are depicted *within* the diegesis; in the latter they *are* the diegesis. Yoked to corporate greed and colonial pillaging, the film implicates operational media in a dominating and hostile military occupation. By contrast, the representation of Pandora is one of ecoharmony and beauty— even though this representation of the planet relies on similar digital spatial renderings as the RDA pseudoscreens.

Digitally animated 3D cinema, as an expansion of perspectival tools of image mapping, dictates that space be conceived of and rendered as an informational schematic in order to be reproduced. Like CGI more generally, it relies upon visual nominalism. Leon Gurevitch has pointed out how the symbiosis of CG animation and visual nominalism is a key part of contemporary product design. "As 3D CGI literally becomes an engineered visual space, the development of processes initiated during the Renaissance poses new questions," he states, and he accordingly goes on to stress how every visual object in a computer-generated milieu is detachable and industrially designed, and so in effect a "product placement."[42] Visual nominalism thus links war and consumerism, radar and product design, targeting and CG blockbuster. *Avatar*'s 3D CGI is another form of visually nominalist, operational mediation, even if the narrative and aesthetic of the film aims to free this form of visuality from these negative connotations. Digital spatial rendering is used to create a seductively immersive and overtly beautified landscape emphasizing verisimilitude and spiritualism rather than colonial mapping and precision targeting.[43] The representation of Pandora thus seems to run counter to statements like Kittler's, as it instead encourages connection with the (alien) world and depicts or even makes possible a deep(er) connection with matter. Extraneous information seems not to have been stripped away here, but added in abundance.

If the diegetically presented display technologies provide primitive versions of the much more advanced digital modeling processes that produce Pandora and the Na'vi themselves, then these mutual bases must be acknowledged. Far from incidental, the 3D displays used by the human characters reveal foundational presumptions around stereoscopic spatial renderings and their possible applications, in particular the CG animation of which so much of *Avatar* consists. *Avatar*'s pseudoscreens may foreground futurism, the stereoscopic capacities of the film itself, and, through a logic of opposition, the better form of seeing practiced by the Na'vi, but the alignment of these pseudoscreens with military practices and enframing procedures tells a deeper story. Although the film stages an ideological conflict between the militaristic human characters and the compassionate natives of Pandora, the hologrammatic displays by the former reflect the technological basis of the latter. The screens may be relatively "primitive" and schematic, lacking as they do verisimilitude and photorealism, but their aesthetic horizon is the photorealistic terrain of Pandora and its inhabitants.

This affinity is revealed by an analogous reliance on virtuality and incorporeality. In CG animation, both world and performances are reduced to point clouds and trajectories, and the RDA's dimensional maps of Pandora highlight this process, operating as mise-en-abymes of stereoscopic rendering. So, in the film's diegesis, military, corporate, and research personnel all use stereoscopic media to map, understand, and dominate the landscape of Pandora, while the film's exhibition *as* digitally rendered stereoscopic media expands the reach of this technology and brings it into the perceptual now. The gaseous perception of Pandoran vision is in play in both cases, but rather than increasing our sense of presence within an ethereally beautiful, alternative ecology, in the RDA's pseudoscreens the incorporeality of the visual field is connected to systems of instrumental control that are very far from the transcendental freedoms espoused by the Na'vi. The stereoscopic, digitally rendered ontologies of both pseudoscreens and of *Avatar* indicate how closely this film is aligned with what James Der Derian terms the military-industrial-media-entertainment network: a prevailing confluence of technology, corporate manufacturing, and media spectacle.[44] The film not only narratively represents something of the workings of this network and its reliance upon stereoscopic simulations of space, but as a stereoscopic simulation of space the film itself is also a contributing node of this network. *Avatar*, like the other films that will be explored in the next two chapters, actively performs and pushes for stereoscopic visual culture, but at the same time this 3D propagation occurs as a result of broader changes in ideas of images and mapping that are fomented in range of contexts, including those of surveillance and the military.[45] *Avatar* is both an active force encouraging the adoption of 3D technology, and a significant trace of an already-present and wide-reaching simulationist stereoscopic imaginary.

VISUALIZING HOME TREE
. . . .

The diegetic displays of the film underscore the connections between RDA and the filmmakers, between the ways in which the diegetic corporation uses 3D visualizations of space in order to control it, and the spectacular, produced, and controlled 3D space of Pandora itself. In Pandora we, the viewers of the 3D narrative feature film, are immersed in a volumetric, detailed, almost ethereal computer-generated space the apparent physical matter of which the virtual camera can slip through without incident; then, in scenes in the human corporate headquarters, we are shown diegetic technology that performs the same task—albeit at a notably lower rate of resolution—and through which the camera similarly slips with asomatous freedom. Various representations of Home Tree, the site of a Na'vi village, illustrate this well.

This enormous structure contains seemingly natural hollows, and various scenes take place here between Jake, Neytiri, and the village elders. These were filmed on a mostly bare stage using the SimulCam and are presented in the final film with verisimilar digital graphics (fig. 3.4). Elsewhere, we see this tree rendered as a hologram on an interactive tabletop in RDA's headquarters. Here, it is subtly translucent, consisting of microdotted lines and ridges in the manner of a LIDAR scan, and is surrounded by floating blocks of text and block lines of various colors indicating measurements, trajectories, and atmospherics (fig. 3.5). Selfridge introduces it when briefing Jake about the importance of relocating the Na'vi so that the unobtanium beneath it can be mined. After some fiddling—the luddite Selfridge surrenders the controls to a more competent underling—the table is used to navigate the surface of the planet and alight on Home Tree in order to visually demonstrate that unless the natives move before the mining equipment arrives, the relocation will be by force. The transplane model is thus effectively aligned with enframing and productionist metaphysics. It enables not just mapping, but also a better understanding of profit margins, deadlines, and other systemic imperatives, discourses that all visually cluster around it, much like the individuals of the corporate and military command structure.

This hologram table and its representation of Home Tree then shifts to openly militaristic later when Jake uses it to provide information to the armed contractors as part of a Faustian pact to get back the use of his legs. He enthusiastically describes the interior, load-bearing structure of the tree, doing so by gesturing within the model and describing a circle with his hand inside its glowing luminescence. His hologram-enabled descriptions provide valuable tactical information, and so the scene indicates how this three-dimensional

3.4 Home Tree as visualized using CGI in *Avatar* (2009).

3.5 Home Tree as visualized by the RDA for military purposes in *Avatar* (2009).

rendering of Home Tree is functioning as a kind of expanded "immutable mobile." As described by Bruno Latour, immutable mobiles are key to science and industry: "Scientists start seeing something once they stop looking at nature and look exclusively and obsessively at prints and flat inscriptions. In the debates around perception, what is always forgotten is this simple drift from watching confusing three-dimensional objects, to inspecting two-dimensional images which have been *made less confusing.*"[46]

Immutable mobiles are representations of information that can be moved, exchanged, and reproduced through different scales and contexts without apparent loss of fidelity. As Latour shows, linear perspective mobilizes knowledge, permitting data to circulate visually in seemingly unproblematic ways and without information loss or apparent distortion. There is, in scientific rhetoric, little that cannot be recorded and disseminated in this fashion.[47] Here, we see Home Tree subjected to this procedure; for Latour such mobiles may by their nature be two-dimensional planar renditions of a more awkward, less easily toyed with, embodied universe of three-dimensional tactile experience, but contemporary technology allows these mobiles to themselves become 3D, even while retaining their instrumental, abstract qualities. That is, the logics of 2D representation are used to build virtual 3D space, and this 3D space is then treated just like a 2D mobile.

If space itself becomes an immutable mobile in this display table, then the destructive possibilities of this rendering are demonstrated later when antagonist Colonel Quaritch (Stephen Lang) launches an attack on Home Tree. In shots created using sophisticated digital modeling and rendering software, a fleet of RDA helicopters approaches Home Tree, which is depicted as a verisimilitudinous, photorealistic structure within an equally convincing landscape. Using Jake's information about the tree's deep structure, Quaritch's missiles cripple its foundations and send it crashing to the ground. In light of these consequences, the earlier scene of Jake's briefing underscores how volumetric spatial renderings function as useful, data-rich simulations of space that can be put to work, enframing, controlling, even destroying the spaces they simulate.

Meanwhile, the operationally mediated and constructed nature of Pandora itself (and not just its simulation by the RDA) is helpfully demonstrated via the representation of Home Tree in a short paratext—a deleted scene in which Jake, in his Na'vi body, goes on a vision quest. This scene is available on some DVD and Blu-ray editions and exists as a previsualization only—a kind of moving digital storyboard with notably crude graphics. Sitting somewhere between the RDA table schematic and the filmmakers' visualization of Home Tree, in these visuals we witness the deep structure of the tree and of *Avatar*'s CGI images more generally. This paratext shows the manner in which further extensive digital effects artistry (both automated and manual) and rendering procedures are necessary to turn raw, overtly operational and nominalist simulations into the kind of perceptually realistic, immersive content we see in

3.6 A deleted scene from *Avatar* (2009) reveals Pandora's schematic underpinnings.

the released film. Such unfinished scenes reveal the extent to which the "realism" associated with effective CGI work and stereoscopic impressions proceeds from yet also conceals the nominalist mapping and operationalization described above.

In the deleted scene, Jake is infected with a hallucinogen and seems to move to a higher plane of consciousness. This is no mere intoxicated mirage: the spiritual truth of Jake's vision is validated by the narrative fact that the spirit animal he witnesses—the dragon-like toruk—later becomes his tamed companion through Jake's sheer force of will. This is a prophetic vision. Crucially, the otherworldly plane Jake enters when drugged is represented as a wireframe-like schematic, the geometrically ordered undergirding of objects and spaces becoming visible (fig. 3.6). The visuals suggests that Jake is seeing through material reality to the pulsing energy flows of Home Tree and the transcendent realm from which these flows emanate. We can presume that these shots would, if kept in the film, have been developed to resemble to a greater or lesser extent other shots from the finished film in which Pandora becomes semitransparent and throbs with visible electrochemical energy. In either case, in their unfinished form these images closely resemble the hologram of Home Tree used by Jake during his tactical briefing for RDA and the military. Such a connection is not coincidental, but in fact speaks to the film's ultimate privileging of nominalist, simulative imaging. Even though a hallucinogenic vision quest might be the personification of embodied and nonrational perception, in the film the truth-value of this quest is asserted through the rendering of Home Tree as a transparent schematic. The use of operational media by spatial aggressors may not be so surprising, but its presence not only in the deep structure of all the film's Pandoran scenes (CGI is after all built from nominalist conceptions of space) but also Jake's transcendental vision of the planet shows how the film itself considers operationalization to be a more truthful and revealing form of spatial perception.

THE COSTS OF ACCESS

The deep structure of *Avatar*'s lush, photoreal Pandoran environments reveals much about the film's surface-level association of operational mediation and visual nominalism with a commodified, enframing, hostile form of world-knowledge. *Avatar*'s narrative emphasis on ecologically respectful living and denigration of corporate agents like RDA allows it to argue that stereoscopic 3D can be a tool for revealing green issues and propagating ethical environmentalism, an argument that Ellen Grabiner and James Der Derian, among others, see as successful and cogent.[48] More critically, Thomas Elsaesser identifies this strand of *Avatar* as part of what he calls the film's "access for all" approach, seeing it essentially as a marketing device. He argues that Hollywood cinema's willed openness to textual interpretation for the purposes of audience inclusion is here taken to extremes. He describes the key to the film's commercial success as its inclusion of "astonishingly different, in fact contradictory and even incompatible, access points for viewer identification which *Avatar* managed to combine, or rather, compress into a single storyline and textual system."[49] This results in the film preaching an anticorporate, pro-green message even as it revels in costly industrial display technologies. As Elsaesser sums up, "The technologies that are responsible for the beautiful flora and fauna of Planet Pandora—beautiful thanks to the effects that 3-D imaging creates—are the same technologies as used by Pandora's enemies, bent on destroying this beauty, by harvesting it in either material (unobtainium) or immaterial (knowledge) form."[50]

As this reference to knowledge collection makes clear, these pseudoscreens do not just point to the military uses of digital 3D, but also the place of such mappings and visualizations in contemporary scientific exploration and explanation. It is not just Selfridge and Quaritch who use these technologies, but also the expedition led by Augustine—the former may seek material resources by any means, but the latter's harvesting of information in the form of scans, experiments, and even the avatar programme aligns the seemingly benign scientists with a similarly voracious view of Pandora as little more than a source of quantified knowledge. This is revealed by the mutual emphasis both groups place upon operational mediation, as when Jake's neural pathways are "mapped" and visually presented on a pseudoscreen before his first avatar experience (fig. 3.2). Furthermore, not only do the scientists rely on interplanetary transport, retrofitted equipment, and genetic resources that have all been donated by RDA, but we might reasonably conjecture that it was exactly the sort of interplanetary scientific mission that is here sympathetically rendered that discovered the presence of unobtainium in the first place and even determined its hyperusefulness as a fossil fuel. While economies of abstract scientific data-collection and the experience of simulative virtual presence propagated by stereoscopy both assert a kind of transcendent experience that leaves physical concerns behind, the physical implacably remains, being used to manufacture, house, and run the hardware, software, and networks that make abstraction from matter possible.

All of which indicates how the overt narrative "message" of the film is somewhat refuted by its aesthetic reliance upon technologies tied to ideologies of conquest and destruction. In Heideggerian terms, the film-as-object cannot get away from an enframing worldview, as the mechanisms of 3D CG cinema rely on visual nominalism and the extraction of form from matter. Space is something to be measured, quantified, and even destroyed once its material presence has been recorded and re-presented as an instrumental replacement for itself (whether in the context of scientific extraction and cataloging, or corporate mining and exporting).[51]

In the deleted scene described above, just before Jake downloads himself to his avatar to go on his vision quest, Augustine tries to convince him that he can never actually become a Na'vi, that he is deluding himself that he can be part of a tribe that will never accept him. Above all, this is because a Pandoran existence is not "natural," but, in Jake's case, is made possible by corporate intervention. "Our life out there takes millions of dollars of machinery to sustain. You visit, and you leave," she counsels. Immersive media are seductive, and operational media make space more knowable, flexible, and user-friendly. Yet Augustine's words alight upon a far-too-little acknowledged truth of such media—they rely upon vast energy resources and physical infrastructures both human and technological. Indeed, in the fictional diegesis of *Avatar* it is reasonable to assume that propelling a human consciousness into a genetically engineered avatar body requires reserves of energy best found through processing the very unobtainium that Jake is fighting to keep in the ground. As much as the divorcing of form from matter makes our experience of Pandora seem transcendent and immaterial (indeed, this is crucial to the planet's appeal and use), the process itself both within the film and *as* the film is very much dependent upon material fuels and processes. Nonetheless, the final cut removes this dialogue.[52] As a result, little friction is offered to the "myth of immaterial media" that the film otherwise propagates.[53] Like many accounts of digital technology in industrial, commercial, and public discourses, Jake and *Avatar* efface corporeal realities, heralding the frictionless plastic pleasures of an operationally mediated, digital 3D landscape.

• • •

In his review for *Film Quarterly*, Joshua Clover suggests that *Avatar*'s "bally-hooed three-dimensionality" only truly makes sense when read through a lens of industrial mastery that defines its writer-director: 3D offers "a new space for James Cameron to assert dominion over—armed only with a quarter-billion dollars and all the technological augmentation it can buy."[54] While the film's story and characters repeatedly assert the importance of the natural world and a harmonious, reciprocal relationship with it, the stereoscopic pseudoscreens/mise-en-abymes tell a different story. *Avatar* crystallizes dominant ideas of spatial simulation and disembodied agency in the digital world, a fact perhaps unsurprising given its preeminent place in digital 3D film culture. The shop window for digital 3D at the beginning of its widespread dissemination, *Avatar* announces the capacity of the technology to render spectacular, meticulously detailed, artificial three-dimensional zones of virtual presence.

As sympathetic protagonist and key agential narrative presence, Jake himself cues up for spectators how they should respond to their experience of this 3D film. Although humanly static when plugged into the technobiological avatar matrix, he uses telepresence to immerse himself in a kind of virtual paraspace: Pandora becomes a site of possibility and freedom that solves his real world concerns.[55] As a surrogate of the " 'immersed' 3D film viewer," Jake educates us as to the appropriate responses to this form of vision and presence.[56] These include not just excitement and wonder, but a literal falling in love that prompts him to abandon his prior physical being and live within the simulated world of Pandora. Like many other users and scholars of VR and virtual simulated environments more generally, he experiences immersion as a kind of pleasurable, enriching "enchantment."[57] Yet while the world that enchants him may be perceptually realistic, it is created as a purely digital space, whose responsiveness, luminescence, and immaterialty all make its alternative ontology overtly apparent.

The divestment of corporeal matter is a key aspect of digital culture and its simulations, but as we have seen it has a much longer history in relation to stereoscopic media. If Oliver Wendell Holmes believed that unshackling form from matter is always inherently useful, then *Avatar* updates and shares this view. Jake's desire to live within simulated space speaks not just to the aesthetic pleasures of this space, but also its teleological conception within contemporary technoculture: the ultimate fantasy of the simulation is that it will replace reality. Divorcing form from matter allows form to take more enticing shapes and seems to unchain human perception from the heavy drag of matter and corporeal concerns. While *Avatar* joins this presumed teleology with an ecological message of anticapitalist resistance, this narrative deflects attention from the propagation of a visual regime predicated on technological enframing and instrumental simulation. The very real terrestrial devastation that continues to be wrought by the kinds of technological prostheses featured in the film and their material demands, infrastructural needs, and energy requirements is elided by the ephemeral CGI visuals and the narrative of transcendent avatar use, all of which make matter seem literally and figuratively immaterial, and so endlessly traversable and even irrelevant.

Avatar's use of 3D can be seen as part of a larger effort to map and control space through digital tools in the twenty-first century. The underlying attraction of such tools seems to lie not exactly in their (re)creation of terrestrial or alien natural environments, but in their matterlessness, their generation of an ethereal milieu through which we float or glide. Simulation is not geared solely around emulation of the world, but the ordered extraction of those things apparently not useful or wanted about this world—including the heavy burden of corporeal existence. If *Avatar* is about how environmental devastation and corporate capital can today make us "ashamed to be human," then the film alleviates this shame through a transcendent immaterialism enabled by immersive digital simulations and 3D stereoscopic rendering.[58]

4

IMMERSION

. . . .

Entering the Screen

he sustained and excessive use of digital screens in *Avatar* reflects the world of the film's production: not only do many of us attend to television screens in our homes and cinema screens in our evenings out, but we are encouraged in the context of both work and pleasure to endlessly navigate the screens of our smartphones, laptops, desktop computers, and tablets. Looking beyond these personal devices, we also encounter a staggering array of screen or screen-like displays as we move through the public and privatized spaces of the contemporary city.[1] This, then, is a "multi-screen world" in which screens of all sizes have become ubiquitous and continue to proliferate.[2] If the end of the twentieth century witnessed the arrival of "ambient television"—Anna McCarthy's suggestive phrase for the increasing use of television beyond domestic environments and in ways that shaped cultural spatial logics—then perhaps the early twenty-first century is the era of the compulsive screen.[3] Today, after all, interactive screens have displaced many alternative modalities of encountering information or media. Television may still be "ambient" in airports, waiting rooms, and spaces of consumer leisure, but if lingering in such locales for any length of time we are more likely to fiddle with our phone or tablet than attend to these site-specific displays. This profusion of haptically responsive screens constructs an increasingly enveloping environment of digital mediation, an environment that demands tactile engagement and way-finding. Conceived not solely as displays but as interfaces in which data can be logged, accessed, and otherwise worked with, these screens demand specifically spatialized forms of navigation.[4]

As this chapter will show, contemporary 3D cinema is connected to and properly understood alongside broader developments in screen practice that seek to free media from the screen itself. The screen, rather than a site of abstract data, is conceived of as a virtual world, one that might intermingle with and even replace the material world. If in the last chapter simulation roughly named the process by which the world is reconfigured as data, then immersion here names processes by which the user might be placed *within* this data (and, in the following chapter, surveillance names those processes of monitoring and data collection that make all this possible). While representational media have long sought to escape the perceived confines of the screen, contemporary digital technologies demonstrate a qualitative leap in this regard.

Placing digital 3D in the context of volumetric data visualization and the rise of augmented reality (AR) and virtual reality (VR) systems, this chapter explores the ways in which real-world immersive technologies and their aesthetics are in dialogue with 3D mediation.[5] As with *Avatar*, the fictional technologies depicted by the films explored below disclose contemporary presumptions around what computer interfaces are and what they are for, while the presentation of these technologies in cinematic 3D underscores the centrality of a stereoscopic aesthetic to twenty-first-century technoculture, methods of data visualization, and our relationship to online environments. Both the films and other media described below work together to drive the adoption of stereoscopic mediation within and beyond the cinema. In the films discussed, this occurs through twinned approaches of normalization (3D is depicted to be everywhere), advertising (3D dataspaces are seductive and beautiful), and instrumentalism (3D interfaces help solve mysteries and advance plots). In this way these films partake of a kind of stereoscopic imaginary that is shared by other visual media: they depict *in* digital 3D prevailing and constitutive ideas *regarding* digital 3D, in particular the advantages it seems to offer over the planar screen for the management of information, and its presumed destiny as a culturally mandatory media form.

The chapter begins by surveying various 3D blockbusters that depict screens that are stereoscopically deep, or extend into real space. These advanced screens or screen-like interfaces assert futurism and highlight 3D spectacle; they also— more important—speak to the imagined uses of stereoscopic simulations in the present moment. Following this, I describe how the enveloping nature of these on-screen simulations evokes VR and its own instrumental replacement of material reality. Although it is certainly true that digital 3D and VR differ in their capacities for interaction and communal use as well as in their affective qualities, they are equally focused on replacing the world with a simulated volumetric environment that goes beyond the confines of the image. Their alliance is underscored and deepened by films like *Insurgent* (2015), which emphasize the ubiquity of virtualization, and by tie-in paratexts like the VR experience *Insurgent: Shatter Reality* (2015), which extend this virtualization further into the consumer's experiential orbit.

SCREENIC PROTOTYPES

The 2014 action melodrama *Need for Speed* depicts a range of television monitors, computer desktops, and mobile phone interfaces. In its 3D presentation, when these screens are glimpsed as elements of a broader diegetic reality—when seen in the context of their setting and on-screen characters—they are planar, as would be expected given the present-day setting. However, when these displays are cut into—when their content fills and effectively takes the place of the film itself—they become stereoscopic. This is the case even when these images are clearly being recorded by a monoscopic camera source (for instance, a diegetically glimpsed, single-lensed GoPro camera). Monoscopy gives way to stereoscopic depth at the intersection of any screen, and in this way this converted 3D film operates at the boundary between 2D and 3D visual culture. *Need for Speed* shows the presence of 2D screens, but looks toward a more stereoscopically oriented screen environment. Through its own approach to converting its originally captured 2D images, it contributes to the presence and propagation of 3D media across a range of consumer devices (including GoPros, webcams, and mobile phone screens).[6]

Need for Speed is far from singular in this regard and points to the way a stereoscopic interface imagination pervades contemporary cinema. Incidental screens in numerous 3D films are depicted in similar ways, with stereoscopic space shown to be latent within what appears, diegetically, to be a 2D screen. If 3D exhibition allows for the screens within films to themselves become 3D, then this occurs partly to further signal 3D cinema's own stereoscopic possibilities. More than this, though, 3D screens-within-screens work to normalize 3D screen culture at a time when this has yet to fully manifest in commercial and industrial spheres. Films like *Need for Speed* contribute to 3D visual culture both in their own 3D-ness and in the embedded 3D content they present—2D *screens*, the world of such films assert, are, should, or will soon be exclusively or predominantly 3D *interfaces*.

4.1 Computer space extending into the z-axis in *The Amazing Spider-Man 2* (2014).

As a way of propagating this stereoscopic screen culture, diegetic 3D displays assert that the illusionistic depth we encounter in computer screens is actually real depth. Screens may be flat, but through cinematic stereoscopy this flatness is apparently revealed to be just a limitation of current, non-3D interfaces. The interior of our devices shown to be a volumetric data space, one to which we can, with the right (3D) technology, gain access. This can be rendered subtly—as will be shown in *The Amazing Spider-Man 2* (2014) and *Insurgent*—or the depth (and beauty) of stereoscopic data spaces can be aggressively foregrounded through the more spectacular sequences found in *Iron Man 3* (2013) and *Prometheus* (2012). In either case, 3D is used to reveal the spatial depth of digital data, the diegetic technologies in these science fiction films operating as visualized prototypes for our (apparently) impending stereoscopic screen culture.

In *The Amazing Spider-Man 2*, a character uses a computer screen built into a desk to access a memory stick. We are shown his navigation of the narratively important information in both an over-the-shoulder shot and a reverse angle shooting up through the translucent desk/screen. The initial angle shows that the screen is not only illusionistically deep but avowedly dimensional, with windows organized along a stereoscopically receding z-axis (fig. 4.1). The underneath shot accentuates this, presenting these windows as existing in actual tangible depth beneath the screen, layered in negative parallax space. Similarly, in *Insurgent*, a wall-mounted transparent screen is shown to contain information receding in stereoscopic depth, and a reverse shot from behind and through the screen perceptually verifies that this organization-in-depth is no illusion but a spatial fact. Behind the screens of these films lie actual, material depths of layered information. The interfaces not only present data in depth, but are made by 3D effects into literal windows into three-dimensional virtual worlds. In 2D screenings this depth is indicated through overlap and focal cues, but 3D screenings emphasize the actual manifest depth by replicating it stereoscopically, layering these windows and their content at a range of z-axis positions.

Avengers: Age of Ultron (2015) expresses this realized depth more overtly, taking us fully within the digital data space. Early on in the film a screen provides information on the so-far-unproductive development of a sentient defense computer; suddenly, we see the portentous command-line notification "Integration Successful" and the screen goes black. Slowly, fractal stacks of translucent cubes appear within a limitless black void. These cubes move toward the screen as the artificial intelligence Ultron (visualized as a hovering orange spark) accesses and organizes the information apparently contained within them. Images (photographs, news clippings, maps) appear on the sides of the cubes, all of this information positioned briefly at the screen plane while Ultron absorbs it, before each cube then drops away into recessive stereoscopic depth as the AI continues to navigate its way through the volumetric space of the digital archive. If the faces of the cubes, like the monitor at the start of the scene, show us the kinds of interface experiences that we can recognize from our own computer use (albeit in more complex forms), then the deep space through which Ultron hovers shows us where this data might be imagined to originate. We may attend to planar material on our screens, but the Euclidean volume depicted in *Age of Ultron* asserts that the source of this material is spatial, and that literal spatial navigation within it is more efficient and instantaneous than our flat interfaces.

The CG-animated feature *Wreck-It Ralph* (2012), meanwhile, takes place almost entirely in the immersive volumetric environments within the screen spaces of various arcade games. To introduce this world, the virtual camera tracks toward an arcade machine, moving unexpectedly but smoothly through the glass surface of the monitor, revealing that what the screen pictures is in truth not a picture but a three-dimensional space. This shot demonstrates the spatial qualities of contemporary CG animation, as contrasted to the planar organization of earlier computer animation (of the kind found in arcade games). The film goes on to stereoscopically explore numerous heterogeneous CG game environments—from first-person shooter simulations to driving games—in ways that highlight propulsive navigation of volumetric spatial terrains. The screens of our games, the narrative asserts, are windows on three-dimensional universes, and this narrative scenario is echoed in the 3D exhibition of the film itself, which spatializes what has for the most part been a historically 2D cinema screen.[7]

Such sequences assert that computer data is inherently spatial and volumetric. Characters use or live within cutting-edge screens that broadly resemble those that we encounter in work and domestic life, but that also seem to be extensions and developments of them. This associates the *implied* depth of mainstream contemporary (2D) screen technology with the actual impression of depth provided by stereoscopic exhibition. These scenes all evoke the notable opening shot of *The Matrix* (1999), in which the camera moves inexorably toward the command-line interface of an apparent screen only to plunge into this interface and reveal that the glowing green text is cavernously deep and infinitely more complex than its surface presentation implied. All these examples show a pervasive belief that the illusion of depth manufactured by screen interface design *is in fact real depth*. It is in such fathoms that digital information is thought to reside—the digital screen, not an illusionistic arrangement, is considered an access point into a deep space of data. In this context, 3D exhibition allows these and other films to suggest that the information we engage with on our computer screens is inherently spatial, with the reverse shots taken from within computer space proposing that layered planar representations are three-dimensional virtual objects in space. The illusion of the screen's window-ness is avowedly shown *not* to be an illusion.

As shown in the last chapter, *Avatar*'s spatialized pseudoscreens spill forward into the surroundings of the characters, data being manipulated like ephemeral objects. *Avatar* is far from unique in depicting near-future screens in this manner, and similar or even more notable scenes of hologrammatic interaction can be found in films like *TRON: Legacy* (2010), *John Carter* (2012), *Prometheus*, *Iron Man 3*, *Star Wars: The Force Awakens* (2015), and many others. In key scenes in these films, rather than the screen revealed to be spatially deep, data is instead brought into the material world of on-screen characters, as rooms are filled with glowing data-rich schematics marveled at by on-screen agents.

For instance, *Iron Man 3* features a sequence in which the protagonist Tony Stark (Robert Downey Jr.), a billionaire inventor, reproduces the site of an apparent bomb blast using hologram technology in his laboratory. Moving through the simulated scene as though it were real, albeit ephemeral space, he manipulates it and expands incidental details, simultaneously augmenting the scene with additional data and schematics (fig. 4.2). The film makes very clear that this is a functional procedure. Only by attending to the crime scene in this virtual fashion can he discover a vital clue (he never visits the actual site of the bombing, Mann's Chinese Theater in Los Angeles). Recreating the position of one of his employees who was wounded in the blast, Stark's holograms produce lines that extend from both the victim's eyes and his pointing hand. At the convergence point of these lines he finds (the simulated evidence of) a soldier's dog tags, which he discovers by digging (actually, swiping) through layers of the simulation. Detection is here a matter of trigonometry, which is made possible, and even encouraged, by the use of an operational volumetric representation. With some verbal commands and sweeping hand gestures the crime scene becomes a map of the mainland United States, and Stark identifies sites with similar "energy signatures" to the LA blast. Pulling a particular one forward, the associated information (digital press clippings, police reports, crime scene photographs) manifests in a floating cloud for his sorting and prioritization.[8] At another point in the film, the villain Aldrich Killian (Guy Pearce) similarly demonstrates his new genetic modification technology by projecting a live hologrammatic rendering of his brain. This display fills the office of company director Pepper Potts (Gwyneth Paltrow), and although Killian initially brings up a volumetric map of the universe apparently by mistake (which is nonetheless "strangely mimetic" to that of the brain, he comments), he nonetheless confidently navigates through this display using hand gestures, showing Potts how the brain has an "empty slot" that can be "upgraded" using bioengineering (fig. 4.3). In 3D presentations, both of these glowing spatial interfaces are dispersed across positive and negative parallax, providing experiences of digital data that is as immersive and volumetric as those enjoyed by the characters in the film.

Similarly, in *Prometheus* an android named David (Michael Fassbender) explores an alien spaceship and activates a surveillance recording and navigation display; the room in which he stands is suddenly populated with ethereal holograms, including an enormous rotating orrery. Luminescent wireframe celestial objects and their orbital trajectories again fill up positive and negative parallax space, drifting fluidly around the amazed android. This scales up the tabletop hologrammatic map that the human characters of this film were earlier shown using in their spaceship, and the more advanced capacities of the aliens become explicit through this demonstration of even more expanded, screen-less, immersive interfaces. At the end of the sequence, David even cradles the holographic representation of Earth in his hands,

4.2 Manipulating digital data in *Iron Man 3* (2013).

4.3 A hologram depicts the human brain in *Iron Man 3* (2013).

testifying to the haptic qualities of the orrery, and its power to influence the fate of humankind.

In sequences such as these, pseudoscreen technologies unshackle data from planar coordinates, turning space itself into a piece of operational media. The usefulness of these interfaces is highlighted, while the employment of extensive stereoscopic depth helps to advertise their aesthetic and communicative power. As Miriam Ross describes, such moments function as advertisements "for removing the predominance of the hard-bodied flat screens that have hosted moving images for over a hundred years," their 3D manifestation offering a sense of "how these screen environments may feel at a time when they are not yet realised."[9] In *Iron Man 3*, *Prometheus*, and elsewhere, the futurism of an interface is directly correlated with its holographic and immersive capacities, and these in turn are aligned with power, knowledge, and revelation. As a cinematic exhibition technology, then, digital 3D visualizes the next step in interface capacity. The 3D holograms in these films may not be interactive for the viewer, but the performance of interactivity undertaken by the on-screen characters indicates the alignment of 3D display and data manipulation in ways that propagate the presumed efficacy of this alignment.

Crucially, while science-fictional, these interfaces are still just about recognizable, and so can be understood as what David Kirby calls "diegetic prototypes": fictional demonstrations of a technology that push for the creation of that technology in the real world. As Kirby outlines, such filmic prototypes offer a kind of "virtual witnessing," working to embed fictional technologies within the social sphere through representations that emphasize necessity, normalcy, and viability.[10] Stereoscopically deep screens like those found in the films described above certainly do this work, showing the pleasures, power, and even the pseudoexistence of such screens (in the form of 3D cinema) in the present moment.

AUGMENTING REALITY

By interpreting the real world and the data-screen world as equally and similarly spatially organized, even coextensive, these films reflect technologies outside the cinema that likewise encourage this spatial interpretation of digital data. So, while they are often attractively futuristic, the technologies of these films and their visual properties are nonetheless recognizable, and in particular resemble contemporary virtual and augmented reality systems. As such, and in line with Kirby's work on "diegetic prototypes," they offer a kind of bridge toward near-at-hand developments in these areas and powerfully demonstrate the efficacy and usefulness of these speculative developments.[11] This normalizes such interfaces, as does the depiction of them using stereoscopic exhibition, a depiction that itself recapitulates the logic and appeal of a data space that is not confined to the screen, and which allows viewers to vicariously experience the thrill of entering the screen and manipulating data in three dimensions.

Outside of the cinema, similar assertions around immersing oneself in data are made by the so-called "data observatory" in the Data Science Institute at Imperial College London. Opened in 2015, and financed through a combination of educational and commercial interests, this enveloping panoramic display synchronizes 64 1k monitors to create a 313-degree visual field and employs Microsoft Kinect input devices to track the movements of visitors. It is used to visualize "big data" sets like those arising from bitcoin transactions or around large-scale migration. It is also, in a seemingly different vein, used to display enveloping visuals of unusual environments, like a composite digital still taken from the surface of Mars by NASA's Pathfinder robot. As the website attests, the observatory "provides an opportunity for academics and industry to visualise data in a way that uncovers new insights, and promotes the communication of complex data sets and analysis in an immersive and multi-dimensional environment."[12] More open and comumunally minded than the cloistered experience associated with VR technologies, but nonetheless still providing an immersive environment of data images, the Data Observatory is predicated on the apparent need to be *within* the virtual databases of contemporary digital information storage, as only in this way can this information be properly understood and interpreted. Meanwhile, digital stills like that provided by Pathfinder highlight the synchronicity of the visualization of big data and enveloping virtual terrains. That is, we are encouraged to think of real-time bitcoin transaction information as a space, like Mars, that may be highly remote, but that we can step inside using the powerful prosthesis of the observatory.

In more mainstream contexts, touchscreen technology removes the cognitive gap previously present between action-input and screen-output (such as when using a mouse or keyboard), replacing this with a system of haptic gestures. Using fingers to swipe, pinch, or stretch screen-based programs links digital data objects with corporeal objects by indicating that each can be managed in similarly tactile ways. In a related fashion, motion trackers that can detect the precise movements of users have become commonplace. Most visible in the Xbox's Kinect sensor and the Wii's remote control, but also crucial to VR systems, these trackers allow for the more effective intermingling of digital and physical space, as our fully embodied movements direct the navigation of a digital avatar or cursor.[13]

This melding of the real and the virtual is most accomplished in AR technologies. These add digital elements to the visual field captured by an enabled device: our own movement of the device (along with its screen and camera) provides embodied navigation through a remediated world, which is now enriched with computer-sourced data that we can see on the screen. Although dedicated AR headsets like Google Glass proved commercial failures upon their initial release in the early 2010s, the interfaces remain culturally pervasive through their use on tablets and smart phones.[14]

A recent notable example of widespread AR adoption is the game *Pokémon GO*. Based on a longstanding media franchise that has multiple transmedia elements—including previous video games, trading cards, films, and television shows—*Pokémon GO* expands the franchise's consistent emphasis on exploration, archiving, and social play. While earlier *Pokémon* iterations encouraged players to swap trading cards or connect their Nintendo Game Boys together in order to collect and exchange the titular creatures, the AR version allows players to "catch" digital Pokémon that seem to be roaming free in the world. The game proved so enormously popular that it generated multiple news stories and media scares in its launch year of 2016.[15] Rather than construct an alternate space for gameplay like many other computer games, AR games such as *Pokémon GO* make the player's surroundings into an interactive gamespace. In order to be a master in the virtual world, players must explore and to an extent interact with the physical world around them. This allows lived public space that is usually reserved for other purposes to become a site of ludic entertainment. In a more operational fashion, many estate agents and web-based property companies now offer AR apps. In these, users to hold their phone or tablet up to the homes around them and are rewarded with recent listing prices, among other useful information.[16] Like *Pokémon GO*, the real and the virtual here intermingle through the screen, for similarly acquisitive purposes.

AR systems use the screen as an access point into a wealth of data that is apparently embedded within the world around us but that can only be read through the use of an enabled device and our own investigative movements. They aim to immerse us within "a screenless, surfaceless and frameless image"—something of a paradoxical intention, but one that speaks to our apparent desire to divorce the form of the screen (with its virtual models, touch-based haptic interfaces, and glowing seductiveness) from the matter to which it has heretofore been shackled (be this a wall upon which visual material is projected, or the thin glass and invisible metallic electrical conductors of the contemporary touchscreen).[17] Creating a "seamless blend of real and virtual space," AR embeds the kind of digital material previously associated with the screen within the real world, even if the screen still mediates this material.[18] Like a data x-ray of sorts, the screen does not so much enrich our field of view as it seems to reveal the "true" data-based underpinnings of our surroundings.[19]

Given this logic, it makes sense to think of the still-surviving screen as being more obstructive than functional. In the context of AR especially, the screen, as a tool for interfacing with an environment rich in digital, nominative, embedded information, is increasingly inadequate. In AR, digital data becomes (perceptually) concordant with the real, material world; in light of this hands-on tactility, the screen becomes an antiquated, encumbering material object. Screens themselves may now be relatively unshackled, able to be held in our hands and moved around the world rather than fixed to a desk or wall, but they still seem to *screen* us from those programs we access and those files we manipulate with so much haptic palpability. In Latourian terms, the abstraction of the two-dimensional (planar) mobile is no longer sufficient in an age when screen-based mediated material surrounds us and mobilizes a vast array of our daily activities and so is endowed with a spatiality that expands and escapes the screen. Like Ultron, we want to float within fractal data sets, provided access to rawer, seemingly more intuitive and properly immersive interfaces.

SHATTERING REALITY

If AR intermingles real and virtual worlds, then VR entirely replaces the former with the latter. VR places users within a digitally mediated scenography, one that can be navigated with prostheses like data gloves, wands, handheld controllers, or motion-capture sensors. Even if in some cases this interaction is limited to moving one's viewpoint, this still provides a sensation of embeddedness in the virtual world. Further immersion is offered through the fact that this world is frequently presented stereoscopically—VR headsets like the Oculus Rift and HTC Vive include a separate screen for each eye, and even economic alternatives like Google Cardboard split the user's mobile phone screen into two parts in order to provide depth cues through binocular disparity.

Blockbuster 3D cinema has close associations with VR, from the explicit subject matter of films like *Ready Player One* (2018) to the tie-in stereoscopic VR experiences offered alongside *Spider-Man: Homecoming* (2017), *Blade Runner 2049* (2017), and *Insurgent*, the last of which will, along with its VR paratext *Shatter Reality*, be the focus of this section. This transmedia terrain demonstrates the importance of 3D to digital media beyond the cinema, as well as pointing to the propagation of 3D visuality in personal media devices. These

VR cinematic paratexts also further stress the operational and nominalist nature of stereoscopic simulation—they create virtual worlds that we can perceptually enter, but that remain purely visual, comprehensively mapped, and conceivably surveilled at all times. Prior to exploring how VR functions in this way, though, it is necessary to outline the medium's immersive traits, and its limitations in this regard.

For all the rhetoric regarding VR's spatial world-creation, it still relies on screens to deliver its content. Although they are much closer to the user, and so perceptibly disappear, and although they are part of a larger technological nexus (a nexus that potentially includes controllers and motion sensors), screens nonetheless remain the site of visual representation in VR.[20] Like the more distantly contemplated 3D screens of television and cinema, VR manufactures space illusionistically through perspectival and stereoscopic cues that are delivered via a (twinned) planar surface. But, through sheer proximity, VR's spatialization of the screen amplifies the process of screenic immersion already described. As Oliver Grau puts it, VR "install[s] an artificial world that renders the image space a totality . . . [and] integrate[s] the observer in a 360° space of illusion, or immersion, with unity of time and place."[21] Observer and image are combined in distinctive, powerful ways, and illusionistic space becomes experiential space.

This integration of perception and simulation is most clear in those VR programs that rely on and highlight the co-constitutive act of digital space-creation, such as Google's *Tilt Brush* (2016). *Tilt Brush* offers users of the HTC Vive or the Oculus Rift the opportunity to paint virtual "images" in three dimensions—a controller is used as a proxy "brush" to create volumetric spatial shapes of "paint" in a range of user-chosen colors, styles, and textures. The created 3D artwork exists in virtual space and can be scrutinized like a kind of sculpture by moving around and even through it, and it can also be sent to other VR users. As an experience, *Tilt Brush* is clearly embodied, reliant upon corporeal movement for both the creation of virtual paintings and also their volumetric, sculptural appreciation—these are not images for distanced contemplation, but ephemeral spaces to be plunged into.[22] Movement and even a haptic sense of touch (provided by the VR controllers) work to confirm and amplify the illusionistic virtual space presented by the screens, verifying the all-enveloping nature of this virtual environment while simultaneously highlighting its responsiveness to our own gestures. This is not isolated to *Tilt Brush*: similar claims might be made for other programs like 2016's *Audioshield* (in which a user's own music library is used to create a simple interactive game consisting of fast-moving projectiles that explode [on the beat] when hit) or the same year's *Fantastic Contraption* (in which the user constructs tools and vehicles to transport an abstract shape toward a goal). In all cases space is openly "built" or otherwise influenced by the user through their visual navigation and engagement with it.

Yet no matter how perceptually convincing the virtual spaces of VR may be, they can never offer unmediated psychophysiological perception. Unlike many other simulative media, VR eradicates any divide between physical space and simulated space and essentially equates them with one another. For Lev Manovich, physical space always comes off worse in such a meeting. Even those systems that synchronize physical and virtual space (like AR) always end up privileging the virtual, he argues.[23] So, while a VR user may be moving and acting within physical space, the computerized simulation of space they are seeing supersedes and even overrides this physical reality. As Ken Hillis suggests, whatever pleasure or usefulness VR might offer is therefore conditional on the user's acceptance of "a reduction of the sensory interplay between people and their lived worlds to a concept of 'world picture' from which the non-human natural world has been excluded."[24] Physical space and our multisensory interplay with it may be simulated, but are notable by their concrete absence.[25] The simulation then operates as a kind of coded construct. Even with contemporary technology's capacity for verisimilitude and perceptual realism, VR's "simulated environment" is always "derived from photographic sources, architectural drawings, or rendered entirely with computer-generated designs," all of which for Elsaesser emphasizes the format's links with perspectival projection and geometrical optics.[26] What VR offers is "a *language* of vision, not something that is in any sense actually 'out there.'"[27]

It is reasonable, then, for VR to be considered closer to the mathematical perception of perspectival art than might initially be implied by its apparent (but not actual) supersession of the screen and its appeals to visual interactivity. Although we experience the space presented within VR as an enveloping spatial volume, a "reality," it is fundamentally a symbolic language that our mind translates into an experience of real space.[28] This symbolic nature presupposes a degree of control around the contents and organization of space. Just as a symbolic form delineates what will be found or represented when the world is presumed to be organized in a certain way, so too the creation of VR's digital spaces marginalizes and even eradicates aspects of space and experience that cannot be contained within the assumptions and technical capacities of the medium. If in the last chapter Heidegger identified a modern, machinic mode of perception that automatically considers the world and its contents to be nothing more than a standing reserve of fuel and resources, then here we see that something of the inverse is also true: that which is visible in digital simulation must be programmed in at the level of software. This is, as Leon Gurevitch has proposed in relation to CG animated cinema, "a new spatial logic" in which the contents of the frame consist purely of industrially machined product placements.[29] As a result, not to sound too axiomatic, what appears *in* simulated space can only be that which is simulated *of* a space. Something is always left behind, otherwise the simulation would not be a simulation, it would be the thing itself—as Schröter argues, "The simulation only makes sense when first of all only certain *aspects* of the phenomenon concerning *operative* questions and aims are simulated."[30] A simulation can only be a simulation if it strips away something that is, for the intents and purposes of the operational simulation, unhelpful background noise. When such simulations are "entered" as virtual spaces—as they are in VR—they propagate this operative view as a mode of spatial, embodied existence.

This mode is not incidental, but actively demanded by the digital world in which we live. This is an enframed world, and a world that posits the comprehensive *capabilities* of such technological enframing. This need not be read as a critique of the relative success or usefulness of VR visuals; as Manovich puts it in a slightly different context, "Computer-generated imagery is not an inferior representation of our reality, but a realistic representation of a different kind of reality."[31] Some even see in this difference the possibility for a new appreciation of situated processes of spatial cognition. Mark Hansen, for instance, proposes that VR offers a much-needed "reinvestment" in the bodily act of perception through its capacity for and even reliance upon user mobility, a mobility and embodied involvement heretofore lacking in digital media and theories around it.[32] Further and somewhat counter to this reinvestment, though, VR unavoidably provides the assurance that virtual space is a serviceable replacement not only for now-archaic screen-based interfaces, but also for nonaugmented physical space itself. So, whether or not any given VR world is verisimilitudinous, the technology asserts that its virtual spatiality is equivalent to—or even an improvement upon—the nonscreened spatiality of psychophysiological perception.

This is all articulated in the science-fiction action-adventure *Insurgent* and its VR tie-in *Shatter Reality*, a transmedia experience in which simulation, virtualization, and the experience of immersive data spaces are all insistently normalized, and digital simulation (and its pleasures) overtake the real. As already described, this film features incidental moments that illustrate the imagined depth of computer interfaces. Further to this, and above and beyond its mise-en-scène of abundant 3D screens and holograms, the film also narrates and visualizes the importance of spatial simulation to contemporary digital technologies. This emphasis is echoed and deepened by both the existence and content of the VR experience *Shatter Reality*. Virtualization may be positioned by both film and paratext as in some senses spectacular, but the consistency of the logic of simulation in both reveals the expectation, rather than the novelty, of volumetric spaces built from digital data.

A sequel to *Divergent* (2014) and similarly based on a young adult novel by Veronica Roth, *Insurgent* is set in a dystopian Chicago after an unspecified cataclysmic event has led the population to seal themselves up within unscalable city walls. Tris (Shailene Woodley), a "divergent" (someone who does not fit into this rigidly categorized future society) is captured by malevolent faction leader Jeanine (Kate Winslet) and forced to undergo a series of VR-like tests to open a mysterious, powerful artefact. While Tris undergoes these trials, Jeanine and others monitor her using translucent immaterial interfaces, within which Tris and her virtual surroundings are represented as glowing orange schematics built from pixel-like cubes. When the simulations are all successfully completed at the film's end, the box divulges its contents: a message (delivered via hologram) revealing that Chicago is in fact a kind of simulation or science experiment set up precisely to prompt the development of divergent individuals like Tris.

Insurgent's central narrative, key plot events, and overt moments of visual spectacle all rely upon virtualization. The VR tests Tris undertakes may be convincing visual renditions of the world, but their virtuality is cued up by narration and content: she is plugged in at the beginning of each sequence, and simulations are often outlandish and overtly unreal in content (if not in representation).[33] The illusory nature of these tests allows them to appeal to the kinds of aesthetic experiences scholars like Elsaesser equate with effective 3D. The "thrills and threats of floating, falling, disorientation, and realignment" are displayed in abundance: Tris chases a floating house through the ruins of Chicago, fights her doppelganger in a crumbling, vertiginous space free that seems devoid of gravity, and falls endlessly through a fractally fragmenting cityscape.[34] In each case, real world physics are departed from in order to appeal to the volatile mise-en-scène of the navigable hologrammatic interfaces featured in the likes of *Age of Ultron*, *Avatar*, and *Prometheus*.

The operational nature of these simulations is made clear throughout the film, which frequently cuts between the diegetic VR experience and its exterior monitoring. In a room adjacent to Tris, Jeanine and others watch through floor-to-ceiling glass as Tris's unconscious hanging body is buffeted by invisible forces. They also have access to Tris's virtual hologrammatic double, which

4.4 A holographic control matrix in *Insurgent* (2015).

4.5 The camera floats through an immaterial body double of Tris in *Insurgent* (2015).

records and replays her experiences in a schematic fashion and describes her levels of progress and health like a computer game (fig. 4.4). Three distinct versions of the test's bodily coordinates are therefore in play: one is lived, albeit virtual, experience (Tris's tests, visualized in a verisimilitudinous fashion); the second is physical existence (Tris's dangling body); and the third is digital representation/monitoring (the holographic display matrix). This last is most noticeably brought closer to the viewer through the employment of negative parallax cues, the camera drifting toward Tris's suspended form and in the process moving through the hologram. As with *Avatar*'s SimulCam, these shots assert the immaterial nature of their digital effects (there Pandora's flora and fauna, here holograms), highlighting not only the stereoscopic medium itself but also its sympathy with the ethereal (fig. 4.5). More specifically, in *Insurgent* these shots underscore the symmetrical doubling of the bodily map and the mapped body. Focusing on the constitutive re-creation of preexistent material (the real Tris), and the insertion of this re-creation into systems of measurement and volumetric data capture (the control matrix), these shots reveal the reproducibility of virtual experience. Tris's experience is not singular, but duplicated through data capture. This duplication is then further underscored when Tris's doppelganger is introduced: initially taken to be a reflection seen through the glass separating Tris from the control room, the doppelganger reveals herself to be a separate entity, standing in the space where the holographic matrix would normally be. Once again, a replica of Tris is generated through the VR apparatus, albeit this time a versimilitudinous, rather than graphic, replica.

Ultimately, in the film's narrative, it is only through simulation and virtual realities that the underlying truth of the real world can be discovered. Ironically, this "truth" consists of the revelation that this reality is itself also a kind of virtualization, or operationalization, of space, yet a more concrete virtualization than that experienced by Tris during her tests. Chicago, like the VR simulation of it that Tris experiences, is a test bed, a controlled and surveilled environment. This expands even further the representational frames of simulation with which the film deals. The triumvirate virtual-physical-holographic Tris that is shown during the test sequences is extended further outward into the urban spatial scale. The links thus drawn allow for the realization that, effectively, all space is virtual, even if it is also at the same time concrete. Through all of this, the film subscribes to what has been termed by Orit Halpern and others as the "epistemology of the test bed," a prevailing attitude of "smart" urban planning that places an emphasis on simulation, modeling, and optimization, and that privileges data collection and the future-oriented demoing.[35] This is a digital epistemology, reliant upon fluidity and algorithmic feedback. In echoing this logic, *Insurgent* shows simulation to be an expected part of broader social existence. Not just relegated to Tris's virtual tests, the epistemology of the test bed is explicitly scaled up to Chicago itself in a selfsame manner.[36]

As I have hinted, the aesthetic qualities of the verisimilitudinous sim to which Tris is subjected reflect the aesthetic qualities of the holographic interfaces described throughout this chapter. Emphasis is placed upon hovering and floating; space consists of fragmenting, malleable, virtual elements and is subject to a digital weightlessness that might be familiar from our manipulation of programs and other elements on our computer desktops. The film's consistent, if fleeting and subtle, redoubling of virtual people and spaces with their physically existing counterparts asserts the intermingled nature of virtual

4.6 Direct address in the VR experience *Insurgent: Shatter Reality* (2015).

space and real space. VR, then, is not a site of escape or alterity; rather, it pro-vides access to a terrain that comingles the real (as inspiration) and the digital interface (which provides the basis for the way this space is organized, and dic-tates its operational nature). The film thus articulates immersion and virtual-ization as prevalent "cultural logics" for the digital age, not because they replace reality as such, but because they bring this reality closer to our experiences of digital space and the computerized interface.[37]

This is all strengthened by the promotional tie-in VR game. Tris's simulated tests are the foundations of *Insurgent: Shatter Reality*, an Oculus Rift experi-ence produced by VR content manufacturer Kite and Lightning. In it, the user plays a "divergent" subjected to similar trials: experiencing Jeanine's testing floor in the first person, you watch yourself get strapped into the diegetic VR apparatus and then plunge into simulations of rooftops and train tracks, all while characters from the film speak to you directly, giving you hints as to how to proceed (fig. 4.6). As with some other VR of this kind, the user is statically positioned in space, and, although one's vision is mobile, the absence of a con-troller interface limits the potential for interaction. Indeed, these kinds of immersive entertainments are often called 360° experiences rather than games, and some even avoid labeling them virtual reality. Despite dialogue from in-game characters stating that you have made "impressive" decisions, in actual-ity looking around your surroundings is all you can accomplish, and even this does nothing to change the programmed outcome. Accordingly, the emphasis is on heightened sensation, such as that offered by the feeling that you are within a virtual environment, or by the roller-coaster-like swooping that takes you between locations, or by the more modest pleasure of actors like Kate Winslet and Mekhi Pfeiffer addressing you directly as an (apparently) agential narrative presence.[38] More overt excitement might be found in the vertigo felt as you stand one hundred stories above a simulated Chicago, or the panic encouraged by the sight of a train charging toward you (before it shatters into digital shards just prior to collision).[39]

Surrounding the viewer/user with enveloping simulative space built from images, *Shatter Reality* seeks to be immersive in a manner that extends but is closely connected to the immersive strategies of the 3D film *Insurgent*. An overriding sense of spatial presence is here far more important than any intellectual or tactile "interactivity," which is in either case absent. In this manner, the VR game functions as an extension of the scope and standardization of simulation that defines the film. Through its very existence as VR, *Shatter Reality* emphasizes how the on-screen virtual environments of *Insurgent* are part of a wider, paracinematic terrain of ubiquitous digital simulation. A VR experience posing as a VR experience, *Shatter Reality* aesthetically resembles its source text, but its graphics are at a lower level of resolution than those photorealistic simulations found in the film. *Shatter Reality*'s world is therefore more clearly a simulation, with its computer-generated trees and rubble offering particularly clear traces of their nominalist digital graphics production. This further accentuates what is an already underlined metatextuality. By effectively commenting upon its own existence as a piece of VR media, *Shatter Reality* sidesteps issues of representational verisimilitude, unconvincing digital compositing, and even the foregrounded immobility of the experience itself (after all, the player's unseen virtual avatar is literally strapped into the apparatus by way of introduction). If, in the film, neither spectator nor Tris are expected to fully believe the simulation is "real" for any length of time, then this is even truer of the VR experience.

Between them, then, *Insurgent* and *Shatter Reality* reveal much about contemporary screen use and digital interaction. Hooked into an immaterial space, we experience simulations that might as well be real, since the world we normally inhabit is increasingly saturated by simulative reproductions. These media offer an expanded experience of digital presence, the feeling that we have been given access to the apparently volumetric, nominalist space normally contained within or behind the computer screen, a space controllable and controlled. This access is both pleasurable and, crucially, normal. *Insurgent* offers little contrast between the real and the virtualized. Like *Shatter Reality*, it does not make much of the concealing or duplicitous potential of simulated space. The tendency of VR discourse to assert the superiority of virtualized terrain in comparison with concrete, embodied space is much in evidence in the film, just as it is, predictably, in the ancillary VR paratext. These texts thus indicate how our everyday reality is increasingly filled with and understood through interface technologies that provide us with spatialized images sourced from computer data. This franchise is not seeking to diagnose or critique this situation, even in the somewhat muted and disingenuous manner that *Avatar* did. Rather, it re-presents presumptions and expectations concerning the immersive media environment of the twenty-first century, both reveling in and spectacularizing this environment and treating it as a fait accompli.

The material world is here read as a kind of virtual simulation in and of itself, an expanded, screen-less digital screen. In this vein, *Insurgent*'s 3D conversion makes the film as a whole a simulation of space, and this is highlighted in those moments when we drift through Jeanine's immaterial pixel rendering of Tris's virtual experiences. This hologrammatic display box seems an apt metaphor for the broader logic of simulation at play: emptied out of all but relevant detail, matterless, and part of an operational network designed around repeatable and recordable outcomes, it resembles not only the film's urban test bed, but also its linked VR paratext. *Insurgent* becomes not so much about the shattering of reality as about the replacement of reality with its virtual double, the colonization of material space by the logic of the screen.

• • •

Volumetric, immersive sites are considered the best way for managing the informational "environments" of the digital age. Enveloping data visualizations allow haptic handling of the big data sets contained within digital networks, and so graphic user interfaces and their related screens have become ever more spatialized. In the 3D films described here, the possible futures of these screens, the way they might move beyond any concept of "screen," is visualized. *Avengers: Age of Ultron*, *Prometheus*, and *Insurgent* suggest the better, more powerful experiences that await us in a screen-less world. They remediate the volumetric and holographic dataspaces that we will virtually encounter—but they remediate in reverse, showing a prospective future medium within a currently existing one in a kind of "pre-product placement" or "virtual witnessing."[40]

If films like this push for a particular technological environment, then they do so principally in order to advertise their own value and cutting-edge status, their 3D effects connecting them to the stereoscopic imaginary of today's screen technologies. In 3D, the enveloping and immaterial aesthetic of virtualized interactive space is cinematically emphasized, as is its digital attainability. Although the represented technologies remain circumscribed within a cinematic model of spectatorship, stereoscopic exhibition to some extent bridges the gap between these diegetic prototypes and the kinds of immersive aesthetics and affective involvements offered today by augmented reality technology and virtual reality experiences. These 3D films and their on-screen nonscreens advertise the pleasures and powers of AR-style interfaces that bring digital data into our haptic reach. Operating in alignment with the ideologies of the military-industrial-media-entertainment network referenced in the previous chapter, these films and their diegetic technologies demonstrate what three-dimensional data interfaces are thought to be for—that is, what AR and VR should, or soon will, look like. Far from merely depicting immersive dataspace interfaces, 3D cinema itself therefore pushes toward the existence and diffusion of them within the broader cultural landscape.[41]

In this, 3D joins up with a broader virtualizing logic that sees the world as source material for the building of a more instrumental and pleasurable digital surrogate. Augmented reality apps reveal something of the profusion of computer-sourced data hidden in our surroundings, generating a convincing, useful blend of real and virtual space. While the screen is capable of showing this, it is also obstructive in its limited field of view. The desktop/tablet/mobile screen interface may have moved inexorably toward more convincing depths and volumes over time, but this obstruction seems to only be overcome through immersive VR, which places the user, Ultron-like, within computer data space. This immersion, and its divorcing of form from matter, provides maps that can be lived in and manipulated, expanding the capacities of knowledge by simulating the world *as* a product of knowledge (abstract, immaterial data).

This informational space is, however, highly distinctive. While Jay David Bolter and Richard Grusin describe how in VR the user has "jumped through Alberti's window and is now inside the depicted space," this "space" is still built using perspectival techniques.[42] As such, it is a different kind of space than that experienced in nonmediated vision. Bolter and Grusin propose that "to create a sense of presence, virtual reality should come as close as possible to our daily visual experience," and they demand that in doing so its "graphic space should be continuous and full of objects and should fill the viewer's field of vision without rupture."[43] Such a statement intriguingly reveals the extent to which Cartesian assumptions about (and distortions of) "our daily visual experience" have colonized thinking about space and vision. Panofsky would certainly argue against the assertion that our psychophysiological experience of space is "continuous," "full of objects," and "without rupture," statements that sit far better with mathematical space and perspectival art than they do with embodied vision. Both 3D and VR therefore arrive into a cultural landscape that already presumes space to be organized in this geometric, Euclidean fashion, a presumption propagated by perspectival techniques and their manifestation today in the ubiquitous computer, tablet, or mobile screen.[44]

As we saw in the last chapter, such geometry demands the mapping of space and its contents for the purposes of simulative representation; but, equally, virtualization mobilizes the mapping of that with which it interacts. Any VR experience is a documented, logged experience. As Hillis describes, in virtual environments movements "can be monitored, recorded, reordered, and replayed in a way unavailable to embodied experience and the 'messy' world of contingency and 'natural' intrusion."[45] *Shatter Reality* experiences can be recorded and rewatched; *Tilt Brush* actions are automatically logged in the cloud. The digital 3D film may not offer exactly this kind of monitoring, but it nonetheless functions within a landscape in which the screen or screen-like space is not only watched and experienced, but in many ways watches back. Technologies of stereoscopic capture, conversion, and exhibition play into a logic of mapping and monitoring in ways that have only been hinted at here. In the following chapter, then, my focus will fall more squarely upon the ways in which stereoscopy has been drawn into contemporary systems of surveillance and spatial management, and how these manifest in digital 3D's production methods.

5

SURVEILLANCE

. . . .

Converting Image to Space, World to Data

D igital technology has had a profound effect on surveillance practices. If we understand surveillance as "the collection and analysis of information about populations in order to govern their activities," then it follows that a quantitative increase in the information that can be collected in the digital era compared to prior eras might lead to extended, even entirely novel, modes of collection, analysis, and governing.[1] In this vein, William Bogard proposes that today's "telematic" societies dream of creating a totalizing and transparent visual field, mapping people, places, and events in a comprehensive fashion and predicting all future action through algorithmic forecasting. Bogard asserts that surveillance today relies on "the conversion of persons and social relations into the universal ether of information," and thus that surveillance is a process of simulation: electronic and computational networks collapse time and space and reproduce society as a manageable, predictable model.[2] Mark Andrejevic extends these claims, describing at length not only the ways in which our actions are monitored and logged in a digital age, but also how the operationalization of this information reshapes social and political life. Andrejevic proposes that in an asymmetrical power arrangement, records of our actions—which are stored and interpreted digitally—become privatized commodities, and that this creates a sealed world, an overwhelming "digital enclosure" of corporatized observation and prediction.[3]

The work of these authors therefore indicates how the practices of monitoring and control performed by state and corporate actors resonate with the digital spatial productions of twenty-first-century 3D cinema. In the digital age, screens seem to offer not so much images that are temporal slices of a past time, but present-tense spaces that are rendered as fragments of larger, entirely mapped, and quantified virtual worlds. This mapping is surveillant in nature, and in this chapter I extend many of the claims already put forward in this book concerning digital 3D's instrumental production of space, linking them to this surveillant assemblage.

Like those aspects of digital media already discussed, surveillance relies upon totalization, data collection, and predictive simulation. As such, the links between 3D cinema and surveillance reveal how the goal of seeing everything that is evoked by practices of state- and corporate-controlled social observation does not exist in a separate sphere from entertainment media but rather intermingles with it. As film scholar Catherine Zimmer has pointed out, cinema and surveillance have always been correlated entities. Since its inception, film's documentary capacities have contributed to the disciplinary recording of daily life; the mediated, globalized world is at the same time a surveilled world.[4] This has not changed in the twenty-first century. Digital 3D is, as Thomas Elsaesser argues, an "integral part of the [contemporary] surveillance paradigm," a paradigm predicated not only on observation but on "probing and penetrating, processing and possessing."[5] As a way of presenting more information around space, and doing so in a dematerialized, abstract, and reproducible fashion, 3D can operate as a powerful disciplinary tool.

In what follows, I will show how the so-called "spatial images" of the digital are implicated in contemporary surveillance practices, and I will stress how 3D conversion takes part in this disciplinary imaginary. Virtual space, as we will see in more detail here, visualizes the aggregate data—both spatial and otherwise—that can be harvested from the ubiquity of digitally recorded activity. Demanding the reverse-engineering of spatial coordinates from planar source material, 2D to 3D conversion inverts the workings of perspective and so demonstrates how contemporary digital cinema generates abstract, virtual worlds in which every action is by its nature plotted, measured, and nominally recorded. After exploring both cinematic and surveillant processes of conversion, I consider key films that feature indicative diegetic surveillance technologies and that narrate the manner in which surveillance technology works toward volumetric spatial mapping. These films, like those explored in chapter 4, conceive of the image as a real-time, interactive window on virtual space. This conception functions as a vital step toward the rigorous and intense regulation of space through advanced surveillance techniques. Once again, cinema is shown to both trace and advertise shifts in image culture far beyond entertainment media. Cinema and surveillance methods not only furnish one another with tools for totalized visual mapping, but the former also naturalizes the visual pleasures and apparent efficacies of the latter.

CONVERSION #1: CINEMA

In 3D conversion, two image streams are created from a monoscopic source. The use of conversion allows films to be shot and edited in 2D and then exhibited in 3D in theatrical and home entertainment contexts. Some twentieth-century films like *The Wizard of Oz* (1939), *Top Gun* (1986), *The Last Emperor* (1987), and *The Lion King* (1994) have all been digitally converted in recent years for both cinematic exhibition and home entertainment rerelease. The process is not utilized solely for this kind of revivification, though, and is applied to contemporary films that have made the creative and economic choice to film in 2D. Some full-text conversions in the early stages of the digital 3D era were subject to critical attack (see chapter 7), but nonetheless conversion has become a customary method for creating 3D cinema, whether in the case of entirely converted films or in the use of conversion for certain shots or scenes in otherwise natively shot productions. The latter is more common than might be expected: many native 3D films will include some converted shots or elements. The second shot of *Avatar*, for instance, was converted, since it demanded a close-up of an eye that proved impossible to capture with the film's relatively bulky native rig. *The Martian* (2015), another natively shot science-fiction production, also contained an array of material that was converted for a variety of reasons.[6]

Various industrial actors argue for and against the creative and economic value of conversion. Most vocally, some propose that conversion is inherently always somehow "fake."[7] However, the sharp distinction presumed by such discourses is not reflected in production practices, as indicated by *Avatar* and *The Martian*. In any case, this kind of qualitative assessment is not my concern in this chapter (furthermore, the multiplicity of factors and contexts involved make any such judgements unhelpful). Rather than contribute to these debates, I will focus on the way in which conversion's rendering of the world as a nominal spatial map aligns with digital surveillance practices that work to create "digital enclosures" and "data doubles": immaterial, operational sites in which the online and offline actions of citizens and consumers can be tracked and modeled. To do this, I will consider in turn these two forms of conversion—firstly, the conversion of 2D images into 3D media, and, secondly, the conversion of the world and our experience of it into abstract data—and then show how they relate to one another.

Like other kinds of digital effects production, conversion is an "art of space," to use Sean Cubitt's helpful description.[8] In much the same fashion as CGI, it relies upon visual nominalism and Euclidean spatial architecture; conversion asserts that the image can be reverse-engineered into a space in order to change or augment the contents of this image/space. As Stephen Prince influentially described in the mid-1990s, the convincing integration of digital effects with profilmic material like sets and actors relies on the creation of "perceptual realism": the believable "anchoring" of the digital effect in the perceived three-dimensional space represented by the image.[9] As such, the digital effect always retroactively spatializes the planar filmic image, demanding that spatial coordinates be interpreted so that these can dictate the visualization of the added digital object or terrain. For example, the alien "pseudopod" in *The Abyss* (1989)—an early sustained cinematic blending of digital object and profilmic environment—can be convincing only thanks to the painstaking efforts of animators to ensure that its physical structure, luminescence, and texture correspond to the photographed location in which it is visually placed. This correspondence is crucial to the digital effect's realism, its ability to be taken as a constituent part of the film's world rather than a later, ontologically distinct addition to this world.

3D conversion similarly requires that the planar image be turned into a mathematical Euclidean space. To do this, the shape, movement, and location of delineated objects and surfaces need to be calculated. This can be achieved through collating the information provided by numerous views of a filmed space (the motion parallax of a tracking shot reveals depths through the relative movement of layers, for instance), hypothesized through educated guesses on the part of digital animators, or produced automatically using depth generation software. Outside of these retroactive interpretations of the filmed image, depth values might be obtained by physically measuring sets, objects, and even actors with literal laser precision, generating abstract digital models. The coordinates produced by these various methods are used to create "depth maps" (sometimes gray scale, sometimes wireframe models). These present the geography of the contents of a shot, regimentally interpreting the planar image as a three-dimensional virtual schematic (fig. 5.1). This then guides the animation of a second view of a scene positioned at a slightly offset angle, or the manufacture of two entirely new streams of moving images; in either case, the monocular source material becomes a set of twinned image streams, one for

5.1 A 3D depth map as used in the conversion of *World War Z* (2013) by Prime Focus World, available here: https://www.youtube.com/watch?v=f7DuxignGYI (accessed September 30, 2019).

each eye. The creation of this new material requires the animation of those aspects of the scene not originally recorded. Those parts of objects and spaces that the additional lens of a stereoscopic camera (had it been present) would have seen all need to be animated frame by frame, generated through keyframe techniques, or created by an automated algorithm. These additions need to be photorealistic: the image streams must align identically and evince no distinctive differences (beyond their necessary coordinated spatial offset). With appropriate polarization, these image streams create 3D cinema in a way that usually seeks to be indiscernible from native 3D shooting.

It is worth pausing over two examples of this alchemical transition in order to demonstrate how it works in practice. In an article for the website fxguide, Mike Seymour explores a single, indicative shot from *John Carter* (2012). This action-adventure film was a 3D release converted by Cinesite, and it was not only filmed in 2D but captured on 35 mm film with anamorphic lenses (both of which pose challenges to conversion).[10] As Seymour outlines, the process began with the film strip being digitally scanned; the movements of the camera and the contents of the image were then tracked and their spatial parameters mapped. This data provided information around lens distortion, the exact dimensions of which needed to be ascertained in order for a second view to be successfully generated. Missing details—namely, the edges of objects newly "revealed" by the second angle—were introduced via digital animation. During this process visual features of the planar image such as film grain and lens flare were either removed completely, or heavily reengineered in order to synchronize with the added impression of stereoscopic depth. (In the case of *John Carter*, Cinesite first removed most of the grain from their digital intermediate, then—having manufactured a second image stream—they used a grain-simulation programme to digitally reintroduce grain to the left and right eye views, modifying offset values in order to "place" grain within 3D space). Finally, CG props, figures, and backgrounds were added to both image streams by animators, their left and right eye divergence being automatically calculable given the prior mapping of the image.[11]

In other instances, a conversion company may start working on a film during shooting rather than waiting until postproduction. This was the case with Prime Focus World and *Edge of Tomorrow* (2014). For this high-concept science-fiction film, the company captured high-resolution LIDAR scans of important sets and undertook a facial cyber scan of star Tom Cruise's head. For scenes set within environments that could not be scanned, 3D models were built using software packages like Nuke (which extrapolates depth relations by calculating the relative movements of 3D survey points in the image). These scans and extrapolations were then used in the conversion process in order to ensure accuracy and consistency of depth and shape. Operating as volumetric maps, the filmed planar footage is wrapped upon them like a kind of skein.[12] Here, then, both human physiognomy and built sets were subjected to laser-accurate mapping for the purposes of exact dimensional replication, the specific shape of Cruise's head being considered by Prime Focus, the film's director Doug Liman, its financing studio Warner Bros., and presumably Cruise himself to be an important aspect of *Edge of Tomorrow*'s commercial and creative appeal.[13]

These examples indicate how conversion removes ambiguities related to the planar constitution of source images, generating a complete understanding of the geography, dimensions, and proportions of that which is being represented. If perspectival visual nominalism in pictorial art history allowed depth to be turned into illusionistic flatness, then here it enables flatness to be turned into depth. Captured images become volumetric, calculated spaces, and these spatial attributes are then conveyed to viewers through stereoscopic exhibition. Computer software is vital, whether building virtual spaces from laser scans, or algorithmically interpreting the spatial data latent in captured images. Indeed, the regimented delineation of image coordinates and values that is pixilation (described in chapter 2) is fundamental to 3D conversion's processes of measurement and duplication. Thus, making the image digital is a vital first step in making the image spatial. While films shot and stored on celluloid may be converted (as was the case with *John Carter*, and the numerous conversions in which the source material pre-dates today's era of digital filmmaking), this occurs only after they have been digitized and is a process always enacted using digital tools. Even if the films in question are entirely free of digital effects, such processes effectively make all converted films, whatever they were before, into computer animated media.[14]

This digital spatialization of the image is not unique to 3D conversion. Light-field camera technology, for instance, seeks the same result, albeit by capturing space at the filming stage instead of producing it later using conversion. Originating in the "integral photography" of Gabriel Lippman in the 1900s—in which both capture and presentation rely on an array of thousands of microlenses that record different viewpoints of a scene—light-field systems do away with the traditional single lens associated with many optical capture devices.[15] Instead they record a vast number of potential viewpoints, one or even several of which will then be chosen after filming has taken place. This potentiality is pitched as improving creativity and image quality. Lytro, a camera developer, market their light-field model as being able to ensure every shot is perfect: focus, shutter speed, frame rate, and even the precise angle of the shot all become malleable values that can be adjusted in postproduction thanks to the amount of data that is captured on set. What the camera effectively records is space itself, allowing the angle at which this space is subsequently viewed to be decided later and carefully finessed. While originally aimed at a consumer market, light-field technology is currently being positioned by the company as crucial to mainstream digital production methodologies. As Lytro's chief product officer Ariel Braunstein states in a promotional video, "Video until now has been a 2D medium, and computer graphics tend to be three-dimensional. Cinematographers and visual effects artists are doing amazing things, but they have to struggle through the fact that these are two different mediums. What light-field allows you to do, is that it integrates two worlds. It turns every frame in a video into a three-dimensional model."[16]

Through this technology, the shot itself becomes a spatialized digital effect. As a result, embedding new digital effects into this now-spatial world supposedly becomes that much easier. Meanwhile, by capturing spaces rather than images and allowing, even demanding extensive postcapture exploration, light-field technology is valuable in the production of immersive VR media (Lytro offer a dedicated VR rig, called Immerge). Like 3D conversion, then, light-field systems further argue for the capacity of digital equipment to offer totalized visual recordings of space, overcoming ambiguities or blind spots associated with monoscopic capture.[17]

CONVERSION #2: THE DIGITAL ENCLOSURE

In an article on the widespread standardization of space that occurred across the twentieth century, Nigel Thrift argues that tracking, integration, and calculation increasingly define the way we encounter our surroundings.[18] Instrumental to all of these is computing. Ever-present processes of digital mapping and algorithmic management, Thrift proposes, will "become a new kind of surface, fitted to activity-in-context like a glove is fitted to a hand."[19] Digital systems allow for increased accuracy in the capture of data, vastly extend capacities of storage, and offer a platform for the useful aggregation and analysis of all this information.[20] The "track-and-trace" model engendered by all these changes represents a kind of conversion of lived experience into abstract data and a conversion of space into its simulated double.[21]

The widespread adoption and commercialization of Global Information Systems (GIS) and Global Positioning Systems (GPS) and the ubiquity of consumer electronic devices fitted with receivers that record location are endemic of this change.[22] Further to this, digital networks collect information about a range of other activities. Radio-frequency identification (RFID) tags monitor a growing ensemble of consumer products both on and off the shelves; facial recognition software captures information about those who pass through airports and other securitized locations; mobile phones collect the movements of their owners throughout the day; consumer loyalty cards log purchasing decisions and offer targeted coupons; internet browsing history and the content of email exchanges alter not only the nature of embedded adverts but also search query results; and so on. Consumers often surrender this information willingly. As José van Dijck argues, the "datafication" of society has normalized the surrendering of data and metadata to corporate and state agents, in return for consumer or social benefits.[23] This is not so much surveillance as it is a new form of automatically consented information collection: "Whereas surveillance presumes monitoring for specific purposes, dataveillance entails the continuous tracking of (meta)data for unstated preset purposes."[24]

Mark Andrejevic expands this argument, suggesting that the adoption of digital technology by state, corporate, and individual agents and the enactment of dataveillance all creates a "digital enclosure," an "interactive realm wherein every action and transaction generates information about itself."[25] This is not just neutral monitoring, but a kind of entrapment. Andrejevic likens it to an increasingly globalized Taylorist factory, as information about our decisions, microdecisions, and even our hesitations are collected, privatized, and then used both for purposes of social control and "to encourage us to consume as much as possible."[26] The physical world is thus turned into a "customizable interior" as wired devices and their users "respir[e] information" within monitored zones, their actions recorded and used to predict future behavior.[27] We have become locked into offering up our data whether we want to or not, addicted to digital screens that turn every moment into a productive moment, every transaction into a monitored transaction. In line with his earlier work on observational techniques as a shifting cultural phenomenon, Jonathan Crary more recently argues that constant screen use has reshaped how we engage with the world. The "contingency and variability of the visible world are no longer accessible," he contends, having been disabled through "processes of homogenization, redundancy, and acceleration" wrought by computerization and screen culture.[28] Digital images, whatever aesthetic properties they may have, operate in this "24/7" world as ways of "maximizing the amount of time spent in habitual forms of individual self-management and self-regulation."[29] That is, they pull us inexorably toward those very interactive, consumerist networks that are maintained through our clicking, commenting, and scrolling, and that in turn offer us targeted pleasures based on predictive behavioral modeling.

Crary argues that this computerized, track-and-trace present places the meaningfulness of everyday life—defined by its "fugitive anonymity," or tendency toward the unproductive and unmonitored—under threat: a life in which "one's gestures are all recorded, permanently archived, and processed with the aim of predetermining one's future choices and actions" is a new and hollowed out form of living.[30] Offering more concrete evidence of this change, in *Google and the Culture of Search* (2013) Ken Hillis, Michael Petit, and Kylie Jarrett use the ubiquitous search engine to show how the digital registration and organization of knowledge reorders knowledge itself.[31] While they may seem politically and culturally neutral, Google and its ilk actually restructure the world and our experience of it, doing so in line with corporately owned, profit-oriented, and far-from-unbiased algorithms. This might be most overt in moments when technology's racial or gender biases reveal themselves, as in the kinds of radically different results one user found when searching in 2016 for images of "three black teenagers" (dour police mug shots) on the one hand and "three white teenagers" (grinning, clean-cut students) on the other.[32] But this restructuring goes deeper, operating at a powerful, metaideological level. As a kind of open-access world surveillance, internet searching—by proposing that everything worth knowing is "on the Web"—equally alters our impression of reality such that any "list of [search] returns increasingly becomes equivalent to what we *can* know."[33] The registration and codification of knowledge allows it to be "searchable," and in the process knowledge that escapes codification becomes devalued or even culturally invisible. Meanwhile, that which is codified is increasingly subject to pervasive monitoring. If we choose to make Google our go-to site for knowledge acquisition, then we surrender to Google all data regarding how we acquire and use knowledge (from what we search to what we then click on, to what actions we then take, whether purchasing a product, joining a mailing list, or never revisiting the site). This kind of data capture is always switched on and operates in real time.[34] It thus helps build the digital enclosure Andrejevic describes, while also shaping and reshaping the (ideological) contours of this enclosure.

Comingling with the world it encloses, this digital enclosure also operates as a duplicate of this world, such that William Bogard proposes that social control today is enacted via, and works incessantly toward, a total simulative logic. Simulation, Bogard argues, is a kind of "*panoptic imaginary*," and both surveillance and simulation "are means of exposure, training, preparation, and deterrence."[35] Echoing Andrejevic, he asserts that contemporary surveillance ultimately has a rather simple aim: "To develop a closed system, where all processes can be translated and managed as flows from and back into information."[36] This is perhaps most clear in contemporary warfare and the use of surveillance drones. As Grégoire Chamayou stresses, while they may be used to deliver lethal attacks, unmanned aerial vehicles are also tools of observation. Drones operate under principles of permanent overwatch, synoptic viewing, data fusion, endless archiving, and predictive modeling, their vision fused with wider networks of data and other drone feeds in order to both monitor the present and calculate likely future actions.[37] Akin to invisible, militarily controlled CCTV cameras, their recorded images are extensively cross-referenced, and out of this surveillance assemblage life-and-death decisions are made.[38] Dronized omniscience takes the form of a totalizing, synthesized gaze, and a great deal of effort is expended in the private sector to inflate the scope of drone-based cameras from single-sensor, limited-field-of-view devices to integrated multicamera systems like the ARGUS-IS, a drone-mounted camera that offers images of 1.8 billion pixels that cover 100 km² of ground area.[39] This aerially captured content is then augmented and enriched with other material—including CCTV, satellite observation, and even the "picture" metaphorically formed from a person's biographical data—to manufacture an inescapable spatial image.

This second-order world, this cybernetic shadow of prediction and modeling, is profoundly important to contemporary military, consumerist, and bureaucratic systems. But its influence is far from inconspicuous or obscured. Not confined to corporate boardrooms, military briefings, and police stations, the kinds of visual content that spatialized surveillance makes possible feed back into the public sphere, becoming part of the consumer landscape.[40] This is because the simulations created through data gathering and processing are not rigid echoes but customizable, potentially personalized visual universes. Just as augmented reality apps described in the previous chapter like *Pokémon GO* augment the screen-accessed world by adding new data to it, so too the world can be reshaped after its surveillant mapping—a process that can be nearly invisible. For instance, a Google translation app converts the text that might be encountered in a foreign country (e.g., a road sign, the list of ingredients on a packet of processed food) into the user's own language. Digital code operationally simulates the user's surroundings in a more user-friendly guise and replaces psychophysiological vision with a volumetric, personalized simulation.[41] This kind of nominalization—the identification of discrete objects for analysis and, if deemed necessary or desirable, for adaptation or replacement—subjects the visual field to more intense forms of commodification. Translating foreign text may seem neutral enough, but simulations of this sort can function according to more overtly consumerist dictates. Witness the work of Mirriad, a technology company whose software can be used to replace the contents of moving-image media, in particular films and television shows. From background billboards to drinks containers all the way up to the cars driven by on-screen characters, Mirriad can replace one logo, brand, or object featured in a specific broadcast instance with another.[42] This allows advertising to be region-specific (with different content seen in different national territories), and to even be future-proofed, with reruns of old TV shows featuring diegetically embedded ads for now-contemporary products.

In these instances, image mapping and augmented reality software convert the extensible world and screen media into Euclidean spatial volumes in order to integrate them with one another and modify the content of both. This involves externalized and often algorithmically automated control. It is in this context that we must place 3D conversion. The mapping of space, objects, and people enacted by conversion and related technologies like light-field cameras and content personalization is in important respects a way of ordering and controlling that which is captured. These tools thus operate as part of the broader conversion of space described by Andrejevic and Bogard. As we have seen in the previous chapter, 3D's simulations of space in mainstream cinema similarly function as operational, immaterial sites of virtual presence. Surveillance theory then highlights how the production of these virtual spaces correlates with the production of a simulated double of the world in which any ambiguities of space or action are removed, and whose contents can even be switched around as market forces dictate.

Datafication and the digital enclosure thus radically develop the panoptic disciplinary society famously described by Michel Foucault. Space is further segregated and observed, its people and contents all the better delineated and effectively tagged in order to eradicate ambiguity and expand possibilities for social management.[43] Indeed, the changes wrought by computational and digital technology upon modes of surveillance are such that Gilles Deleuze proposes that in the late twentieth and early twenty-first centuries Foucault's "disciplinary societies" have been displaced by a "control society" that is more flexible and diffuse.[44] For Deleuze, the site-specific logic of discipline associated with the former has been replaced by the latter's all-encompassing, fluid network of computerized control, in which the most crucial knowledge is "the position of any element within an open environment at any given instant."[45] The key space of discipline is no longer the school, shop, factory, or prison monitored by a visible authority figure or surveillance tower. Instead, all of social space is now subject to invisible, automated disciplinary control through its reflexive, ordered spatial simulation. The key space of discipline becomes not a specific site, but a simulated, second-order world that echoes, records, predicts, and ultimately shapes and controls that which occurs in real space.

Certainly, we can identify a world of difference between the volumetric virtual creations of 3D cinema and the actual daily workings of RFID tags, computerized commerce, online cookies, and facial recognition software. Yet both digital 3D conversion and surveillance practices privilege simulation—particularly data-rich, spatialized simulations that remove the opaque, the unquantifiable, and the ambiguous and rely on exact measurement in standardized Euclidean space.[46] Paul Virilio has described the links between war and cinema, and how both are led by a logistics of perception that works toward an ideal of limitless visibility, "a general system of illumination that will allow everything to be seen and known, at every moment and in every place."[47] Converted 3D cinema continues this mutually reinforcing relationship—as cinema has moved to a spatial, digital medium, so have the logistics of perception employed in warfare and surveillance. So, while Akira Mizuta Lippit describes the 1945 bombing of Hiroshima and Nagasaki as a kind of immense photograph—with total visibility (a tremendous flash of light) leading to total destruction—twenty-first-century strategic control is found not in a photograph or an image but in a three-dimensional, immutable mobile, an economical abstract model of space and its contents, fashioned to enable distanced contemplation and manipulation.[48] This mode of seeing is enabled by computational tools that offer instant, uniformly formatted information and can be harnessed to monitor just about anything. 3D conversion relies upon and propagates these tools, offering in the mainstream entertainment ecology what might be termed a surveillant or even dataveillant visuality, one premised on total simulation and in which visualization is not only representation but also an act of spatial management.

THE SCIENCE FICTION OF SPATIAL SURVEILLANCE

Writers like Virilio, Bogard, and Andrejevic all argue to varying extents that we must attend to the sought-for futures of surveillance practices. The actual surveillance that is carried out day to day with existing tools is one thing, but crucial too is the "dream" of total transparency and spatial access toward which surveillant practices seem to be always reaching. In the remainder of this chapter, I will accordingly look to key science-fiction films that visualize surveillance technologies of total transparency. Cinema has a long history of depicting 2D-to-3D conversion and frequently places this practice in the service of near-future systems of effective, spatialized, inescapable surveillance, key examples being the Esper machine of 1982's *Blade Runner* and the Snow White machine of *Déjà Vu* (2006), as well as the proliferation of spatial images in the digital 3D releases *Prometheus* (2012) and *RoboCop* (2014).[49] The diegetic tracking and monitoring tools of these films trace changing ways of thinking about the image-as-space, predicting and then embellishing the technological transformation of flat representations into efficacious and predictive simulations: the conversion tools employed have more than a passing resemblance to real-world tools like 3D conversion and Google Street View, underscoring the links between military, entertainment, and consumerist spatial images.

Like the rest of *Blade Runner*, the Esper has been the subject of considerable academic attention, firing critical imaginations in outsize proportions to its role in the plot.[50] In the only scene in which it features, protagonist Rick Deckard (Harrison Ford), a detective hunting humanoid "replicants," feeds a photo found at a crime scene into the Esper and verbally instructs the machine to negotiate the image as it is reproduced on an in-built screen. His zooming and panning eventually reveals the image of a sleeping woman—a replicant—in the depths of the photo. That a computer might aid in image magnification is perhaps not surprising or all that noteworthy, but when Deckard tracks across a convex mirror at the center of the captured image, this action startlingly reveals depth disparities through motion parallax—that is, different layers of space within the photographed room move and overlap one another at different speeds during the lateral movement. This effect suggests the screen image is shifting its viewpoint around a physically existing deep space rather than tracking across a frozen image.[51] More than just magnification, the Esper seems to penetrate and somehow reproduce the photographically captured space, allowing it to reveal previously hidden parts of the represented room (e.g., a woman's reflection in a mirror). Scott Bukatman may describe the scene as "a hypnotic meditation on the power of cinema," but the Esper's transformation of the screen barrier into a now-permeable membrane speaks today more specifically to the seeming capacity for digital images (whether cinematic or not) to provide access to completely mapped, quantified spaces.[52]

As Mark Hansen notes in his own analysis of this scene, the photographic image is transformed into an arbitrary view of a captured volumetric environment.[53] Planar, photographic source material is, through the Esper's scanning and digitization, rendered spatial. Thus, what we see here, just prior to the widespread adoption of digital cameras and the explosion of commercial and domestic computing, is, for Hansen, the assertion of "a radically new understanding of the photographic image as a three-dimensional 'virtual' space."[54] Images may have always been windows of one kind or another, but now they become present-tense and interactive thanks to technological augmentation. Computer vision dethrones "the particular perspectival image in favor of a total and fully manipulable grasp of the entire dataspace, [and] the whole repertoire of possible images it could be said to contain."[55] Essentially, computerization of representation here equals spatialization, resulting in new navigational possibilities.

In the later *Déjà Vu*, diegetic surveillance technology goes one step further—rather than providing spatial access to planar images, it functionally reproduces the space-time continuum itself. This technology is called Snow White and is introduced as a complex computer system able to show past events on a bank of translucent monitors. This surveillance has its limitations: the moment screened is always roughly four days previous, and the area screened must be within a few miles of the machine's location in the present (restrictions necessary for the vicissitudes of the plot). When in action, Snow White creates navigable, penetrative montages that move from aerial urban views to side-on street perspectives, through closed doors and into private apartments. As in any cinematic experience more generally, events that are historical and seemingly recorded are thus made concurrent with the present through their temporally displaced relay via a screen. More pertinently to this chapter's concerns, this recorded history is represented as a single, ultranavigable, real-time world-space. Investigators wiggle joysticks and tap keyboards to explore a limited but extensive visual and audial world, monitors showing a virtual camera's plunge through time and space.

Blade Runner's desire to recreate a spatialized view of a historical event is thus progressed and literalized, once again yoked to national-security imperatives. The shadowy government controllers of this machine present it as a satellite observation and data-harvesting network, and this is highly convincing: Snow White's visuals generally appear to be stitched-together fragments of surveillance footage from multiple sources, employing satellites, street cameras, and wireframe schematics.[56] As Catherine Zimmer describes it, the technology is "far-fetched, but still theoretically possible and certainly consistent with principles of computer imaging and assemblage theories of surveillance."[57] Assemblage theories emphasize the joined-up nature of contemporary monitoring, with different cameras, audio sources, and databases all feeding into a single monolithic system. Such theories urgently respond to the overt desire of state and corporate agents to synthesize all observation practices and technologies into a larger whole, a fusion that exponentially increases surveillant capacity.[58] Snow White appears to be a consummation of this surveillance synthesis: the aesthetic of its screen is implicitly integrationist, as it seems to load disparate fragments, diagrams, and views at a rate just slow enough to be perceived as a kind of spatialized, actively navigated bricolage.

As a technology of spatial access, it is not so far-fetched—the interface strongly resembles Google Street View, which was launched in 2007, the year after *Déjà Vu*'s release. Street View visualizes streets from a vehicle- or pedestrian-eye view, providing a totalized representation through which one can navigate via mouse clicks or screen swipes. Described by Ben Campkin and Rebecca Ross as "part map, part video game, and part travelling down the road," Street View seeks to create a panoramic experience of urban and extraurban (but usually road-accessible) space.[59] Digital photographs taken both from a fleet of Google vehicles and donated by users of the program are all stitched together with visual warps that assert the continuity of pictorial material. The impression sought (if not always achieved) is that of uninterrupted space, not subdivided viewpoints. The objective utility of the graphical map is productively combined with a sensation of virtual presence, and this visual world is augmented with further information regarding location, road names, and businesses that are pictured.[60]

Functionally identical in terms of both interface and aesthetics, Snow White may seem to science-fictionally extend Street View's visualization capacities through both space (accessing the *inside* of houses) and time (accessing the past). However, the gaps between the technologies are not so wide as might be expected. Since 2010 Google has offered businesses and cultural institutions "indoor Street View," which makes the interior of premises navigable in the same way as exterior streets.[61] Starting in 2014 Google has also offered a feature allowing users to view specific historical Street View archives, making available to the interested Googler their home street's appearance in previous years, for instance.[62] This hints at the logic of absolute spatial visualization and access that lies at the core of Street View, a logic only partially disrupted by its legal need to blur faces and logistical inability to capture up-to-date images of every street in the world (as of 2018 vast areas of Russia, China, the Middle East, and Africa were yet to be mapped).[63]

Both Snow White and Street View propose that vast amounts of disparate information can be usefully centralized and coordinated to provide totalized rendering and omniscient access. As Ingrid Hoelzl and Remi Marie hint, Google's underlying database logic is at work in Street View: the company already generates a kind of "total image" of the world, and Street View is a borderless, interactive visualization of this totality.[64] Just as in the consumer context Street View amalgamates multiple images, cartographic data points, and consumer-facing information into a seemingly navigable space, so too Snow White seems to unify all possible source material—camera feeds, audio sources, infrared scanning, satellite data—to produce what can be explored as space itself (albeit space on a screen). That this system is later revealed in the film to be a time machine that provides a literal moving window into the world four days prior is perhaps not so radical a departure from its cover story as surveillance assemblage; after all, surveillance seeks to operate as a virtual time machine of sorts, preventing crimes before they happen through speculations of future behavior predicted from recordings of past actions. Snow White may have been created by accident, but it is explicitly aligned with a longer history of optics and global surveillance: the lead project scientist describes how research to "enhance the sensitivity of optical telescopes" led (somewhat improbably) to a breakthrough in warping "the very fabric of space." The extension of human optics that begun with the telescope in the seventeenth century here transitions into the visualization of all space and time.[65]

As a culmination of long-standing strategies of visualization and spatial mastery, it is again perhaps not surprising that the space Snow White screens can be physically accessed. When, roughly halfway through the film, suspicious protagonist Doug Carlin (Denzel Washington) shoots a laser pointer at one of the system's screens, the laser breaches the temporal gulf between him and the surveilled events, becoming visible to those who are being observed in the past. This demonstrates once again how the screen loses meaning as a compositional, representational device in an era of digital simulation, being reconfigured instead as an increasingly permeable barrier between the physical world and the totalized data space it depicts (or, rather, that it provides a literal window upon). Subsequently, Carlin sends first a handwritten note and then himself back in time using the machine. In doing so he literalizes the way that surveillance's detection functions according to a logic of prevention: he ends up stopping the very terrorist attack the aftermath of which he has been investigating. In light of this, Garrett Stewart proposes that time-travel films like *Déjà Vu* and the similarly themed *Source Code* (2010) participate "in a uniquely post-9/11 fantasy of retroactive surveillance and prevention while redefining the cognitive sensorium of human epistemology in the process."[66] To this list we might add the science-fiction blockbuster *Minority Report* (2002), in which a group of "precogs" witness murders before they occur, and the crime procedural television show *Person of Interest* (2011–16), in which an artificial intelligence with access to all surveillance databases and computer-stored data helps solve crimes before they happen. In the former, a slick interface allows the protagonist to navigate the various splintered shards of which the prophetic visions consist, while in the latter, occasional glimpses show the artificial intelligence's vision as one of spatialized data sets and a simulative rendering of contemporary New York. As such, a key aspect of the redefined "cognitive sensorium" that Stewart points to is the spatialization of surveillance images, the plunging of the protagonist (via digital interfaces) into an interactive, personalized present-future.

In all these examples, technologies of spatial surveillance, for all their ethical gray areas (which are often gestured to but rarely dwelt on at length), simply *work*. This successful functioning is linked to and communicated through the generation of what can be termed *spatial images*: virtually composited, hypernavigable spatial simulations. Subject to a broader "algorithmic turn," the image becomes a constructed "image-space," one useful for monitoring and detection.[67] The Esper, once science fiction, now finds a contemporary cousin in Street View, and even more direct relations can be detected not only in the area of 3D conversion but also forensic science: recently developed software called sv3DVision can use a single photograph of a crime scene (along with a single spatial measurement to delineate scale and camera position) to extrapolate a three-dimensional environment from this one image. In this way, even if little visual evidence was initially collected at the scene, the aftermath of a crime can be visualized from a range of angles and perspectives, aiding court presentations of such evidence.[68] So, much like Deckard, forensic investigators can today use a single image as an access point to a greater selection of views, the extensiveness of which asserts full spatial recording and aids policing. Just as Snow White finds a contemporaneous corollary in Street View, so too the Esper's spatially surveillant imaginary has been realized less than three decades later by the makers of a police tool that works toward total visibility through the same means of image access.

This dream is built on the promise of 2D-to-3D conversion, the promise that the image is a(n accessible) space. If 3D reconfigures the screen into a spatial, but still mathematical, terrain, then conversion acutely highlights this translation, and, as outlined above, it can be considered dataveillant in nature. Certain contemporary 3D films then explore these connections. *Prometheus* and *RoboCop*, as I now argue, articulate the connections today between dataveillance, cinema, and 3D, and they do so in ways that go beyond just their diegetic technologies. These films and their ilk, as Adam Brown and Tony Chalkley describe, exemplify a widespread cinematic tendency "to naturalise the concept and aesthetics of surveillance for the viewing public(s)."[69] Crucially, the kinds of aesthetics they naturalize are stereoscopic and spatialized. As such, these films operate as visible markers of changes in image-making, surveillance, and spatial representation that, as further shown in chapter 3, go far beyond entertainment media. They make use of and visually foreground contemporary tools of spatial mapping that are surveillant in nature, linking these tools to spectacle and efficacy.

In science-fiction horror film *Prometheus*, a crew of astronauts follow an ancient star map found on Earth to an alien world, where they discover a weapons facility created by a powerful race known as the Engineers. The film populates its 2089 setting with a multitude of simulative and surveillant technologies, some of which have been touched on in the previous chapter. Most overt in this regard is perhaps a 3D model of the alien facility: as drone-like orbs affectionately termed "pups" sweep through its corridors, their data is used to assemble, layer by layer, a tabletop 3D hologram (fig. 5.2). This process is observed by various characters across the film's second act, the construction of this map indicating that a virtualized rendering of the new terrain is necessary before the characters can understand or properly occupy it. The film implicitly endorses this assumption through its depiction of inevitable spatial surveillance in many other contexts, including a VR style headset that can provide visual access to the dreams of others; holographic alien surveillance footage; a versimilitudinous, hologrammatic "space box" used to deliver a recorded message; and medical technology visualizing the inside of the body for the purposes of invasive surgery.

5.2 The creation of a 3D model is the subject of much attention in *Prometheus* (2012).

This film's future not only features constant surveillance and monitoring, but also points directly to 3D conversion and its presumed ubiquity. The production may itself have employed principally native 3D capture, but the schematic and interactive holographic interfaces of the mise-en-scène suggest the kinds of carefully mapped, digitally articulated spaces of conversion. More directly, David watches *Lawrence of Arabia* (1962) during the journey to the alien planet, and the version he watches has been converted to 3D. David repeats the film's dialogue and styles his hair after star Peter O'Toole, and the scene he is shown watching—in which Lawrence describes his life philosophy using a burning match—is exhibited on a curved screen and offers stereoscopic layers of depth.[70] Like the volumetric hologram of the alien facility, the cinematic interface showing *Lawrence of Arabia* offers an original that has been converted into a 3D digital replacement of itself—in the former, concrete space is rendered as a spatial schematic; in the latter, the film image is rendered as a 3D continuum. It is as though stereoscopic spatial rendering is the only possibility in the future imagined by *Prometheus*, as it occurs across entertainment media, exploratory mapping visualization, and even alien CCTV technologies.[71]

If *Prometheus*'s intergalactic milieu might deflect attention from this surveillant visuality, then a film released two years later embeds this mode of observation within more recognizable terrain. 2014's *RoboCop*, a remake of the violent 1987 satiric action film of the same name, offers a sustained exploration of processes of spatial surveillance and ambivalently traces their relationships to various systems of power. Only given planar release in the United

States, Europe, and other markets, the film was converted to 3D for its release in China, where it was a significant financial success.[72] This act of conversion is particularly notable in that the film itself depicts the use of various conversion-like technologies, all of which are yoked to procedures of surveillance and state-sanctioned violence.

Set in 2028, the film concerns Detroit police officer Alex Murphy (Joel Kinnaman), who, after being injured by a car bomb, is turned into the eponymous cyborg by enormous robotics company Omnicorp. Both RoboCop and the world in which he lives are saturated with augmented reality-style interfaces and information. News shows, medical labs, and corporate boardrooms feature floating screens that seem immaterial until called on to provide content, sketching all empty space as a kind of mediatized zone. Meanwhile, Murphy's robotized vision provides a surveillant and simulative mode of observation that is particularly evocative of conversion. To prepare for live-fire training, for instance, Murphy uses visual depth mapping technology to generate a Euclidean model of his warehouse surroundings. From his point of view, we see a sonar-like pulse create a wireframe schematic; the camera then moves slickly around this schematic to visualize the position of enemy drones. Murphy's gaze seems to be able to float, disembodied, through the abstract model he has created. Seconds later, the film itself depicts the warehouse in a highly analogous fashion, with a virtually cinematographed shot sweeping through the building's rafters. This latter digital effect, manufactured through the crew's LIDAR scanning of the location and subsequent production of a verisimilitudinous digital model, is effectively a scaled-up version of Murphy's own procedures of tactically minded virtual mapping.[73] Both show what would otherwise remain concealed and virtualize space in order to provide greater, smoother, operationalized visual access to it. The volumetric rendering and vectoral navigation of Murphy's cyborg mappings therefore assertively give him much more information than would planar, perspectival representations or nonaugmented embodied vision. Effectively allowing him to see around corners, they make him a better law enforcement machine.

This reaches an apotheosis later in the film, when Murphy's disembodied digital vision is inescapably linked to 3D conversion practices. Investigating his own attempted murder by car bombing, Murphy returns to his old house and uses his now computerized perception to search for clues. His operational vision first highlights evidence linked to the case, such as burn marks on his driveway; seeming to find this insufficient, he then identifies four nearby CCTV cameras that have useful vantage points on the scene and uses these to generate a wireframe model of his house. Each camera provides a new angle and thus fleshes out the virtual representation. For instance, a house-mounted camera provides dimensional information for the front of his car; when the view changes to that of a street-mounted camera, we see that the back of the car lacks accurate detail—until, that is, Murphy embeds the spatial data gleaned from this second source, and so on. We are shown Murphy's point of view throughout this process and see how the virtual construction is assembled and honed as new information is gleaned from each differently situated camera feed, the triangulation of the cameras providing Murphy with enough visual information to produce a detailed three-dimensional schematic (figs. 5.3, 5.4, and 5.5). As if this were not comprehensive enough, he turns his manufactured wireframe into a lifelike reconstruction and sets it in motion (as this happens, the phrase "rendering environment" flashes on the screen, as though he were a digital effects technician, or a video game player). He thus employs the logic of conversion to spatialize historically recorded surveillance images. Just as 3D conversion companies and artists can use data from various angles to reverse-engineer qualities of depth, shape, and positioning, so too Murphy's dronized vision amalgamates divergent surveillance images into a simulated space.

This moment demonstrates not only the apparent necessity and efficacy of no fewer than four overlapping CCTV cameras on a quiet suburban street, but more crucially indicates the usefulness of integrated multicamera surveillance and its creation of spatial images. Each CCTV stream alone is deemed insufficient to reveal the truth of the matter; it is only through their unification and the production of an amalgamated virtual environment that Murphy can fully perceive what happened after he was knocked unconscious. If all this demonstrates the mutually informing nature of conversion techniques and surveillance practices, then the shots that immediately follow integrate this visuality with cinematic representation. Once Murphy has built his model, the film repeats an earlier shot from the film, when the car bomb initially went off. But, while this earlier scene showed little after the explosion itself, here Murphy is able to effectively walk into the shot and look around at the aftermath of the bombing. The schematic he has created from CCTV feeds has apparently generated a verisimilitudinous simulation of the past from which he can glean new information: he watches his wife rush out of the house to attend to his own bloody body, and he even provides himself with nominalist, augmented pop-ups of her emotional condition (stress, tension, and hysteria are all quantified). That the film here repeats the same shot of Murphy stepping toward his car, only this time as an explicitly rendered simulation, constructs an equivalence between the film's diegetic material reality and the virtual recreation of this reality via the totalized surveillance assemblage. That is, the resemblance of reality and virtuality encourages us to think of the film itself as something

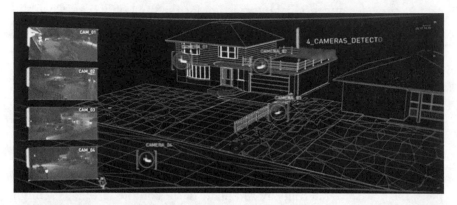

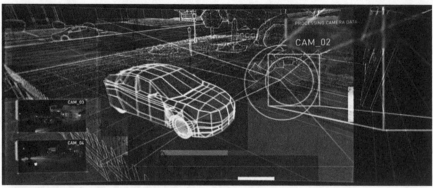

5.3, 5.4, AND 5.5 Four CCTV cameras allow for the creation of an immersive 3D recreation of the past in *RoboCop* (2014).

of a simulation, with every shot having been *rendered* rather than *filmed*. Alternatively, we must conclude that the simulation can effectively do business for the film, and cinematic strategies of representation generally (a conclusion similarly encouraged by *Insurgent*). In either case, the capacity for pervasive surveillance technology to generate verisimilitudinous, navigable space is foregrounded.

This scene must be seen in light of Murphy's more general ability to access the surveillant assemblage. Throughout the film, he identifies suspects through their glimpsed fingerprints and his instant access to state surveillance records, and he is able to track their recent movements exactly through his recourse to CCTV feeds and facial recognition software. The online, real-time image-space that his vision can produce is in this way populated by "data doubles," pragmatic replications of people that consist of pure information (accessed here through AR-style pop-ups).[74] This imagined, but believable, twenty-first-century surveillance apparatus allows Murphy not only to solve crimes with incredible speed, but also to call up the past on demand, stepping inside it like a virtual reality. In this way, Murphy's RoboCop embodies the modern surveillance state and its radical capabilities. Endowed with a seemingly objective vision of all of Detroit, he turns the proliferating databases, sensors, and visual recordings of the telematic society into a unified, nominalist simulation. Reflecting reality—but in a manner that is virtualized, info-enriched, and very acutely goal-oriented—this simulation converts material and social existence into an "ether" of centralized and privatized information.[75] Murphy may be a sympathetic protagonist within a highly personalized drama of trauma and investigation, but his functioning as RoboCop is distinctly that of an agent of the state, one with privileged access to various records and endowed with the algorithmic capacity to synthesize them to discern guilt and innocence. As a corporate project used for the maintenance of social order, he has been given apparently singular access to the digital enclosure's "privatized overlay" of harvested and collated information.[76]

In films like *Blade Runner* and *Déjà Vu*, the kinds of hyperobserved virtual spaces contemporary technology can create are powerfully visualized and shown to be effective in maintaining social order. *Prometheus* further propagates a world in which all events are rendered as spatial simulations, while *RoboCop* directly foregrounds the ways instant digital mapping and 3D conversion function in service of the surveillance state. The invented technologies of these films rethink the image from a recording *of* time to an access point *into* real time and reconstituted space, access that is articulated through the lens of state security and that is used for detection and predictive prevention. As evidence of the practices and possibilities of digital monitoring technologies, these filmic spatial images reveal the usefulness for law enforcement of totalizing spatial (and temporal) maps. As the uptake of digital surveillance outside the cinema becomes more inclusive and wide ranging, they proliferate onscreen. Furthermore, as 3D becomes a central part of mainstream cinema exhibition, the connections between surveillant spatial images and stereoscopic entertainment media become ever more pronounced. And, as might be expected of films that are themselves using 3D and conversion as key forms of cinematic spectacle, the narratives commend the capacity of this technology to capture, replace, and control space.

• • •

Surveillance extracts data from context and reproduces it in a more manageable and spatiotemporally distant form: security cameras provide selective views on space that are accessed remotely and can be replayed; databases record online activity and reduce individuals to their informated, algorithmically processed data doubles. In these and other ways surveillance always operates as a simulation of space. In the contemporary moment, these simulations tilt toward virtual volumetric renderings that are built from an assemblage of data sources. *Blade Runner* and *Déjà Vu* outline an imagination of surveillant spatial images that will become actualized in the digital era, while *Prometheus* and *RoboCop* reveal how this imaginary engages technologies of 2D-to-3D conversion. If spatial images become more normalized as aspects of surveillance technology in science-fiction cinema across the digital era, these later films show how the aesthetics and logics of spatial images themselves increasingly extend beyond just their use as part of diegetic machinery. 3D, as I have implied, is in the digital era employed as part of a surveillant visuality, one in which vision is inflected by instrumental imperatives and mobilized by the ontology of digital production methods.[77] If for Zimmer and others cinema has always been inherently surveillant, then today 3D conversion practices highlight the links between digital cinema and a qualitatively different kind of monitoring.

Both digital surveillance methods and 3D conversion practices render the image into a literal window onto a spatial world. In digital 3D cinema, the screen is no longer an image but an accessible virtual space, a process that conceives of the world as a geometrically ordered site of recorded and recordable, reproduced and reproducible data. This, in turn, is exactly the kind of regimented, tagged, abundant data offered by the monitoring of the digital enclosure and its simulation of space and action. This digital enclosure sits atop and duplicates real space, turning it into a source of quantifiable actions (e.g., purchases, GPS coordinates, daily routines, networks of known associates). Digital monitoring achieves the same kind of work as Heidegger's "standing reserve": it turns all actions, purchases, clicks, movements, and hesitations into sources of information, a massive databank that algorithmic processing converts into a resource for greater securitization and commodification. In its mainstream, CGI-reliant incarnation, digital 3D cinema offers something of a visualization of an analogous virtual world—a computed, nominalist enclosure of exact coordination. In such a world, objects become not only monitorable but flexible, as indicated by technologies like those offered by Mirriad and Google Translate, which modify the visual field and re-render space in alternative, commodified ways.

Just as both the content and production methods of early cinema traced the beginnings of modernity's visual capture and sorting of daily life for disciplinary ends, so too the digital 3D of films like *Prometheus* and *RoboCop*, as well as chapter 4's *Insurgent* (not to mention countless others), reflects surveillance practices in the twenty-first century. The digital filmmaking and 3D conversion used in these films relies upon the same methods as tools like sv3DVision and facial recognition software. Meanwhile, the diegetic technologies in the films point to how surveillance practices actually exist and how they are imagined, but also reveals something of how these practices look and feel: they are slick, polished, often beautiful, and never wrong. Digital 3D cinema recapitulates and underscores the rhetoric that 3D virtualizations offer more *comprehensive* and more *effective* records of time and space than any currently existing alternatives. This is quite different to proposing that 3D offers a more realistic form of visual address. What was previously, in planar surveillance, hidden from view is—through the spatialization enabled by conversion-like technologies—brought dazzlingly to light. 3D cinema thus argues powerfully and spectacularly for the value of the spatialization of the image. Nonetheless, much like Google's search algorithms, for all that digital 3D may seem neutral, a way of expanding cinematic realism by bringing a greater range of spatial cues into play, it is anything but. As with Google, the fundamentals of 3D conversion "constitute statements about reality that have the ability to influence reality itself."[78] Digital 3D creates mapped spaces that subtract matter from form and reconceptualize space itself as imagistic, perspectival, and, in the case of conversion, built from algorithmically interpreted data sets. As I have shown in this and the previous two chapters, this installs nominalization, operationalization, enworlding, and mapping as necessary predicates for the existence of space in the first place. In the process, psychophysiological perception and material space are marginalized.

ParT 3

MONSTROUS SPACES

In the digital age, 3D cinema functions as an emblem of the changes wrought by computerized technology on visual culture. Part of a technocultural nexus of operational mapping, the virtualization of space, and surveillant simulation, 3D effectively extends the structuring logics of perspectival art beyond planar renderings of illusionistic depth, moving them into volumetric space: in digital effects, virtual reality, and contemporary stereoscopic blockbuster cinema, perspectival processes of exact geometric measurement and visual nominalism structure the production of space. Nevertheless, despite all this regimentation, 3D's particular optics necessitate an embodied and unstable mode of film viewing, one with intensely ephemeral and haptic qualities. Offering a "unique type of visuality that cannot be found elsewhere," digital 3D media are composed of (twinned) images, but they are not received imagistically.[1] As already described in chapter 2, both digital media and stereoscopic 3D in their own way escape the definitions and ontologies historically associated with the word "image," and in the following three chapters I build on this, approaching digital 3D cinema in ways not enslaved to planar interpretive models.[2] If part 2 was concerned with 3D's mode of production and its relationship to systems of simulation and spatial control, part 3 turns toward 3D's mode of reception or observation in order to account for 3D's uniquely distortive visual effects and their consequences.

For all 3D's importance in the military-industrial-media-entertainment network, the kind of objectivity and mastery it seems to promise is far from assured. The map is never the territory, and even the map itself must be viewed from somewhere.[3] Vision is always embodied, and the embodied reception of digital 3D cinema produces unfamiliar and at times intimate optical spatial experiences. Digital 3D film production, in particular that which involves CGI and 2D-to-3D conversion, relies upon geometric ordering and creates a kind of Cartesian cube; however, the manner in which this space is manipulated by filmmakers and perceived by viewers renders it distorted and unstable. The space of digital 3D may be mapped, as part 2 has shown, but this map becomes monstrous through its realization as an optical illusion and through the challenges stereoscopic media pose to expected perceptual norms. Furthermore, if 3D is somehow both perspectival (in constitution) and distorted (in reception), then these paradoxically copresent systems of visual representation are quite different in either case from what might broadly—if problematically—be called "everyday" or "real life" perception. Everyday vision involves our emplacement within a spatially extensible milieu, an experience that is unlike the spaces of 3D, which are built from but rework and explode imagistic source material. As a result, stereoscopic visuality is best considered a third category, distinct from both planar visuality and lived experiential visuality.

The following three chapters consider this third category in detail, explaining how, even though digital 3D reinforces Cartesian visuality at the production stage, the reception of it introduces a range of aesthetic effects that cannot be reconciled with this sort of geometric, carefully quantified spatial perception. Each chapter begins by describing a unique aspect of stereoscopic media visuality and then connects this to digital 3D cinema in particular and the peculiar spatial impressions it can offer. Chapter 6 explores the relationship of digital 3D to the screen plane, using the examples of depth racking and lens artifacts to show how 3D retains but also radically refigures filmmaking techniques associated with planar cinema, and how this refiguring defamiliarizes the screen. Chapter 7 examines the distortions of space generated by 3D, noting that these are not only ever-present but highly malleable. Finally, chapter 8 looks at 3D's unusual intimacy, which results from the format's almost imperceptible but vital tendency toward the proximate and the bounded. In each case, 3D effects are shown to not simply "add" depth, but to reconfigure mediatized spatial experience in powerful, subtle, and significant ways.

6

DEFAMILIARIZATION

....

Rethinking the Screen Plane

D igital 3D is reliant upon imagistic logics, but it also escapes and confounds these logics. It is partly for this reason that stereo-scopic media have historically struggled to exist alongside planar media equivalents. In the case of commercial narrative cinema, 3D is both broadly similar to 2D (both are built from images, and 3D films are released alongside otherwise identical 2D versions) and radically, problematically different. Often improperly interpreted as an attempt to increase some vaguely defined idea of visual or spatial "realism" (i.e., as an improvement in verisimilitude), 3D is deemed a failure for not straightforwardly solving what are pitched, in such an equation, as the dimensional deficiencies of planar media. But while 3D may share many qualities with 2D, their similarities and coincidences must not distract from the very different visual operations stereoscopic media undertake, nor from the unique aesthetic effects digital 3D cinema can and does produce.

In this chapter, I explore the difference of 3D by focusing on the manner in which it negotiates, adapts, and above all *defamiliarizes* the screen plane. This is somewhat different from the spatialization of the screen discussed in chapter 4. There I considered how digital media tend toward an aesthetic experience in which users/viewers feel as though they have been brought within the terrain of digital data itself. Here I alight upon the ways in which the act of stereoscopic *perception* can paradoxically subvert the enframing procedures previously discussed. I indicate how digital 3D relies upon a distorted spatial continuum, a continuum that escapes the dichotomy normally applied to 3D of in-front-of or behind-the-screen. Certainly, depth effects can protrude (leading to diagnoses that this is 3D's sole aesthetic divergence from planar cinema) or recede (an aesthetic associated with heightened immersion), but 3D films can and do have a far more nuanced relationship to the screen than this. Indeed, 3D cinema simultaneously retains, revises, and undermines the core ontological and aesthetic presumptions of the screen itself. To demonstrate this, it is necessary first to return to the stereoscope and its problematic realism, as this can helpfully inform our reading of the plane in digital stereoscopic cinema.

"THERE NEVER REALLY IS A STEREOSCOPIC IMAGE"

Erwin Panofsky, John Berger, and Bruno Latour have all suggested that perspectival planar images offer a kind of two-way translation between image and space.[1] Yet, for all its apparent efficacy and veracity, the rendering of space as plane will always result in the eradication of some information. Perspectival art might use spatial coordinates for its composition, but it can never yield unequivocal spatial data in the other direction. While the monoscopy and immobility of perspective are cartographically useful traits, they introduce ambiguities of distance and shape. As E. H. Gombrich describes, in perspective the 2D representation of a three-dimensional object "does not give us adequate information about the object concerned, since not one but an infinite number of related configurations would result in the same image."[2] The shapes and volumes involved may often be intuitive—the larger of two pictured similar objects will be intuited as closer, for instance—but this should not blind us to the inherent ambiguities involved in perspectival rendering. Just as a shadow cast on a wall can *imply* the shape of an object but never actually guarantee that this implication is correct, so too the perspectival images assert information about size and depth positioning without providing a concrete way of verifying these.

These ambiguities are highlighted by optical illusions that rely on them, such as the Ames room. Appearing from a specific vantage point to be a simple right-angled cube, this room is in truth a strange diamond configuration; when viewed through a pinhole or a monocular camera, occupants of the room appear giants in one corner and miniatures in the other. In this instance, perspective's apparent cues radically fail. While it is tempting to describe the space of the Ames room as distorted, it is actually our perception that is working to disfigure an unorthodox configuration into a seemingly more normal right-angled box. This imposition of normalized perception is then unsettled but not quite overridden by the strange changes of size that occupants appear to undergo—we read the contents of the room as proportionally unstable long before we perceptually intuit the actual shape of the space (if we ever do). In everyday vision, embodied movement and binocularity provide the verifications that are missing from perspectival art and the Ames room.[3] That is, we rarely misconstrue our lived surroundings, thanks to the depth information provided by stereopsis and the shifting spatial perspectives contributed by bodily repositioning. The Ames room must be observed with a single eye (or through a monocular camera feed) because both stereoscopic vision and the physical repositioning of the observer reveal something of the strange, unexpected dimensions of the space, giving vital clues as to its actual constitution.

By providing binocular depth cues, 3D stereoscopy seems to offer more verifiable spatial data than does the perspectival plane. The depth cues of stereoscopic media should remove the plane's ambiguities, and, relatedly, reflect more closely our own embodied experience of space. Accordingly, commentators throughout 3D's history have suggested that stereoscopic media might provide more "realistic" content than planar alternatives. Since realism has a privileged position in art historical narratives and many popular assessments of artistic value, it is not surprising that from the early propagation of the nineteenth-century stereoscope, stereoscopic media's qualities (and indeed, artistic *quality*) were being read through this lens. Wheatstone's original experiments arose from his interest in monocular representation and the apparent difficulty painting had in depicting proximate objects, which always seemed less realistic or believable than distant landscapes. As a scientist, Wheatstone primarily sought data on the physiology of visual perception, yet through short-circuiting normal optical operations in order to discover more about them he also laid vital groundwork for interpretations of stereoscopic media that see them as inherently more realistic than monocular alternatives. In other words, in using the gap between everyday perception and art to discover more about the former, his enquiries tangentially assisted the latter in its implied and presumed goal of mimesis. Foreshadowing the application of photography to the stereoscope, Wheatstone suggested in the 1830s that the right amount of "attention" in the drawing and painting of the hand-sketched twinned images used in the mirror stereoscope would serve to make real things and their stereoscopic representations indistinguishable.[4] This implicit articulation of a realist optic and his constant references to art and representational veracity all indicate the extent to which his experiments were influenced (somewhat automatically and probably unknowingly) by mimetic imperatives.

Upon migration into the commercial sphere, the stereoscope became further associated with representational verisimilitude. Prevailing ideas of vision and representation that the stereoscope unsettled in a laboratory context were quickly reinstated, even embellished, when the apparatus was placed in Great Exhibitions, department stores, and living rooms. In these promotional and domestic settings, the stereoscope did not enact "the strange and epistemologically dubious way" that subjective sight works.[5] On the contrary, it imparted "a confidence in vision and in the transparency between the object and its representation," with two (dissimilar) pictures being apparently better than one, providing as they did an even more realistic, all the more believable, visual recreation of reality.[6] Stereoscopes and stereocards were sold on the basis of their ability to show unusual or far-off sights and places in a manner akin to witnessing them with one's own eyes.[7] Oliver Wendell Holmes accordingly stated that thanks to its depth impressions the stereoscope could "produce an appearance of reality which cheats the senses with its seeming truth."[8] Similarly, visual theorist Hermann von Helmholtz suggested in 1867 that stereoscopic photographs "are so true to nature and so life-like in their portrayals of material things" that any later encounter with the reproduced object in real life yields no new information about its form and shape.[9] For Holmes and Helmholtz, as for countless others, the key to the stereoscope's spectacle and cultural value lay in its convincing illusion of reality.

This positivistic understanding of stereoscopic mediation—the presumption that it accurately discloses a stable external world—eventually found its way into 3D cinema. Unfortunately, as chapter 1 has demonstrated, the equation of stereoscopic film exhibition with mimetic representation leads to hostile evaluations of 3D precisely because it seems to fail at this level. 3D media "feed our addiction for realism but leave it somewhat unsatisfied," as Brian Winston indicatively outlines.[10] Roger Ebert's widely circulated objections to 3D films in 2010 and 2011 similarly centered on the fact that 3D is clearly *not* like natural vision and never can be. As Ebert asserts, 3D requires human vision to work in ways it was not designed to and is therefore "inherently brain-confusing."[11] He cites editor and sound designer Walter Murch, who complains firstly that 3D glasses "gather in" the image, making it seem smaller, and secondly that the focus and convergence points of our vision—points normally always in sync—become independent variables: we must focus on the screen, but our eyes converge at distances that may be in front or behind of this screen.[12] This is an entirely novel perceptual procedure, and thus for Ebert and Murch a problematic and frustrating one.

These criticisms are in many respects accurate, or at least built on accurate foundations. 3D cinema, like the stereoscope before it, demands atypical perceptual work on the part of the observer. 3D may produce visual impressions endowed with spatial cues that are absent from planar media, but it generates these perceptual spaces using polarized or otherwise perceptually separated pairs of images, images that can function without their partner as 2D "versions" of the 3D scene. This is quite different from embodied vision.

Even if we admit to the stereoscopic nature of sight, it does not then follow that in this embodied situation each individual eye sees a 2D image. Wheatstone may himself assert exactly this, and it may be common to presume that the "2D photograph" and the "retinal image" are so identical as to be unproblematically equatable.[13] But each eye does not see imagistic pictures exactly; rather, each eye interprets an unstable constellation of light and color from an extensible environment. As Robert Hughes has described, vision is not so much a perspective painting as it is a "mosaic," a meeting of multiple relationships produced by saccadic eye movements.[14] The measured plane, static surface, and mastering detachment of the image is alien to the corporeal investment (and continual reinvestment) in our surroundings that is prompted by any observance of lived spatial surroundings.[15] When functioning in unison our two eyes do not reconcile competing monocular impressions, but construct spatial impressions from rapid foveal glimpsing, binocular cues, and a host of other stimuli. 3D media may evoke this kind of spatial emplacement through the use of twinned images and binocular disparity, but this is a visual-spatial experience of a fundamentally different kind. In 3D media we are faced not with materially felt, saccadically scanned surroundings, nor with a tactile volumetric experience beyond and around us. Instead, we encounter an ephemeral, imagistically enabled illusion created in collaboration with our perceptual apparatus.[16] Despite the censures of Ebert, Murch, and others, this is no reason to condemn the medium in favor of its planar equivalent. Indeed, planar cinema itself is similarly unlike everyday vision according to the terms sketched here.

While 3D media diverge from everyday sight, they also reveal crucial aspects of our embodied vision that are often unremarked upon. Revealing "the agency of the mind in visual perception," the stereoscope showed that we could not take what we saw at face value, since what seems to be a space might in truth be two carefully rendered diagrams;[17] in short, it demonstrated that "vision occurs independent of reality."[18] In the nineteenth century, this was an important intervention into debates not only around perception but also neurology and philosophy.[19] Furthermore, it was, and still is, a revelation that does not fit comfortably with artistic practice that seeks realism and verisimilar representation as artistic ends in and of themselves. After all, if vision and the world are somewhat independent of one another, then vision becomes highly subjective and fluid, and "realism" loses purchase as a constant, definable category. As Laura Burd Schiavo describes, Wheatstone's creation "insinuated an arbitrary relationship between stimulus and sensation," challenging "centuries of thought that had assumed correspondence between objects and their retinal projections."[20] While previous visual paradigms had suppressed the subjectivity of the viewer, stereoscopic media seemed to disclose it in a direct, even revolutionary, manner.

In this way, the nineteenth-century stereoscope destabilized conceptual models of a stable, ordered external world, whether this world was generated through embodied vision or through planar rendering. For Crary, stereoscopy showed that the monocular, objective visual representation associated with the map and the plane was a fiction of visual mastery rather than its scientific attainment. The stereoscope's manipulation of the physiological fact of binocular disparity exposes the provisional nature of the content perceived by each eye (or delivered by a planar image), while its generation of stereoscopic spatial impressions proves that the physiology of the viewing subject is a crucial part of their perception of the world. As he puts it: "There is no longer the possibility of perspective under such a technique of beholding. The relation of observer to image is no longer to an object quantified in relation to a position in space, but rather to two dissimilar images whose position simulates the anatomical structure of the observer's body."[21] The illusion of depth that the stereoscope provides couples the observer with the apparatus and presents a fused, contingent, utterly subjective optical production. This is very different to the singular and seemingly objective point of view constructed by photography and perspectival images. Instead of a geometric scene upon a plane that can be measured, and so mastered, the stereoscope provides a visual experience that is embodied and ephemeral, that exists, in Martin Jay's words, "nowhere but in the mind."[22] In the stereoscope, and in any stereoscopic media, we cannot passingly "glance" at content the way we can with planar material. Instead, we must put on a prosthesis of some sort, situate ourselves such that the binocular fusion can occur, and willfully commit to the media experience.

In his own nineteenth-century account of the stereoscope, David Brewster describes how it generates the effect of relief through a rapid succession of moments of coalescence: our eyes sequentially unify different parts of the scene presented one after another as they wander across it.[23] Crary concludes from this comment that "there never really is a stereoscopic image," that the visual experience the stereoscope provides is "a conjuration, an effect of the observer's experience of the differential between two other images."[24] The very phrase "stereoscopic image" is therefore oxymoronic, as it places stereoscopic media into a monocular optical bracket in which they do not fit. This is not solely a semantic distinction: stereoscopic content is *not* two side-by-side or overlain images; it is their fusion and surmounting by our own perceptual apparatus.

Like the stereoscope, 3D cinema does not transparently recreate reality and so make objectively existing space more visible. Instead, it eradicates presumed correspondences between the observer and that which is observed, creating an unreal space through a novel mode of perception. 3D films generate a visual illusion in which the observer's perceptual apparatus is implicated, a physiologically produced sensation entirely particular to stereoscopic media. Far from bringing mediated visual representation closer to the perceptual conditions of a viewer's life outside the media artifact, stereoscopic representation—in tandem with its viewers—creates ephemeral yet strangely material-seeming optical illusions quite different to images *or* real life experiences. Stereoscopy is a mutual production of media, apparatus, and observer; the correct arrangement of these generates the sensation of deep, layered space. This results in a media experience that is immediate, proximate, and sensorially affecting in ways very different from 2D media, as I will now examine through a comparison with anamorphosis.

ANAMORPHIC SPACE AND THE 3D CONTINUUM

Despite 3D's variance from 2D, the screen remains an organizing principle within many interpretations of the format. This is clearly shown in the way that critical accounts of 3D consistency alight upon the metaphors of the window and the frame, metaphors also commonly used in relation to planar narrative cinema.[25] As Thomas Elsaesser and Malte Hagener sum up, foundational theories of cinema from both formalists (such as Rudolf Arnheim and Sergei Eisenstein) and realists (such as André Bazin) "implicitly accepted the cinema as a window on the world and as a frame on a preconstituted reality."[26] The window metaphor "implies a diegetic world that extends beyond the limit of the image"; meanwhile, the metaphor of the frame "delineates a filmic composition that exists solely for the eyes of the beholder."[27] The screen is hypothesized as a limit point in either case, a barrier between the world of the viewer and that of the viewed media. 3D's added binocular cues are often seen to work in accordance with this structural metaphor. It is tempting to see 3D as creating a world in depth behind the (now-disappeared) screen, one that can occasionally reach out through the window in moments of negative parallax. However, this approach risks schematically reducing 3D depth to operating *either* in front of *or* behind it, *or* both, at various times during a film text. Such concrete binaries—the screen is violated, or it is not; the scene is deep, or it is not—can marginalize the greater array of spatial effects present in 3D cinema. Stereoscopic values are rarely either plus, minus, or absent; 3D media do not solely protrude, recede, or (when doing neither) exist at the level of the plane (in which case they are no longer 3D). Instead, stereoscopic depth is better thought of as a continuum, a fluctuating spatial scale that visually exists in front of, behind, and at the screen plane. This continuum can be usefully explored via a short detour into pictorial art history, and the technique of anamorphosis.

Anamorphosis creates images that appear distorted or illegible, but that resolve into normality either when an optical tool is employed (catoptric anamorphosis) or when the observer physically changes their vantage point (oblique anamorphosis). Anamorphic art uses perspectival geometry to achieve these effects: an original, classically structured image is overlain with a right-angled grid that can then be translated into a deformed grid with the same number of squares but very different geometry. The original composition, copied square by square and stretched, compressed, or tapered in the process, then retains its fundamental structure even as its topology radically shifts. Probably the most famous example is Hans Holbein the Younger's *The Ambassadors*, a painting from 1533 that features an oblique anamorphic skull in its lower quarter, a skull that presents initially as a skewed gray smudge and only resolves into "normal" dimensions when the viewer stands adjacent to rather than in front of the large canvas (fig. 6.1). This painting, as many scholars have argued, uses perspectival ordering to create a convincing spatial representation in relation to the titular figures and most of their surroundings even as it also uses anamorphosis to divulge the potential for other, apparently warped perspectives that run aggressively counter to this representational order.[28]

If Crary claims that stereoscopy "signals an eradication of 'the point of view' around which, for several centuries, meaning had been assigned reciprocally to an observer and the object of his or her beholding," then anamorphosis offers a useful prior indication of the intentions and consequences of a similar kind

6.1 Hans Holbein the Younger's *The Ambassadors* (1533), a key example of anamorphosis.

of "eradication."[29] Both 3D and anamorphosis rethink the screen plane, making this normally stable illusionistic surface into a multidimensional experience that exceeds this surface; while in each case a particular kind of "point of view" might be eradicated, the screen itself is not. Stereoscopic cinema expands beyond and rethinks the screen to the extent that it seems to negate fixed coordinates, but it is still projected upon and technologically contained within this screen.[30] Like anamorphosis, 3D is screen-based and perspectival, even as at the same time it seems to deny the supremacy and accuracy of the very perspectival measurements upon which it relies. 3D cinema is monstrous in much the same fashion as Holbein's skull: in either case, an optical illusion upsets the presumed view of reality that lies at the core of Western codes of image representation, hinting at the extent to which stable, objectively perceived space (whether represented through planar painting or 2D cinema) is a fiction.

If 3D expands beyond the screen upon which it is projected, then it is imperative to deduce what rules and limitations govern this expansion. Instead of the cinema screen being a window on a world, it becomes a vehicle for spatial content in a pseudoanamorphic manner, generating a shifting and ultimately nonrealistic spatial terrain. In the same manner that anamorphic art seems to exist in something of an alternate epistemological mode than the planar, perspectival illusion, 3D cinema is not "framed" and has the potential to colonize space both in front of and behind the screen. The former is best considered a kind of pyramid the tip of which is the viewer's eyes; the latter is a box-like shape the far edge of which is not infinity but a point some perceptual distance from (yet still anchored to) the screen—namely, the distance at which binocular vision becomes redundant.[31] The potential space of a 3D film is thus a kind of continuum, a latent zone of presence that may or may not be perceptually filled up during any shot or sequence.[32] The dimensions of this spatial continuum undermine assertions that the screen is a window.

As Ron Burnett suggests, 3D cinema offers a very different experience from 2D cinema because in the former "information [is] scattered across ambiguous spaces that require scanning, viewing, and continual adjustment to spatial and temporal shifts."[33] Part of the ambiguity Burnett points to results from 3D's illusionistic nature—it *seems* to offer space, but if we move our heads to look *around* objects they refuse to reveal more spatial information. Those minor head, neck, and eye movements that in embodied vision divulge potentially negligible but always accessible spatial information and confirm our embeddedness in a material space operate quite differently in 3D. Any optical repositioning by the viewer during a 3D film screening uncovers not greater volume cues, but rather the illusory, imagistically built spatiality in play, as the perceptual fusion of the twinned image source material shifts and realigns without revealing more spatial information. This points to the alternative, entirely optical nature of stereoscopic spatiality, a spatiality built from images rather than actually present spaces. Taking up different viewing points within the cinema does not vary the spatial information, but it does change the perceptual experience of the 3D film—closer to the screen and depth effects diminish; further to the left or right hand side of the screen and volumes become significantly less pronounced (i.e., flatter) creating a so-called cardboard-cutout effect.[34] All of this potential variation produces what Philip Sandifer calls a "highly erratic and arbitrarily shaped space."[35] This is not the experience of space we have when looking through a window, but a space of distortion and perceptual instability.

If the window metaphor is insufficient because of the distinctive spatial traits of stereoscopic media, then so too it is unsatisfying to think of the screen as a boundary or limit point that may be occasionally violated. Certainly, filmmakers evince a general tendency to place many elements of the film world in positive parallax, on the perceptual "other side" of the invisible screen. This implies a barrier, one that is oddly reaffirmed through its negation—those moments when 3D cinema addresses the viewer and "breaks" the frame. Personified by *House of Wax*'s paddleball entertainer, but found more recently in *The Legend of Tarzan* (2016) when an ostrich snaps its beak irritably at the viewer, or *Guardians of the Galaxy Vol. 2* (2017) when an arrow shoots toward the viewer, as well as other films too numerous to list, 3D is for many defined by these moments of direct address or rupture. Seen by many as distracting "novelties" or even "destabilizations" that are contradictory to the goals of immersive, story-based entertainment, in these moments the coherent, self-contained world of narrative feature filmmaking seems to give way (albeit briefly) to a cinema-of-attractions-style, front-facing, viewer-aware modality.[36] Such interpretations reveal the pervasiveness of planar image culture and its related expectations; they also imply that 3D only occasionally undertakes such "violations" and that they always operate in certain ways, something I argued against in chapter 1.

Negative parallax in 3D cinema does not inherently or automatically work in this rupturing fashion. In *Beowulf* (2007), for instance, landscapes and other backgrounds are placed overwhelmingly at the screen plane, and as a result anything else in the shot (e.g., figures, props, buildings) is positioned in negative parallax space. Here the screen functions not as a window but as a backdrop, the very rear of an imagined theater space, with the stage of action brought assertively forward into the perceptual space of the cinema. *Beowulf* thus reverses the presumed correspondence between screen and world—from the viewer's perspective the 3D continuum does not *start* at the screen, but ceases at it. Meanwhile, many other 3D films offer spatial compositions somewhere between the extremes of screen as window and screen as backdrop. In such cases, the volumetric world of the diegesis seems to be spatially present simultaneously in front of, at, and behind the screen. *Avatar*, as many scholars and critics pointed out, uses positive parallax powerfully but, as shown in chapter 3, the film nonetheless consistently employs compositions that place figures and objects within negative parallax space. Elements like ferns, foliage, and even people are equally staged in emerging space, with the film's world as a result spilling out in front of the screen in ways that are not aggressively oriented toward direct address, but that offer a subtler experience of palpable (but unfocused-upon) space. Equally, over-the-shoulder shots—which are frequent in the film—often situate a character's shoulder in foregrounded negative parallax space. For example, as Jake briefs the RDA about his first

6.2 A character is positioned in negative parallax, but not in a manner that "violates" the screen, in *Avatar* (2009).

adventure with the Na'vi he is placed prominently in negative parallax, with the other figures in the scene placed roughly at (or just behind) the screen plane (fig 6.2). Jake is not "violating" anything here; he is instead part of a volumetric composition taking in that which is both in front of and behind the invisible plane upon which the media content is being projected.

For Barbara Klinger, negative parallax is "the cinematic equivalent of the exclamation point in language, lending forcefulness to that which is articulated and soliciting the audience's special attention."[37] Meanwhile, Kristen Whissel proposes that in today's digital 3D cinema emergent elements are inherently tied to "'affective seeing' (a mode of perception organized around heightened emotion and sensation)."[38] Both suggestions thankfully view negative parallax effects as more than just direct address. But I argue that the defamiliarization of the plane in digital 3D means that those elements that protrude need not do so in even this kind of showy or enunciative manner, nor that they always operate as markers or enablers of a kind of heightened emotional response.[39] They are, rather, just traces—albeit perhaps the most overtly visible traces—of the holistic transformation of the planar screen into an extensible, highly malleable perceptual space.

For this reason, it is productive to think of 3D as creating what Miriam Ross terms a "membrane," Alla Gadassik calls "voluminous surface," or what I term a "latent continuum."[40] In this way, 3D's generation of a consistent, if fluctuating, impression of stereo depth is emphasized. Ross's and Gadassik's terms point to the bulging, bending, and bowing of 3D cinematic space, while the word continuum by subtle contrast stresses not the modified surface dimensions but the expansive and distinctively ephemeral spatiality of 3D. The addition of the word "latent" here then aims to underscore the presence of potential, if unused, depth. This is an aspect of 3D's spatiality that is often disregarded, although two comparative examples from planar cinema helpfully indicate the importance of vacant or unexploited space. 2D films might include shots in which areas of the frame contain little of interest (and so might be out of focus or dimly lit) but these areas nonetheless still exist as fundamental parts of the shot, contributing to graphical design, structured ambiguity, or diegetic context. Likewise, off-screen spaces might themselves by definition not be visualized, but they can be activated through glances, compositional codes, and sound cues, becoming as a result a kind of structuring absence.[41] Textual analysis must take note of such partially "empty" frames or the pointed deployment of off-screen space, and, similarly, even though the continuum of stereoscopic space may not be filled in its entirety in any given shot or across any given film, it remains a latently present volume of spatial possibility.

3D filmmaking, then, rethinks the plane and how it might function in the creation of illusionistic representational content. Neither window, frame, nor boundary, the screen in 3D is rather the vehicle for a latent continuum of potential space. As a result, instead of using the coordinates of 2D cinema and perspectival art to map 3D aesthetics as they play out for viewers, it is better to deploy anamorphic terms: disrupting the stability of the visual field and film world, 3D introduces an experience of spatial dimensions that is wholly distinctive. Generating objects and spaces that are simultaneously both present and not, 3D is anamorphic in its subversion of expected visual norms, as well as in its simultaneous supersession of and reliance upon the screen plane. In 3D cinema, the plane is *defamiliarized*—a term that makes different claims than those suggestions that the screen is "eradicated" or made "invisible." The screen is still there not only as the material site of projected media (3D films are not holograms: they require a site of projection), but also as the structuring foundation of each of the twinned image streams (each of which is imagistic, planar). Nonetheless, the 3D film is not illusionistically presenting space *upon* a surface: the screen remains vital, but no longer functions in a strictly perspectival, geometric manner. Just like anamorphic art, perspective and planar logics may structure and coordinate the media experience of 3D cinema, but they become mobilizers of a form of visuality that escapes these codes. In this way, 3D undermines expectations regarding the screen plane and its functioning, turning this plane into a multidimensional spatial continuum.

THE SPECTER OF THE SCREEN

A better understanding of this latent continuum can be reached through an assessment of those moments when 2D aesthetics intersect with 3D spatiality. Elsewhere, I have described how 3D films "negotiate" methods of composition and editing associated with 2D cinema and have argued that 3D stylistics are in many ways "tamed" to accepted, normative, planar models of editing and cinematography.[42] Here, however, I wish to focus on the subtler ways in which 3D films adopt but reconfigure certain aspects of contemporary 2D film style. Although, as we have seen, digital 3D films offer expanded spatial compositions, they also cling to certain aesthetic approaches associated with planar cinema. Firstly, 3D cinema may seem to dematerialize the screen but it simultaneously preserves the screen as a site of meaning in its adoption of rack focus techniques and the linking of these to stereoscopic depth in a process I term "depth racking." Secondly, 3D retains a sense of the monocular camera as an interpretive framework through the regular deployment of lens-based artifacts and blemishes. In these ways the screen is strangely retained, although not, I argue, in a manner that refutes my claims regarding the presence of a 3D continuum that functions in anamorphic, not perspectival, ways. The lingering aesthetic influence and importance of the screen produces distinctive, distorting effects that helpfully point not to the similarity between 3D and 2D but to their radical difference.

As already discussed, 3D depth demands that our eyes converge and focus at different points. This is unlike everyday life (in which our sight simultaneously focuses and converges on objects) and 2D cinema (in which we simultaneously focus and converge on the screen). However, 3D cinema can evoke these other modes of viewing by situating objects of interest at zero parallax—the site of the screen. In these cases, our focus and convergence are aligned, as we are essentially viewing 2D material. Throughout *Avatar*, for instance, visual elements that contain motivated narrative or affective information are often situated at zero parallax. From the eyes of characters (which tend to draw direct attention), to important props and crucial aspects of architecture and space, the stereoscopic depth arrangement consistently—if not universally—correlates the intended site of the viewer's gaze with the screen plane. This is especially the case in scenes in which character and narrative are emphasized over spectacle and action. In Prince's words, this approach avoids presenting viewers with "discomfiting image fusion tasks," since the likely subject of the gaze is aligned with what is considered the most comfortable part of the stereoscopic visual field.[43]

Avatar is not alone in this—many mainstream digital 3D productions arrange the stereoscopic continuum this way, uniting the site of intended attention for the most part with the plane.[44] If this tethering of concentration with zero parallax preserves the specter of 2D within 3D cinema and propagates the continued relevance and supremacy of that which exists at the site of the screen, then the use of these kinds of screen-oriented compositions can nonetheless also incidentally produce a significant visual-spatial distortion, one which highlights the extent to which 3D cinema not only expands the screen but also manufactures a distinctive, malleable, and above all unusual kind of spatial experience. This is the recalibration of depth values within a continuous shot, a process that, while common and uncontroversial, speaks to digital 3D cinema's ongoing struggle to combine 2D and 3D compositional logics.

To use *Avatar* as an example again, the wandering camera in this film often drifts from person to person, tracks through space, or racks focus between multiple objects in a single shot, depending on where the filmmakers think our attention should be. The shifting point of intended attention in such shots poses a challenge to the zero parallax approach. This challenge is met by realigning the stereoscopic continuum during a shot, fluidly altering depth relations to position each new attention point at the screen plane. During a briefing scene, for instance, the camera begins by focusing on Jake and Selfridge in the midground, before racking focus to Quaritch in the background when he speaks (figs 6.3 and 6.4). The focus pull works to transfer our attention from one character to the other in both 2D and 3D versions of the film; in 3D, however, the depth relations of the shot also alter: Jake and Selfridge begin at zero parallax, but when the lurking Quaritch becomes the center of attention the other characters are shifted into negative parallax as Quaritch is brought forward to zero parallax. We apparently plunge a few feet into space to get closer to Quaritch, but at the same time Jake and Selfridge remain visible and occupy the same amount of space in our visual field. This spatial sleight of hand may be minimally noticeable as a 3D effect, but from a sensory perspective it is, to say the least, rather unusual. In such moments (and they recur across *Avatar* and a large body of digital 3D cinema) it is almost as though the shape of space itself warps and twists before our eyes, albeit in subtle and physiologically unaccountable ways.

6.3 AND 6.4 A rack focus in *Avatar* (2009) is accompanied by the repositioning of stereoscopic values.

In this example from *Avatar*, stereoscopic depth changes in line with a focus rack, and the similar intentions of each technique encourages the realignment of the 3D continuum in this manner to be considered a kind of "depth racking." Like a focus pull, it seeks to transfer audience attention from one site of the screened space to another, but it operates in a spatial rather than planar fashion.[45] (This said, it is important to note that depth racking can occur independent of focal changes, as in shots with a less shallow depth of field than the above example, or when the camera physically moves from one composition to alight on a new object of interest at a different depth, and these other examples also occur throughout *Avatar*.) Director James Cameron may claim the importance of biological mimicry in 3D cinema—"Everybody's got two eyes, even down to the insect world," he insists as proof of 3D's realism—but depth racking shifts the volumetric dimensions of represented space in a highly nonnaturalistic fashion.[46] In everyday perception we might focus on objects at different depths in turn, but in such moments our eyes change their convergence point to match where our new focus rests; when digital 3D cinema racks depth, focus and convergence (already operating, as we have seen, with relative independence) shift their relationship within the parameters of a single shot. This demonstrates even more directly their disconnection from one another in this medium and produces a perceptual space that is unstable and subject to highly unusual reorientation.

Similarly, the latent continuum of a 3D film can be shrunk and expanded as demanded by creative imperatives or concerns for audience comfort. For example, the depths of shot are sometimes lessened—or "dialed down," in stereographer parlance—around a fraction of a second prior to and immediately after a cut. This, like depth racking, is geared toward the optical well-being of the audience: the viewer is not shown radically different spatial information in instantaneous succession, but rather eased into and out of potentially variant depth experiences. As Prince outlines, this strategy presumes that the "perceptual resources" a viewer brings to a 3D film are somehow limited and so should not be exhausted through demands for excessive "work," such as is apparently demanded by significantly varying depths between quickly edited shots.[47] Cutting from one extensive spatial arrangement to another is, in this view, deemed perceptually demanding in a way that experiencing space as a kind of accordion that can deflate and inflate rapidly apparently is not. 2D is again used to anchor 3D: the potential textual threat posed by 3D perception is apparently lessened by its translation through a 2D filter at moments of highest visibility.

All of this accentuates the extent to which, despite the fact that digital 3D manifestly reconfigures the nature of the cinema screen, the presence of the screen is retained in some respects as a site around which spatial relations are organized. This allows 2D and 3D stylistic codes to intermingle—or, to take a more detrimental view, speaks to the way 3D's radical aesthetic potential might be diluted in a media environment in which 2D aesthetics and compositional strategies are historically and culturally pervasive. Complexly negotiating its relationship to both planar media and everyday vision, depth racking reveals how 3D filmmaking admits to some of the elasticities and ambiguities of the latter, while being entangled within the discursive terrain and visual expectations of the former. A little-explored but key aspect of digital 3D cinema practice, depth racking shows how the spatial compositions of 3D respond to and rearticulate representational codes associated with the screen and points to the way stereoscopic composition distorts space, thanks to the influence of 2D aesthetic expectations.

Another echo of the 2D screen can be found in the presence of lens artifacts. These are resolutely not points of explicit audience interest, but, like depth racking, they confound spatial expectations and indicate the complex relationship of 3D to the screen plane. Appearing in a wide range of films from realist dramas to blockbuster science fiction, artifacts indicate the presence of the lens: this may be in the form of light flares, or blemishes that dirty up this lens (often caused by diegetic rainwater or other fluids). But in digital cinema this is a lens that in many cases did not materially exist, or, if it did, the artifacts that reveal it are themselves digitally generated effects. In the words of David Fleming and William Brown, the artifacts of digital cinema are "surplus features," visual effects that seek to connect digital cinema to its analogue antecedent by "simulat[ing] a familiar 'cinematic view' of 'recorded' events," even if these events have been digitally generated and rendered without the involvement of a camera.[48] These lens artifacts impersonate not only indexicality, then, but a specifically analog, messy kind of indexicality.[49]

While flares and dirt blemishes would seem to be counterintuitive to the polished aesthetic of commercial filmmaking, they carry with them a certain kind of realist credibility and have found extensive purchase in contemporary digital cinema. *Pacific Rim* (2013), for instance, includes many shots in which skyscraper-tall robots do battle with similarly enormous alien monsters. In these scenes, often at night and in rain, droplets of water constantly intersect with the lens of the camera, creating a layer of congealed spray through which the viewer beholds the spectacular action. These fully CG-rendered shots therefore rely on the lens artifacts (along with shaky handheld framing) to ground the fantastical combat. This might productively be considered an updated version of Prince's "perceptual realism," in which realism now includes not only the rendering of digital objects in film space, but also the rendering (through artifacts) of the lens that is supposedly filming them (even if this lens is an entirely virtual, simulated construction). If the screen is a window, then lens artifacts like this make the glass of that window tangible: the barrier between audience and represented world is emphasized through the evocation of a transparent partition with which fluid intersects.

In 3D, however, the barrier implied or constructed by artifacts is more nuanced. Not fixed to a certain point—zero parallax, say—artifacts often exist at a range of negative parallax depths, including, sometimes, multiple depths at once. The aforementioned shots in *Pacific Rim* layer artifacts throughout the continuum, activating its latent potential across multiple z-axis sites, including a range of points within negative parallax space, zero parallax, and occasionally positive parallax. The result is a multiply tiered, overlapping spatial patchwork of fluctuating ephemeral patternings. Far from unique to this film, such an approach to fluid-based artifacts is common in digital 3D cinema and can be applied in ways that are either overt or understated. For instance, films like *300: Rise of An Empire* (2014) and *Point Break* (2015) create extremely nebulous compound layerings of screen-like partitions through their placement of blemishes and droplets at notable moments, while *Beowulf*, *Life of Pi* (2012), and *Gravity* (2013) employ subtler and more sporadic moments in which parts of the negative parallax stereoscopic field are splattered with variable blemishes of fluid.

Implying the presence of both a screen and a (monocular) filming apparatus, artifacts undermine many claims the 3D film might make regarding its creation of an entirely immersive, binocularly perceived diegetic world. At times, *Pacific Rim* and other films place artifacts much further into negative parallax than they do any other filmic elements, and this extreme proximity encourages the interpretation of the blemishes less as marks upon the camera lens and the traditional screen plane than as marks upon the polarized glasses that viewers wear during 3D exhibition. Camera-lens artifacts are in this way reconceptualized as glasses-lens artifacts.[50] However, while the glasses metaphor might seem a compelling replacement for the screen metaphor, it fails at the levels of alignment and spatial variability. Firstly, alignment: just as they are in 2D, in 3D these artifacts are not accidental but rigorously managed by postproduction techniques. If converted, a film will either retain existing blemishes but duplicate them for the second, newly created image-stream; if native, all blemishes will likely be CG productions, since they will not harmoniously align across the twinned lenses of a stereoscopic camera rig. In either case, artifacts are engineered in order to be spatially "placed." Under real conditions, water spray impacting our eyewear would take very different forms across left and right lenses. (Just such a realistic, differential experience of such artifacts is offered by 2014's *Goodbye to Language*, which as a result conjures a far more

6.5 Lens flare arcs through the stereoscopic continuum in the title screen for
The Martian (2015).

chaotic and confusing visual field than the carefully placed artifacts of digital
blockbuster cinema; see chapter 7). Secondly, the existence of blemishes at several points along the z-axis simultaneously suggests a tiered, compound-screen
arrangement, one that does not make logical sense according to conventional
experience of space and vision. Ideas of the screen and related codes of (digitally enabled) realism may remain in play, but they are radically reconceived,
the spacing and even the nature of the implied screen/window boundary being
transformed, as it becomes both screen and space, continuum and terminus.

In a similar fashion to these water stains, light flares must be reconfigured
from imagistic elements to spatial ones in digital 3D cinema, a reconfigura-
tion that allows them to arc gracefully through the stereoscopic continuum.
The opening shot of *The Martian* (2015), for instance, is a slow pan over the
planet Mars, the sun in the distance; lens flare appears across the frame as the
film's title slowly materializes, and the diagonally composed artifacts glint at
a range of depths, some highly protrusive, others at the screen plane, the
remainder at various depths in between (fig. 6.5). This digitally created shot
includes flare to provide perceptual realism (e.g., flare appearing as we would
expect it to if a camera panned across a distant sun) and also to create a sense
of stereoscopic depth that would otherwise, in a shot this distant, be absent.
Prevalent in 3D releases like *Man of Steel* (2013) and *Star Trek Into Darkness*
(2013), among many others, lens flare colonizes the latent stereoscopic volume
of a shot, effectively mapping the ephemeral spatial terrain that the 3D film
has available, providing a shimmering, dispersive element for the viewer to look

through and around to the represented world beyond.[51] As is the case with blemishes, flares can be brought heavily into negative parallax space, since most viewers will focus their attention upon the contents of the scene rather than these artifacts.

If depth racking speaks to the ways in which the 3D continuum is anchored to the plane, then by contrast the persistent presence of lens artifacts in 3D cinema shows how screen-based codes of realism are expanded into stereoscopic space and accordingly reimagined as spatial elements. Inspired by aesthetic strategies that pre-date the widespread adoption of digital 3D, artifacts demonstrate how the screen plane is paradoxically retained and confirmed, even as it is also transformed. They show that the screen has not exactly "disappeared," that we are not peering into a holistic world-beyond. They instead insinuate that the planar screen and its associated image logics (and reality effects) have been imported and recalibrated to survive 3D presentation, and, moreover, they allow the contemporary 3D film to negotiate the medium's potential for negative parallax without resorting to direct address.

Lens-based artifacts navigate the liminal terrain not only between analog and digital cinema but also between planar and stereoscopic exhibition, and they highlight the extent to which the screen quite literally changes shape in digital 3D. While artifacts may, as they do in analog and 2D cinema, assert a kind of perceptual realism, this is a perceptual realism that makes little perceptual *sense* in digital 3D, as artifacts exist at a range of depths and even become volumetric shapes in some instances. In this way, though artifacts, like depth racking, speak in some ways to the lingering presence and importance of the screen in 3D cinema, they do so in a manner that points to 3D's radical difference from 2D, rather than to any similarity or equivalence.

• • •

3D's uniqueness within the media landscape stems in part from its intricate and novel relationship with the screen. 3D cinema creates an ephemeral, unstable zone of perceptual space that expands beyond the planar confines of the screen, but it also preserves aspects of film language that are screen defined and screen dependent. The 3D film is not just a window, nor is it any longer a screen, but some strange combination and supersession of the two: an anamorphic, multidimensional continuum that skews planarcentric expectations around the mediation of space. As such, although the monocular ambiguities of perspectival representation might seem overcome by 3D's stereoscopic cues, this does not necessarily make 3D a more "realistic" rendering of embodied visual experience. The phrase "3D image" may be oxymoronic, but the logic of the image remains crucial to 3D even as it is simultaneously annulled and transformed. Like anamorphic art, 3D overcomes yet still relies upon the screen in order to exist in the first place. Being attentive to the continuing presence and importance of the screen in 3D cinema in this way does not undermine claims that 3D is a radically different form of visuality from planar media. Rather, it allows us to begin considering how 3D negotiates and rethinks this plane in significant ways.

As such, the specter of 2D cinema aesthetics, as it were, can be seen to haunt digital 3D. 3D films exist within a broader 2D media environment and so employ similar filmmaking devices like rack focus, and even faux-verité effects like lens artifacts. However, 3D cinema fundamentally reorients how such devices work. Films like *Avatar* may use depth racking in order to somehow align a 2D illusionistic device (focus) with a stereoscopic one (spatial position) but in the process they undermine the realism and naturalism that might otherwise be claimed of stereoscopic exhibition. Depth racking may site important elements at the screen for the sake of physiological comfort, but this results in a radically malleable impression of visual space, conjuring an elastic visual field that can wend and warp at the staidest of narrative moments. While the placement of immaterial, nonconcrete elements and artifacts in negative parallax might evoke the holograms of films like *Iron Man 3* and *Insurgent*, the different constitution of these elements focuses more attention upon 3D as a distinctive, distorted experience. Certainly, like those digital spatial models, lens artifacts are generated digitally in contemporary blockbuster 3D cinema and placed within stereoscopic space in highly intentional ways and thus proceed from a similar ontology of strict, algorithmic visual control. Even so, inclusion of these artifacts, like depth racking, defamilarizes the screen plane through the employment and manipulation of a continuum of overlapping, latently ever-present spaces.

Defamiliarize, not dematerialize: while 3D might conveniently be thought to *remove* the pane of glass from the window that is the cinema screen, this removal is not complete, nor is it unambiguous. Many digital 3D films retain the supremacy of the plane by keeping objects of interest at zero parallax, while the presence of artifacts in negative parallax space paradoxically reinstates the screen even as it is apparently overcome. These aesthetic features produce a 3D experience in which the screen plane is *not* reducible to a metaphorical "window" onto a stereoscopic world that recedes in depth. Thus, for all its supposed *addition* of depth cues, 3D does not (re)instate a greater impression of realism to our media images. Stereoscopic media may seem to do duty for embodied everyday vision, but the visual experience they offer is just as far from every-day vision as it is from planar images. Like anamorphosis, 3D rethinks the screen, making it multidimensional and unfamiliar. But 3D goes further than anamorphosis in this regard. It is, after all, an ultimately nonimagistic media form in which space is not received as geometry but perceived as a latent poten-tial volume, monstrous in its perceptual alterity. The plane becomes a lengthy volume of potential space, space that does not perceptually exist in a perspec-tival recession but is instead a kind of ephemeral continuum that begins at the viewer's 3D glasses and extends to an artificial vanishing point beyond the screen. So, although 3D imports realist effects like lens artifacts from 2D cin-ema, this translation is neither easy nor unproblematic. This reveals something of the strangeness of stereoscopic space and the 3D "screen," as we can see when emphasizing not the geometric spatial mapping of the medium but its nonim-agistic, nonobjective ephemeral qualities. If 3D's continuum unsettles planar conventions, as this chapter has shown, then it also radically (if subtly) dis-torts naturalized ideas around space, a theme I take up in the next chapter.

7

DISTORTION

. . . .

Unfamiliar and Unconventional Space

The differences in the way viewers perceive 2D and 3D content are marked, and they can make 3D appear problematically, unwelcomingly monstrous. In contrast to the seductively ethereal spatial simulations of the films of part 2, with their assertions of accuracy and usefulness, 3D's perceptual experience of spatial surplus can seem at other times objectionably peculiar, even painful. As Akira Mizuta Lippit explains, "3D cinema is, in the idiom of its detractors, grotesque, a mutilation of the placid surfaces of Apollonion art."[1] In this chapter, I consider such grotesque examples of 3D, since it is when the format is at its most Dionysian that it reveals the monstrous aspects of its foundational optical situation and the extent of its difference from the Apollonian values of its digital production methods.

3D's detractors find its potentially shocking alterity—its appeals to the subjective and the irrational, its excessive and possibly gratuitous spatial impressions—to be at odds with what art, or cinema, should be: rational, ordered, cemented within a screen. I have already questioned this dichotomy, and for all 3D's potential and actual *strangeness* as a visual mode, this can only ever be a relative term. 3D's spatial productions may be very different from those of planar media, but in both cases the embodied visual experience of space is being distorted. 2D media crush the extensible experiential world into a geometric plane; its images may be evocative of our embodied physiological perception of space, but they are by no means identical to it. The distortions of 3D media are simply less normalized, and so potentially more overt, and so, often, critiqued as aberrant. Yet this abnormality offers a valuable opportunity.

If a particular example of 3D filmmaking diverges so much from expectations regarding screen-mediated visual material that it becomes prominently, even radically, unusual, then it is possible to glimpse the more pervasive alterity of 3D exhibition generally, its strangeness relative to 2D templates.

To explore 3D's distortions in more detail, then, this chapter first attends to the haptic nature of stereoscopic media and then analyzes the malleability of stereoscopic depth effects, and the ways in which spatial flexibility speaks to the distinct visual operations engendered by the 3D format. As I described in the last chapter, effects like depth racking and lens artifacts indicate how digital 3D is not blandly yoked to realist imperatives, and how it operates across a latent continuum that is always present, whether it is all in use or not. 3D, as also shown in chapter 1, does not appear briefly in order to address the viewer before then disappearing, but is always present in some form or another. Accordingly, if 3D space cannot be considered either present or absent, correct or incorrect, then the actual and potential variations in the scale and makeup of this visual space must be accounted for in any analysis of 3D media. Every stereoscopic depth composition in a 3D film is a concerted, creative choice—even if it might sometimes appear naturalistic, uninteresting, or effectively invisible.

Although by no means a prominent way of thinking about 3D, some key accounts of the format are attuned to this spatial variability and its importance. In relation to predigital 3D, Sheldon Hall has explored the way Alfred Hitchcock uses the varying scale of the 3D continuum to throw light on plot mechanisms in *Dial M for Murder*, and William Paul has discussed how the emergence effects of *Kiss Me Kate* are indebted to renowned theater presences Bertolt Brecht and David Belasco.[2] Through such work, these scholars make claims for the artistic integrity of (some) 3D depth. More recently but in a similar vein, Lisa Purse and Scott Higgins have each offered readings of *Hugo* (2012) that highlight how the film's stereo depth is adapted creatively to suit thematic ends (alighting on the way the film shifts productively between claustrophobically constricted and expansively enveloping depth impressions).[3] Similarly, Caetlin Benson-Allott has investigated the metaphysics and depth strategies of *Coraline* (2009), a film whose 3D is often singled out by critics as expressively rewarding, and Miriam Ross and Owen Weetch each offer book-length studies of the diverse effects and uses of stereoscopic depth.[4] All of this work rightly emphasizes the extent to which stereoscopic space is a manipulable value, one that offers as many opportunities for creative intervention and decision-making as other aspects of contemporary cinematography (such as color grading, image sharpness, brightness, and so on). Never stable or naturalistic, stereoscopic depth is shown by these studies to be subject to adjustment and fluctuation.

These scholars single out moments of expressive 3D, yet the extent and power of the format's particular visuality is made most overt in a different context— namely, those moments in which the twinned images that make up any 3D media are insufficiently coordinated. As our eyes angle to perceive spatial objects that are not corporeally present, focus and convergence, normally linked, become uncoupled; if the dual image streams of 3D projection are not exactly aligned both spatially and temporally, this uncoupling can lead to visual stress. Images with a vertical mismatch, or angled obliquely to one another, or chronologically out of step (as could be the case in analog 3D screenings relying on two separate film reels) can result in what is commonly termed "eyestrain." This is a loosely defined condition characterized by headaches and/or nausea, thought to result from the need for the eyes and brain to do a greater amount of work to comprehend the overly divergent visual material presented in such cases. It is a physiological response described in numerous historical accounts of 3D cinema prior to the digital era.[5] It continues to be raised as an issue, the most widely cited descriptions of its effects and frustrations coming courtesy of Roger Ebert and Mark Kermode.[6] This is despite the fact that contemporary digital production pipelines work to mitigate those misalignments that previously affected analog 3D production: today, misalignment is most commonly associated with those films that pre-date the digital era, or with cheap or hasty contemporary 3D conversions, or with natively shot films that lack the financial resources for extensive, digitally aided postproduction image-tinkering.[7] But eyestrain might equally result from intended spatial compositions, including those that contain extensive disparities between focus and convergence points (such as when a viewer's gaze converges for a sustained amount of time on an object that protrudes aggressively from the screen).[8] In either case, it is commonly considered undesirable, a trace of poor craftsmanship in the production or exhibition of a given film.

However, I would like to stress how 3D cinema's ability to induce physical discomfort testifies to the visceral, literally bodily reactions upon which it relies. Words like "eyestrain" and sensations such as headaches and nausea highlight how stereoscopy involves the body and its systems of perception to a greater extent and in different ways than do planar media.[9] Despite its intense connections with Euclidean spatial imaginations and digital image coordination, digital 3D cinema, like the stereoscope before it, offers a visual experience that is haptically embodied, highly novel, and perceptually destabilizing. These qualities come to the fore in those moments when 3D space either does not seek or does not achieve anything resembling spatial naturalism. In this chapter, I find these moments respectively in an art-house text and a block-buster text. In drama-cum-essay-film *Goodbye to Language* (*Adieu au langage*, 2014), the monstrosities of 3D filmmaking and exhibition are openly interrogated, as the film aggressively and purposefully reveals the distortions of which the format is capable. While this film has been applauded for "thinking" in 3D in this way, I will show that similarly bold and revelatory distortions can be found in the less renowned *Clash of the Titans* (2010). This 3D conversion also has monstrous stereoscopic values, but these are the result of apparent creative mismanagement rather than auteurist creative purpose. Nonetheless, each of these films in their own ways demonstrate the "spatial seeing" that defines stereoscopic media and makes it a revelatory and entirely distinctive mode of optics.[10] The widely divergent production practices and cultural standings of these films, meanwhile, helps to stress the consistency of this spatial seeing. *Goodbye to Language* and *Clash of the Titans* amp up 3D's already abnormal optics, and in the process they indicate 3D's difference from planar media, and how 3D creates distinctive perceptual experiences in which the physiology of viewing and the dimensionality of space are made strange. This is not solely true of cinematic 3D, though, as a return to scholarship on the stereoscope and its own monstrosities can usefully show.

HAPTICS AND SPATIAL SEEING IN STEREOSCOPIC MEDIA

One of the key features of the stereoscope was its removal of the physical and psychological distance between viewer and view. John Plunkett, for instance, may place the stereoscope within a broader lineage of immersive art that also includes the panorama and diorama, but he also proposes that it particularly highlighted the "phenomenology of vision" by accentuating the activity of the perceiver in personally generating what they perceive. The stereoscope, for Plunkett, thus questioned assumptions "concerning the relationship between the material and the ideal, the internal and the external, imagination and reality."[11] Writing about this aesthetic of intermingled boundaries in relation to pornographic stereocards, Colette Colligan coins the term "stereograph effect." Unlike "the reality effect" that Roland Barthes associated with the accumulation of "useless detail" in the nineteenth-century novel, the "different form of realism" offered by the stereograph effect is "dimensional and perceptual, rather than mimetic and symbolic," a realism in which the previously stable "sign" acquires "fathoms and depths" and is not subsumed within hierarchies of meaning.[12] Finally, in her book on the Victorian imagination, Isobel Armstrong proposes that the stereoscope demands the abandonment of the "classical gaze" through its revelation of the instability of the relationship between subject and object.[13] The "strangeness" of its depth effects prompts the user, to varying degrees, to be aware of the slippage between perception, media, and self.

For all these writers, then, stereoscopic media escape the mastering gaze. The 3D scene is not a received fact of external topography, but rather seems to emerge from within our own mental landscape as a "conjuration" of tricked perception.[14] Plunkett accordingly suggests that the stereoscope operates as a "haptic, sensuous, sculptural mode of viewing," and he is not alone in making this connection to haptics.[15] Influentially described by art historian Aloïs Riegl, haptic perception is a tactile kind of looking that sinks into texture, as opposed to the detached survey of form and space offered by optical perception.[16] As Laura Marks puts it, "The eyes themselves function like organs of touch" in haptic looking, with surface characteristics rather than spatial depth emphasized.[17] In this way, the separation of (looking) subject and object (of the look) that is associated with normalized, objective, Cartesian viewing practices is rejected. As such, applying the label "haptic" to stereoscopic media works implicitly and intriguingly against claims of spatial naturalism, realistic depth, and windows-on-the-world. Instead, a haptic reading seeks to account not only for the sense of tactility in stereoscopic media, but also the way this tactility is copresent with ephemerality: notwithstanding the volumes assured by binocular cues, the objects and spaces depicted are, just as in planar media, inherently out of reach and literally untouchable. Making the eyes function as organs of felt tactile sensation, stereoscopic media may offer a kind of "visualisation of tangibility," but whatever impressions of tangibility they tender is also complicated by the simultaneous *in*tangibility of the represented content.[18]

I will explore this intangibility in more detail in the next chapter, but for the time being I want to stress how the sense of presence conjured by stereoscopy does not result in a straightforward impression of reality. Rather, it offers a sensation of an unusual, overflowing, uncertain reality that is both present and not present, and in which the act of visual perception is made strange. As Crary suggests, although the stereoscope creates a sense of tangibility, "it is a tangibility that has been transformed into a purely visual experience."[19] He describes how, as a result, popular nineteenth-century stereographs offer a "vertiginous uncertainty" around distance, and how even their empty spaces have "a disturbing palpability."[20] Furthermore—and underlining their haptic nature—stereoscopes create a scene that cannot be taken in all at once. Users must glance around the represented scene, accumulating something of a cohesive sense of space from that which is nonetheless "a fundamentally disunified and aggregate field of disjunct elements."[21] As Crary argues, the result is "a patchwork of different intensities" imbued with "hallucinatory clarity," but that "never coalesce into a homogenous field."[22] Art critic Rosaline Krauss calls this saccadic scanning a "physico-optical traversal of the stereo field."[23] The stable visual field promised by planar image culture is refused, replaced by constantly in-process foveal fabrication.

Stereoscopic media puzzlingly commingle representation and embodied perception, and they disconcertingly transmute our sense of touch and our spatial awareness into entirely visual categories. These overlaps and substitutions are intrinsic to 3D's particular visual experience, and if Crary calls this "hallucinatory," such a word speaks not only to stereoscopic media's novelty in an imagistic visual culture but also the affective power of these media. Even Oliver Wendell Holmes—who championed the positivism of the stereoscope and argued for its detail-laden beauty—had to make recourse to engulfing, overpowering mental states like hypnotism and dreams to portray its experiential effects: so entrancing is the stereoscope for Holmes that he describes it as offering a "dream-like exaltation of the faculties, a kind of clairvoyance, in which we seem to leave the body behind us and sail away into one *strange* scene after another."[24] Frequently, Holmes's purple prose pulls him away from the realism he purports to valorize:

> The first effect of looking at a good photograph through the stereoscope is a surprise such as no painting ever produced. The mind feels its way into the very depths of the picture. The scraggy branches of a tree in the foreground run out at us as if they would scratch our eyes out. The elbow of a figure stands forth so as to make us almost uncomfortable. Then there is the frightful amount of detail, that we have the same sense of infinite complexity which Nature gives us.[25]

Comments on detail, depth, and nature may be of a piece with Holmes's realist itinerary, but his descriptions of scraggy tree branches and elbows that threaten our corporeal bodies and discomfortingly invade our personal space all point to something else. Yes, these embodied responses refer to a convincing representation of reality, but, more than this, such descriptions highlight the potent and unusual aspects of stereoscopic scenes, how they can unsettle us in a contingent and incomplete manner. Elbows "almost" make us uncomfortable; tree branches seem "as if" they could touch us. Whatever photography offers, the stereoscope seems to offer in a more embodied, immediate fashion. Thus, when Jib Fowles speaks of how stereoscopic views are "more vivid and engrossing than any two-dimensional photograph" and proposes that they have a "magnetic" appeal that accounts for their nineteenth-century popularity, he is not just talking about levels of detail or added spatial data, but about a tactile, optical phenomenology that is abnormal and fascinating.[26] This is reiterated by Krauss, who suggests in an essay on the nineteenth-century stereo photography of Timothy O'Sullivan that our experience of stereoscopic scenes is "insistent and inescapable," "a kind of tunnel vision," and a "heightened" visual experience.[27]

Rod Bantjes provides a comprehensive analysis of this aspect of stereoscopic media in his article "Reading Stereoviews: The Aesthetics of Monstrous Space." Alighting upon the spatial distortions of the stereoscope and its divergence from other representational forms, Bantjes argues that, in comparison to the "metric space" of Renaissance perspective, stereoscopic space has a "bizarre spatial logic" that makes it "monstrous and un-parseable."[28] He further suggests, like Armstrong, Plunkett, and Colligan, that the nineteenth-century stereoscope historically revealed how "the real" and our inculcated ways of perceiving it were (and still are) arbitrary rather than immutable. While stereoscopic photography may have existed within what Bantjes terms a "covert technological assemblage" (35) inherited from perspective—an assemblage privileging architectural logic and the "trigonometry of the eye" (37)—it was nonetheless capable of very different operations.

These alternative spatial impressions become visible in the work of certain stereoscopic photographers. So, while many stereophotographers elected to capture wide shots of buildings and their facades, or interior shots of rooms both domestic and industrial, or staged scenes of an unfolding drama—all compositions and subjects familiar from perspectival art—the format was also used in other, more "monstrous" ways. For instance, Bantjes describes stereophotographs by Claude-Marie Ferrier and George Washington Wilson that seem to abandon architectural logic, activating a different kind of spatial seeing: that of unexpected depths, shapes, and recessions. These stereocards, Bantjes sums up, were unlike preexisting spatial representations in pictorial media, offering "a great deal to see that, by the standards of Classical representation, might be considered monstrous" (54). Crucially, these stereocards were most likely designed to be looked at in two formats: first as planar images, and then (through the stereoscope) as dimensional scenes. Part of the pleasure to be taken from them, as Bantjes outlines, was a shift in spatial values that could be profoundly unexpected. For instance, in Ferrier's *Caverne de glace a Rosenlaui*, a glacier is photographed in such a fashion that in its planar form it is difficult to ascertain or fully comprehend the depths and shapes in play, depths and shapes that are then thrillingly revealed through stereoscopic perusal. What seems to be a foregrounded protruding piece of glacier ice is discovered through the stereoscope to be a slight but deep opening into recessive space, an example of the possible surprises on offer (47). In this way, stereocards can forcibly point to the difference between 2D and 3D representation, indicating how the spatial seeing of stereoscopic media is not mere augmentation and deepening.

Accounts of cinematic 3D can equally alight upon its capacity to rework expected spatial realities in monstrous ways. Miriam Ross has drawn on phenomenological film theory to describe the haptic encounter offered by stereoscopic exhibition, proposing that, more than just a haptic cinema, 3D is best considered a "hyper-haptic" experience. If haptic cinema, as Marks describes, involves the eye "grazing" across the image rather than "gazing" at it, then 3D's hyper-haptic visuality replaces or extends this through a kind of perceptual engulfment, with the eyes grasping at fluctuating, ephemeral spatial impressions that overwhelm the observer at a tactile, embodied level.[29] Yes, 3D emphasizes space and volume, but "the viewer's body is located within and in relation to, rather than separated from, the [3D] film."[30] This involvement, Ross asserts, goes beyond traditional accounts of haptic cinema. More than amplification, this is a difference of degree: as a haptic experience, 3D may be textural and perceptually subjective, but it is also persistently *strange*—whatever haptic immersion it offers occurs alongside persistent visual alienation.

This is something various scholars have been at pains to point out for many years, even if the precise nature of this strangeness has proved difficult to pin down. In the 1950s, André Bazin suggested that 3D creates "ghastly or impalpable" impressions of space that are inherently unreal-seeming.[31] Sergei Eisenstein, writing in 1948, welcomed such effects, and was excited by the way the 3D cinema screen "'swallows us up' . . . or 'pierces' us with unprecedented force."[32] Contemporaneously discussing the same kinds of 3D films Eisenstein would have seen, Ivor Montagu describes how on his trip to the Moscow stereokino in the early 1940s objects in negative parallax were "melodramatically accentuated" even if they were as simple as static tree branches or lanyards.[33] Montagu then hypothesizes about other shots that, in 3D presentations, may change their fundamental implications and emotional consequences: "A big close-up might endow a nose with the menace of a crow-bar, instead of showing a simple characteristic; a hand held forward might appear monstrous and plain gestures become endowed with unexpected menace."[34] The optical experience offered by stereoscopic cinema can be so insistent, and so insistently peculiar, that it recalibrates for Montagu what the film text *means*. More recently, scholars like Barbara Flueckiger and Lance Duerfahrd discuss this strangeness in terms less dependent on emergence. For Flueckiger, bodies in 3D cinema can "los[e] solidity or rigidity and becom[e] rubbery or even semifluid," while Duerfahrd calls the world conjured by 3D viewing one "never before seen or experienced," and he emphasizes 3D's potential for hallucinogenic or trip-like qualities and the way 3D collapses boundaries between represented bodies and spaces.[35] Finally, Caetlin Benson-Allott uses the Freudian idea of the uncanny to think about the new kind of digital realism 3D offers in place of indexicality. She proposes that the virtual depths of *Coraline* "render RealD visible as a dematerialized inscriptional space in which relationships between form and matter, ideal and embodiment, can be worked out," and she intriguingly asserts that what 3D gives us is "reality, uncannily enhanced."[36]

The "ghastliness" of 3D cinema persists in the digital era. Ross, Duerfahrd, and Benson-Allott rightly claim it as a powerful aesthetic tool across both analog and digital 3D filmmaking.[37] Such strangeness may be opposed to the exacting simulations and their focus on mapping, replication, and prediction described in the second part of this book. Indeed, for Bantjes, 3D media might be effectively labeled *either* "architectural" *or* "monstrous" depending on content and compositional approach, with the latter the province of experimental or avant-garde photographers. However, I propose that these terms might be used instead to point to those twinned visual modes that stereoscopic media rely upon simultaneously, particularly so in the case of cinema. As I have already outlined, the mapped and monstrous aspects of 3D filmmaking are not mutually exclusive, but paradoxically bound together in ways that demand closer investigation. The architectural model of stereoscopic depth found in the contemporary cinematic production of 3D (evidenced in the use of conversion and digital effects technologies and their reliance on mapping and quantification) nonetheless always coexists with its monstrous qualities.

Expanding on Bantjes, I thus propose that all 3D in some ways explores "spatial seeing" and our "arbitrary space-making," in the sense that 3D offers a distinct form of visuality in which these aspects of visual experience are at stake.[38] So, although the presence, potentialities, and provocations of the kind of spatial seeing that I, too, am labeling monstrous may be downplayed in the depth strategies of many films, this spatial seeing is a fundamental aspect of 3D media. No matter how regimented a stereoscopic composition might be, through its stereoscopy it brings into play the kind of haptic, hyper-haptic, heightened, or strange seeing described here, a process that, as seen in the last chapter, defamiliarizes the screen and recalibrates visual perception in ways unaccounted for by mathematical *or* psychophysiological perception. Capable of producing radical anxiety, and hardly congruent with narrative cinema's emphasis on legibility and coherent categories of space and time, these distortions are always present but nonetheless come to the fore in specific 3D films in instructive ways, as I will now show.

PALPABLE STRANGENESS: *GOODBYE TO LANGUAGE*

One of digital 3D cinema's most overtly "monstrous" texts to date, the 2014 pseudoessay film *Goodbye to Language* has received considerable scholarly attention for this and other reasons. In line with prevailing taste cultures, the involvement of canonized auteur Jean-Luc Godard—who wrote and directed the film as an expansion of his contribution to the 2013 portmanteau project *3x3D* (which also featured sequences by Peter Greenaway and Edgar Pêra)—has naturally made the film the subject of sustained analysis.[39] However, few critics have offered traditional textual readings of the expressive application of 3D depth in the film; it is as though the oblique style, density of allusions, and sheer range of unusual 3D effects make such an analysis of *Goodbye to Language* impossible.[40] Instead, scholars assert that the film's analytical implacability is something of the point, and that this is intimately linked to its use of the 3D format, what it has to say about this format as a mode of communication, and, indeed, what the film has to say about communication in general. As Yaron Dahan puts it, *Goodbye to Language* is significant, but not so much because it is "a film *in* 3-D as it is a film *about* 3D [*sic*]."[41]

For David Bordwell, the use of 3D is creative and exciting enough to demonstrate that the medium "is a legitimate creative frontier," an intriguing comment given his previous skepticism.[42] Daniel Fairfax similarly describes how, given 3D's association with costly blockbuster spectacle, it is ironic that "it is the work of a reclusive 83-year-old director, operating on a miniscule budget, that unlocks the true aesthetic potential of the technique."[43] Of what does this "true aesthetic potential" consist? Intriguingly, in this film's 3D, this potential is avowedly separate from the long takes, deep focus, and wide angles that might be expected. *Goodbye to Language* refuses to associate 3D with a Bazinian idea of "total cinema"; as Ross argues, it stands apart "from the teleological imperatives of contemporary mainstream industries with [their focus on] greater resolution, frame rate, dynamic colour range and the implied realism these technologies offer."[44] The "imperfections" that the film offers in place of this technological polish and that will be explored in a moment are not mistakes or present for their own sake. Rather, as Andrew Utterson suggests, these anti-Bazinian 3D features are used by *Goodbye to Language* as "one means of reframing cinema, both literally and metaphorically," in the digital age.[45] Even with this emphasis on cinema, this places the film in dialogue with a range of moving-image artists—such as Ken Jacobs, Jodie Mack, and Lucy Raven—who use 3D in their practice as a method for highlighting the act of observation and to provide nonnaturalistic, knowingly imperfect, or even purposefully painful visual experiences.

Utterson and others generally agree that the 3D in *Goodbye to Language* successfully flouts or rethinks a presumed set of expectations, reimagining the aesthetic parameters of the format.[46] This is somewhat to be expected in light of Godard's previous work. "Having upended the rules of film language in *Breathless* (1960), Godard does it anew here," states Amy Taubin, and she is far from alone in linking the radical jump-cutting in the earlier film to the use of 3D here.[47] As Florence Jacobowitz and Richard Lippe explain, since Godard has long been preoccupied with "film as a language system (communicating through sound, image, word, metaphor)," it makes sense that his use of 3D foregrounds the presence and process of stereoscopic mediation.[48] Famed for destabilizing norms of narrative, editing, character, and plot, and for rejecting classical Hollywood concepts of coherence and motivation, Godard is understood to offer a similarly critical look at the medium of 3D, interrogating how it works, the kinds of spaces it produces, and its connection to social, historical, and political worlds. All of this, per the film's title, is bound up with the idea of meaningful communication. However, the film's assessment of 3D as a communicative system is somewhat open ended: whether *Goodbye to Language* valorizes 3D cinema as a useful modern artistic development, or positions it as yet one more obfuscating device that alienates people from one another, is (perhaps unsurprisingly) left somewhat open to interpretation.

What is certain is that 3D is employed as a method of unsettling our visual experience, a strategy shared by other aspects of the film. Narratively, *Goodbye to Language* aims to disconcert by eschewing both identifiable characters and chronologically unfolding situations. Even if the viewer is able to demarcate the two couples at the center of each "section" (labeled 1/Nature and 2/Metaphor), and even if they also loosely understand the relationship difficulties both couples seem to be encountering, and even if they are further able to comprehend the way one or both couples adopt a stray dog named Roxy, then the presentation of all this material is nonetheless highly oblique. The same is true of the dialogue, which proceeds via citation and reference, and always feels overtly disjointed (a common strategy of Godard's).[49] Meanwhile, the variety of cameras and shooting approaches that are employed is matched by the variety of filmed situations and the diversity of quoted or excerpted media (including clips from other films, news broadcasts, poetry, philosophy, and literature), all of which are edited together in a fashion that stresses intellectual rather than emotional, spatial, or intuitive connection. The film's use of 3D—which encourages the direct perception of this exhibition medium as an aesthetic spatial effect and a technological process, rather than as a pseudoinvisible representational vehicle for narrative content—then joins up productively with this wider textual terrain.

Throughout the film, stereo depth is palpable in ways that go far beyond naturalism. Spatial compositions, emergence, and disparity are all dictated not by realism or comfort, but by a playful experimentation that seems to be led by no more formal methodology than the desire to exhaust visual possibility. For Bordwell, the film's depth effects deny two principal demands that are placed on stereoscopy in more conventional filmmaking: its need to "guide us to salient story points" in the manner of other stylistic techniques, and its need to be a "relatively realistic" window onto a world.[50] Neither guide nor window, *Goodbye to Language* instead places 3D within quotation marks, making 3D felt as a filtering technological system. This awareness is achieved in part through the frequent activation of the entire continuum of stereoscopic space (a compositional tactic that might be employed at key moments by other 3D films, but that is consistent here in a manner that is distinctive).

An early, simple over-the-shoulder shot of a woman looking at her lap and manipulating the touchscreen of a mobile phone, for instance, positions the character's ear strongly in emergent, negative parallax space, and the phone and ground in extensively recessive deep space (fig. 7.1). This shot might have offered subtle contours and a sculptural sense of volume that seemed naturalistic, but instead it aggressively confronts the viewer with stereoscopic cues. The extent of the continuum employed and the divergence between planes of content mean that it takes a few moments for us to get our bearings on the shot and its spatial scale. Discarding visual comfort, the magnitude of the differences between those elements most pronounced and those most recessive is such that disharmony sets in if a viewer's glance moves quickly between the foregrounded head and the more distant phone. These elongated spatial values might seem appropriate for entry into an expansive, exotic milieu—*Avatar*'s Pandora, say—but the content here is an everyday gesture and setting,

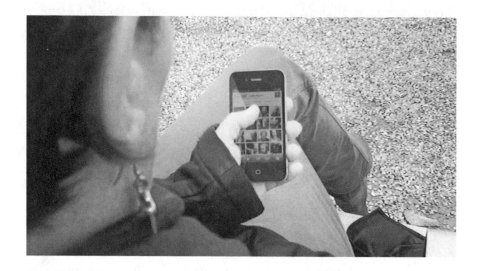

7.1 The stereoscopic continuum is filled up in *Goodbye to Language* (2014), with the space between a character's ear and feet colonizing the entirety of 3D space.

domestic in both content and scale. The highly elongated spatial scale is made even more unusual through the angle of the composition: the camera points sharply downward toward a pavement and also to an extent inward. As in some of the stereocards discussed by Bantjes, here "the architectural horizon tilt[s] out of view."[51]

In this shot and throughout the film, then, the stereoscopic continuum is colonized in such a manner as to be visually disturbing. Such an approach runs overtly counter to any reading of 3D built around naturalistic depth cues, viewer comfort, or even ostentatious spectacle. In *Goodbye to Language*, we are often made aware of our perceptual contribution in generating the volumes on display, with the enormous gulf between near and far meaning that attending to one spatial layer results in the other layers visibly becoming disharmonious, splitting and "buzzing" as two separate, overlain visual forms. This may occur in our peripheral vision, but it is potent enough to be actively felt and to explicitly distract. The audience is not invited to passively watch in visual comfort, but, rather, forced to feel complicity in ongoing perceptual acts that threaten to fracture and optically assault them from moment to moment. Shots at times exist in kaleidoscopic flux, refusing to harmonize into an impression of shape and volume; backgrounds quiver irreconcilably, and foregrounds demand cross-eyed binocular acrobatics (fig. 7.2). Moreover, thanks to the

7.2 Backgrounds quiver and foregrounds demand cross-eyed viewing, in *Goodbye to Language* (2014).

native 3D shooting, elements like ripples on water, or artifacts of out-of-focus light in the background of shots, vary between cameras, meaning that they shimmer evanescently due to conflicting visual information across the image streams.[52]

In accordance with Crary's description of the stereoscope, 3D space is revealed by the film to be "a fundamentally disunified and aggregate field of disjunct elements," a hallucinatory patchwork that, though bordering on a naturalistic space, "never coalesce[s] into a homogenous field."[53] Other stereoscopic texts often seek to disguise or downplay this disjunction; *Goodbye to Language* forcefully embraces it. This approach to 3D fits with the film's broader attention to issues of mediation and the subjective reception of the external world, an attention also manifested in its numerous explicit, even didactic, discussions of literature, technology, art, and philosophy. By highlighting the tools and consequences of stereoscopic cinematic mediation—in particular its capacities for distortion—the film uses the medium to flag up the act of 3D depth-creation specifically and cinematic spectatorship more generally. This creation is treated as problematic and fraught: when a voice-over announces that mankind is blind to the world, an accompanying stereoscopic shot stubbornly remains two oscillating, fragmentary shards that do not—but *almost*—cohere into depth and legibility, and in this way we are given a 3D-specific demonstration of this blindness. Stereoscopic values are deployed as reminders of the deceptions and fallacies involved in mediated sight, as we are constantly aware that what we witness is an act of digitally processed communication, one that might be more or less "successful" from moment to moment.

The presence of the 3D apparatus is further stressed by the use of what might be termed a "poor image" aesthetic. For Hito Steyerl, poor images are those that are widely shared on low-fidelity platforms, such as AVIs and JPEGs, and have undergone reformatting, reediting, and recompression. These poor images show their poverty in visible pixilation, temporal glitches, or other distortions. They are the "debris of audiovisual production," the visual fatigue and noise of which function in direct comparison to the "flagship store" of the rich, sharp image: cinema.[54] Certainly, in line with Steyerl's comments, *Goodbye to Language* insists upon imperfection and imports this into the stereoscopic sphere: the alignment of the twinned images does not seek the kind of polished and harmonious spatial field for which the majority of 3D films overwhelmingly aim. This is both a creative choice and, relatedly, the direct result of a distinctive, improvisational production methodology. The credits list a variety of cameras, from the Canon 5D Mark II to cheaper equipment like GoPros and the Sony MHS FS3 Bloggie pocket 3D camcorder, all of which were mounted on homemade wooden camera rigs.[55] Little effort was made to stylistically harmonize the shots captured by these various stereo rigs, and the film even includes home video footage by the film's cinematographer Fabrice Aragno of his children running through trees in Umbria, a shot Aragno only gave to Godard to demonstrate the potential of the medium, and that he did not expect the director to add to the film.[56]

Among this aesthetic diversity, the kind of carefully aligned, fluidly sensuous spatial creation and navigation associated with mainstream digital 3D filmmaking makes a few fleeting appearances. Firstly, shots from polished Hollywood productions *Fright Night* (2011) and *Piranha* (2011) are very briefly excerpted.[57] More conspicuously, a crane shot over an empty car park has been filmed with a pair of Canon 5D Mark IIs and offers the most commercially normative expression of depth creation, visual clarity, and fluid camera movement. Given the film's themes, this shot perhaps unsurprisingly begins with the unmistakable shadow of the crane and camera rig in the foreground. In this way, while the presence of 3D's aesthetic distortion is unusually minimized for the moment, such distortion is replaced by an alternate on-screen technological trace of the 3D capture apparatus. The composition may be spatially coherent and stereoscopically comfortable, but it includes within itself a disavowal of its autonomous existence as a spatial world. The artifice of our spatial perception is thus again underlined.

Cutting between a range of low-tech material, prosumer footage, and polished content in this way creates an insistent sense of visual variation. Alongside the extensive and excessive use of the stereoscopic continuum, this results in what Bryant Frazer calls a "physically uncomfortable viewing experience" in which the viewer's eyeballs are "yanked around" in challenging and exhausting ways.[58] This is all part of the film's denial of a realist paradigm, a denial Godard himself expresses in interviews, as he questions the assumptions made of 3D by critics, filmmakers, and audiences: "They think 'We have two eyes, so if we put two cameras, we will. . . .' But it's wrong. Quite simply, if you close one eye, you still see space. I can still see you in three dimensions, more or less well depending on one's eye. Therefore to put two cameras like that, it has no . . . it's a trick."[59] There are two moments that demonstrate the presence of this "trick" even more forcefully than the film's aggressive depth compositions or the fleeting presence of the camera's shadow, moments in which the curtain is pulled away and the mechanisms behind 3D are more potently exposed. In each of the film's two numbered "sections" a short scene occurs in which the two stereoscopic cameras recording the twinned imagistic source material of the 3D film split apart: the right-hand camera rotates slowly on a central axis in order to follow one character, while the left-hand camera remains fixed on another character who is static. The viewer of the stereoscopic film no longer sees a space unified by their own cognitive apparatus; instead, they see two different images (one with each eye), and can choose either to attend to them both, which may be painful, or to close their left or right eye in turn, looking at a particular strand of the unfolding action (while still hearing both on the film's soundtrack). In both scenes, the shot(s) shortly resolve back into depth several seconds later when the mobile characters return to their earlier positions, the rotating camera realigning with the other, static camera (figs. 7.3 and 7.4).

3D thus comes under the most intense scrutiny at those points in which it is torn asunder. For Nico Baumbach, these moments rethink the form in a way that adds a kind of third term to the two most fundamental (albeit somewhat reductive) stylistic categories of film studies: "It is simultaneously a new kind of sequence shot and a new kind of montage (a marriage of Bazin and Eisenstein)."[60] Meanwhile, Ross argues intriguingly that this approach does not deny the tactile and haptic qualities that she has explored in 3D cinema more generally, and that it might even offer a more acute sense of involvement, albeit an uncomfortable one: "If palimpsest layering is one of the visual tools most likely to encourage a haptic, tactile, sense of vision in spectatorship, this form of compositing images produces a type of ultra haptic [experience] that is both fascinating and almost completely unbearable."[61]

7.3 AND 7.4 The twinned cameras of the native 3D rig split off in different directions (top), then resolve back into depth when they realign (bottom), in *Goodbye to Language* (2014).

These moments are yoked to the normative creation of stereoscopic depth in that they begin and end with aligned images and the perception of stereoscopic spatial volume. We experience the shocking sensation of visual space buckling and tearing apart, in the process becoming planar and multiple. By placing the fundamentals of the stereoscopic illusion under extreme stress, these scenes reveal how 3D space is built from offset planar image streams, the alignment of which is a matter of concerted technical work and creative production activity. The film's stereoscopic illusion outside of these scenes is then made unsound: already excessive and even uncomfortable, 3D depth becomes fragile, in danger of once again being rescinded at any moment. These scenes place a trauma at the heart of *Goodbye to Language*'s 3D, revealing and stoking what might be called a *separation anxiety*. They achieve this directly and radically at the moment of their unfolding, but this unbuckling, raised as a possibility, then haunts the rest of the film, quietly undermining our faith in the stereoscopic illusion.

If these separation scenes disturb 3D viewing practices, the duplicated planar experience they offer functions as more than just a revelation of 3D's ontology. These scenes also, I argue, point more deeply to the ontology of all pictorial representation, whether planar or stereoscopic. The detour that they perform away from the traditional, aligned use of twinned cameras for the creation of 3D depth emphasizes not only the presence of the 3D technological apparatus in this film and 3D cinema more generally, but also destabilizes planar images themselves as points of reference, since, through their divergence, overlap, and eventual reconvergence, 2D images are revealed here as potentially always dimensional. As the twinned cameras of native stereoscopy detach and then realign, 2D and 3D media do not operate as contrasts, nor is the former positioned as a conventional standard with the latter announcing itself as a digital augmentation or enhancement. Instead, the film reveals how 2D is always layered within the spaces of digital 3D, and, equally, how all 2D media have—under the right conditions of duplication, coordination, and exhibition—the latent potential to become 3D. An image is rearticulated as half of a stereo equation, a monoscopic viewpoint in which the perception of stereoscopic depth is undeveloped but potently conceivable—all that is required is another monocular image at the correct angle. This same presumption underlines 3D conversion, discussed in chapter 5, and as shown then it speaks to a particular spatialization of images and screen mediation in the digital era. What *Goodbye to Language* brings to this is not only a stronger, more palpable impression of the manner in which stereoscopy exists as a latency within any image. Also, and more distinctively, the film points to the fact that there is only a small camera swivel between ordered 3D depth and apparent visual chaos.

The film's production methods and compositions therefore destabilize expectations around stereoscopy (and by extension pictorial images as well). Its exhaustive exploration of the stereoscopic continuum as well as its willingness to obliterate this continuum by tearing twinned images away from alignment (and then suturing them back again) reveals the artificial construction and contingent nature of 3D space. In these ways, the film returns to Wheatstone's original intentions and ideas around the stereoscope—namely, that it should interrogate vision. As Bantjes sums up, the stereoscope's "coalescence of dissimilar forms seem[s] to imply an indeterminate and troublingly subjective process of space-making," and certainly *Goodbye to Language* equally alights upon the unstable subjectivity of 3D technology.[62] Escaping a realist paradigm allows the film's depth effects to be both intellectual and affectual, mobilizing as they do a range of thematic meanings and expanding the film's commentary on both illusion and allusion. This is not to claim that these stereoscopic depths cannot simultaneously provoke haptic appreciation, as Ross has noted. However, this haptic quality is sculptural in the more literal sense of the word than is normally applied to 3D space. That is, the spatial impressions of the film are intentionally produced as artistic, visibly *displayed* aspects of media form. So, just as a sculpture might emphasize its constituent material (be it iron, wood, glass, etc.), this film stresses and revels in the immaterial material of stereoscopic depth. Working with stereo cues in an avant-garde manner, *Goodbye to Language* interrogatively cracks open multiple conceptual avenues for thinking about 3D as a representational form. Key to this project is the admission and embrace of 3D both as a technology of spatialized visuality, and as an optical illusion, an inherently distorting and distorted representation of space.

"YOU NEVER FORGET YOU'RE WATCHING 3D:"
CLASH OF THE TITANS

Notwithstanding the critical attention it has received, it is important to note that, broadly speaking, the distorted and distorting effects displayed throughout *Goodbye to Language* are not confined to this film alone, although it certainly underlines them with peculiar force. If Bantjes hopes his exploration of early stereoviews will "bring attention to an innovative and transformative pictorial language which until now has received almost no critical attention," then much the same might be said of *Goodbye to Language*, which forcefully highlights 3D's transformative reworking of the visual field.[63] Indeed, this film's entire visual approach is predicated on an embrace of 3D aesthetics as a malleable, unconventional spatial system. But, while *Goodbye to Language* highlights these aspects of 3D in ways that have encouraged scholarly praise, such revelations are not the provenance of auteur-led, avant-garde cinema alone. The sustained and intentional way in which this film distorts our expected, normalized experience of 3D is certainly unique, but to valorize its use of the format risks rendering invisible the fact that the stereoscopic distortions it embellishes are a constituent part of any stereoscopic exhibition, albeit in often less pronounced forms.

As I am arguing throughout this part of the book, 3D is always in some sense monstrous, a fact that comes to the fore through close analysis of techniques like depth racking and lens artifact placement (chapter 6), or pervasive impressions of miniaturization and proximity (chapter 8). As such, it is vital to note that *Goodbye to Language*, for all its idiosyncrasies, amps up a strangeness that is constantly present in 3D exhibition, even if it is normally tamed through an association (although a highly problematic one) with conventionalized ideas of planar representation and spatial perception. That is, if *Goodbye to Language* aggressively emphasizes the artifice and abnormalities of 3D exhibition, then it can only do this because artifice and abnormality are inherent in the way in which the medium is perceived. Put simply, the film offers distorted distortions.

To demonstrate this, it is useful to look briefly to another film that, in its own way, also offers distorted distortions, but that has a very different cultural and critical standing than a Godardian essay film. Released around four months after *Avatar*, the action-adventure fantasy epic *Clash of the Titans* was neither shot nor planned as a piece of 3D cinema, but was converted to capitalize on the enormous success of Cameron's Pandoran blockbuster. This was a far from critically successful tactic. Although it made nearly $500 million at the global box office (from a production budget around a quarter of that amount), and although much of this box office came from 3D showings, *Clash of the Titans'* use of the format was widely derided.[64] Its "chintzy stereo-vision effects,"[65] which looked "you've-got-to-be-kidding bad," prompted negative comments from the majority of reviewers.[66] Many were pleased to call out the conversion as the economic decision it was—*Time* critic Richard Corliss is indicative, in an article headlined "Cash of the *Titans*," when he describes the film as being "retrofitted [to 3D] with no other purpose than greed."[67] Prime Focus World, the company who converted the film, now openly accept the shortcomings of its stereoscopic effects, distancing their present work from *Clash of the Titan's* questionable reputation. Even the film's director Louis Leterrier is on record calling it "famously horrible."[68]

The speedy ten-week conversion produces stereoscopic effects that are noticeably unusual and at times even outright bizarre.[69] Compared to some other blockbuster 3D releases, most notably *Avatar*, *Clash of the Titans* is conservative in its population of the stereoscopic continuum, using a minimal range of depth cues and pegging its content close to the screen. The film certainly never comes near the kind of extensive, aggressive population of stereo space witnessed in *Goodbye to Language*. Nonetheless, its 3D is perceptibly nonnaturalistic. This is most overt in the layered organization of depth. Throughout the film, planes are split across the z-axis in ways that create multiple planar layers rather than rounded volumes. This results in a widely commented on (and condemned) cardboard cutout effect: characters, objects, and settings all appear to be flat elements, propped up across slightly variable depths like a layered paper diorama.

In this, the film demonstrates the aesthetic of cutout planes arrayed in deep space that was, for Crary, also a key aspect of the stereoscope and its visual presentation.[70] As Crary implies, this layered space was not a fault of the apparatus, merely a distinctive outcome of its mode of visual organization. Indeed, in some cinematic contexts, such aesthetics can be commended. Bordwell, for instance, enjoys the use of "coulisse"-like effects in digital 3D and the way planes can "prettily drift away from each other" in films like *Drive Angry* (2011).[71] Meanwhile, Pam Cook appreciates similar effects and their thematic resonance in Baz Luhrmann's *The Great Gatsby* (2013), a film whose "pop-up book" look she compares favorably to the director's earlier, 2D *Moulin Rouge!* (2001).[72] The cutouts of *Clash of the Titans*, being by contrast unintentional and not wedded to creative imperatives, are perhaps more unnerving than these examples. Rather than prettily arranged planes drifting relative to one another, the viewer is given volatile spatial segmentation that seems only haphazardly related to other visual cues. As binocular vision is activated by stereoscopy, it is simultaneously rejected by the flatness of the arrayed planes and by compositions that, unlike *The Great Gatsby*'s careful layering, are often muddled and even spatially incoherent.

This apparent planar layering in stereo space is the most overt trace of the film's somewhat coarse conversion and the easiest explanation for its discomfiting visual impressions. More acute monstrosities can also be found, though. For instance, when in close-up shots more contoured volumization of a figure is attempted, the 3D conversion produces not curved undulation but rather a stepped gradation that, although effectively visually *invisible*, is still *perceptible*. So, an early shot of protagonist Perseus (Sam Worthington) sites his face and chest at zero parallax, while his neck recedes in slight positive parallax (fig 7.5). This gesture toward the natural curves of the human body is undone by the seemingly sharp delineation between two distinctly defined depth values, a delineation that subtly detaches the character's neck from his body and sinks it an inch or so backward. In other moments, medium shots of characters place the *content* of their faces and bodies at the screen, but the *outlines* of these same faces and bodies at slight positive parallax; again, the intention is

7.5 The curves of the human body become sharp, unnatural values in *Clash of the Titans* (2010).

to provide shape and undulation, but the result is an odd optical discrepancy, actors given subtly shimmering, receding halos of spatial explacement.

Other examples of similarly strange depth impressions are not hard to come by. In another shot, framing may place Perseus at frame left in the middle distance and one of his companions at frame right close to the lens and out of focus, but the apparent spatial gulf between these characters that is asserted through staging and focal information is defiantly not replicated in 3D depth. Stereoscopic effects push the rocky background into slight positive parallax but place both figures at zero parallax (fig. 7.6). Despite their clear z-axis distance from one another, the two figures populate the same layer of the stereoscopic continuum. At other times, characters are made to appear stereoscopically at the same depth as their surroundings, even though other visual-spatial information provided by light, focus, and staging asserts their distance from these surroundings (fig. 7.7). All of this prompts subtle spatial disorientation. Shots last for only a few seconds at most, meaning their dimensional strangeness is not necessarily perceptible in the moment. It is difficult to instantly parse the structure of these stereoscopic depths and volumes and what makes them off-putting, diverging so subtly and yet so profoundly as they do from the kind of naturalistic spatial rendering we might expect. Viewers instead likely recognize that something spatially shifty is afoot, without being given the opportunity to discover the nuances of this oddness. A cognitive gap is thus opened up between spatial expectations and the film's 3D rendering.

Clash of the Titans therefore offers a particularly manifest example of the "derangement of the conventional functioning of optical cues" that Crary

7.6 The in-focus character on the left and the out-of-focus character on the right, although at different focal planes, are placed at the same stereo plane in *Clash of the Titans* (2010).

7.7 Again, two characters arrayed across z-axis space are situated at the same stereo plane as one another—and the even more distant background terrain—in *Clash of the Titans* (2010).

describes in relation to the stereoscope, with binocular cues here operating effectively autonomously in respect to other markers of distance, such as (in this case) focal cues and relative size.[73] The film is not alone in this. Other fast or parsimonious conversions contain similar incongruities: for instance, a shot in Korean action melodrama *A Better Tomorrow* (2010) shows one character gripping the bars of a fence, but the 3D conversion places him at some distance from the fence he seems to be so vehemently clutching. The conversion of *The Huntsman: Winter's War* (2016), meanwhile, appears to use such a mismatch intentionally. When Queen Freya (Emily Blunt) begins to summon magic in her hand, the circling, sparkling glints that manifest her growing power are not spatially positioned in the same plane of slight negative parallax that contains Freya, but rather appear in distant positive parallax, overlapping with and contradicting the spatial placement of background scenography. The mismatch here is presumably sought, conjuring an impression of otherworldly power, and it is (literally) out of place with the film's otherwise implicitly naturalistic depth compositions.

Clash of the Titans, then, is not unique in offering a 3D experience that runs counter to the demands of both spectacular visual pleasure and spatial naturalism. However, although its conversion was scorned by reviewers, disliked by the film's director, and even critiqued by the company responsible, these stereoscopic effects cannot be ignored (indeed, both in the sense that they should not be dismissed, and in that they are hard to see past). The 3D conversion of the 2D footage may broadly speaking follow the logics of geometric mapping and Cartesian visuality described in chapter 5, but the speed and nature of the work undertaken has laid bare the way in which our perception of digitized space can undermine its order and clarity. *Clash of the Titans* occupies a key place in the visual history of stereoscopy, offering a moment in which digital 3D cinema's overt strangeness found a mainstream audience on a global stage (if not a willing one). To admit to the presence of these visual oddities is not to defame the 3D medium. Rather, it should prompt awareness of the manner in which stereoscopic media are always offering unique productions of space. Responding to but not exactly reflecting other spatial cues, and failing to coherently resolve into naturalistic depth, the 3D of *Clash of the Titans* generates a novel perceptual experience of unreal, unexpected space.

As such, this derided conversion is certainly analogous to Godard's natively shot *Goodbye to Language*. In both cases, 3D's expected evocation of realistic depth is unsettled by optical effects that remain conspicuously present, if not always exactly visible. That is, the technoperceptual apparatus of stereoscopic mediation is underlined—not through the kind of direct address with which this kind of underlining is often associated (think of *House of Wax*'s paddle-baller), but through a persistent sense of *strangeness*. To be clear, I am not claiming that the creative approach, audience, or 3D production methodologies of *Clash of the Titans* and *Goodbye to Language* are in any way identical. Furthermore, it is clear that their differences in these areas have led—quite reasonably—to opposed cultural appraisals of their distorted visuals. Godard's film is a bracing aesthetic exploration; Leterrier's is a frustrating visual cacophony. Yet when Ross states that *Goodbye to Language* is "about the displeasures of viewing and the impossibility of knowing through sight," and that it explores 3D as "a new alienating rather than immersive technology," her words might be correspondingly applied to *Clash of the Titans* (albeit with less intentionality behind these displeasures and their alienations).[74] Similarly, Jonathan Romney's praise that "you never forget you're watching 3-D" during *Goodbye to Language* can be redirected at *Clash of the Titans*, and if this Hollywood blockbuster is much less concerned with "keeping all [3D's] possibilities in play all the time" than Romney claims *Goodbye to Language* is, then the earlier conversion nonetheless helpfully disturbs discourses stressing the accuracy and truth-value of the 3D conversion process and of digital stereoscopic rendering in general.[75] Just like *Goodbye to Language*, *Clash of the Titans* fractures the smooth surface of digital 3D cinema and its holographic, ephemeral immersiveness, stressing instead 3D's "derangement" of perceptual norms.

In their own very different ways, then, these two films reveal those spatial distortions that 3D is always already undertaking. Their perceptual experiences of space may be unusual, but they are best considered amped up versions of 3D's spatial operations more generally. In spite of the reliance upon Cartesian ideas of space in the production of digital effects (chapter 3), the volumetric simulation of space (chapter 4), the application of conversion technologies (chapter 5), and the linking of all of these to a conceptualization of embodied human sight that understands it as functioning in much the same way, our perception of stereoscopic cinema actually works to generate forms of space that are quite unlike either Cartesian cubes or psychophysiological space. In a conversion like *Clash of the Titans* and a self-aware essay on mediation like *Goodbye to Language*, the somewhat tangential, contingent, and unstable nature of the stereoscopic illusion moves to the metaphorical foreground. We struggle to reconcile the twinned image streams and the odd spatial effects they produce, and if we never forget we are watching 3D, then this offers an indication of the visceral, palpable, ultimately peculiar spatial experience 3D provides.

● ● ●

In 3D, the act and activity of vision may be highlighted, but it is a strange form of vision that specifically encompasses and even relies upon visual distortion (with distortion naming that which departs from normalized spatial perceptual experiences). Marginalized, downplayed, and even actively fought against by a media industry that frequently deploys representational realism as a marker of authenticity and even creative credibility, these unstable aspects of

3D seem anathema to the mapped Cartesian cube of the stereoscopic data imaginary. Yet they persist throughout the history of the format: as an optical illusion that creates a hallucinatory visual field of disjunction, the reception of 3D always renders them a monstrous spatial experience, diverging from embodied sight and planar media.

Even so, to use 3D's monstrosities as an alibi for the format's dismissal would not only be highly questionable (since planar media offer plentiful distortions of their own); it would also be irresponsible, omitting a form of cinema exhibition from analytical attention on the grounds of its very difference from expected norms. The distortions of 3D visuality may be obscured in many histories of 3D and downplayed within specific media texts, but they are fundamental. To discuss the distortions of 3D in detail is not necessarily to label them aesthetically displeasing or textually aberrational, nor is it to demean 3D space as false or inaccurate, but rather brings to light the distinctive and fluidly changeable nature of stereoscopic depth.

The films analyzed in this chapter have all revealed stereoscopy's inherently distorting nature. *Clash of the Titans* might do this somewhat by accident, but *Goodbye to Language* employs distortions for thematic ends, not only rupturing 3D space at key points, but also amping up stereoscopic depth cues to such an extent that these are read throughout as implicitly or explicitly monstrous. That such distorting effects are produced by a medium that seems to be so closely aligned to a more familiar and conventional planar cinema only adds to the impression of uncanniness. In those moments in *Clash of the Titans* when characters visibly distant from one another along the z-axis nonetheless occupy the same stereoscopic depth plane, or in *Goodbye to Language* when the two cameras diverge and become overlapping but separate image streams, we glimpse the deep structure of stereoscopic media and gain greater awareness of their technical nature and distorting capacities. These films thus hint at the visual strangeness of 3D, and reveal how stereoscopic depth is a manufactured and inherently malleable construct rather than a naturalistic value.

Both these films, regardless of their different modes of production and audiences, equally "think" in 3D (even if the "thoughts" of *Clash of the Titans* are far from articulate). To achieve this they emphasize the "monstrousness" of 3D space in their compositional approaches and show how the removal of ambiguity that might be a natural expectation of 3D exhibition is, in fact, far from assured. In these films, architectural optics are at times either warped out of expected shape or almost entirely abandoned in favor of an intensely off-kilter stereoscopic aesthetic. And even those depth compositions that do function in recognizably architectural ways do not always maintain an uncomplicated, Cartesian spatial legibility. We have heard how for Montagu plain gestures and forms can in 3D take on the "menace of a crow-bar," and this is true not just for protrusions: in *Goodbye to Language* the recessive depth of the corner of a living room is imbued with a sharpness and a strangeness that is unsettling, while *Clash of the Titans* creates palpably unreal layering's of space that have a visceral effect.

Yet, outside of these examples, 3D's distinctive optics are often hidden behind geometric, architectural compositions in which depth is already intuitively presumed through the application of perspective codes, and in which stereoscopic presentation offers few acute surprises. The films examined in part 2 aim to wed 3D to a visuality of mapping and control, downplaying its distortions, and in this they are typical of the majority of mainstream 3D films, as these tame the strangeness at the core of our reception of it in order to use 3D alongside systems of continuity editing and composition that have been developed with 2D narrative media in mind.[76] As a result, although the distortions of 3D are present in their stereoscopic release, many 3D films do not *rely* on these distortions. *Goodbye to Language* is something of an exception in this case—through to its experimental form and alternative, low-tech production approach, this film makes 3D reception a key part of its overall project. Contrastingly, *Clash of the Titans* is perhaps only bearable for some viewers in its 2D form, and the distortions here are the result of rushed and poorly coordinated conversion rather than validated creative agency.

But if many 3D releases seek to be servants of two masters (in terms of exhibition), such negotiations must not lead us to disregard 3D visuality's particular qualities. Many 3D films are doubtless spatially communicative and coherent in 2D, but the more creatively and distinctly a film manipulates its stereoscopic values the more the tonal and narrative emphases that such manipulations serve (if any) will suffer in 2D contexts. The sequences and shots described in this chapter uncover these aspects of the medium, highlighting its monstrous aesthetic effects. As a third category distinct from planar media and everyday perception, stereoscopic media generate spaces that escape normalized spatial expectations. It is not strictly speaking necessary to read 3D somehow against the grain to discover these distortions, since they are an inherent part of stereoscopic media. This fact becomes even more pronounced when we pay attention to digital 3D cinema's negotiation of size and scale and its associated appeals to intimacy, which are the subject of the next chapter.

8

INTIMACY

· ·

The Boundedness of Stereoscopic Media

Mainstream digital 3D cinema is often linked to large format screens, multiplexes, and colossal visual spectacle. However, 3D is far from anathema to the small and the intimate. Across the last two chapters I have argued that 3D media are a distinctive form of visuality that defamiliarize the plane as a site of compositional meaning and distort visual space. 3D relatedly tends toward the scalar reduction of its contents, shrinking its represented worlds and bringing them perceptually closer to the viewer. As Miriam Ross suggests, stereoscopic media are not "at a distance in the same way that flat (2D) images are," and instead "rely on a sense of proximity in order to function."[1] 3D cinema, she states, "present[s] optical illusions which are frequently *extremely close* but simultaneously not quite there."[2] Stephen Prince hints at how this sensation of closeness involves the rescaling of spatial dimensions when he describes how digital 3D films invoke binocular cues "under viewing distances for which they do not operate in natural life."[3] This mismatch invariably amplifies proximity: binocular cues associated with near-at-hand viewing are applied even at times when these are not physiologically accurate. Distance, involving as it does the leveling off of the disparity between left and right eye views, is contrary to the innate functioning of 3D. By contrast, miniaturization and proximity are crucial.

This offers creative opportunities. Ron Burnett proposes that if digital 3D cinema "seems close to the eyes," then this closeness operates "more in the sense of a dollhouse effect (miniaturization) than in terms of real proximity," a diminution of the filmed world that can be marshaled to intriguing aesthetic ends.[4] André Bazin suggests that the characters in *House of Wax* (1953) some-times seem like "Lilliputians" thanks to the 3D exhibition, but nonetheless—and possibly relatedly—he praises this film for making "the ultimate worth of the third dimension perceptible."[5] But 3D's miniaturizing visuality is con-demned by others. Walter Murch complains that 3D "gather[s] in" what it represents, making it "seem half the scope of the same image when looked at without glasses."[6] Rather than a creative possibility, 3D's closeness and small-ness here become an inconvenience and aesthetic flaw. Similarly, Christopher Nolan, a purveyor of high-brow blockbusters, describes how he finds the format "too small scale and intimate in its effect": "I prefer the big canvas, looking up at an enormous screen and at an image that feels larger than life. When you treat that stereoscopically, and we've tried lots of tests, you shrink the size so the image becomes a much smaller window in front of you."[7] The kind of big screen experience sought here is apparently poorly served by 3D exhibition, precisely because 3D tends toward the small, the intimate, the "gathered in."

Murch and Nolan are typical of academic and industrial commentators who automatically consider miniaturization a problem and so mark it as a poten-tial pitfall of stereoscopic media to be avoided at all costs (or, at the very least, downplayed or disguised). Digital 3D, as personified in films like *Avatar*, is touted instead as a medium of immersive, overwhelming impressions of spa-tial abundance. But as Charles Wheatstone knew when he invented the origi-nal mirror stereoscope in the 1830s, vistas and distances were best served by planar media (in his case painting) whereas binocular cues were vital only for that which was close as hand.[8] So, even though 3D cinema might depict the distant and grand, these depictions are often presented in a way that brings them *closer*, and, correspondingly, makes them *smaller*, frequently *enclosing* them within the viewer's peripersonal space. These technoaesthetic traits must not be considered errors or representational failures. As distortions, they are simply, as Robert J. Silverman puts it in relation to the scalar variations of the stereoscope, "*unfamiliar* and *unconventional*" when set alongside existing, more mainstream models of representation.[9] Neither trivial nor irrelevant, the shrinking and enclosing effects of 3D cinema, much as with the similar effects of the stereoscope, have rarely been analyzed in an extended fashion.[10] While miniaturization may arise in discussions (and particularly critiques) of 3D filmmaking, it is rare that this leads to more concerted explanation and explo-ration of this aesthetic effect.

In this chapter I seek to redress this absence. I begin by analyzing the ways in which stereoscopic media miniaturize content and draw it perceptually near.

Debates raged among nineteenth-century stereoscopic photographers regarding the spatial rescaling that was possible through the manipulation of the interocular gap, and whether such rescaling was a justified creative act. This historical conversation around 3D optics is highly attuned to the format's unique spatial impressions. As such, it provides valuable background to an exploration of the malleability of 3D cinema's depth cues in relation to scalar play: as I will show, impressionistic smallness can be employed in tandem with other mutable cinematographic effects to propagate narrative, textual, and emotional meanings. Further to this, stereoscopy's proximate visuality can also work to extend 3D's haptic gaze and even create impressions of constriction and enclosure. This is the case in *Love* (2015), and the majority of this chapter will show how this sentimental drama not only links physical closeness with intense bodily and emotional intimacy—and so highlights the libidinal, pornographic nature of 3D's proximate aesthetic—but also how the film stresses the absence, intangibility, and confinement that lie at the heart of 3D's virtualized simulations.

DIMINUTION AND CLASPING

As shown throughout this book, public reception of stereoscopic media has been far from stable. Part scientific experiment and part popular amusement, part realistic reproduction and part novel visual experience, the stereoscope provoked disputes concerning not only human vision, but also what the apparatus itself should specifically be for, and how it might fulfill this declared purpose. These disputes were informed by, and themselves often sought to inform, the aesthetic approach of stereoscopic photographers. In the 1860s, enthusiasts like Oliver Wendell Holmes believed strongly in the veracity, accuracy, and beautiful detail of photography and, by extension, applauded the apparent augmentation and improvement of these in stereoscopic photography.[11] But, as much as Holmes might have thought that the stereoscope freed visual form from material matter, he equally admits that many people "suppose that they are looking on *miniatures* of the objects represented, when they see them in the stereoscope."[12] A few decades later, in 1899, Eadweard Muybridge offers a brief but telling comment to this effect in the preface to his *Animals in Motion*. Describing a moving-animal study made with stereoscopic cameras (the twinned image streams of which were placed on opposing zoetropes within a Wheatstone-style mirror stereoscope in order to produce a moving stereoscopic scene), he states that it offered "a very satisfactory reproduction of an apparently solid *miniature* horse trotting, and of another galloping."[13] Muybridge was no stranger to the stereoscope, having previously worked as a stereophotographer and even a maker of stereopanoramas.[14] Therefore his recognition, and apparent satisfaction, with the miniaturizing effect should be seen not as the surprised pleasure of a novice, but as the calibrated intention of a specialist. In these instances, then, the stereoscope could somehow offer both an exact (and scientifically useful) replication of sight and also shrink the world it represented.

Before exploring the aesthetic dimensions of these scalar reductions and their relevance to contemporary digital 3D filmmaking, it is necessary to describe in turn the two distinct but linked ways by which this reduction comes about. The first, and most relevant, is that the twinned cameras of the stereoscopic apparatus might be placed farther apart than human eyes, recalibrating perceptions of size. The second is the condition of stereoscopic viewing, which places the scene literally in the viewer's hands and within a few inches of their eyes. Between them, these produce an effect of diminution in the stereoscope that might not be strong enough to become the medium's defining trait, but that is persuasive and pronounced enough to demand critical inquiry.

Interocular distance—the gap between the twinned images of a stereo rendering—is a potentially flexible value, restricted only by the size of the camera apparatus (or, if the two images are taken sequentially with the same single-lens camera, not restricted at all). However, David Brewster—whose place in stereoscopic history has already been described in chapter 1—notably argued that interocular distance must be kept fixed at 2.5 inches, mimicking the gap between the eyes of an average adult human. Not only the creator of a popular stereoscope, Brewster also designed a stereocamera, purposefully engineering it with the two camera lenses fixed 2.5 inches apart. Further to this overt appeal to human physiology, Brewster would later also assert that the apertures used in the lenses of his stereocamera must be the same size as the human pupil.[15] As Silverman stresses, the analogy between (stereo) camera and human body propagated by Brewster was a distinctly cultural and even religious one, owing "much of its power to the notion that the divinely constructed human form offered the model for the most efficient application of physical principles."[16] Truth and aesthetic value were linked through physiological appeals, an anthropomorphic and theistic model privileging the human body. Stereographs captured in Brewster's preferred human-mimicking manner would, for him, present their contents in an identical fashion as these contents would appear to individual observing the material in person—except, we might crucially note, for the absence of movement and color, and any added effects of blur and grain that might arise from photographing, developing, and printing the twinned images of the stereocard.

If this was the correct use of the apparatus for Brewster and many others, then Crary describes how this tendency toward replicating human biology to some extent dictated the kinds of scenes photographed and their impact on the viewer. Subjects had to be chosen that offered stereoscopic impact with a 2.5-inch interocular. Accordingly, Crary proposes that "the most intense experience of the stereoscopic image" was to be found in stereocards of object-filled spaces like living rooms or museum exhibits stuffed full of bric-a-brac, as these offered a Brewster-friendly wide range of convergence points at various proximate depths (fig. 8.1).[17] But, while it may be the case that such a busy, enclosing space was aesthetically suited to stereoscopic rendering, stereocards offered a far greater variety of scenes than this, including open landscapes and mammoth objects (fig. 8.2).[18] These were nonetheless often endowed with palpable stereoscopic depth, an effect that could be achieved through the photographer's abandonment of human physiology as a conceptual framework. As a French guide to optical phenomena describes in 1868: "Theoretically, the interval of the two points of view [of a stereophotograph] ought to be two inches and a half, that being the average distance between the two eyes; but in practice it is better to increase it in the case of portraits or other near objects to about twelve inches, and in that of views to even several feet."[19]

8.1 A cluttered stereocard scene. Courtesy of the Bill Douglas Cinema Museum, University of Exeter, item 63350.

The Seven Sisters waterfall leaping over the jutting bluff, seen across the Geirangerfjord, Norway.

8.2 A Realistic Travel Publishers stereocard depicting an open landscape (Seven Sisters waterfall in Norway). Courtesy of the Bill Douglas Cinema Museum, University of Exeter, item 72734.

An 1890 guide to stereoscopic photography further describes how, amid the differences of opinion around interocular variability, the photographer must make an informed decision:

> Suppose that an observer standing before a landscape desires to have a ste-
> reoscopic picture of it *with the same relief* seen in nature; it is very evident
> that the optical angle of the eyes, and that of the lenses should be the same,
> and therefore, that the lenses should be placed as far apart as the eyes are. If
> the landscape be at a great distance, relief will be extremely feeble, perhaps
> imperceptible, but it will be exact. . . . Relief may be increased; and to make
> it as pronounced as possible, it would be necessary to suppose the landscape
> reduced to a small scale, *and placed at the minimum of distinct vision.*[20]

By widening the gap between the twinned images and using alternative lenses on the cameras, the multiple convergence points or layered depths that Crary describes are created where they are not palpably present within the unmediated perception of a scene.[21] In this way, the stereoscope could make more open and distanced environments closely resemble the kind of cluttered space Crary references.[22] Moreover, placing the cameras further apart makes the viewer into something of a giant. As our interocular expands to several inches or wider, we perceive our own bodies to be that much larger, and so the represented content seems that much comparatively smaller. Referred to as "hyperstereo," thanks to its greater or embellished depth impressions, Sheenagh Pietrobruno describes how under these conditions "objects and people both near and far seem to pop up as though they were part of a model, whose scale appears smaller than life-size dimensions."[23] In this way, explorers climbing the Swiss Alps are made to appear as tiny figures, shrunken individuals hauling them-selves across a landscape that seems spatially treacherous and extended (fig. 8.3); and the Sphinx in Egypt—its actual mammoth size confirmed by a person sit-ting upon its neck—is made into something that could be touched by our reaching hands rather than a distant gargantuan landmark (fig. 8.4).[24]

8.3 AND 8.4 Hyperstereo makes figures appear miniaturized in these two stereocards. Courtesy of the Bill Douglas Cinema Museum, University of Exeter, items 72677 and 48349.

Wheatstone comments that "the mind is not unpleasantly affected" by such an incongruous, nonnatural approach to depth, and miniaturization certainly offers aesthetic pleasures.[25] Susan Stewart, in one of the few extended scholarly studies on the topic, contends that the enjoyment apparently offered by miniatures of all kinds results from their break with the everyday, their creation of an entirely separate time and space in which reverie can occur apparently undisturbed.[26] Claude Lévi-Strauss, meanwhile, proposes that all miniatures "seem to have intrinsic aesthetic quality," and, moreover, that any artistic production is essentially a miniature, whether through being literally reduced in scale or through the reduction of other dimensions ("volume in painting, colour, smell, tactile impressions in sculpture," for example).[27] Such reductions allow the observer greater comprehension, and so have an innate visual appeal. As such—and as Pietrobruno argues—the stereoscope's rendering of a huge object such as a building or a monument as a kind of authenticated, indexical cameo of itself offers aesthetic intrigue, rendering the real into the fanciful and fantastical.[28] The stereoscope could thus produce "magical" experiences of "tiny treasures" for nineteenth-century audiences, creating enclosed and miniature spaces that were akin to dollhouses, toys, cameo carvings, cartes de visite, and handheld daguerreotypes.[29] So, even though Brewster and others appealed to nature and the supposedly stable, sovereign perceptual faculties of the normalized human subject, the stereoscope's capacity for perceptual falsification and pleasurable reduction was far from culturally invisible, or exclusive to this apparatus.[30]

Another aspect of the stereoscope that contributes to a sense of visual diminution—and that occurs whether or not interocular values have been widened beyond average human physiology—is its condition of viewing: the way a viewer peers through small apertures at photographs that are only a few inches from their eyes. While stereocards might depict a range of distances, the plane of focus upon which the content is presented is always proximate to the viewer. Optical convergence is therefore highly acute, even if the content being represented implies greater distances and more parallel binocular angles. As Crary puts it, optical cues are being fundamentally "deranged": while cues such as object occlusion, atmospheric hazing, and perspectival composition may all assert expansive distance, the cue of convergence will always communicate the impression of extreme closeness.[31] Although the scene presented may be a wide shot or a vast landscape, the impression of proximity wrought by the very closeness of the medium is always implicitly evident. A book that accompanies a turn-of-the-century collection of stereocards describes how the miniature effect some people discern "is due mainly to their constant remembrance of the small card a few inches from their eyes" and proposes that this can be overcome with care and practice, the viewer in this way "acquir[ing] rapidly the power of such [correct] interpretation."[32] But this is somewhat disingenuous. The correct interpretation proposed here is not really attainable; the stereoscope's impression of proximity is an intrinsic part of its media presentation—so much so that this closeness cannot be adequately separated out from the medium's claims of verisimilitude or realism.

This perception of an extremely close-by media surface encourages what Silverman calls a "kinaesthetic" experience, one of quasi-tangible physical connection.[33] As Holmes describes when seeking to sell the realism of the stereoscope, this apparatus allows us to "clasp an object with our eyes, as with our arms, or with our hands, or with our thumb and finger, and then we know it to be something more than a surface."[34] This kind of "clasping" is an indication of the haptic "spatial seeing" of the stereoscope, its apparent comingling of touch and vision. More pertinently, clasping can literally only happen with that which is in arm's reach: to clasp is to cradle or clutch, to appreciate through tactile handling. Clasping occurs only within what is termed "peripersonal space" in accounts of human cognition; indeed, the peripersonal, as opposed to the extrapersonal, is defined as that which can be reached without bodily repositioning.[35] Holmes's description of clasping with the eyes therefore indicates how the stereoscope brings content into our peripersonal orbit, even if only visually. He may intend his description as a marker of stereoscopy's realism, its replication of embodied sight, but in the process he points to an intense intermingling of sight, corporeal sensation, and felt closeness that is entirely distinctive to the stereoscope and its stereoscopic media progeny.

For Rosalind Krauss, the already "heightened" experience of stereoscopic space is further accentuated by the apparatus of the stereoscope itself, which masks peripheral vision and powerfully focalizes concentration in a technological manner, constructing a "channel of vision" that is highly circumscribed.[36] This channel is explicitly corporeal and close, since the stereoscope user literally holds or otherwise touches the apparatus feeding them media content—it is at their tactile command. Handling a stereoscope demands that the user bring the media device into contact with their own bodies, with many stereoscopes surrounding their eyepieces with a shaped surface upon which the forehead and cheekbones rest. If, as John Mack asserts in *The Art of Small Things*, the hand is "often at once the measure and the container of the miniature," then the gripping of the apparatus in this case is far from an immaterial detail.[37] Moreover, this clasping provides a sense of control and ownership. For Jib Fowles, one of the pleasures of the stereoscope was that, even when depicting immense landscapes, these sights did not tower over the user, but, rather, the user towered over them.[38] The stereoscope, then, is haptic not only in its visual effects, but also in its literal handling as an object with which the body interacts.

The stereoscope's impression of diminution—produced both by interocular effects and the physical and perceptual nearness of the device itself—must not be considered incidental, accidental, or unimportant, even if in the case of specific stereocards this impression might be imperceptible, subtle, or downplayed. And if the stereoscope's miniaturizing aesthetic joined up with other Victorian apparatuses of diminution such as dioramas, peep shows, and microscopes, then its recalibration of visual content was nonetheless still unique.[39] Represented worlds could be felt as physically existing (yet still virtualized) spaces within the user's peripersonal orbit, between their eyes and hands, hands that are not even stretched at arm's length but are close and clasping. These aspects of miniaturization and closeness demonstrate how the stereoscope provides not simply visual reproduction but visual reproduction brought into perceptual proximity and tactile belonging. This has been interpreted as the reason for the stereoscope's marginal position relative to 2D media: Crary gives the stereoscope's hands-on interface as a reason for its loss of cultural ground to photography, a media form that better "recreated and perpetuated the fiction" of a disembodied, distanced visual field.[40]

Digital 3D cinema, although embedded in very different cultural contexts and employing somewhat different viewing practices than the stereoscope, similarly appeals to the miniature and the proximate in ways that are far from minor or irrelevant. 3D films may not demand the kind of tactile handling required by the stereoscope (although they do necessitate glasses, which are a kind of echo of this tactility), but they nonetheless offer a similarly "clasped" spatial universe. Although 3D cinema may be projected onto immense screens (it has a particularly close association with IMAX and other large format theaters), it still reorients visual perception in ways privileging the close and the small, an aesthetic effect that can be explicit or implicit and deployed to a range of ends.

Just as in the case of earlier stereoscopic media, 3D cinema's visual inclination toward the close and the small has been read as a technical fault to be wrestled with. The complaints of key industry personnel have already been noted, while, in his article on what he calls "sustainable" 3D depth, Scott Higgins objects that, for all its grandiosity, a film like *Avatar* occasionally struggles to overcome the medium's tendency toward miniaturization. He points to a telephoto-style digital effects shot of a fleet of helicopters set against a distant sunset; emerging in negative parallax, these vehicles do not seem to be helicopter-sized objects hovering in the theater, but miniatures of helicopters that are apparently within arm's length of the viewer. He takes such graspable "phantom helicopters" to be problematic for the film's visual economy of spectacle and thus considers them a regrettable aesthetic mistake, evidence of the format's "difficulty with representing scale."[41] Equally, Barbara Flueckiger argues that all live-action 3D films "show the problem of size rendition to varying degrees," describing this as one of the "well-known problems of stereoscopic cinematography."[42] Hyperstereo, for these scholars, is a danger to be avoided.

But this is not the full story. Hyperstereoscopic shots like those of *Avatar*'s helicopters show how binocular depth can be brought into play at scales beyond which it might be expected. Given the telephoto nature of the composition, the flying vehicles should by rights be perceptually coterminous with the background, since both object and surroundings are beyond the distance at which binocular depth cues function. Yet stereoscopic values have been manipulated to lift these aircraft from their surroundings, producing a volume of empty space around them.[43] Doing so rescales the helicopters and their diegetic world in significant ways. This is not a filmmaker falling foul of the aesthetic "dangers" inherent in 3D; rather, the model-like helicopters intentionally provide dimensional palpability. On the one hand, this allows the vehicles to be visually threatening, moving into negative parallax space on their mission of destruction. On the other, if the helicopters become smaller, then this evocation of diminution might reorient their associations, as they become toys of a careless and childishly irresponsible human military force, or a swarm of pestilent locusts. In any case, what we see is not a dimensional error, but a considered stereoscopic choice, one with thematic and expressive consequences.[44]

Scholars can sometimes forgive or even welcome 3D's scalar play. *Coraline* offers carefully calibrated impressions of depth and size that intermittently embellish and disavow the film's production ontology as a stop-motion animation featuring miniature 1/6-scale puppets and sets. Released in early 2009, almost a year before *Avatar*, the film was celebrated by David Bordwell, who called it the best 3D film he had ever seen (a title later taken by 2014's *Goodbye to Language*—see chapter 7). In an influential blog post, he praises *Coraline*'s innovative modulation of depth cues, and the way these help to delineate the two contrasting worlds around which the story revolves.[45] This work is similarly taken up respectively by Higgins, Prince, Sarah Atkinson, and Jesko Jockenhövel, who all to varying extents comment favorably upon this film's use of 3D.[46] Higgins in particular concludes that its stereoscopic effects are laudably

"sustainable." Bound to "character-oriented narrative tasks," stereoscopic miniaturization is deployed consciously: the plot concerns a young girl who enters
another world, and the film's stop-motion animation along with its 3D effects
create a sense of peering into our own model world or dollhouse.[47]

But *Coraline*'s diorama-like aesthetic is not unique, nor uniquely meaningful. Much earlier, *House of Wax* not only offered Lilliputian characters—it
also accentuated the model-like nature of 3D visuality. Scenes in the eponymous attraction include displays of wax figures arranged against planar backgrounds; this setup is more than coincidentally mirrored in the film's own aesthetic strategies, as it turns rooms into boxes with the fourth wall removed
and carefully arranges characters throughout these enclosed spaces in a theatrical fashion. Meanwhile, 3D's evocation of the close at hand, the proximate,
the claspable is widespread in stereoscopic cinema. All digital 3D filmmaking—
whether native or converted—can manipulate interocular distance and angles
of convergence and so underscore the perceptual closeness of 3D. In the midst
of praising *Coraline*, Higgins may claim that "grand-scale spectacle films must
avoid miniaturization like the plague," but this is not quite the case.[48] Occasionally, the manipulation of interocular and the deployment of hyperstereo
is tied to diegetic contexts: in *Ant-Man* (2015), the use of hyperstereo for
sequences when the titular superhero shrinks to miniscule, even subatomic
proportions effectively communicates the altered spatial scale of the action.
Similarly, in *Jack the Giant Slayer* (2013), shots taken from the points of view
of the giants provide 3D viewers with a literal giant's-eye view through the use
of interocular expansion, human characters rendered ant-sized and pathetic
to our swollen gaze. In a different context, the natively shot documentary *Pina*
(2011) purposefully gives the impression that some of its staged dance performances take place in a diorama-like box, with wide shots of the literal stage
employing interocular values broad enough to slightly miniaturize the per-
formers and their surroundings. This visual impression is paid off some way
through the film when a fade to black takes the viewer from the real, subtly
miniaturized stage to an actual miniature model of that stage, with dancers
using this model to think about Pina Bausch's dance choreography.[49]

In spite of these examples, it is more common for digital 3D cinema to use
this device for much the same ends as those envisioned by Brewster, who did
concede that it was acceptable to expand the distance between the twinned
photographs of a stereocard of a "colossal" statue in order to gain a "better and
more relieved representation" of it.[50] So too contemporary filmmakers manipulate interocular distances in order to produce the most appealing visual material in the context of any given scene. This is the case for *Avatar*'s helicopters,

for instance, or the aerial establishing shots of cities in films like *xXx: Return of Xander Cage* (2017) or *Skyscraper* (2018), which provide palpable gaps between buildings through the use of greater binocular divergence than is physiologically normal for such distant views. In such moments, 3D cinema subtly asserts its 3D-ness even at times when this would otherwise withdraw. Elsewhere, *The Green Hornet* (2011) manages stereoscopic depth to allow a cross-fade between a wide shot of a mansion and a much closer view of a coffin to evince the same binocular values (an effect that has required that the mansion be subtly miniaturized). Such moments may not explicitly be about the diminution of content, but they engage in miniaturization in order to maximize their 3D impressions—a tendency that further speaks to the entwining of 3D and a miniaturized, proximate spatial experience.

STEREO SEX

Miniaturization does not just make things smaller, it also makes things closer and so generates a potent sense of intimacy. In the case of 3D cinema, this intimacy is amplified through the perceptual work of the viewer. But this sense of closeness is not straightforward—haptic intimacy is proffered, but never fulfilled. To demonstrate this, the remainder of this chapter will explore proximity rather than smallness, offering an extended analysis of the natively stereoscopic *Love*. This film does not engage in the kind of hyperstereo discussed above, nor does it tend toward creative depth fluctuation and expressive manipulation. *Love*'s stereoscopy is instead consistent and, in terms of interocular distance, physiologically naturalistic. This does not mean it is uninteresting, though—as I will argue, the film's treatment of 3D is a fundamental part of its aesthetic and thematic project. Far from uncomplicatedly engendering impressions of spatial presence and haptic closeness, *Love* implicitly returns to early complaints around 3D, its tendency to, as Brian Winston puts it, "feed our addiction for realism [yet] leave it somewhat unsatisfied."[51] The film does this in order to sketch a world of frustrated relationships and physical yearning.

As I will propose, it is not so much the desire for *realism* that is summoned by the 3D of *Love* than it is a craving for human and environmental bonds, for the *really existing* presence of another person who shares our peripersonal purlieu. 3D has always seemed to promise this copresence—and has always reneged on this promise. The paddleballer in *House of Wax* may have insisted on terrorizing us with a projectile aimed at our tonsils but he was nonetheless addressing *us*, threatening and promising a closeness and physical intimacy in his struggle to broach the space between media and viewer. His emerging paddleball may have attempted this in a highly gimmicky manner, but this sequence ultimately speaks to a consistent facet of 3D projection—namely, its sought-for intimate connection between spectator and spectacle. Moments of emergence and direct address such as those described in chapter 1 can, in this context, be seen as traces of 3D's proximate and connective tendencies, what Kristen Whissel calls the format's "promis[e of] a transcendent, tangible connection between spectator and image across spatial, material, and temporal divides."[52] But 3D can only point to or evoke this physical connection in a virtual fashion; it cannot actually accomplish such a fusion of viewer and media. *Love* alights upon this insurmountable obstacle and thereby stereoscopically depicts bodies and volumes in ways that stress not so much presence, but, rather, absence and longing.

Screened out of competition at the Cannes Film Festival in 2015, *Love* was written and directed by Gaspar Noé, whose previous films *Irreversible* (2002) and *Enter the Void* (2009) were both nominated for the Palme d'Or. Regarding a failed relationship between film student Murphy (Karl Glusman) and artist Electra (Aomi Muyock) in contemporary Paris, the film's modest subject matter, improvisational dialogue, and spare visual approach all accentuate the intimate and personal. As it begins, Murphy is in a loveless relationship with Omi (Klara Kristin), with whom he has a young son; a phone call leads him to think back on his earlier relationship with Electra, and this is seen in extended flashbacks. Murphy contemplates how different this time of freedom was compared to his current, constricted life, and the flashbacks are replete with extended and graphic scenes of lovemaking between Murphy and Electra (with Omi joining them at one point for a threesome). Apart from explicitly rendering these sexual exploits—the focus of much of the film's marketing—*Love* offers little in the way of overt spectacle. Focused on everyday people and mundane events, the film ends on a note of pessimism regarding Murphy's entrapment in a claustrophobic, dour, loveless existence.

Although it tends overall toward a naturalistic 3D approach, *Love* still pointedly gestures toward its 3D mode of presentation, alighting upon analog attractional models. A tongue-in-cheek title card cues up 3D presentations of the film ("the theatre management warns you . . . put your glasses on . . . Love' will start in a few seconds"), while prominently placed in Murphy and Electra's apartment is a poster for Andy Warhol's *Frankenstein 3D / Flesh for Frankenstein* (1973). The kitsch nostalgia of these quotations exhumes aspects of cinematic 3D normally marginalized in digital productions, especially art-house fare and high-budget blockbusters. These diegetic references to cinema history are nonetheless joined by others for 1915's *The Birth of a Nation* (another poster on Murphy's wall), and 1968's *2001: A Space Odyssey*, which he states is one of his favorite films. In this way, even in its apparently tackiest guise, 3D becomes part of tapestry of cinematic invention, existing alongside canonized evolutions in film art. The medium's importance is not just historical, though, as demonstrated when cinephile and budding director Murphy uses an analog stereoscopic still camera to photograph Electra. This act suggests he prefers (native) 3D to its planar alternative (although he is never shown actually making any films). This reflexive technological display, to which I will return below, proposes that 3D, even when not yoked to tools of cutting-edge digital mediation, nonetheless remains a prominent part of visual culture.

Love also points toward another aspect of 3D that is somewhat obscured (or perhaps repressed) in discourses around the format's digital presence: the persistence of stereoscopic pornography. Explicit stereocards were available throughout the nineteenth and early twentieth centuries, appealing to a range of audiences.[53] As Colette Colligan describes, the rise of the stereoscope in Victorian culture went hand-in-hand with "a parallel international trade in hardcore stereographs," and these cards even "dared to show more erotic spectacles than other visual media of the period."[54] For Lynda Nead, the use of the stereoscope for pornographic material is apposite, given the structure and nature of the apparatus:

> The extreme naturalism and illusion of solidity . . . along with the intensity of the viewing experience, seemed to make [stereoscopes] especially well adapted to the production of sexualised images of the body. In the stereoscope there was a perfect synergy between the supply of and demand for sexualised vision. The viewer not only participated in the generation of the image, but seemed to eliminate entirely the boundaries between [spectator and media].[55]

The stereoscope was a significant technology for pornography because it "offered the possibility of total immersion in semi-private sexual reverie."[56] While 3D cinema provides a different kind of viewing situation than the stereoscope, this has not stopped filmmakers from harnessing it for the dissemination of similar material, nor prevented audiences from seeking it out. Erotic feature *The Stewardesses* made a remarkable $26 million at the box office in 1969 from a $100,000 production budget, for instance, and sparked a wave of imitators in the 1970s.[57] More recently, erotic 3D features *Sex and Zen: Extreme*

Ecstasy (2011) and *Naked Ambition 2* (2014) have been financially successful in Asian markets.

Like these other films, *Love* on one level uses its 3D to enhance titillation, seeking to provide sexual arousal in a more direct and exciting form than 2D alternatives. And, like these other examples, *Love* is not afraid of linking this titillation to 3D's direct address possibilities. Indeed, the film most directly conjoins sexual explicitness with 3D exhibition in its depiction of an ejaculating penis. In this shot, the onscreen member fills the screen and is pointed directly at the viewer; semen (both real and digitally generated) launches into negative parallax, at which point the shot promptly ends. Predicated on a model of 3D built around nonnarrative spectacle and bodily address, this moment offers a hardcore version of *House of Wax*'s paddleballer, showing off the 3D exhibition(ism) of the film in an explicitly conspicuous and just plain explicit fashion ("Careful sir, keep your head down or I'll tap you on the chin" indeed).

If both pornography and 3D are, for many critics, about display and visual pleasure, then it is appropriate that 3D's presumed negative parallax "money shot" here becomes a literal money shot (the porn industry term for a shot featuring ejaculation). In this moment, hardcore pornography's taboo-breaking visuality is wedded to the aesthetic "climax" of 3D technology's direct-address potential. As such, this shot demonstrates how, if on-screen explicit sex escapes the bounds of decency, then so too the stereoscopic delivery of this content overflows the bounds of the 2D image. As with the paddleballer, there is something very knowing to this: given the debates around 3D's novelty and limitations since at least *House of Wax*, *Love* is clearly paying homage to 3D's cinema-of-attractions expectations and the technology's associated disreputability. Asserting the questionable, crass, even scandalous appeal of frame- and narrative-breaking projectiles, this vulgar vignette offers a kind of autocritique of the medium's supposedly indulgent properties.[58]

However, this moment of direct address is brief, and the rest of *Love* highlights a very different stereoscopic approach. Explicit sexual acts may be featured throughout, but during them our attention is not drawn to genitals and ejaculation. Instead, we are shown faces, gestures, and fluidly shifting bodies. Careful composition situates characters at the center of the frame visually and roughly at the screen plane spatially. This stereoscopic placement results in no lunges into negative parallax. Shot mostly from above (and sometimes upside down, or on an unusual diagonal slant receding from the camera), these scenes also offer minimal surroundings—the angles are tight enough that little other than the bed and its human contents are visible. This accentuates the shapes of the bodies on display and the shifting patterns of the sheets around them,

8.5 Minimal spatial contexts and undulating bodies during the sex scenes of *Love* (2015).

and the sustained takes are not interrupted with facial or bodily close-ups of any kind. With both little recessive depth and only minimal, delicate extrusions into negative parallax, the 3D staging of these sexual encounters privileges on-screen interpersonal connections and their dramatic intensity (fig. 8.5).

In their sexually explicit 3D spectacle, these scenes may be thought to evoke erotic stereocards. Their frankness is certainly comparable, yet they diverge aesthetically. A significant number of erotic stereocards embellish the female form with an array of surrounding detail—the spectacle of sex is augmented and flanked by the spectacle of dressing tables, mirrors, baroque Victorian furniture, and even ornate decorative wallpaper.[59] Emphasis is placed not just on the visual excess of female nudity, but also a broader spatial plenitude. A similar approach is taken in *The Stewardesses*, a film that, in Lance Duerfahrd's useful description, chooses to accentuate spaces and objects in lieu of soft-core sex, offering a "lazy eye" or "strabismatic" form of viewing that displaces the centrality of lovemaking and pulls attention toward mise-en-scène and optical cacophony.[60] *Love* provides a less cacophonic, less copious spatial experience. Appealing not so much to the detail-rich mise-en-scène and covetous, insatiable gaze of erotic stereocards and much other 3D pornography, the film is best placed alongside the more apparently cultured and contemplative observation prompted by sculpture stereophotography. Situated at the opposite end of the spectrum of cultural taste than erotica, these stereocards would often isolate carved figures from any surroundings using a dark background sheet, stressing as a result the folds and contours of the artwork. For instance, a

8.6 A London Stereoscopic and Photographic Company stereocard featuring Pietro Magni's sculpture *The Reading Girl*. Courtesy of the Bill Douglas Cinema Museum, University of Exeter, item 40120.

stereocard taken at London's International Exhibition of 1862 by the London Stereoscopic and Photographic Company shows Pietro Magni's sculpture *The Reading Girl* framed against a background of black curtains, the folds of which are just discernible (fig. 8.6). The composition captures the entirety of the sculpture, and stereo values are controlled so as to provide a potent sense of the shapes and undulations of the marble figure. Here, just like in many erotic stereocards, the female form is offered for contemplation, although the fine art context allows this act of lengthy observation to be implicitly edifying rather than lascivious.

Like the subgenre of sculptural stereophotography, *Love* focuses on the curves of the reproduced bodily form, stereoscopy's spatial spectacle giving way to a more modest but no less significant tactile intimacy and accentuation of bodily form over spatial milieu.[61] 3D's tendency toward the claspable is marshaled in a sexually explicit context, not to invite salacious visual devouring, but to generate the sensation that we have privileged, spatio-optic access to the bodies on display. Like nineteenth-century stereophotography of sculptures, *Love*'s onscreen copulators do not just provide voyeuristic visual access to that which is a cultural taboo, but offer to the 3D viewer the pseudosensations of touching, feeling, and caressing, thanks to the cross-wiring of the optic and the haptic. The film, as I will now show, proceeds to deconstruct the desire for and meaning of these pseudosensations.

LIBIDINAL 3D AND INTIMATE ENCLOSURES
. . . .

If *Love* luxuriates in the intimacy offered by 3D, it does not do so naively. Noé suggests that he was inspired to use 3D thanks to his use of a cheap stereoscopic camera to film his mother shortly before she died; reviewing these shots, he felt "they looked so real," and that they "were far more touching than a regular 2D film."[62] While the director appeals to a conventional and familiar model of stereoscopic realism here, his association of this material with family, empathy, and death is instructive. Certainly, *Love*'s sexual explicitness associates 3D with a certain kind of ultimate exposure, the rawness and accuracy of relentless visual access and excess. But the film's deeper yet entirely linked concerns cluster around connection, memory, and loss, which it uses both hard-core content and 3D aesthetics to think through. In this light, the inclusion of unsimulated sex is less a promotional stunt or strategy for viewer arousal than it is a further device for thinking about mediation, truth, and the particular qualities of 3D representation.

The depiction of this explicit material using long, static shots aims to bring viewers into emotional and physical intimacy with the characters, as we are given little to focus on except for the shifting, undulating curves of the displayed bodies, which are rendered as subtle haptic shapes. 3D places us within the world of these characters, but not in a manner that might encourage the use of a word like immersion—more suitable to *Avatar*'s enveloping digital space, or *Insurgent*'s holograms—but more in the sense of what Colligan, in relation to stereocards, calls a "libidinal investment" built around "fathoms and depths."[63] The depth we are offered in these cases is not just representational; it is somehow overwhelming, and so it functions as a kind of mediatic or formal corollary to the obscene intensity of the hard-core sexual content. As Plunkett describes, stereoscopic media offer a kind of virtual viewing that "remove[s] the physical and psychological distance between the viewing subject and the scene portrayed [. . . and so creates] a mobile self which extend[s] itself beyond the local, corporeal limits of the body."[64] For Gavin Adams, stereoscopic pornography thus offers not only "a sensual quality of possession" but also "a haptic invasion of the observed object."[65] Through stereoscopy, touch (or, rather, virtual touch) is introduced to pornographic material in a way that seems to supersede the visually mediated nature of the sexual act. This makes the explicitness on display doubly provocative: not only are we witness to the aroused genitalia and unsimulated sex of strangers, but we also feel as though we are touching—or at least within touching distance of—this taboo material.

Thanks to the manner in which they reorient touch and vision, Colligan proposes that, in effect, there is something *inherently* pornographic about all stereoscopic media. The comingling of seeing and feeling, vision and touch, along with, I would add, stereoscopic media's palpable experience of close physical proximity, all produces an experience that powerfully crosses experiential categories and normal taste boundaries.[66] As Linda Williams describes, pornography excavates the absence it frantically and monomaniacally seeks to overcome. In relation to planar cinema, the filmic observation of sexual acts "distances us from the immediate, proximate experience of touching and feeling with our own bodies, while at the same time bringing us back to feelings in these same bodies."[67] This is not just about visual access, but closeness and a kind of quasi-possession. The "close-range reception of highly intimate and once private sexual acts" is not tangible ownership for Williams, but something else—there is no physical contact between viewer and image (as much as this may be craved) and this imperceptible but uncrossable gulf "is constitutive of whatever our relation to these [sexual] images may be."[68] This description of screened sex is highly apposite to 3D, which equally offers a paradoxical experience of both plenitude and absence. Stereoscopic media may overcome, to some extent, the absence of physicality within the 2D image, but they still offer an incomplete experience if compared to embodied physical presence (especially, we might note, in the area of intimate personal encounters). Indeed, the virtualization offered by 3D is not just of simulated spaces and scenes, but of impressions that are themselves *virtually* real, potently on the border between the real and the psychogenic. This is a "not-quite" experience that, like pornography, points to the gap between actual physical contact (or spatial experience) and its mediated surrogate.

In this vein, Jay David Bolter and Richard Grusin remark that the stereoscope, for all its realistic rendering of space, "made the user aware of the desire for immediacy that it attempted to satisfy," and so it was only able to offer "a more or less ironic comment" on this desire.[69] Bolter and Grusin's observation may for them point to an aesthetic *problem* inherent to stereoscopic media (and in this may echo Winston's earlier cited complaint that 3D "feed[s] our addiction for realism [yet] leave[s] it somewhat unsatisfied"), but the "ironic comment" 3D proffers in relation to the media landscape must not be so quickly passed over.[70] Indeed, this virtuality is, as has been shown, crucial to the dreams of immaterial, surveillant, data-rich futures imagined in the films explored in chapters 3, 4, and 5. Despite *Love*'s very different aesthetic and industrial positioning, it resurfaces as a key concern. Stereoscopic virtuality is once again located as a key aspect of contemporary culture; although, to use Bolter and

Grusin's terms, the dissatisfaction and the irony of 3D come to the fore, rather than its efficacy as an immersive optical tool. Ultimately, the peculiar intimacy mobilized by the 3D screening situation is not naively employed to increase connection or titillation. Instead, 3D is used to problematize mediation and, through this, the act of physical and emotional connection in a mediated culture. More so than other representational media, 3D seems to create and accentuate the absence that lies at the heart of any visual depiction of the world. Here, this absence is underscored by apparent, illusory spatial plenitude and a haptic, visualized sense of touch.[71] As such, the film's 3D, as Noé states in the press kit, aligns with a thematic focus on "lost love" and fruitless nostalgia.[72] Simply put, quite unlike *Avatar* and many other digital 3D films—and in spite of Noé's own proclamations above regarding 3D's realness—*Love* pointedly does not buy into the rhetoric of its own presentation. Rather, it unearths the ways in which this kind of optical experience, far from being an immersive and rewarding encounter, is by contrast a hollow and unsatisfying surrogate for authentic human connection.

This is most clearly demonstrated in a scene in which the older Murphy, fearing Electra is dead but desperate to see her again, indulges his cravings by looking at some stereophotos he took of their time together. Murphy loads these into a foldable plastic stereoviewer, and as the film switches to his point-of-view we see shot after shot of Electra cavorting for him in their bedroom, wearing little. Like the technological mise en abymes of *Avatar, Insurgent*, and *RoboCop*, this scene draws our attention to the film's own medium of representation, but it does so in a very different way and to very different ends. The folding stereoviewer points decidedly away from digital futurism and high-definition, pseudoholographic 3D.[73] Indeed, although the stereoviewer in many ways resembles a VR viewer, the most appropriate reference point is perhaps the Victorian peep show. This, as Nead outlines, held a special appeal that was not unconnected to the stereoscope, which "unlike other forms of public amusement . . . offered the possibility of seeing secrets. Bent over and peering into the eyehole, the peepshow offered the viewer a particularly acute and physical form of voyeurism."[74] Murphy seeks not titillation, like a peep show user, but something deeper and more specific. This undertaking is, for the audience at least, a failure: Murphy's photos are presented to us not as 3D scenes but as unreconciled stereo pairs, the twinned images shown side by side in their raw format (fig. 8.7).[75] This denies the viewer the full extent of the libidinal access to Electra that is currently being sought through the use of the stereo viewer. Murphy—who presumably *is* able to see the binocular cues of the stereo shots in a way that viewers are not—is deploying 3D as a visual surrogate

8.7 An unreconciled stereo pair of Electra in *Love* (2015).

for an absent material referent. Making Electra claspable as a proximate, present object both sates and further frustrates his yearning. Yet such claspability is rejected by the film's own exhibition at this point, as it refuses us the haptic, sensual 3D experience Murphy seeks, and that we have ourselves been prompted to revel in across the rest of the film.

While this is a very different kind of enframing than that witnessed in *Avatar*, it still speaks to a Heideggerian productionist metaphysics, a conception of the world as a collection of resources. In this case, the resource being mined is affective: Murphy's use of the stereoviewer speaks to his desire (connected to his status as a budding if lackadaisical filmmaker) to capture and store Electra's form, divorced from her matter, for later perusal at a distance. As such, this scene's laying bare of the twinned-image constitution of the stereoscopic illusion undermines not only the film's own broader representational strategies but also any use of 3D in the contemporary moment. 3D may apparently offer "more" visual information than 2D, but it cannot literally take us to new worlds, or actually return to us things that are physically lost. Here, the inclusion of raw, side-by-side stereo pairs at a moment when the film directly gestures toward its medium of production and exhibition places the falsity and frustrating intangibility of 3D mediation under a microscope. By visually offering only what we might call the *unconsummated* material of the potential stereoscopic experience, *Love* exposes 3D's technological optical creation of sculptural intimacy as a trick, a false balm for lost loves and an unsatisfying retreat from present concerns.

This strategy is, finally, connected to the film's treatment of space. The foregrounding of sculptural shape provokes an intense and unusual perception of proximity. This is both welcoming and estranging—an enveloping visual world may be offered, but it is one that becomes claustrophobic and unpleasant. To achieve this, *Love* accentuates another aspect of 3D's peculiar aesthetics, one closely related to its scalar, diminutive optics. Noé's own words hint at this aspect when he suggests that in stereophotos "one has the feeling of having retained an almost living part of the [subject photographed] *inside a small box*."[76] If 3D content can, as we have seen, be subtly "diorama-like," then these box-like impressions are not an effect imposed upon the medium but one innate to its proximate aesthetic. The viewer is made to feel as though they peer, up close and intimately, into a miniature space built just for them, a space bounded and enclosed.

Far from just shrinking content or bringing it perceptually closer to us, the space generated in this fashion can become stifling, thanks to the limits that 3D exhibition places upon perceptual distance. Just as those things that emerge from the screen can only emerge so far before becoming stereoscopically irreconcilable, so too positive parallax depth is reined in by perceptual limitations. The twinned image streams can only diverge so much before their perception as distance would be overtaken by their radical splitting (an effect witnessed in *Goodbye to Language*, where, as described in chapter 7, positive parallax depth is amped up to excessive and uncomfortable levels). In everyday viewing situations, stereoscopic perception falls off with increasing distance, until each eye sees an identical impression. This, as shown, was the reason Wheatstone thought 2D paintings were entirely suitable for landscapes, since they echoed the way we perceive these under conditions of embodied viewing. Yet 3D cinema does not work this way; its depth perceptions are tethered to the focal point of the eyes—namely, the screen, and it is *here*, not the far distance, that image streams are identical. Depth either in front of or behind the screen can then only be constructed through divergence from this stable, fixed site. Horizons and other far-off elements become therefore simultaneously far and near: visual cues like focal blur, atmospheric hazing, and occlusion may imply distance, but binocular cues are in play that denote relative closeness. Positive parallax does not reach infinity as many claim, but actually forms a kind of visual barrier that is a perceptual stone's throw behind the screen.

Love exposes these limits, accentuating the perimeter of stereoscopic media's depth impressions. Environments may recede in z-axis depth, being perceptual spatial volumes that surround the film's characters (who are often at the screen plane), but they do not speak to spatial plenitude and freedom. In line with this, if people in the film move around, these movements occur via delimited pathways. For instance, an older Murphy stalks the small rooms of his apartment as though looking for a way out, curving back on himself through

8.8 Stereoscopic restriction in *Love* (2015).

the oppressive walls, finding no escape. The size of this apartment is such that the shape of each room is stereoscopically palpable: these spaces are not backgrounds, but perceptible spatial enclosures felt at the edges of the frame. Flashbacks to his relationship with Electra might by contrast take to the streets and parks of Paris, but the consistent center-framing and languid pace of these scenes accentuates a kind of listless ennui and a restrictive spatial terrain: the lovers walk narrow paths and often end up at dead ends. When Murphy and Electra visit a café, the wall behind them may contain a brightly colored mural of a lake and flamingos, but the flatness of this drawing asserts the unattainability of this kind of free, open space and so reflects the stereoscopic spatial strategies of the film more generally (fig. 8.8).[77] Along with the limited field of view of the lovemaking scenes, this generates a pervasive sense of confinement, with the puppet-box aesthetic crafting stereoscopically tight rectangles of space.

This spatial entrapment is perhaps most pronounced in the film's final scene. Murphy, coming to the realization that Electra has likely committed suicide, sits in his bathtub under a running shower and sobs. The tiles around the bath, lit a sickly red, enclose him within a hellish gridded box (fig. 8.9). Binocular values perceptually place the viewer at the site of the camera, next to the bathtub, not at the site of their cinema seat, several tens of feet from what might otherwise be considered a window-like screen. As a result, felt distance between viewer and screen is essentially eradicated. The bathroom walls may be in positive parallax space, but they are perceived as proximate and thus still "claspable" in their stereoscopic constitution; they are near at hand, not beyond the rear wall of the cinema, and so are felt as tactile spatial impressions in ways

8.9 Enclosing space in the final scene of *Love* (2015).

that make them highly proximate, within touching distance. The screen becomes not a window *over there*, showing a world beyond the screen, but a box *right here*, showing a milieu in felt proximity to the viewer's physiognomy.

As a result of this reorientation of perception, in 3D cinema a distant sky can be endowed with the same stereoscopic qualities—that is, be situated at the same positive parallax depth—as a nearby brick wall. Both the sky and wall function as an enclosing limit point to a stereoscopic world, a limit point that must, like the edges of the frame in a 2D film, be present in some form or another. *Love* subtly highlights this aspect of stereoscopy throughout, meaning that even those distant vistas of Paris glimpsed in the film when Murphy and Electra meet in the Temple de la Sybille in the Parc des Buttes Chaumont seem to function not as horizons or far-off vanishing points, but as enclosing edges. As Murphy and Electra's relationship deteriorates, the claustrophobia of this box—both for the characters and the spectator—becomes more noticeable. Like Coraline, Murphy seems sealed within a miniature universe, albeit one that has not been miniaturized through hyperstereoscopic effects. Instead, the very visuality of 3D seems to delimit space, pulling walls and distances close and restraining action and possibility. Culminating in the final bathroom scene, we are encouraged to read the stereoscopic continuum as a perceptual space-box, perhaps even a prison. The fact that 3D creates not extensible psychophysiological space, but rather an enfolding horizon barrier, is put to use constructing a world of tragically limited experiences and emotions.

Ultimately, even in the face of its displays of sexual consummation, *Love* links 3D with a *lack* of consummation, an absence of genuine physical and emotional connection. In many ways, the film updates and adopts Baudelaire's scathing 1859 comment upon the arrival of stereoscopy in nineteenth-century Paris: "It was not long before thousands of pairs of greedy eyes were glued to the peepholes of the stereoscope, as though they were the skylights of the infinite. The love of obscenity, which is as vigorous a growth in the heart of natural man as self-love, could not let slip such a glorious opportunity for its own satisfaction."[78]

Self-love, solipsism, hunger: *Love* argues that these traits continue to haunt and define stereoscopic media a century and a half later. If people seek the "skylights of the infinite" through 3D, then Baudelaire and this film in their own ways express skepticism that such higher plenitude is available, stressing instead—as both do—physical gratification and solitary enclosure. It is only fitting that Electra makes a ghostly appearance in the film's final moments, a spectral presence manifesting in an unobtrusive edit in order to hug Murphy's weeping form in the bathtub. This echoes an earlier haunting, when Electra appeared leaning lovingly on Murphy's shoulder while he looked at stereophotos of her. If these photographs placed Electra within the "enclosed box and hidden scenes" of the peepshow, then now Murphy has placed himself within this same box, an act that offers only the cold comfort of a willfully virtualized, solipsistic existence.[79] Murphy's photographs conjured Electra, but only virtually; now, we discern Murphy's own virtuality.

In the world these characters inhabit, tenderness itself seems to be always incomplete, only ever attempted rather than properly achieved. The whole that is made of the pair Murphy-Electra in the extended flashbacks is as evanescent, and as hollow, as the 3D visual whole conjured by the reconciliation of the film's projected twinned image streams. So, while certain reviewers complain that despite the 3D on display the film lacks emotional "depth" (thanks in part to the improvised performances and the loose, temporally fractured plotting), this would seem to be entirely the point, something that is purposefully and ironically emphasized through the use of stereoscopic cues.[80] The always-out-of-reach-ness of the illusory stereoscopic world is teased out in an expressly down-to-earth milieu, and 3D's virtual dimensions are associated with Murphy's nostalgic, hopeless pining for another time and space. As much as the film explores and celebrates the physicality of love, then, it also seeks to expose the limits of any kind of mediated re-presentation of this physicality. Murphy's frustrated desires—particularly around stereoscopically reliving or revivifying Electra using his portable stereoviewer—illustrate the irreconcilable loss that occurs when form is divorced from matter, and this character's use of 3D here can be seen as somewhat analogous to internet pornography, in which interactive possibilities extend the corporeal self while maintaining physical (not to mention emotional) distance. As such, the film does not buy into rhetoric around 3D that applauds its apparent ability to do duty for embodied existence through binocular cues and evocations of haptic closeness. Nor does it extend claims around the usefulness of simulation and virtual presence propagated by many other 3D films. Instead, *Love* acknowledges these aspects of the format in order to associate 3D with a society of frustrated desire, selfishness, and the emptying out of spatial possibility, turning 3D's intimate proximity into a sustained perceptual prison.

• • •

In the last three chapters I have argued that we should think of stereoscopic space as an extended, latent continuum; however, I have also noted that the contours of this continuum do not match up with our embodied experience of space. Binocular cues, as they are delivered in 3D cinema, do not reflect real physiology. Rather, they rework it, conjuring an experience of space that is familiar, yet also unnerving and incongruous. So, while today's 3D relies upon digital tools of quantification and geometric alignment, our reception of these films produces illusory, unusual spaces. An awareness of the perceptual mismatch between our impressions of actual extensible space on the one hand and the felt impression of the stereoscopic space of 3D cinema on the other forces us to conclude that the stereoscopic continuum cannot be placed within the psychophysiological space of everyday perception; instead, it is a perceptual space all its own. This is not so radical a proposition. If we accept that stereoscopic space is a distortion, then it should come as no surprise that its spatial perceptions cannot be layered onto and within lived space.

If 3D is a radically separate, different kind of space that is nonetheless folded within lived space, then an elemental part of this difference can be found in the way the format unsettles expected optical cues regarding size and closeness. The result, as indicated in this chapter, is a complex impression of intimate proximity. While vastness may be sought or implied by any given film or shot, the binocular disparity of stereoscopy can only ever generate diorama-like enclosures that are in some senses visually "claspable," or near at hand. This attribute may be subtle to the point of effective invisibility through the manipulation of interocular distance, but it is inherent to stereoscopic media, and indeed was the very genesis of Wheatstone's creation of his original mirror stereoscope. Horizons are placed beyond the screen plane in positive parallax, but such vistas are tethered to a proximate model of vision. By wedding visual content associated with distance to stereoscopic values associated with the near at hand, digital 3D cinema turns distance into closeness, a spatial transfiguration that carries with it the perception of diminution. This prompts more metaphysical sensations around haptic connection but also ephemeral absence. Through the manipulation of stereo values, these impressions can be downplayed and modified as creatively needed, serving various aesthetic and thematic goals.

3D's activation of binocular cues that specifically relate to proximity have here been placed in the context of the format's distortive visuality. However, this aspect of the medium also connects with and contributes to the digital virtualizations and surveillance practices discussed in part 2 of this book. The digital enclosures and operational simulations described there, after all, similarly demand the perceptual reduction of represented content. This may be a literal shrinking, as in many of the onscreen holograms of *Avatar* and *Insurgent*, or it may be visual streamlining, the removal of unnecessary detail in the world's operationalization. Simulating the world through the creation of a digital double not only seeks greater simplicity, control, and predictability, it also engenders a proximate malleability—that is, it allows the user to shift the parameters or inputs of the model, granting them god-like power over a world rendered diminutive, claspable, and thus subservient. In *Avatar*, Pandora is shown to be a pleasurably ethereal space of immaterial possibility, and the film's linked use of 3D asserts that this is a medium of space and exploration (and, in the same operation, a medium for mapping, pillaging, and replacing material space). For all its radical thematic, cinematic, and stereoscopic differences, *Love* returns us to the Cartesian space-box of digital cinema, but it does so in order to argue for its constricting, unsatisfying qualities. The stereoscopic imaginary may be one of effective spatial substitution, but the reception of stereoscopic material reveals the insufficiency of this substitution through its rendering of space as distorted and intangible. In *Love*, stereoscopic media's ability to divorce form from matter is once again emphasized; however, the film stresses that the form is not the matter, and that the instrumental spatial surrogate we are offered can be an enclosing and solitary world. This film therefore further reveals how the monstrosities of 3D's visual distortions are wrapped up in and concomitant with its spatial mappings, the two modes or interpretive approaches far from mutually exclusive.

CONCLUSION

· · · · · · · · · · · · · · · ·

Seeing in 3D

Vision is mediated, both technologically and socioculturally. It is structured by codes and conventions that predetermine what we see and how we see it, not to mention what we do with this visual information. These practices have a history. Our ways of seeing transform over time subtly but profoundly, and this modifies the content and parameters of our visual field. This evolution is enacted in visual media. Painting, photography, film, and digital imaging all reveal dominant or standardized methods of seeing; as such, these media also track how these methods change, charting what Jonathan Crary calls an "ongoing mutation in the nature of visuality."[1] I believe it is productive to understand this mutation not only in optical but also spatial terms. Visual mediation invariably entails spatial interpretation. Pictures of the world therefore trace shifts not only in vision but in what Henri Lefebvre calls "spatial codes": distinct means of reading, interpreting, and living in space.[2] As the nature of visuality mutates and the technological landscape in which this takes place changes, so too the nature of space must also transform.

The contemporary era of digital mediation uncovers this fluid nature no less than did earlier moments of historical media change, such as the codification of perspective in the Renaissance, or the popularization of photography in the middle of the nineteenth century. Scholars have argued convincingly that these past transitions reveal with particular clarity the manner in which our visual and experiential fields of comprehension irrevocably alter thanks to social and technological forces, forces that visual mediation both responds to and is installed within.[3] As in these earlier shifts, today's digital media must prompt questions regarding the continuities and discontinuities between developing ways of producing visual space and those approaches that are being supplanted by these new techniques, a task this book has undertaken. My subject has been digital 3D cinema, but thinking about the prominence, industrial production, and aesthetics of this media form has demanded a consideration of its relationship not only to recently developed digital systems such as virtual reality, but also models of visual organization that have longer histories like planar media, perspectival art, and anamorphosis. By situating the production and exhibition of digital 3D cinema within this matrix of aesthetic, technological, and cultural frameworks, I have sought to chart the mutation in vision of which stereoscopic exhibition is a part (a mutation which is neither sudden, nor absolute).

RESHAPING SPACE, REALIGNING VISION

As computer technology and digital tools have reshaped (the mediation of) vision, space, and the interface of the two in the twenty-first century, digital 3D has become a crucial way of representing the world. Stereoscopic cinema operates at the intersection of vision and its technological and cultural reorientation today: though part of a wider landscape of vision, mapping and spatial representation, 3D's relationship with social codes of vision is highly revealing. This said, it is no symbolic form in the way that Panofsky has described perspective. 3D's technological prominence is by no means universal, and its cultural embeddedness seems, superficially at least, far from assured—but this does not make analysis of it any less urgent. In cinematic contexts, 3D is marked by novelty, marginality, and a general sense of "distinction," all of which points to the manner in which cinema is structured by 2D visual modes. This separateness also traces how cinema—both as industrial practice and as normalized media experience—continues to negotiate the wider technological and social fields of digital imaging (i.e., digital renderings of space). This negotiation— the way 3D cinema adopts, adapts, reconsiders, or discards codes of image and space inherited from 2D planar media—tells us much about how we expect our twenty-first-century media to look and feel, what we expect them to do, and how we expect them to do it.

While frequently described in cultural and academic discourse as a peripheral media, digital 3D cinema actually overlaps with and makes highly evident a widespread technological nexus that privileges volumetric, virtualized simulations and procedures of quantified, totalized mapping. As I have claimed, contemporary digital 3D relies on precision-tooled image management to create renderings of space in which dimensions and actions are plotted and geolocated. This is a model of realism and visual accuracy based upon a kind of Cartesian cube. But I have also described how digital 3D cinema is, simultaneously, a highly distinctive form of visuality that, through our perception of it, generates unorthodox and unstable spaces. 3D is acutely haptic and embodied. It is an optical illusion that destabilizes distinctions between observed image and lived-in space and is, as a result, a unique optical experience. Digital 3D has thus been read in the preceding pages as a tool for spatial administration and monitoring *as well as* an atypical form of media presentation that privileges ephemerality and subjectivity. The former defines its production, and is stressed by films like *Avatar*, *Insurgent*, and *RoboCop*, with their use of digital effects and conversion processes to create comfortable and immersive simulated environments. The latter is made manifest in 3D's reception and is revealed by films like *Goodbye to Language* and *Love*, which excavate rather than conceal the distortions that arise in stereoscopic media optics. Therefore, 3D cinema represents space in ways that can—and should—be read as paradoxically mapped and monstrous.

3D is not alone in offering distortions of space and vision: any medium of representation shapes space and our experience of it according to specific technological and spectatorial conditions of presence. No less than 3D, planar media rework space according to rules and systems that are in many ways alien to embodied, psychophysiological perception. Perhaps most influentially, perspectival geometry asserts that the world is a Euclidean extension full of discrete objects, and it proposes that this world can be adequately, even functionally rendered as an illusionistic arrangement upon a flat surface. Physiologically, this disregards spatial movement and the binocular nature of stereoscopic vision, discursively installing a market-oriented idea of space as a cultural norm. Perspective's spatial code depends upon nominalism, Cartesianism, and the supremacy of the eye, and it has proven so influential that it is effectively synonymous with "realism"—a culturally preferred, "common-sense" representational style that, of all the options available, apparently seems closest to embodied visual perception and, so, goes by mostly unnoticed.[4] To be perspectival is to be accurate is to be invisible.

In the digital era, this conception of the image as a site and source of quantified spatial data is deepened and extended, and in part 2 I showed how digital 3D, as a medium of spatial mapping and control, builds on perspectival foundations. The digital in digital 3D does not, therefore, point only to the ways in which digital tools make the production and exhibition of 3D cinema easier and to an extent cheaper than was the case during the celluloid era. The importance of the digital to today's stereoscopic media is more profound. Digital 3D conceives of the world as a Euclidean data space that can be effectively simulated for operational purposes; this makes it a kind of epitome of digital media more generally. Propagated as cutting-edge spectacle by major commercial film studios, digital 3D also aligns with a wider military-industrial-media-entertainment network in which stereoscopic visuality and quantified mapping work hand in glove operationalizing vision and space.

The connections between 3D and other technologies and representational practices in the digital age is displayed prominently in science-fiction film-making. On-screen technologies in a range of films—holograms, data spaces, virtual realities, and other nominalist mappings—respond to and enter into dialogue with 3D production methodologies, operating as "diegetic prototypes" that not only hypothesize about the manner in which existing technologies in this vein will develop, but powerfully perform for global audiences the usefulness and viability of such future developments.[5] Characters live within and haptically manipulate data, and in presenting this process the films give viewers a sense of the same activity. This helps advertise 3D spectacle and holographic and VR technologies to audiences. These films use 3D to propagate the possibilities and pleasures that such apparently screen-less digital spaces might offer. In remediating and publicizing this kind of digital interaction 3D disavows its longer history as a mode of cinematic exhibition and aligns itself instead with visual paradigms of VR, AR, and interactive data immersion. Ultimately, these films and their invented devices demonstrate foundational assumptions and desires around today's screens—namely, that they should become (and, indeed, in many senses already *are*) enveloping, three-dimensional environments of operational information and simulative rendering. This is not a case of 3D cinema forging a path that handheld and industrial screens then also pursue, nor is it the case that military visualizations come first, and other screen media follow suit. Rather, this stereoscopic visual culture of data-access develops simultaneously across various media contexts and hardware.

For all its enormous uptake in the global cinema landscape today, its encapsulation of many currents in digital cultural practice, and its avowed importance in military-industrial-entertainment contexts, 3D cinema is nonetheless spatially and temporally demarcated, a separate-seeming media form to be chosen, or not, at any given time. This seeming marginality prompts many scholars, as we saw in chapter 1, to consider 3D abnormal, nonstandard, or even deviant, useful only for better defining what "proper" (2D) cinema is. By contrast, I contend that any sense of novelty that adheres to 3D is better thought of as an opportunity to approach the visuals and spaces it creates as something fascinatingly strange, worthy of sustained interrogation precisely because what is offered seems to be an alternative and unorthodox world. 3D cinema in the twenty-first century may rely on the kind of careful image management and Cartesian spatial quantification that also—and not coincidentally—defines perceptually realistic digital effects production, but it also conjures visions and spaces that distort. What they distort is not only the standardized, planar film image but also Cartesian space more generally, as well as embodied vision, or what Panofsky has called "psychophysiological sight."

3D's distinction goes well beyond the "addition" of binocular depth to planar cinema, or any other augmentation it might be thought to enact upon the image. Indeed, interpretive models of 3D aesthetics built on the concept of the supplement are misguided. As Crary has inspired me to argue, 3D is fundamentally nonimagistic. Digital 3D's expanded operationalization of the image, its extension of immutable mobiles into perceptual three-dimensionality, may be a gesture toward a kind of Euclidean extensible space, but it is a move that cannot be entirely accomplished, thanks to 3D's inherent reshaping of space and perception. So, while 2D cinema's own reshapings have become effectively unseen visual standards (from the bare bones of planar representation to the more ornate but variable standards governing aspects of film form like cinematography, framing, and editing), 3D still carries with it the charge of novelty. This allows its distortions to be somewhat more visible than those of other representational media, even if they are downplayed by a majority of 3D filmmakers and commentators. Analysis of 3D must therefore be informed by, but by no means shackled to, planar models of textual interpretation.

Although many scholarly accounts of 3D cinema prior to the digital period propose that 3D "violates" or "breaks" the screen plane at key points, I have taken a different approach. If 3D distorts, it does so in a far more comprehensive manner than simply rearranging a given text toward direct audience address at occasional points. Thinking of the 3D screen as a window turns emergence into a disruptive threat and stealthily propagates a reading of 3D built around realism, windows-on-the-world, and naturalistic depth production. This radically underestimates the distinction of 3D's spatial experience. While some scholars (and many filmmakers) retain the plane by privileging it as a site of spatial organization and textual importance, I asserted in part 3 that it is crucial to think about 3D cinema in more expansive ways. Stereoscopic media rearticulate the screen, rendering it not a surface but the mobilizer of a latent spatial continuum, albeit one with surface-like qualities. As with anamorphic art, this continuum relies upon the enduring physical presence of the screen and perspectival logics of visual organization for its construction, but in the process it explodes, rethinks, and undermines the stability of screen, surface, and perspective. Far from being irreconcilable with exacting simulations of space, these monstrous qualities are in fact predicated on them. In the same manner that anamorphic paintings unsettle the very geometric systems of perspectival spatial management that have been used in their creation, 3D media rely on planar, coordinated image pairs to produce perceptual spaces that supersede the logic and workings of the image. It is through this connection with planar media that 3D is equally made unlike everyday sight; despite its addition of binocular depth, and the overt tendency of many 3D films to cleave closely to visual naturalism, 3D exhibition is unlike everyday psychophysiological vision. The latent continuum of stereoscopic space is ephemeral and distorted. Although it combines traits of embodied vision and screen media, it is nevertheless entirely separate from both.

DISASSEMBLAGE

In this book, I have not only sought to account for the presence of digital 3D today, but also attempted to critically examine its aesthetics in ways that expand our knowledge of the format and the tools at our disposal for its study. I have drawn on a wide range of films from the digital era, and my selections have been led principally by how useful the text in question is for demonstrating the ideas under discussion. However, I have also tried to provide a sense of the diversity of 3D filmmaking and the value of exploring normally neglected texts in more detail. My goal here has not been just to substitute the existing 3D canon—which is ultimately limited and unsatisfying—with a wider and more representative sample of films. I have also endeavored to reveal the enormous range of filmmaking with which 3D currently intersects. In 2016 alone, for instance, contemporary 3D encompassed everything from the converted superhero blockbuster *Batman v Superman: Dawn of Justice* to the intimate monochromatic documentary *One More Time with Feeling*, the Disney/Pixar CG-animated family sequel *Finding Dory*, and the technologically ambitious social satire *Billy Lynn's Long Halftime Walk*, to mention only a few of the forty or so films widely released that year in theaters in 3D. In the same vein, in the preceding pages I have analyzed 3D megablockbusters like *Avatar*, notable scholarly successes like *Goodbye to Language*, and generally unheeded post-conversions like *Insurgent* and *RoboCop*. In this way I have intended to show that 3D is not just one genre or style, and that it does not function in just one way. Furthermore, each of the films analyzed here, and indeed any 3D film, must be considered as a *specifically 3D text* if this aspect of its existence and aesthetic is to be fully cognized. The 3D film is always a distinct and divergent textual artifact. Even if the 2D version of a given film has greater critical, academic, and industrial purchase, the 3D version must be treated on its own terms.[6] After all, the core traits of the medium are managed, sidelined, embellished, or problematized by each 3D film in its own unique fashion.

In any case, 3D cinema is never simply emergence, immersion, spectacle, realism, or augmentation, and so it should not be described as such. Scholars like Laura Burd Schiavo and Rod Bantjes have explained how the stereoscope, for all its challenge to perspective and the image, was at the time of its widespread use nonetheless still hemmed in by existing cultural norms, norms that circumscribed the content of stereophotos and how these were perceived.[7] Bantjes calls this a "covert technological assemblage" and describes how it presumed and asserted that images must work in certain ways.[8] A comparable assemblage is at work today, although I have claimed it is just as much social and cultural as it is technological. As with the stereoscope, understandings of digital 3D cinema are influenced by a wider discursive terrain that is dominated by 2D content. Proclamations of 3D's difference are quickly subsumed under the sign of gimmickry, a process engendered only minimally through the films themselves but more thoroughly through popular discourse and even critical theory. Meanwhile, associations with planar cinema are constantly reaffirmed, in particular through copresent releases and generally similar viewing practices, an equivalence that subtly undermines the very existence of 3D by making it apparently additional or alternative, and thus potentially redundant. But the uniqueness of stereoscopic space remains. Therefore, while I have attended to these previous scholarly readings of 3D throughout *Spaces Mapped and Monstrous*, I have also sought to liberate 3D from this planar assemblage, respecting not only the cultural and visual dominance of 3D in many contexts, but also its marginal position as an unconventional form of visual-spatial perception.

There is, nonetheless, a wealth of critical work still to be done in this regard. This work must also seek to salvage 3D from another kind of covert assemblage, that of the discipline of film studies, which has fitfully and insufficiently engaged with 3D cinema even as the format has existed as an ever-present force throughout the history of moving-image media. Future analysis of 3D must continue to disassemble those structures with which it is habitually imbricated—in particular the structuring oppositions of spectacle and novelty, and verisimilitude and binocular veracity—as well as those deeper, reflexive, and often conservative assumptions regarding what cinema (of any form) is, was, or can be.

3D is a significant aspect of contemporary digital visuality, speaking to changing ideas around what images are and how they function, as well as how space is mapped, interpreted, and engaged with. As a key index and mobilizer of the changes to vision and space in the digital era, it is vital that digital 3D cinema's own particular perceptual mode is fully recognized and investigated. To dismiss 3D cinema is to neglect the extent to which any and all mediation reworks and reprocesses the world encountered in embodied perception in ways both obvious and subtle. It also prevents scholars from undertaking the vital work of interrogating a media technology that is part of the reorganization of spatial perception and visual culture in the twenty-first century. This is not to say that one day all cinema and all images will be delivered in 3D, holographic, or VR form. It is, more realistically, to argue that however marginal 3D may seem, it will continue to engender and reflect important technological and social attitudes around vision and space.

NOTES

INTRODUCTION

1. On these logics, see, for instance, David Rodowick, *The Virtual Life of Film* (Cambridge, MA: Harvard University Press, 2007); Richard Grusin, "DVDs, Video Games, and the Cinema of Interactions," in *Multimedia Histories: From the Magic Lantern to the Internet*, ed. James Lyons and John Plunkett (Exeter: Exeter University Press, 2007), 209–21; Vivian Sobchack, *Carnal Thoughts: Embodiment and Moving Image Culture* (Berkeley: University of California Press, 2004); and Nick Jones, "Quantification and Substitution: The Abstract Space of Virtual Cinematography," *Animation* 8, no. 3 (2013): 253–66.

2. There are many aspects of digital 3D that I will only glance at or that will not be found in these pages at all. For instance, although 3D involves ticket surcharges and is partly used by studios to counter the threat of piracy, the economics of 3D production and exhibition are outside my purview. Equally, an exploration of the place of 3D within a globalized media culture, and its very different uses and reception across national contexts, will not be encountered in what follows.

3. To elaborate: the term "digital 3D cinema" does not here, as it sometimes does elsewhere, describe only films that have been converted to 3D from 2D using digital software, or just CG-animated 3D features. It is, rather, a comprehensive phrase pointing to 3D cinema that is shot, stored, and screened using digital equipment.

4. The same is true, of course, for predigital technologies and systems, which conceptualized space and experience in their own linked but delineated ways, and in this context the artistic tool of perspective will be a crucial reference point in what follows.

5. Paul Virilio, *War and Cinema: The Logistics of Perception*, trans. Patrick Camiller (London: Verso, 1989); Paul Virilio, *The Vision Machine*, trans. Julie Rose (Indianapolis: Indiana University Press, 1994); James Der Derian, *Virtuous War: Mapping the Military-Industrial-Media-Entertainment Network*, 2nd ed. (New York: Routledge, 2009); Pasi Väliaho, *Biopolitical Screens: Image, Power, and the Neoliberal Brain* (Cambridge, MA: MIT Press, 2014).

6. See, for instance, the following articles: William Paul, "The Aesthetics of Emergence," *Film History* 15, no. 3 (1993): 321–55; William Paul, "Breaking the Fourth Wall: 'Belascoism,'

Modernism, and a 3-D *Kiss Me Kate*," *Film History* 16, no. 3 (2004): 229–42; and Philip Sandifer, "Out of the Screen and into the Theater: 3-D Film as Demo," *Cinema Journal* 50, no. 3 (2011): 62–78.

7. Miriam Ross, *3D Cinema: Optical Illusions and Tactile Experiences* (New York: Palgrave Macmillan, 2015); Owen Weetch, *Expressive Spaces in Digital 3D Cinema* (Basingstoke: Palgrave, 2016); Yong Liu, *3D Cinematic Aesthetics and Storytelling* (New York: Palgrave, 2018); Kristen Whissel, *Parallax Effects: Stereoscopic 3D Cinema and Media* (forthcoming).

8. Jihoon Kim, "Introduction: Three Dimensionality as Heuristic Device," *Convergence* 19, no. 4 (2013): 391–95, 391. There are further writers working in this vein. No one has written more comprehensively and lucidly about the long history of 3D technology and its complicated workings than Ray Zone in his books *Stereoscopic Cinema and the Origins of 3-D Film 1838–1952* (Lexington: University of Kentucky Press, 2007) and *3-D Revolution* (Lexington: University of Kentucky Press, 2012). Meanwhile, Keith M. Johnston's work offers a detailed description of the medium's critical reception, in particular in Britain, in "'Now Is the Time (To Put on Your Glasses)': 3-D Film Exhibition in Britain, 1951–55," *Film History* 23, no. 1 (2011): 93–103; "A Technician's Dream? The Critical Reception of 3-D Films in Britain," *Historical Journal of Film, Radio and Television* 32, no. 2 (2012): 245–65; and "Pop-up Footballers, Pop Concerts, and Popular Films: The Past, Present, and Future of 3D TV," *Convergence* 18, no. 4 (2013): 438–45. Leon Gurevitch is also a key voice articulating the place of 3D in contemporary media culture; see his articles "The Birth of a Stereoscopic Nation: Hollywood, Digital Empire and the Cybernetic Attraction," *Animation* 7, no. 3 (2012): 239–58; and "The Stereoscopic Attraction: Three Dimensional Imaging and the Spectacular Paradigm 1850–2013," *Convergence* 19, no. 4 (2013): 396–405.

9. Jussi Parikka, *What Is Media Archaeology?* (Cambridge: Polity, 2012), 2.

10. Jens Schröter, *3D: History, Theory, and Aesthetics of the Transplane Image* (New York: Bloomsbury, 2014).

11. Thomas Elsaesser, "The 'Return' of 3-D: On Some of the Logics and Genealogies of the Image in the Twenty-First Century," *Critical Inquiry* 39, no. 2 (2013): 217–46, 221.

12. See Bernard Mendiburu, *3D Moviemaking: Stereoscopic Digital Cinema from Script to Screen* (Burlington, MA: Focal, 2009), 24; and Cynthia Freeland, "On Being Stereoblind in an Era of 3D Movies," *Essays in Philosophy* 13, no. 2 (2012): 550–76, 552–53.

13. Jonathan Crary, *Techniques of the Observer* (Cambridge, MA: MIT Press, 1990). Further references will be given parenthetically.

14. Schröter, *3D*, 4–27.

15. Rod Bantjes, "Reading Stereoviews: The Aesthetics of Monstrous Space," *History of Photography* 39, no. 1 (2015): 33–55, 53.

16. E. H. Gombrich, *Art and Illusion: A Study in the Psychology of Pictorial Representation* (London: Phaidon, 1968).

17. Jonathan Beller, *The Cinematic Mode of Production: Attention Economy and the Society of the Spectacle* (Lebanon, NH: Dartmouth College Press, 2006).

18. Henri Lefebvre, *The Production of Space*, trans. Donald Nicholson-Smith (Oxford: Blackwell, 1991).

19. Akira Mizuta Lippit, "Three Phantasies of Cinema—Reproduction, Mimesis, Annihilation," *Paragraph* 22, no. 3 (1999): 213–27, 213.

20. Richard Maltby, *Hollywood Cinema,* 2nd ed. (Malden, MA: Blackwell, 2003), 235–36. The Technicolor films of the 1940s and 1950s were spectacular because they were vibrant and unusually colorful, and not because they reflected the color of cinema patrons' everyday lives more faithfully, for instance.

21. Adrian Pennington and Carolyn Giardina, *Exploring 3D: The New Grammar of Stereoscopic Filmmaking* (New York: Focal, 2013), 5. Industrial naming practices economically reiterate

such claims: the company that made popular 3D exploitation film *Bwana Devil* (1952) was called Natural Vision, and fifty years later the 3D rig designed by cinematographer Vince Pace and director James Cameron was named the Reality Camera System—see Stephen Prince, *Digital Visual Effects in Cinema: The Seduction of Reality* (New Jersey: Rutgers University Press, 2012), 216–17. It might not be surprising that proponents of 3D applaud its apparent biological mimicry of embodied vision—see, for instance, Ray Zone, *3-D Filmmakers: Conversations with Creators of Stereoscopic Motion Pictures* (Lanham, MD: Scarecrow 2005), 143–44. However, even those hostile to the format draw on this presumed equivalence. In *Film as Art* (Oakland: University of California Press), art critic and film theorist Rudolf Arnheim, who was highly influential in establishing cognitive models of film theory, proposes that stereoscopic exhibition dilutes cinema's meaningful composition of objects within the frame precisely because it moves cinema unhelpfully close to "real life" perception, and thus away from the pleasures and possibilities of constructed art. For more on this, see my "L'illusion partielle de la 3D: distorsions spatiales, stéréoscopie et *Au Coeur de l'océan*," in *Stéréoscopie et Illusion*, trans. Frank Boulège, ed. Miguel Almiron, Esther Jacopin, and Giusy Pisano (Paris: Septentrion University Press, 2018), 213–27.

22.   André Bazin, "A New Stage in the Process: Math Equations for 3D," in *André Bazin's New Media*, ed. and trans. Dudley Andrew (Oakland: University of California Press, 2014) 235–42, 214; André Bazin, "Will Cinema Scope Save the Film Industry?" in *Bazin at Work: Major Essays and Reviews from the Forties and Fifties*, ed. Bert Cardullo, trans. Alain Piette and Bert Cardullo (New York: Routledge, 1997), 77–92, 88.

23.   In the context of film analysis, a caveat is necessary here: while many 3D films described were viewed both at the cinema and on commercially available 3D Blu-rays, the latter have been relied upon for close reading of 3D depth arrangements. While differences may exist between cinematic and home entertainment depth arrangements (more likely in the case of remastered analog 3D films), I have considered these to be beyond the scope of the current project in terms of close reading.

24.   Rosalind Krauss, "Photography's Discursive Spaces: Landscape/View," *Art Journal* 42, no. 4 (1982): 311–19, 314.

25.   The phrase "psychophysiological space" derives from Erwin Panofsky; see chapter 2.

26.   I take this word from Rod Bantjes, whose work on stereoscopy is explored in detail in chapter 7.

27.   This is not as problematic as it may seem at first—stereoscopic media have been explored by other scholars as simultaneously optic and haptic in a related fashion. See David Trotter, "Stereoscopy: Modernism and the 'Haptic,'" *Critical Quarterly* 46, no. 4 (2004): 38–58, 41–42.

28.   This argument is also made in David Phillips, "Modern Vision," review of *Techniques of the Observer* by Jonathan Crary, *Oxford Art Journal* 16, no. 1 (1993): 129–38, 137.

1. HISTORY

1.   Anthony Lane, "Third Way: The Rise of 3-D," *New Yorker*, March 8, 2010, http://www.newyorker.com/magazine/2010/03/08/third-way (accessed September 30, 2019); Mark Kermode, *The Good, The Bad, and The Multiplex* (London: Random House, 2011); Thomas Doherty, "3-D Is Comin' at Ya!," *Chronicle of Higher Education*, September 18, 2011, http://www.chronicle.com/article/3-D-Is-Comin-at-Ya-/128979 (accessed September 30, 2019).

2.   André Bazin, "The Myth of Total Cinema," in *What Is Cinema?*, vol.1, trans. Hugh Gray (Berkeley: University of California Press, 2005), 17–22.

3.   See Kristin Thompson's various accounts: "Has 3-D Already Failed?," *Observations on Film Art*, August 28, 2009, http://www.davidbordwell.net/blog/2009/08/28/has-3-d-already-failed/ (accessed September 30, 2019); "Has 3D Already Failed? The Sequel, Part One: RealD-lighted," *Observations on Film Art*, January 20, 2011, http://www.davidbordwell.net/blog /2011/01/20/has-3d-already-failed-the-sequel-part-one-realdlighted/ (accessed September 30, 2019); "Has 3D Already Failed? The Sequel, Part Two: RealDsgusted," *Observations on Film Art*, January 25, 2011, http://www.davidbordwell.net/blog/2011/01/25/has-3d-already-failed -the-sequel-part-2-realdsgusted/ (accessed September 30, 2019). The long lag time between *Avatar* and its sequels, as well as the cessation of the production of 3D-enabled televisions for the consumer market in 2016, add fuel to this fire.

4.   Akira Mizuta Lippit, "Three Phantasies of Cinema—Reproduction, Mimesis, Annihilation," *Paragraph* 22, no. 3 (1999): 213–27, 216.

5.   Leon Gurevitch and Miriam Ross, "Stereoscopic Media: Scholarship Beyond Booms and Busts," in *3D Cinema and Beyond*, ed. Dan Adler, Janine Marchessault, and Sanja Obradovic (Toronto: Public Books, 2013), 83–93, 84.

6.   While a range of recent scholarship aims to account for 3D's contemporary resurgence and prominence and takes a holistic view of 3D's sustained aesthetic effects, this writing will not be my focus in this chapter. Key examples include Miriam Ross, "The 3-D Aesthetic: *Avatar* and Hyperhaptic Visuality," *Screen* 53, no. 4 (2012): 381–97; Miriam Ross, *3D Cinema: Optical Illusions and Tactile Experiences* (New York: Palgrave Macmillan, 2015); Barbara Klinger, "*Cave of Forgotten Dreams*: Meditations on 3D," *Film Quarterly* 65, no. 3 (2012): 38–43; Barbara Klinger, "Beyond Cheap Thrills: 3D Cinema Today, the Parallax Debates, and the 'Pop-Out,'" in *3D Cinema and Beyond*, ed. Dan Adler, Janine Marchessault, and Sanja Obradovic (Toronto: Public Books, 2013), 186–99; Thomas Elsaesser, "The 'Return' of 3-D: On Some of the Logics and Genealogies of the Image in the Twenty-First Century," *Critical Inquiry* 39, no. 2 (2013): 217–46; and Owen Weetch, *Expressive Spaces in Digital 3D Cinema* (Basingstoke: Palgrave, 2016).

7.   Nicholas J. Wade, *Brewster and Wheatstone on Vision* (London: Academic Press, 1983), 1.

8.   Wade, *Brewster and Wheatstone on Vision*, 27.

9.   Charles Wheatstone, *The Scientific Papers of Sir Charles Wheatstone* (London: Taylor & Francis / Physical Society of London, 1879), 226.

10. Wheatstone, *The Scientific Papers of Sir Charles Wheatstone*, 227.

11. Jonathan Crary, *Techniques of the Observer* (Cambridge, MA: MIT Press, 1990), 128.

12. Crary, *Techniques of the Observer*, 128.

13. Laura Burd Schiavo, "From Phantom Image to Perfect Vision: Physiological Optics, Commercial Photography, and the Popularization of the Stereoscope," in *New Media, 1740–1915*, ed. Lisa Gitelman and Geoffrey B. Pingree (Cambridge, MA: MIT Press, 2003), 113–38, 127.

14. Rod Bantjes, "Reading Stereoviews: The Aesthetics of Monstrous Space," *History of Photography* 39, no. 1 (2015): 33–55, 34.

15. See Ray Zone, *Stereoscopic Cinema and the Origins of 3-D Film, 1838–1952* (Lexington: University of Kentucky Press, 2007), 9; and Wade, *Brewster and Wheatstone*, 42–43.

16. John Plunkett, "'Feeling Seeing': Touch, Vision, and the Stereoscope," *History of Photography* 37, no. 4 (2013): 389–96, 392.

17. Wade, *Brewster and Wheatstone*, 33.

18. Schiavo, "From Phantom Image to Perfect Vision," 123; Zone, *Stereoscopic Cinema and the Origins of 3D Film*, 10–12.

19. See Helen Groth, "Kaleidoscopic Vision and Literary Invention in an 'Age of Things': David Brewster, Don Juan, and 'A Lady's Kaleidoscope,'" *ELH* 74, no. 1 (2007): 217–37.

20. Wade, *Brewster and Wheatstone*, 35; Helmut Gernsheim and Alison Gernsheim, *The History of Photography: From the Camera Obscura to the Beginning of the Modern Era* (London: Thames & Hudson, 1969), 255.

21. As described in Edward Earle, "The Stereograph in America: Pictorial Antecedents and Cultural Perspectives," in *Points of View: The Stereograph in America—A Cultural History*, ed. Edward Earle (New York: Visual Studies Workshop, 1979), 9–21, 13; and Robert J. Silverman, "The Stereoscope and Photographic Depiction in the Nineteenth Century," *Technology and Culture* 34, no. 4 (1993): 729–56, 730.

22. Crary, *Techniques of the Observer*, 118.

23. Schiavo, "From Phantom Image to Perfect Vision," 113–14.

24. Plunkett, "'Feeling Seeing,'" 392–93.

25. John Plunkett, "Depth, Colour, Movement: Embodied Vision and the Stereoscope," in *Multimedia Histories: From the Magic Lantern to the Internet*, ed. James Lyons and John Plunkett (Exeter: Exeter University Press, 2007), 117–31, 120.

26. Jib Fowles, "Stereography and the Standardization of Vision," *Journal of American Culture* 17, no. 2 (1994): 89–93, 91.

27. Plunkett, "Depth, Colour, Movement," 120.

28. Fowles, "Stereography and the Standardization of Vision," 92.

29. Leon Gurevitch, "The Stereoscopic Attraction: Three-Dimensional Imaging and the Spectacular Paradigm, 1850–2013," *Convergence* 19, no. 4 (2013): 396–405, 399.

30. Alan Thomas, *The Expanding Eye: Photography and the Nineteenth-Century Mind* (London: Croom Helm, 1978), 15.

31. Even admitting the difficulty in assessing ongoing popularity, Thomas's description of the stereoscope enjoying "a vogue for a decade or so" in the 1860s is radically inaccurate. As has been noted, Queen Victoria's use of a stereoscope in 1851 drove a high volume of European sales earlier than this, while Fowles ("Stereography and the Standardization of Vision") describes the "rage" waning only in 1910, and Gurevitch ("The Stereoscopic Attraction") in 1930. Finally, Edward Earle describes how the years 1903–5 witnessed more patents for stereoscopes than any other time—hardly the mark of a "craze" that had been dead for thirty years. See Earle, "Interpretive Chronology—Stereos, American History, and Popular Culture, 1850–1915," in *Points of View: The Stereograph in America—A Cultural History*, ed. Edward Earle (New York: Visual Studies Workshop, 1979), 23–87, 76.

32. See Gurevitch, "The Stereoscopic Attraction," 402; and Jens Schröter, *3D: History, Theory, and Aesthetics of the Transplane Image* (London: Bloomsbury, 2014), 203.

33. Sean F. Johnston, "The Cultural Landscape of Three-Dimensional Imaging," in *Techniques and Principles in Three-Dimensional Imaging: An Introductory Approach*, ed. Martin Richardson (Hershey, PA: Information Science Reference, 2014), 212–32; Meredith A. Bak, "Democracy and Discipline: Object Lessons and the Stereoscope in American Education, 1870–1920," *Early Popular Visual Culture* 10, no. 2 (2012): 147–67.

34. William Paul, "The Aesthetics of Emergence," *Film History* 15, no. 3 (1993): 321–55, 333; Geoff Ogram, "Analogue and Digital Stereo-Photography," in *Techniques and Principles in Three-Dimensional Imaging: An Introductory Approach*, ed. Martin Richardson (Hershey, PA: Information Science Reference, 2014), 59–86, 63.

35. Mark J. P. Wolf, "Z-Axis Development in the Video Game," in *The Video Game Theory Reader 2*, ed. Bernard Perron and Mark J. P. Wolf (New York: Routledge, 2009), 151–68, 158.

36. A point made by Gurevitch, "The Stereoscopic Attraction," 403.

37. See Gurevitch and Ross, "Stereoscopic Media." This list might be expanded with Gabriel Lippmann's integral photography and the popularity of stereoscopic media within the Third Reich among other further cultural uses of stereoscopic media. For more information on

these and other uses, see Schröter, *3D*; and S. Johnston, "The Cultural Landscape of Three-Dimensional Imaging."

38. Zone offers an exhaustive list of these throughout his *Stereoscopic Cinema and the Origins of 3D Film.*

39. Richard C. Hawkins, "3-D," *Quarterly of Film Radio and Television* 7, no. 4 (1953): 325–34, 327.

40. F. Marion, *The Wonders of Optics*, trans. Charles W. Quin (London: Sampson Low, Son & Marston, 1868), 215.

41. Daniel L. Symmes, "3-D: Cinema's Slowest Revolution," *American Cinematographer* 55, no. 4 (1974), 406–7, 434, 456–57, 478–85, 409.

42. André Bazin, "The Return of *Metroscopix*," in *André Bazin's New Media*, ed. and trans. Dudley Andrew (Oakland: University of California Press, 2014), 248–50, 249.

43. Oliver Grau, *Virtual Art: From Illusion to Immersion* (Cambridge, MA: MIT Press, 2003), 153.

44. Zone, *Stereoscopic Cinema and the Origins of 3D Film*, 141–43.

45. Howard Rheingold, *Virtual Reality* (New York: Touchstone, 1991), 67; Michael Kerbel, "3-D or Not 3-D," *Film Comment* 16, no. 6 (1980): 11–20, 12.

46. See Keith Johnston, "A Technician's Dream? The Critical Reception of 3-D Films in Britain," *Historical Journal of Film, Radio, and Television* 32, no. 2 (2012): 245–65.

47. A trip to one of these is described in Ivor Montagu, "The Third Dimension: The Future of Film?," in *The Cinema 1950*, ed. Roger Manvell (New York: Arno, 1978), 132–39. See also Symmes, "3-D," 456.

48. Paul, "The Aesthetics of Emergence," 324.

49. Peter Lev, *The Fifties: Transforming the Screen, 1950–1959*, vol. 7 of *History of the American Cinema*, ed. Charles Harpole (Berkeley: University of California Press, 2003), 110.

50. Zone, *Stereoscopic Cinema and the Origins of 3D Film*, 78.

51. Noël Burch, *Life to Those Shadows*, ed. and trans. Ben Brewster (London: BFI, 1990), 6–7.

52. David Bordwell, Kristin Thompson, and Janet Staiger, *The Classical Hollywood Cinema: Film Style and Mode of Production to 1960* (London: Routledge, 1985).

53. Schröter, *3D*, 62n45.

54. Schröter, *3D*, 143n76. Further references will be given parenthetically.

55. Philip Sandifer, "Out of the Screen and into the Theater: 3-D Film as Demo," *Cinema Journal* 50, no. 3 (2011): 62–78.

56. See Tom Gunning, "An Aesthetic of Astonishment," in *Viewing Positions: Ways of Seeing Film*, ed. Linda Williams (New Brunswick, NJ: Rutgers University Press, 1995), 114–33. Sandifer is not alone in evoking this attractional model in relation to 3D, a model that insists upon the outdatedness and apparent unviability of the format in narrative cinema contexts. See, for instance, discussions in Paul, "The Aesthetics of Emergence"; and Carter Moulton, "The Future Is a Fairground: Attraction and Absorption in 3D Cinema," *CineAction* 89 (2013): 4–13.

57. Sandifer, "Out of the Screen and into the Theater," 74.

58. Sandifer, 78.

59. Paul, "The Aesthetics of Emergence"; William Paul, "Breaking the Fourth Wall: 'Belascoism,' Modernism and a 3-D *Kiss Me Kate*," *Film History* 16, no. 3 (2004): 229–42.

60. Paul, "The Aesthetics of Emergence," 331.

61. Alexander R. Galloway, *The Interface Effect* (Cambridge: Polity, 2012), 38.

62. Annette Kuhn and Guy Westwell, *A Dictionary of Film Studies* (Oxford: Oxford University Press, 2012), 149.

63. Scott Higgins, "3D in Depth: *Coraline*, *Hugo*, and a Sustainable Aesthetic," *Film History* 24, no. 2 (2012): 196–209, 198.

64. David Bordwell, "The Classical Hollywood Style, 1917–60," in *The Classical Hollywood Cinema: Film Style and Mode of Production to 1960*, by David Bordwell, Janet Staiger, and Kristin Thompson (London: Routledge, 1985), 1–84, 3–4; see also Paul, "The Aesthetics of Emergence," 321.

65. However, when applied to more prestigious fare, as in the case of the lavish musical *Kiss Me Kate*, 3D was apparently unpopular and even more problematic. Not only based on a successful Broadway play but also a meta-adaptation of Shakespeare's *The Taming of the Shrew*, *Kiss Me Kate*'s musical and literally theatrical subject matter permits reflexive play with direct address, allowing it to use stereoscopic emergence selectively and expressively to differentiate performing styles and in doing so define characters (see Paul, "Breaking the Fourth Wall," 239). Nonetheless, the film struggled to establish itself within the marketplace as a relatively respectable 3D product and was mostly seen in 2D, as described by Thomas Hishack in *The Oxford Companion to the American Musical: Theatre, Film, and Television* (Oxford: Oxford University Press, 2008), 403.

66. Paul, "The Aesthetics of Emergence," 332.

67. Described in detail by Caetlin Benson-Allott, "Old Tropes in New Dimensions: Stereoscopy and Franchise Spectatorship," *Film Criticism* 37, no. 3, and 38, no. 1 (2013): 12–29.

68. Sandifer, "Out of the Screen and into the Theater," 76; Sheldon Hall, "Dial M for Murder," *Film History* 26, no. 3 (2004): 243–55, 246.

69. Paul, "Breaking the Fourth Wall," 230; see also Sandifer, "Out of the Screen and into the Theater," 77.

70. Hall, "Dial M for Murder," 252; see also Kerbel, "3-D or Not 3-D," 19.

71. Sandifer, "Out of the Screen and into the Theater," 76.

72. Sandifer, 76–77.

73. See Johnston, "A Technician's Dream."

74. An argument made by Kristin Thompson in her previously cited blog posts.

75. The superhero genre perhaps offers the clearest expression of this, as films produced by the likes of Twentieth Century Fox, Warner Bros., and Marvel Studios are consistently released simultaneously in 2D and 3D, finding audiences in both formats and being generally successful commercial products that consolidate the production, marketing, and exhibition strategies of Hollywood cinema in the twenty-first century. Moreover, the conversion to 3D of previously planar blockbusters like *Jurassic Park* (1993; rereleased 2013), *Titanic* (1997; rereleased 2012), *Star Wars: Episode 1—The Phantom Menace* (1999; rereleased 2012), and *2012* (2009; rereleased in 2012 in China only) reveals implicit assumptions about the potential for stereoscopic depth values to be productively applied to films that were shot and edited without these values in mind.

76. John Belton, "Digital 3D Cinema: Digital Cinema's Missing Novelty Phase," *Film History* 24, no. 2, (2012): 187–95, 194.

77. Higgins, "3D in Depth," 198.

78. Higgins, 207.

79. David Bordwell, "Coraline, Cornered," Observations on Film Art, February 23, 2009, http://www.davidbordwell.net/blog/2009/02/23/coraline-cornered/ (accessed September 30, 2019).

80. Higgins, "3D in Depth," 201; Stephen Prince, *Digital Visual Effects in Cinema: The Seduction of Reality* (New Brunswick, NJ: Rutgers University Press, 2012), 215–16.

81. Higgins, "3D in Depth," 207. Bordwell's brief but oft-cited description of *Coraline*'s nonnaturalistic spaces seems predicated on the fact that the film's dimensional distortions are discernible in the planar images he includes within his blog post: the "gestalt flip" he specifically highlights as an innovation in the film's representation of space is itself a quintessentially

planar illusion (we cannot tell if a cube's corner is pointing towards us or receding, precisely because depth effects are lacking)—see Bordwell, "Coraline, Cornered."

82. Higgins, "3D in Depth," 207.

83. Another typical assessment is found in Delia Enyedi's conclusion to an article on *Dial M for Murder* and *Goodbye to Language* (2014): "The rare instance when 3D technology strived to surpass the *uncomfortable* position of stylistic problem and become somehow *invisible* as a special effect has been in the hands of a film auteur" (emphasis mine). Enyedi, "Auteur 3D Filmmaking: From Hitchcock's Protrusion Technique to Godard's Total Immersion Aesthetic," *World Academy of Science, Engineering, and Technology: International Journal of Innovative Research in Science and Engineering* 11, no. 3 (2017): 644–48, 646.

84. Further demonstrating the links between 3D and digital effects, *Avatar, Hugo, Life of Pi*, and *Gravity* all also won the Academy Award for Visual Effects in their respective years. It is worth noting that as well as being industrially validated through such awards all of these films, with the notable exception of *Hugo*, were hugely profitable, grossing in excess of $600 million worldwide.

85. Perhaps unsurprisingly, there is no Academy Award for stereography. This omission hints at a broader difficulty in introducing 3D skills and technical language into the discursive landscape of the film industry and commentary, and the tendency to deal with this difficulty by displacing these skills and techniques into the realms of existing categories (effects production, cinematography) and personnel (directors, cinematographers).

86. Chuck Tryon, "Digital 3D, Technological Auteurism, and the Rhetoric of Cinematic Revolution," in *Special Effects: New Histories/Theories/Contexts*, ed. Dan North, Bob Rehak, and Michael S. Duffy (London: BFI, 2015), 183–95, 184.

87. See Miriam Ross, "Spectacular Dimensions: 3D Dance Films," *Senses of Cinema* 61 (2011), http://sensesofcinema.com/2011/feature-articles/spectacular-dimensions-3d-dance-films/ (accessed September 30, 2019); Ross, "The 3-D Aesthetic"; Miriam Ross, "Stereoscopic Visuality: Where Is The Screen, Where Is The Film?," *Convergence* 19, no. 4 (2013): 406–14; Ross, *3D Cinema*; and Ross's website, www.miriamruthross.wordpress.com (accessed September 30, 2019).

88. Elseasser, "The 'Return' of 3-D."

89. Ariel Rogers, *Cinematic Appeals* (New York: Columbia University Press, 2013), 181.

90. Schröter, *3D*, 35; see Jacques Derrida, *Of Grammatology*, trans. Gayatri Spivak (Baltimore: Johns Hopkins University Press, 1976).

91. Paul, "The Aesthetics of Emergence," 327–28.

92. Paul, 322–23.

93. Paul, 322–23.

94. Ross, *3D*, 199.

95. André Bazin, "*The House of Wax*: Scare Me . . . In Depth!" in *André Bazin's New Media*, ed. and trans. Dudley Andrew (Oakland: University of California Press, 2014), 251–53, 251.

96. Bazin, 253.

97. Sergei Eisenstein, "Stereoscopic Films," in *Notes of a Film Director*, trans. X. Danko (London: Lawrence & Wishart, 1959), 129–37, 132.

98. Eisenstein, 136.

99. Nick Jones, "Variation within Stability: Digital 3D and Film Style," *Cinema Journal* 55, no. 1 (2015): 52–73.

100. Bob Furmanek and Greg Kintz, "An In-Depth Look at *Dial M for Murder*," *3-D Film Archive*, n.d., http://www.3dfilmarchive.com/dial-m-blu-ray-review (accessed September 30, 2019).

101. Elsaesser, "The 'Return' of 3-D," 237.

2. VISUALIZATION

1. Erwin Panofsky, *Perspective as Symbolic Form*, trans. Christopher S. Wood (New York: Zone, 1991).

2. Leon Battista Alberti, *On Painting*, trans. Cecil Grayson (London: Penguin, 1972), 48.

3. Panofsky, *Perspective as Symbolic Form*, 42–43.

4. Alberti, *On Painting*, 56, 87.

5. Robert Hughes, *The Shock of the New* (London: Thames & Hudson, 1991), 16.

6. Panofsky, *Perspective as Symbolic Form*, 66.

7. Ernst Cassirer, *The Philosophy of Symbolic Forms*, vol.1: *Language*, trans. Ralph Manheim (New Haven, CT: Yale University Press, 1955); Ernst Cassirer, *The Philosophy of Symbolic Forms*, vol.2: *Mythical Thought*, trans. Ralph Manheim (New Haven, CT: Yale University Press, 1955); Ernst Cassirer, *The Philosophy of Symbolic Forms*, vol. 3: *The Phenomenology of Knowledge*, trans. Ralph Mannheim (New Haven, CT: Yale University Press, 1965); Ernst Cassirer, *The Philosophy of Symbolic Forms*, vol. 4: *Metaphysics of Symbolic Forms*, ed. John Michael Krois and Donald Phillip Verene, trans. John Michael Krois (New Haven, CT: Yale University Press, 1996).

8. Allister Neher, "How Perspective Could Be a Symbolic Form," *Journal of Aesthetics and Art Criticism* 63, no. 4 (2005): 359–73, 359–60.

9. Cassirer, *The Philosophy of Symbolic Forms*, vol. 1, 81.

10. Cassirer, *The Philosophy of Symbolic Forms*, vol. 2, 94.

11. That said, all symbolic forms resemble language in that they are all "structurally conceived semiotic system[s]," a comment that indicates the extent to which Cassirer's thinking is embedded in the burgeoning science of semiotics in the early twentieth century. Neher, "How Perspective Could Be a Symbolic Form," 367.

12. Cassirer, *The Philosophy of Symbolic Forms*, vol. 4, 51.

13. Cassirer, 78–79.

14. As we will see in chapter 5, perspective not only asserts this in its visual style, but also in its mechanics, which aim to provide the possibility for reverse-engineering the volumetric makeup of the recorded space from the structure of the planar surface. Done well, geometrical perspective is a kind of database of spatial relationships and dimensions, all recorded within a two-dimensional frame. (The checkerboard floors of buildings in various fifteenth-century perspective paintings are indicative methods for such coordination, since they provide the viewer with an abstract measuring device, a grid beneath the world of objects for the judging of exact relative position.)

15. His most overt example of its impact involves the natural curvatures of vision that result from the roundness of the human eyeball. These bulging distortions are ever-present at the edges of our visual field, but they are ignored in linear perspective. As a result, we generally ignore them in our sensate existence, since we have been in effect trained not to see them.

16. Oliver Grau, *Virtual Art: From Illusion to Immersion* (Cambridge, MA: MIT Press, 2003), 37.

17. Hughes, *The Shock of the New*, 17. Another compelling account of human vision—and its "welter of dancing light points"—can be found in E .H. Gombrich, *Art and Illusion: A Study in the Psychology of Pictorial Representation* (London: Phaidon, 1968), 45–46.

18. Panofsky, *Perspective as Symbolic Form*, 28–31.

19. Henri Lefebvre, *The Production of Space*, trans. Donald Nicholson-Smith (Oxford: Blackwell, 1991), 79.

20. Lefebvre, *The Production of Space*, 47.

21. Panofsky, *Perspective as Symbolic Form*, 42.

22. Lefebvre, *The Production of Space*, 285.

23. John Berger, *Ways of Seeing* (London: Penguin, 1972), 103.

24. Sean Cubitt, *The Practice of Light* (Cambridge, MA: MIT Press, 2014), 177.

25. Cubitt, *The Practice of Light*, 214; see also Lefebvre, *The Production of Space*, 361.

26. William M. Ivins Jr., *On the Rationalization of Sight* (New York: Da Capo, 1973), 9.

27. Lev Manovich, "The Mapping of Space: Perspective, Radar, and 3D Computer Graphics," Manovich.net, 1993, http://manovich.net/index.php/projects/article-1993 (accessed September 30, 2019), 3.

28. Alberti too was an architect and painter as well as a writer, albeit somewhat less influential in these other fields.

29. Lefebvre, *The Production of Space*, 146. This style becomes all the more prevalent in modern architecture of the twentieth century, but it has its roots in the possibility that form can be treated as a geometric value somewhat separate and distinct from matter, about which more can be found in the next chapter. I explore twenty-first-century blockbuster visualizations of plastically flexible architecture and cities in my "Flexible Cities: Postindustrial Urban Space in *Inception*, *The Adjustment Bureau*, and *Doctor Strange*," in *The City in American Cinema*, ed. Lawrence Webb and Johan Andersson (New York: I. B. Tauris), 223–50.

30. Samuel L. Edgerton, *The Mirror, the Window and the Telescope: How Renaissance Linear Perspective Changed Our Vision of the Universe* (Ithaca, NY: Cornell University Press, 2009), 169.

31. He makes this argument throughout *The Production of Space*.

32. Ivins, *On the Rationalization of Sight*, 12.

33. Manovich, "The Mapping of Space."

34. Hubert Damisch, *The Origin of Perspective*, trans. John Goodman (Cambridge: MIT Press, 1995), 28, emphasis added.

35. Photography need not operate in the manner that it does, evoking the structured space of perspective and construing the surface of the image as a window upon a frozen, indexical moment from a coherent world that is separated from us by time alone. Rather than consider them distortions or stylistic effects, photography might emphasize the patterns of light sent through a structured lens and onto chemically receptive surfaces in all their unpredictability. That such emphasis is found principally in avant-garde or amateur work is indicative of the influence of perspective upon dominant modes of vision, space, and being.

36. Sean Cubitt, *The Cinema Effect* (Cambridge, MA: MIT Press, 2004); Lev Manovich, *The Language of New Media* (Cambridge, MA: MIT Press, 2001).

37. D. N. Rodowick, *The Virtual Life of Film* (Cambridge, MA: Harvard University Press, 2007).

38. Rodowick builds on Stanley Cavell, *The World Viewed: Reflections on the Ontology of Film*, 2nd ed. (Cambridge, MA: Harvard University Press, 1979).

39. Rodowick, *The Virtual Life of Film*, 79.

40. Rodowick, 98.

41. Stephen Prince, "True Lies: Perceptual Realism, Digital Images, and Film Theory," *Film Quarterly* 49, no. 3 (1996): 27–37.

42. Rodowick, *The Virtual Life of Film*, 133.

43. Thomas Elsaesser and Malte Hagener, *Film Theory: An Introduction through the Senses*, 2nd ed. (New York: Routledge, 2015), 194.

44. Jay David Bolter and Richard Grusin explore this process of media resemblance and development in their influential book *Remediation: Understanding New Media* (Cambridge, MA: MIT Press, 2000).

45. William J. Mitchell, *The Reconfigured Eye: Visual Truth in the Post-Photographic Era* (Cambridge, MA: MIT Press, 1994), 5. In a similar vein, Philip Rosen describes the analog-digital divide as a difference between continuous inscription (a brush on a canvas) and

discontinuous inscription (numbers), in *Change Mummified: Cinema, Historicity, Theory* (Minneapolis: University of Minnesota Press, 2001), 302.

46. Sean Cubitt, "Making Space," *Senses of Cinema* 57 (2010), http://sensesofcinema.com/2010 /feature-articles/making-space/ (accessed September 30, 2019). Cubitt rigorously describes the fundamentals of this process, noting not only the presence but also the procedures and consequences of digital tools like bitmaps, color management, and codecs. The invisible undergirding of digital media, these tools informationally quantify the light content that is received by a digital camera sensor, selecting what values to retain and how to retain them in the transference of this information to devices for augmentation, manipulation, and exhibition.

47. Mark Hansen, *New Philosophy for New Media* (Cambridge, MA: MIT Press, 2006), 99.

48. Cubitt, *The Cinema Effect*, 250.

49. Vivian Sobchack notably suggests that "electronic" media lessen moral and physical investment, in *Carnal Thoughts: Embodiment and Moving Image Culture* (Berkeley: University of California Press, 2004), 153–54.

50. Rodowick, *The Virtual Life of Film*, 118.

51. Cubitt, *The Practice of Light*, 7.

52. Cubitt, "Making Space."

53. Rosen, *Change Mummified*, 318.

54. Rosen is not claiming that all digital images function in exactly this fashion. When we visit the cinema to see a digital blockbuster like *Avatar*, we do not expect to be able to manipulate or interact with it while it is being projected, and our trip to the theatre itself is probably at least partly motivated by the film's nonconvergence on simultaneous media platforms (i.e., we will have to *wait* if we want to watch it in the comfort of our own homes via DVD, Blu-ray, or streaming service). There is thus some continuity between analogue and digital media and their landscapes of consumption.

55. Mitchell, *The Reconfigured Eye*, 118. Rosen (*Change Mummified*, 310–11) offers a useful description of this process of digital graphics production:

> A three-dimensional object—say, a building—is conceived as points, lines, and surfaces, and mapped according to Cartesian coordinates (x, y, and z axes representing breadth, height, and depth relations). These coordinates are numerically representable, which means that a three-dimensional model of the object can be stored in computer memory, but as a numerically coded, hence non-perceivable "virtual" object. This object only becomes perceivable by computations that translate it into an image. And if that image is on a two-dimensional surface, such as a computer monitor or some other flat support like printer paper or a conventional movie screen, the encoded solid object can only manifest its three-dimensionality by translation into a perspective projection.

56. See Manovich, "The Mapping of Space," 12.

57. E. H. Gombrich, *The Image and the Eye: Further Studies in the Psychology of Pictorial Representation* (London: Phaidon, 1982), 190–91.

58. Rodowick, *The Virtual Life of Film*, 101–2.

59. André Bazin, "The Ontology of the Photographic Image," in *What Is Cinema?*, vol.1, trans. High Gray (Berkeley: University of California Press, 2005), 9–16.

60. Robert S. Allison, Laurie M. Wilcox, and Ali Kazimi, "Perceptual Artefacts, Suspension of Disbelief, and Realism in Stereoscopic 3D Film," in *3D Cinema and Beyond*, ed. Dan Adler, Janine Marchessault, and Sanja Obradovic (Toronto: Public Books, 2013), 149–60, 150. The difficulties of achieving the exact values and precise replication demanded by 3D stereo

pairing in the analog era may be summed up using the example of film grain. Cherished by cinephiles and rhetorically associated with celluloid's indexical trace of past time, grain is a challenge for analog 3D, which captures left- and right-eye images on separate cameras and film reels with distinct grain patterns. That which might be ontologically, philosophically valued in the analog image is inherently irreconcilable with the ideal requirements of stereoscopic cinema.

61. Stephen Prince, *Digital Visual Effects in Cinema: The Seduction of Reality* (New Brunswick, NJ: Rutgers University Press, 2012), 203.

62. Prince, *Digital Visual Effects in Cinema*, 127.

63. Ben Walters, "The Great Leap Forward," *Sight and Sound* 19, no. 3 (2009): 38–43, 40.

64. Leon Gurevitch, "The Birth of a Stereoscopic Nation: Hollywood, Digital Empire, and the Cybernetic Attraction," *Animation* 7, no. 3 (2012): 239–58, 241.

65. Prince, *Digital Visual Effects in Cinema*, 203.

66. Ironically, digital pipelines provide the kind extended commercialization of stable, reproducible 3D content in the film context that photography provided for still-image content in the 1850s stereoscope. Just as photographic images are easier to align than drawings, digital moving images are easier to align than photographic moving images.

67. Manovich, *The Language of New Media*, 202.

68. Thomas Elsaesser, "The 'Return' of 3-D: On Some of the Logics and Genealogies of the Image in the Twenty-First Century," *Critical Inquiry* 39, no. 2 (2013): 217–46, 238. Further references will be given parenthetically.

69. Rosalind Krauss, "Photography's Discursive Spaces: Landscape/View," *Art Journal* 42, no. 4 (1982): 311–19, 314.

70. The difficulties stereoscopic media encounter in their efforts to enter the home through 3D television sets (which have never been widely adopted or used) is indicative of this.

71. Edward Skidelsky, *Ernst Cassirer: The Last Philosopher of Culture* (Princeton, NJ: Princeton University Press, 2008), 123.

72. Martin Jay, *Downcast Eyes: The Denigration of Vision in Twentieth-Century French Thought* (Berkeley: University of California Press, 1993), 59.

73. Martin Kemp, *Seen/Unseen: Art, Science, and Intuition from Leonardo to the Hubble Telescope* (Oxford: Oxford University Press, 2006), 75.

PART 2: MAPPED SPACES

1. D. N. Rodowick, *The Virtual Life of Film* (Cambridge, MA: Harvard University Press, 2007), 129–30.

2. Rodowick, *The Virtual Life of Film*, 104.

3. SIMULATION

1. John Belton, "Digital 3D Cinema: Digital Cinema's Missing Novelty Phase," *Film History* 24 no. 2 (2012): 187–95, 190–91.

2. For instance, Todd McCarthy's review decried its thematic simplicity, but indicatively admits that on an experiential level *Avatar* is "all-enveloping and transporting," in "*Avatar*" (review), *Variety*, December 10, 2009, http://variety.com/2009/film/markets-festivals/avatar-2 -1200477897/ (accessed September 30, 2019).

3. Miriam Ross, "The 3-D Aesthetic: *Avatar* and Hyperhaptic Visuality," *Screen* 53 no. 4 (2012): 381–97; Owen Weetch, *Expressive Spaces in Digital 3D Cinema* (Basingstoke: Palgrave, 2016),

17–42; Leon Gurevitch, "The Birth of a Stereoscopic Nation: Hollywood, Digital Empire, and the Cybernetic Attraction," *Animation* 7 no. 3 (2012): 239–58.

4. Martin Heidegger, "The Question Concerning Technology," in *The Question Concerning Technology and Other Essays*, trans. William Lovitt (New York: Harper Perennial, 1977), 3–35; Jordan Crandall, "Operational Media," CTheory, 2005, http://www.ctheory.net/articles.aspx ?id=441 (accessed September 30, 2019).

5. Jonathan Crary, *Techniques of the Observer* (Cambridge, MA: MIT Press, 1990).

6. John Plunkett, "'Feeling Seeing': Touch, Vision and the Stereoscope," *History of Photography* 37 no. 4 (2013): 389–96, 396.

7. Oliver Wendell Holmes, "The Stereoscope and the Stereograph," in *Classic Essays on Photography*, ed. Alan Trachtenberg (Stony Creek, CT: Leete's Island, 1980), 71–82, 74. Further references will be given parenthetically.

8. Jens Schröter suggests that stereoscopes mark "the beginning of virtualization" and can by extension be seen as an early version of virtual reality, in *3D: History, Theory, and Aesthetics of the Transplane Image* (London: Bloomsbury, 2014), 379. The obvious (if low-tech) resemblance of the stereoscope to contemporary technologies like Oculus Rift and other VR headsets accentuates this link—in either case, the viewer inserts the upper part of their face within an enfolding apparatus to receive a personalized media experience.

9. Jib Fowles, "Stereography and the Standardization of Vision," *Journal of American Culture* 1, no. 2 (1994), 89–93, 91–92.

10. Brooke Belisle, "Immersion," in *Debugging Game History: A Critical lexicon*, ed. Henry Lowood and Raiford Guins with A. C. Deger (Cambridge, MA: MIT Press, 2016), 247–57, 255.

11. Fowles, "Stereography and the Standardization of Vision," 92.

12. Fowles, 91.

13. Tom Gunning, "Tracing the Individual Body: Photography, Detectives, and Early Cinema," in *Cinema and the Invention of Modern Life*, ed. Leo Charney and Vanessa R. Schwartz (Berkeley: University of California Press, 1995), 15–45, 18.

14. As such, the stereoscope's haptic form of visuality could be just as objectifying as the abstract gaze of the perspectival image; see Plunkett, "'Feeling Seeing,'" 395.

15. On this, see Paul Virilio, *Open Sky*, trans. Julie Rose (New York: Verso, 1997); and Sean Cubitt, *Simulation and Social Theory* (London: SAGE, 2001).

16. On this, the hype surrounding virtual reality is instructive, emphasizing as it does the increased presence, productivity, and excitement of matterless world-experience—see Howard Rheingold, *Virtual Reality* (New York: Touchstone, 1991), and chapter 4 of this book.

17. Although technically presented as the moon of a gas giant, for the sake of simplicity I will refer to Pandora as a planet.

18. Ellen Grabiner, *I See You: The Shifting Paradigms of James Cameron's Avatar* (Jefferson, NC: McFarland, 2012), 62.

19. J. Holben, "Conquering New Worlds," *American Cinematographer* 91, no. 1 (2010): 32–47.

20. Jenna Ng, "Seeing Movement: On Motion Capture Animation and James Cameron's *Avatar*," *Animation* 7, no. 3 (2012): 273–86, 278.

21. William Brown, "*Avatar*: Stereoscopic Cinema, Gaseous Perception and Darkness," *Animation* 7, no. 3 (2012): 259–71, 259; see also Gilles Deleuze, *Cinema 1: The Movement Image*, trans. Hugh Tomlinson and Barbara Habberjam (London: Athlone, 1986), 83–88; and William Brown, *Supercinema: Film-Philosophy for the Digital Age* (New York: Berghahn, 2013).

22. Miriam Ross, *3D Cinema: Optical Illusions and Tactile Experiences* (New York: Palgrave, 2015), 47.

23. Brown, *Supercinema*, 81.

24. James Clarke, *The Cinema of James Cameron: Bodies in Heroic Motion* (New York: Wallflower, 2014), 129.

25. These dreams are most influentially prevalent in William Gibson's *Neuromancer* (London: HarperCollins, 1984) and Rheingold's *Virtual Reality*. The concept of transcendence to a virtual realm in which greater possibilities for human consciousness might be unlocked is cinematically present in everything from *The Lawnmower Man* (1992) to *The Thirteenth Floor* (1999) and *Transcendence* (2014). It is notable that *Avatar*'s representation of Pandora retains the positive elements of the cyberspaces of those films (i.e., it is a site of freedom, thrill and sex) but entirely removes negative connotations surrounding the loss of humanity and the diminishing moral responsibility wrought by digital disembodiment.

26. Sylvie Magerstädt, *Body, Soul, and Cyberspace in Contemporary Science Fiction Cinema: Virtual Worlds and Ethical Problems* (Basingstoke: Palgrave, 2014), 22.

27. Melanie Chan, *Virtual Reality: Representations in Contemporary Media* (London: Bloomsbury, 2014), 147–50.

28. Michael E. Zimmerman, *Heidegger's Confrontation with Modernity: Technology, Politics, Art* (Bloomington: Indiana University Press, 1990), 222, xiii; Heidegger, "The Question Concerning Technology," 14, 17; Jeff Malpas, *Heidegger's Topology: Being, Place, World* (Cambridge, MA: MIT Press, 2006), 281.

29. Lev Manovich, "The Mapping of Space: Perspective, Radar, and 3D Computer Graphics," Manovich.net, 1993, http://manovich.net/index.php/projects/article-1993 (accessed September 30, 2019), 2.

30. Manovich, "The Mapping of Space," 5–6.

31. Lev Manovich, *The Language of New Media* (Cambridge, MA: MIT Press, 2001), 100.

32. Crandall, "Operational Media."

33. Crandall. Crandall's term "operational media" categorizes a different kind of image than that of Harun Farocki's term "operational images," although there are productive overlaps. As Pasi Väliaho describes, Farocki's label points to images like those in use in settings such as CCTV, robotics, and precision weaponry, all of which are "defined not by their capacity to instruct, to give aesthetic pleasure, to entertain, or even to serve as propaganda, but by their operational functions." See Pasi Väliaho, *Biopolitical Screens: Image, Power, and the Neoliberal Brain* (Cambridge, MA: MIT Press, 2014), 64. As with Crandall's operational media, Farocki's operational images are the visible structure of a grid of power that conceives of the world in a fashion that focuses on the management of risk, the visibility of threat, and the production of neoliberal subjectivity. On the operational qualities of the digital image, see also Ingrid Hoelzl and Remi Marie, *Softimage: Towards a New Theory of the Digital Image* (Bristol: Intellect, 2015).

34. Schröter, *3D*, 180.

35. This said, it would not be appropriate to call these onscreen technologies "stereoscopic" exactly, since they are apparently not constructed from twinned image sources; they are more properly hologrammatic, since they exist as virtual entities in space.

36. Friedrich Kittler, *Optical Media*, trans. Anthony Enns (Malden, MA: Polity, 2010), 41. Again, like Gunning above, Kittler introduces this passage as a technical description of photography, rather than stereoscopy.

37. As Lefebvre has argued, commodity production and exchange rely on an abstract space of accumulation maintained by state and corporate forces in which standardized laws and values predominate. Henri Lefebvre, *The Production of Space*, trans. Donald Nicholson-Smith (Oxford: Blackwell, 1991). Although Lefebvre focused on the predigital production of material and social space, his work is nonetheless applicable to a present moment in which more and more data is captured, collated, and interpreted by a range of software and hardware, all of which then feeds back to structure space. See Rob Kitchin and Martin Dodge, *Code/Space: Software and Everyday Life* (Cambridge, MA: MIT Press, 2011).

38. See Ng, "Seeing Movement," 275. In this regard, the deathblow that Neytiri deals to Quaritch at the end of this finale is telling—her poisoned arrow shatters the digital pseudoscreen of his mech suit on its way to his heart.

39. Sallie Anglin, "Generative Motion: Queer Ecology and *Avatar*," *Journal of Popular Culture* 48, no. 2 (2015): 341–54.

40. Chan, *Virtual Reality*, 153–54. See Cameron's "message" at A Message from Pandora, n.d., http://messagefrompandora.org/ (accessed September 30, 2019).

41. Zimmerman, *Heidegger's Confrontation with Modernity*, 223; see also Martin Heidegger, "The Origin of the Work of Art," in *Poetry, Language, Thought*, trans. Albert Hofstadter (New York: Harper & Row, 2001), 17–86.

42. Leon Gurevitch, "Computer Generated Animation as Product Design Engineered Culture, or Buzz Lightyear to the Sales Floor, to the Checkout, and Beyond!" *Animation* 7 no. 2 (2012): 131–49, 132.

43. Thomas Elsaesser also draws a link between *Avatar*'s 3D, its featured on-screen technologies, and operational imaging in the twenty-first century. Thomas Elsaesser, "The 'Return' of 3-D: On Some of the Logics and Genealogies of the Image in the Twenty-First Century," *Critical Inquiry* 39, no. 2 (2013): 217–46, 242–43.

44. James Der Derian, *Virtuous War: Mapping the Military-Industrial-Media-Entertainment Network*, 2nd ed. (New York: Routledge, 2009).

45. While critical of the melding of media and technologies of warfare, Der Derian himself would likely disagree with my reading of *Avatar*, as he has elsewhere defended the film's antiwar credentials and its work in exposing of "the pathologies of the military industrial complex within a wholly new media-entertainment matrix"; see James Der Derian, "'Now We Are All Avatars,'" *Millennium: Journal of International Studies* 39, no. 1 (2010): 181–86, 182.

46. Bruno Latour, "Visualization and Cognition: Thinking with Eyes and Hands," *Knowledge and Society: Studies in the Sociology of Culture Past and Present* 6 (1986): 1–40, 16.

47. Latour, "Visualization and Cognition," 22.

48. Grabiner, *I See You*; Der Derian, "'Now We Are All Avatars.'"

49. Thomas Elsaesser, "James Cameron's *Avatar*: Access for All," *New Review of Film and Television Studies* 9, no. 3 (2011): 247–64, 249.

50. Elsaesser, "James Cameron's *Avatar*," 259.

51. This contradiction is not unique to the film. As has been noted by Chan, *Avatar* is evocative of virtual reality installation *Osmose* (1995) by artist Char Davies, in which the viewer/participant dons a responsive vest and VR goggles and seems to be transported to a computationally constructed virtual world. See Chan, *Virtual Reality*, 129–55. For more on *Osmose*, see Char Davies's own account of her work in "Landscape, Earth, Body, Being, Space, and Time in the Immersive Virtual Environments *Osmose* and *Ephémère*," in *Women, Art, and Technology* ed. Judy Malloy (Cambridge, MA: MIT Press, 2003), 322–37.

52. This is true of the initial cinema release, and both the later special and extended collector's editions.

53. Sean Cubitt, *Finite Media: Environmental Implications of Digital Technologies* (Durham, NC: Duke University Press, 2017), 13.

54. Joshua Clover, "The Struggle for Space," *Film Quarterly* 63, no. 3 (2010): 6–7, 7.

55. On the function of paraspaces in the contemporary action film, see my *Hollywood Action Films and Spatial Theory* (New York: Routledge, 2015), 95–118.

56. Brown, "*Avatar*," 266.

57. Janet H. Murray, *Hamlet on the Holodeck: The Future of Narrative in Cyberspace* (New York: Free Press, 1997), 263.

58. Chan, *Virtual Reality*, 139.

4. IMMERSION

1. See Chris Berry, Janet Harbord, and Rachel Moore, "Introduction," in *Public Space, Media Space*, ed. Chris Berry, Janet Harbord, and Rachel Moore (Basingstoke: Palgrave, 2013), 1–15; and Nanna Verhoeff, "Screens in the City," in *Screens: From Materiality to Spectatorship—A Historical and Theoretical Reassessment*, ed. Dominique Chateau and José Moure (Amsterdam: Amsterdam University Press, 2016), 125–39.

2. Dominique Chateau and José Moure, "Introduction: Screen, a Concept in Progress," in *Screens: From Materiality to Spectatorship—A Historical and Theoretical Reassessment*, ed. Dominique Chateau and José Moure (Amsterdam: Amsterdam University Press, 2016), 13–22, 13.

3. Anna McCarthy, *Ambient Television: Visual Culture and Public Space* (Durham, NC: Duke University Press, 2001), 3.

4. Nanna Verhoeff, *Mobile Screens: The Visual Regime of Navigation* (Amsterdam: Amsterdam University Press, 2012), 13.

5. This is not to say that the screen "disappears" in this spatialization; see chapter 6.

6. This reaches a kind of apotheosis early in the film, when a refurbished car is displayed at a media event using somewhat unlikely holographic technology. For more on 3D conversion, see the next chapter.

7. Flashbacks further reveal that these volumetric terrains are more developed than archaic, screen-based surfaces: a chronologically earlier racing game uses a scrolling backdrop, in contrast to the extensive 3D circuits found in the film's contemporary game where much of the film's later action takes place.

8. Stark's holograms are aesthetically similar to his enriched visual field when wearing the Iron Man suit as well as his use of a Google-glass–style interface for piloting the suit remotely (this last especially prevalent in *Iron Man 3*).

9. Miriam Ross, *3D Cinema: Optical Illusions and Tactile Experiences* (New York: Palgrave, 2015), 140–41.

10. David Kirby, "The Future Is Now: Diegetic Prototypes and the Role of Popular Films in Generating Real-world Technological Development," *Social Studies of Science* 40, no. 1 (2010): 41–70, 42–43.

11. Kirby, "The Future Is Now," 45.

12. Anonymous, "Data Observatory", Imperial.ac.uk, n.d., https://www.imperial.ac.uk/data -science/about-the-institute/facilities/data-observatory-/ (accessed September 30, 2019).

13. See Patrick Crogan, "The Nintendo Wii, Virtualisation, and Gestural Analogics," *Culture Machine* 11, no. 1 (2010): 82–101.

14. Erkki Huhtamo, "The Four Practices? Challenges for an Archaeology of the Screen," in *Screens: From Materiality to Spectatorship—A Historical and Theoretical Reassessment*, ed. Dominique Chateau and José Moure (Amsterdam: Amsterdam University Press, 2016), 116–24, 120–21.

15. A summary of these can be found in Marcus Carter and Eduardo Velluso, "Some Places Should Be Off Limits for Games Such as Pokémon Go," Conversation, July 12, 2016, https:// theconversation.com/some-places-should-be-off-limits-for-games-such-as-pokemon-go -62341 (accessed September 30, 2019).

16. See Emily Morton, "Augmented Reality Property Searches – See It To Believe It!", Foxtons .co.uk, December 16, 2014, http://www.foxtons.co.uk/discover/2014/12/augmented-reality -property-searches-see-it-to-believe-it.html (accessed September 30, 2019).

17. Olivier Asselin and Louis Auger Gosselin, "This Side of Paradise: Immersion and Emersion in S3D and AR," in *3D Cinema and Beyond*, ed. Dan Adler, Janine Marchessault, and Sanja Obradovic (Toronto: Public Books, 2013), 132–41, 140.

18. Asselin and Gosselin, "This Side of Paradise," 135.
19. An articulate parody of this AR aesthetic by artist/content provider Keiichi Matsuda speculates on the overwhelming inflation of augmented content in the near future and critiques the implications of this content for social and spiritual existence. In Matsuda's dystopia, everything from employment to leisure time to shopping to religion is monitored by corporate interests whose presence is explicitly and suffocatingly felt through augmented reality pop-ups and overlays. See Matsuda, "HYPER-REALITY," Vimeo.co.uk, May 16, 2016, https://vimeo.com/166807261 (accessed September 30, 2019).
20. I discuss the proximity of the screen in a range of media in my article "The Expansive and Proximate Scales of Immersive Media," *International Journal on Stereo and Immersive Media* 2, no. 2 (2019): 36–49.
21. Oliver Grau, *Virtual Art: From Illusion to Immersion* (Cambridge, MA: MIT Press, 2003), 13.
22. See Anonymous, "Google Tilt Brush: Impossible Now a Reality?," CNN Style, May 2016, http://edition.cnn.com/2016/05/09/arts/google-tilt-brush/index.html?sr=fbCNN051016google-tilt-brush0210PMVODtop (accessed September 30, 2019).
23. Lev Manovich, *The Language of New Media* (Cambridge, MA: MIT Press, 2001), 113.
24. Ken Hillis, *Digital Sensations: Space, Identity, and Embodiment in Virtual Reality* (Minneapolis: University of Minnesota Press, 1999), 72.
25. Multisensory VR—involving textured touch, olfactory stimulus, and temperature shifts—is available in some site-specific contexts; my discussion here is on the more widely available, home consumer–oriented VR, which is visual and auditory only.
26. Thomas Elsaesser, "Pushing the Contradictions of the Digital: 'Virtual Reality' and 'Interactive Narrative' as Oxymorons between Narrative and Gaming," *New Review of Film and Television Studies* 12, no. 3 (2014): 295–311, 296; see also Jens Schröter, *3D: History, Theory and Aesthetics of the Transplane Image* (London: Bloomsbury, 2014), 342.
27. Elsaesser, "Pushing the Contradictions of the Digital," 299.
28. Elsaesser, 302.
29. Leon Gurevitch, "Computer Generated Animation as Product Design Engineered Culture, or Buzz Lightyear to the Sales Floor, to the Checkout and Beyond!," *Animation* 7, no. 2 (2012): 131–49, 133.
30. Schröter, *3D*, 381.
31. Manovich, *The Language of New Media*, 202.
32. Mark Hansen, *New Philosophy for New Media* (Cambridge, MA: MIT Press, 2006), 105.
33. The only exception is a brief moment in which Tris must recognize that she is still in VR when her partner apparently breaks her out of Jeanine's control; her realization prompts her rescuer's dissolution into multiple tiny shards, and her own completion of the latest test.
34. Thomas Elsaesser, "The 'Return' of 3-D: On Some of the Logics and Genealogies of the Image in the Twenty-First Century," *Critical Inquiry* 39, no. 2 (2013): 217–46, 240.
35. Nerea Calvillo, Orit Halpern, Jesse LeCavalier, and Wolfgang Pietsch, "Test Bed as Urban Epistemology," in *Smart Urbanism: Utopian Vision or False Dawn?*, ed. Simon Marvin, Andrés Luque-Ayala, and Colin McFarlane (New York: Routledge, 2016), 146–68; see also Orit Halpern, Robert Mitchell, and Bernard Dionysius Geoghegan, "The Smartness Mandate: Notes toward a Critique," *Grey Room* 68 (2017): 106–29.
36. The third film in this franchise, *Allegiant* (2016), shows how the privileging of such virtuality leads to ecological devastation beyond the hermetically sealed walls of the simulation, as everything beyond Chicago is revealed to be dangerously irradiated. This is very similar to the way simulations, space, and a global apocalypse are treated by the *Resident Evil* franchise, as I discuss in detail in "This is My World: Spatial Representation in the Resident Evil films," *Continuum* 30, no. 4 (2016): 477–88.

37. Elsaesser, "Pushing the Contradictions of the Digital," 300.

38. As such, *Shatter Reality* would seem to confirm Manovich's proposal that even in VR technologies the immobility associated with cinematic spectatorship remains a fundamental requirement of the media: for all the congruence offered between tactile experience and simulated terrain, ultimately the user is bodily static and can make few, if any, spatial choices. See Manovich, *The Language of New Media*, 107. For an indicative review that hints at the affectual, rather than intellectual or interactive appeal of *Shatter Reality*, see emart, "INSURGENT: Shatter Reality on the Oculus Rift!!!" YouTube.com, March 11, 2015, https://www.youtube.com/watch?v=8VuWRhGuJ7o&nohtml5=False (accessed September 30, 2019).

39. The oncoming train section might be read through the longer lineage of cinematic representational media and their use of similar direct addresses to stimulate audiences of a newly emergent media form. On this, see Steven Bottomore, "The Panicking Audience?: Early Cinema and the 'Train Effect,'" *Historical Journal of Film, Radio, and Television* 19, no. 2 (1999): 177–216; and Leon Gurevitch, "The Cinemas of Interactions: Cinematics and the 'Game Effect' in the Age of Digital Attractions," *Senses of Cinema* 57 (2010): http://sensesofcinema.com/2010/feature-articles/the-cinemas-of-interactions-cinematics-and-the-%E2%80%98game-effect%E2%80%99-in-the-age-of-digital-attractions/#b1 (accessed September 30, 2019).

40. Kirby, "The Future Is Now," 46, 43.

41. This is true whether or not such paracinematic interfaces are themselves stereoscopic, which, in the case of VR, is not always the case.

42. Jay David Bolter and Richard Grusin, *Remediation: Understanding New Media* (Cambridge, MA: MIT Press, 1999), 29.

43. Bolter and Grusin, *Remediation*, 22.

44. On this, see Anne Friedberg, *The Virtual Window: From Alberti to Microsoft* (Cambridge, MA: MIT Press, 2006).

45. Hillis, *Digital Sensations*, xxviii.

5. SURVEILLANCE

1. Kevin D. Haggerty and Richard V. Ericson, "The New Politics of Surveillance and Visibility," in *The New Politics of Surveillance and Visibility*, ed. Kevin D. Haggerty and Richard V. Ericson (Toronto: University of Toronto Press, 2006), 3–33, 3.

2. William Bogard, *The Simulation of Surveillance: Hypercontrol in Telematic Societies* (Cambridge: Cambridge University Press, 1996), 69.

3. Mark Andrejevic, *iSpy: Surveillance and Power in the Interactive Era* (Lawrence: University of Kansas Press, 2007), 132. Scholarly work on digital surveillance—including that by Bogard and Andrejevic—tilts toward the dystopian, breathlessly evoking a smoothly interlocking, externally imposed surveillance assemblage from which there is no escape. While problematic, perhaps this is not surprising given the pace at which observational and disciplinary practices are currently being restructured. Such sensationalist pessimism is proudly on display when Kevin D. Haggerty and Richard V. Ericson describe contemporary life as not only Orwellian, but "augmented by technologies [Orwell] could not have even had nightmares about," in "The Surveillant Assemblage," *British Journal of Sociology* 51, no. 4 (2000): 605–22, 612.

4. Catherine Zimmer, *Surveillance Cinema* (New York: New York University Press, 2015), 6. In the context of media art practice, Miriam de Rosa has shown how Harun Farocki's work makes a similar argument, in "Poetics and Politics of the Trace: Notes on Surveillance Practices Through Harun Farocki's Work," *NECSUS: European Journal of Media Studies* (2014),

http://www.necsus-ejms.org/poetics-politics-trace-notes-surveillance-practices-harun-farockis-work/ (accessed September 30, 2019).

5. Thomas Elsaesser, "The 'Return' of 3-D: On Some of the Logics and Genealogies of the Image in the Twenty-First Century," *Critical Inquiry* 39, no. 2 (2013): 217–46, 245.

6. On *The Martian*, see the description by converters Prime Focus World, at http://www.primefocusworld.com/the-martian/ (accessed September 30, 2019).

7. See the list maintained by Philip Dhingra, "Real 3D or Fake 3D," n.d., https://www.realorfake3d.com (accessed September 30, 2019). Meanwhile, claims about the cost and creative restrictions of shooting natively (which is presumed by some to be more expensive, and more logistically complicated) must be placed in the context of stakeholder self-interest and should not distract from the fact that conversion is an intrinsic part of the contemporary digital 3D landscape.

8. Sean Cubitt, *The Cinema Effect* (Cambridge, MA: MIT Press, 2004), 249.

9. Stephen Prince, "True Lies: Perceptual Realism, Digital Images, and Film Theory," *Film Quarterly* 49, no. 3 (1996): 27–37, 32.

10. Mike Seymour, "Art of Stereo Conversion: 2D to 3D—2012," May 8, 2012, https://www.fxguide.com/featured/art-of-stereo-conversion-2d-to-3d-2012/ (accessed September 30, 2019).

11. Seymour further stresses how lens flares were, in the case of *John Carter*, always removed from the monoscopic source, only to be reintroduced "creatively" (i.e., at modulated magnitudes and depths). See chapter 6 for more on lens artifacts in 3D cinema.

12. Stereo supervisor Richard Baker describes these processes here: https://www.youtube.com/watch?v=teYCL6XRcwM (accessed September 30, 2019).

13. On *Edge of Tomorrow*, see the description by converters Prime Focus World, at http://www.primefocusworld.com/edge-of-tomorrow/, (accessed May 10, 2017). Similarly, the same company's description of its work on *World War Z* (2013) emphasizes the recognizability of star Brad Pitt's features, and the painstaking work they undertook modeling this visage in 3D so that they could apply this depth abstraction to the converted film: http://www.primefocusworld.com/world-war-z/ (accessed May 10, 2017).

14. As Grant Anderson, stereographic supervisor on *The Green Hornet* (2011), states, "When you convert any 2-D movie into stereo 3-D, you have to think of every shot as a visual effects shot." Quoted in Iain Stasukevich, "Adding a Third Dimension to Hornet," *American Cinematographer*, February 2011, https://theasc.com/ac_magazine/February2011/GreenHornet/page3.html (accessed September 30, 2019).

15. Jens Schröter, *3D: History, Theory and Aesthetics of the Transplane Image* (New York and London: Bloomsbury, 2014), 144–164.

16. This video was previously available on the Lytro website (https://www.lytro.com/cinema, accessed March 19, 2017), but is no longer available following Lytro's sale to Google in 2017.

17. This rhetoric of overcoming planar ambiguity is powerfully present in a 2006 SIGGRAPH paper around light field microscopy, in which the advantages of using this kind of spatial optical array for microscopic evaluation is asserted. Again, whatever opacities the monoscopic microscopic image offers are eradicated through the creation of focal stacks and volume rendering, manufacturing a navigable three-dimensional model from what is effectively a single-camera source. The fact that one of the authors of this paper subsequently went to work for Lytro only underscores the inherent connections between science and media technologies, and how both emphasize spatialized image capture. See Marc Levoy, Ren Ng, Andrew Adams, Matthew Footer, and Mark Horowitz, "Light Field Microscopy," *ACM Transactions on Graphics* (Proceedings of SIGGRAPH) 25, no. 3 (2006): http://www.graphics.stanford.edu/papers/lfmicroscope/ (accessed September 30, 2019).

18. Thrift proposes that three systems in particular contribute to an ascendant geolocational model of addressing the world: firstly, "the general availability of technologies which can continuously track position—lasers, various forms of new information technology, wireless, geographical information systems, global positioning systems"; secondly, "a series of formalised and integrative knowledges of sequence arising out of the general application of models drawn from logistics across a wide range of fields"; and, thirdly, "new means of countability [such as spreadsheets] which have provided new possibilities of calculation." In "Remembering the Technological Unconscious by Foregrounding Knowledges of Position," *Environment and Planning D: Society and Space* 22, no. 1 (2003): 175–90, 182.

19. Thrift, "Remembering the Technological Unconscious," 183.

20. Bogard, *The Simulation of Surveillance*, 16.

21. Thrift, "Remembering the Technological Unconscious," 183.

22. Unsurprisingly, GIS and GPS are modes of geographical knowledge derived from the precision targeting techniques of the US military; see Caren Kaplan, "Precision Targets: GPS and the Militarization of US Consumer Identity," *American Quarterly* 58, no. 3 (2006): 693–713, 696.

23. José van Dijck, "Datafication, Dataism, and Dataveillance: Big Data Between Scientific Paradigm and Ideology," *Surveillance and Society* 12, no. 2 (2014): 197–208, 198.

24. van Dijck, "Datafication, Dataism, and Dataveillance," 205. See also Rita Raley, "Dataveillance and Counterveillance," in *"Raw Data" Is an Oxymoron*, ed. Lisa Gitelman (Cambridge, MA: MIT Press, 2013): 121–46.

25. Andrejevic, *iSpy*, 2.

26. Andrejevic, 52.

27. Andrejevic, 118.

28. Jonathan Crary, *24/7: Late Capitalism and the Ends of Sleep* (New York: Verso, 2014), 33; see Crary's earlier works, *Techniques of the Observer: On Vision and Modernity in the Nineteenth Century* (Cambridge, MA: MIT Press, 1990), and *Suspensions of Perception: Attention, Spectacle, and Modern Culture* (Cambridge, MA: MIT Press, 1999).

29. Crary, *24/7*, 47.

30. Crary, 76. When Crary suggests that such a "non-social model of machinic performance" disguises its human costs (9), he seems to be pointing toward the psychic and experiential harm to (relatively solvent) individuals, but his comment could be expanded to include those populations and environments that are damaged by production networks and the build-up of electronic waste through planned obsolescence, not to mention the broader damage to the planetary ecosystem that occurs as a result.

31. Ken Hillis, Michael Petit, and Kylie Jarrett, *Google and the Culture of Search* (New York: Routledge, 2013).

32. Antoine Allen, "The 'Three Black Teenagers' Search Shows It Is Society, Not Google, That is Racist," *Guardian*, June 10, 2016, https://www.theguardian.com/commentisfree/2016/jun/10/three-black-teenagers-google-racist-tweet (accessed September 30, 2019). See also Safiya Umoja Noble's monograph on this topic: *Algorithms of Oppression: How Search Engines Reinforce Racism* (New York: New York University Press, 2018).

33. Hillis, Petit, and Jarrett, *Google and the Culture of Search*, 54.

34. Rob Kitchin and Martin Dodge, *Code/Space: Software and Everyday Life* (Cambridge, MA: MIT Press, 2011), 99.

35. Bogard, *The Simulation of Surveillance*, 19–20.

36. Bogard, 30.

37. Grégoire Chamayou, *Drone Theory*, trans. Janet Lloyd (London: Penguin, 2015), 38–44.

38. Like Chamayou, *RoboCop* takes a dim view of this assemblage, depicting the automated slaughter of terrorists and civilians alike in this future's US-occupied Iran. Murphy escapes

condemnation because his humanity asserts itself over machinic automation, allowing the viewer to root for him relatively unproblematically—despite the fact that his automated abuses of civil liberties through cyborg connectivity go unremarked upon and unpunished.

39. Pasi Väliaho, "The Light of God: Notes on the Visual Economy of Drones," *Necsus*, December 4, 2014, http://www.necsus-ejms.org/light-god-notes-visual-economy-drones/ (accessed September 30, 2019).

40. Stephen Graham makes clear that in this context simulation means not only data extraction and storage, but also the visual presentation of this data:

> Computerised simulation and modelling systems now allow the huge quantities of data captured by automatic surveillance systems to be fed directly into dynamic facsimiles of the time-space "reality" of geographic territories (neighbourhoods, cities, regions, nations, etc.), which can in turn be fed into support new types of organisational change, spatial targeting, and urban and regional restructuring. . . . More and more powerful data surveillance thus becomes spatially visualized and operationalized through sophisticated GIS and, increasingly, Virtual Reality (VR) and computer monitoring technologies. . . . New techniques which blend remotely-sensed data with digital maps and 3-dimensional virtual simulations further strengthen the connections between surveillance and simulation.

> Steven Graham, "Geographies of Surveillant Simulation," in *Virtual Geographies: Bodies, Space, and Relations*, ed. Mike Crang, Phil Crang, and Jon May (New York: Routledge, 1999), 131–48, 132–33.

41. This implantation may reveal itself through its reliance upon the user's mobile screen and camera (through which they access their translated surroundings), but this reminder of the conversion that has taken place is less visible in glasses-based interfaces and the fully remediated worlds provided by VR.

42. Zsofia Szemeredy, "A Short Guide to Mirriad," Mapping Contemporary Cinema, 2015, http://www.mcc.sllf.qmul.ac.uk/?p=1516 (accessed September 30, 2019).

43. Michel Foucault, *Discipline and Punish: The Birth of the Prison*, trans. Alan Sheridan, 2nd ed. (New York: Vintage, 1991), 197.

44. Gilles Deleuze, "Postscript on the Societies of Control," *October* 59 (1992): 3–7; Foucault, *Discipline and Punish*.

45. Deleuze, "Postscript on the Societies of Control," 7.

46. Light-field technology, for instance, has found its way into the surveillance sphere, since it can produce a depth model of a subject's physiognomy, augmenting existing facial recognition software and its reliance on the shape of faces for identification. See Anne Strehlow, "Computer Scientists Create a 'Light Field Camera' That Banishes Fuzzy Photos," Stanford Report, November 3, 2005, http://news.stanford.edu/news/2005/november9/camera-110205.html (accessed September 30, 2019).

47. Paul Virilio, *War and Cinema: The Logistics of Perception* (New York: Verso, 1989), 4.

48. Akira Mizuta Lippit, *Atomic Light (Shadow Optics)* (Minneapolis: University of Minnesota Press, 2005), 109.

49. For a more wide-ranging survey of these kinds of science-fiction surveillance technologies, see my "Expanding the Esper: Virtualized Spaces of Surveillance in SF Film," *Science Fiction Film and Television* 9, no. 1 (2016): 1–23, 10–12.

50. For further discussions of the Esper, see Giuliana Bruno, "Ramble City: Postmodernism and *Blade Runner*," *October* 41 (1987): 61–74, 73; Marshall Deutelbaum, "Memory/Visual Design: The Remembered Sights of *Blade Runner*," *Literature/Film Quarterly* 17, no. 1 (1989): 66–72; Kaja Silverman, "Back to the Future," *Camera Obscura* 9, no. 3 (1991): 108–32, 124; and Barry

Atkins, "Replicating the Blade Runner," in *The* Blade Runner *Experience: The Legacy of a Science Fiction Classic*, ed. Will Brooker (New York: Wallflower, 2005), 79–91.

51. William M. Kolb tellingly reveals that in the original script for the film, Leon's memento was not a photograph but a hologram, in "Script to Screen: *Blade Runner* in Perspective," in *Retrofitting* Blade Runner: *Issues in Ridley Scott's* Blade Runner *and Philip K. Dick's* Do Androids Dream of Electric Sheep?, 2nd ed., ed. Judith B. Kerman (Madison: University of Wisconsin Press, 1997), 132–53, 144.

52. Scott Bukatman, Blade Runner (London: BFI, 1997), 46–47.

53. Mark Hansen, *New Philosophy for New Media* (Cambridge, MA: MIT Press, 2006), 92–93.

54. Hansen, *New Philosophy for New Media,* 93.

55. Hansen, 96.

56. The content of Snow White's screens was made by Digital Air using a camera array familiar from *The Matrix*. Examples of their work can be found on their website, Digital Air, n.d., http://www.digitalair.com (accessed September 30, 2019).

57. Zimmer, *Surveillance Cinema*, 162.

58. Haggerty and Ericson, "The Surveillant Assemblage," 610.

59. Ben Campkin and Rebecca Ross, "Negotiating the City Through Google Street View," in *Camera Constructs: Photography, Architecture, and the Modern City*, ed. Andrew Higgott and Timothy Wray (Farnham: Ashgate, 2012), 147–57, 147.

60. A similar process of photo-stitching and spatial amalgamation was offered by the Microsoft app Photosynth, which was discontinued in early 2017. On this app, see William Uricchio, "The Algorithmic Turn: Photosynth, Augmented Reality and the Changing Implications of the Image," *Visual Studies* 26, no. 1 (2011): 25–35.

61. See Anonymous, "Capture and Publish Your Own Street View," Google Maps, n.d., https://www.google.co.uk/maps/streetview/trusted/ (accessed September 30, 2019).

62. A feature described in Josh Lowensohn, "Google's Street View Now Lets You Step Back in Time," Verge, April 23, 2014, http://www.theverge.com/2014/4/23/5640472/googles-street-view-now-lets-you-step-back-in-time (accessed September 30, 2019).

63. See Anonymous, "Sources of Photography," Google Maps, n.d., https://www.google.co.uk/streetview/explore/ (accessed September 30, 2019).

64. Ingrid Hoelzl and Remi Marie, *Softimage: Towards a New Theory of the Digital Image* (Bristol: Intellect, 2015), 84.

65. In her reading of *Gravity* (2013), Kristen Whissel draws out similar connections in that film between orbiting satellites of digital location, stereoscopic 3D space, and an epistemology of total knowledge: "Parallax Effects: Epistemology, Affect, and Digital 3D Cinema," *Journal of Visual Culture* 15, no. 2 (2016): 233–49.

66. Garrett Stewart, *Closed Circuits: Screening Narrative Surveillance* (Chicago: University of Chicago Press, 2015), 20.

67. Uricchio, "The Algorithmic Turn," 33.

68. Diego Gonzalez-Aguilera and Javier Gomez-Lahoz, "Forensic Terrestrial Photogrammetry from a Single Image," *Journal of Forensic Sciences* 54, no. 6 (2009): 1376–87.

69. Adam Brown and Tony Chalkley, "'Beautiful, Unethical, Dangerous': Screening Surveillance and Maintaining Insecurities," *Reconstruction* 12, no. 3 (2012): http://hdl.handle.net/10536/DRO/DU:30049443 (accessed September 30, 2019).

70. Ironically, in his attack on 3D, Mark Kermode uses *Lawrence of Arabia* as an example of how effective nonstereoscopic parallax can be in planar cinema, alighting in particular upon the iconic desert introduction of Omar Sharif's Sherif Ali. Kermode describes how this scene works just fine without 3D effects and is dismayed at the possibility that it might be ruined by a "bizarrely concocted polarised parallax process." While *Lawrence of Arabia* has yet to

be subjected to such a process in its entirety, in *Prometheus* we see what Kermode feared. In Mark Kermode, *The Good, the Bad, and the Multiplex* (London: Random House, 2011), 123.

71. Moreover, David's replication of O'Toole converts the human into its digital (robotic) replacement.

72. This geographical schism hints at diverging national taste cultures around contemporary 3D and how these are managed through marketing and release strategies—see Patrick von Sychowski, "*RoboCop*'s 3D Success in China Spells Trouble for Imax," Celluloid Junkie, March 12, 2014, https://celluloidjunkie.com/2014/03/12/robocops-3d-success-china-spells -trouble-imax/ (accessed September 30, 2019). *Jason Bourne* (2016) received a similar 3D release strategy but was not a critical success in this regard—see Patrick Brzeski "3D *Jason Bourne* Causes Nausea, Protest in China," *Hollywood Reporter*, August 26, 2016, http://www .hollywoodreporter.com/news/3d-jason-bourne-causes-nausea-923098 (accessed September 30, 2019).

73. Ian Failes, "*RoboCop* Redux: Inside the Film's Biggest Scenes," *fxguide*, February 13, 2014, http://www.fxguide.com/featured/robocop-redux-inside-the-films-biggest-scenes/ (accessed September 30, 2019).

74. Haggerty and Ericson, "The Surveillant Assemblage," 613–14.

75. Bogard, *The Simulation of Surveillance*, 69.

76. Andrejevic, *iSpy*, 132.

77. Bruce Bennett refers to 3D's "imperial" or "cartographic" visuality, a visuality of colonial control displayed in particular in the roving, penetrative, digitally assisted long takes of many CGI-heavy 3D films; the phrase "surveillant visuality" is indebted to this reading. Bennett, "The Normativity of 3D: Cinematic Journeys, 'Imperial Visuality,' and Unchained Cameras," *Jump Cut* 55 (2013), http://ejumpcut.org/archive/jc55.2013/Bennett-3D/text.html (accessed September 30, 2019).

78. Hillis, Petit, and Jarrett, *Google and the Culture of Search*, 53.

PART 3: MONSTROUS SPACES

1. Miriam Ross, *3D Cinema: Optical Illusions and Tactile Experiences* (New York: Palgrave Macmillan, 2015), 17.

2. On digital media, see D. N. Rodowick, *The Virtual Life of Film* (Cambridge, MA: Harvard University Press, 2007), 125–26. On stereoscopic 3D, see Jonathan Crary, *Techniques of the Observer* (Cambridge, MA: MIT Press, 1990), 122; and Jens Schröter, *3D: History, Theory, and Aesthetics of the Transplane Image* (New York: Bloomsbury, 2014), 38.

3. As Martin Jay puts it, "There is no 'view from nowhere' for even the most scrupulously detached observer"; in *Downcast Eyes: The Denigration of Vision in Twentieth-Century French Thought* (Berkeley: University of California Press, 1993), 18.

6. DEFAMILIARIZATION

Portions of this chapter were previously published in Nick Jones, "'There Never Really Is a Stereoscopic Image': A Closer Look at 3-D Media," *New Review of Film and Television Studies* 13, no. 2 (2015): 170–88.

1. Erwin Panofsky, *Perspective as Symbolic Form*, trans. Christopher S. Wood (New York: Zone, 1991); John Berger, *Ways of Seeing* (London: Penguin, 1972); Bruno Latour, "Visualization and

Cognition: Thinking with Eyes and Hands," *Knowledge and Society: Studies in the Sociology of Culture Past and Present* 6 (1986): 1–40. This translation is in many ways fundamental to capitalist spatial management, subdivision, and reproduction. See Henri Lefebvre, *The Production of Space*, trans. Donald Nicholson-Smith (Oxford: Blackwell, 1991), 47. For further exploration of these issues, see chapter 2.

2. E. H. Gombrich, *The Image and the Eye: Further Studies in the Psychology of Pictorial Representation* (London: Phaidon, 1982), 190–91. Jens Schröter makes a similar point in *3D: History, Theory, and Aesthetics of the Transplane Image* (New York: Bloomsbury, 2014), 18.

3. Robert S Allison, Laurie M. Wilcox, and Ali Kazimi, "Perceptual Artefacts, Suspension of Disbelief, and Realism in Stereoscopic 3D Film," in *3D Cinema and Beyond*, ed. Dan Adler, Janine Marchessault, and Sanja Obradovic (Toronto: Public Books, 2013), 149–60, 149.

4. Charles Wheatstone, *The Scientific Papers of Sir Charles Wheatstone* (London: Taylor & Francis, 1879), 233.

5. Rod Bantjes, "Reading Stereoviews: The Aesthetics of Monstrous Space," *History of Photography* 39, no. 1 (2015): 33–55, 34.

6. Laura Burd Schiavo, "From Phantom Image to Perfect Vision: Physiological Optics, Commercial Photography, and the Popularization of the Stereoscope," in *New Media, 1740–1915*, ed. Lisa Gitelman and Geoffrey B. Pingree (Cambridge, MA: MIT Press, 2003), 113–38, 131.

7. Jib Fowles, "Stereography and the Standardization of Vision," *Journal of American Culture* 17, no. 2 (1994): 89–93, 91.

8. Oliver Wendell Holmes, "The Stereoscope and the Stereograph," in *Classic Essays on Photography*, ed. Alan Trachtenberg (Stony Creek, CT: Leete's Island, [1859] 1980), 71–82, 74.

9. Hermann von Helmholtz, *Treatise on Physiological Optics*, vol. 3, trans. and ed. James P. C. Southall (Birmingham, AL: Leslie B. Adams, 1985), 303.

10. Brian Winston, *Technologies of Seeing: Photography, Cinematography, and Television* (London: BFI, 1996), 111.

11. Roger Ebert, "Why 3D Doesn't Work and Never Will. Case Closed," Roger Ebert's Journal, January 23, 2011, http://www.rogerebert.com/rogers-journal/why-3d-doesnt-work-and-never-will-case-closed (accessed September 30, 2019); see also Roger Ebert, "Why I Hate 3D Movies," *Newsweek*, May 10, 2010, http://europe.newsweek.com/roger-ebert-why-i-hate-3d-movies-70247 (accessed September 30, 2019).

12. Quoted in Ebert, "Why 3D Doesn't Work and Never Will."

13. Allison, Wilcox, and Kazimi, "Perceptual Artefacts," 149; see also Wheatstone, *Scientific Papers*, 234.

14. Robert Hughes, *The Shock of the New* (London: Thames & Hudson, 1991), 17.

15. See Schröter, *3D*, 35.

16. Although, of course, 3D media are received *through* our existing optical system.

17. John Plunkett, "'Feeling Seeing': Touch, Vision, and the Stereoscope," *History of Photography* 37, no. 4 (2013): 389–96, 393.

18. Schiavo, "From Phantom Image to Perfect Vision," 113.

19. Jonathan Crary, *Techniques of the Observer* (Cambridge, MA: MIT Press, 1990), 116–36.

20. Schiavo, "From Phantom Image to Perfect Vision," 116.

21. Crary, *Techniques of the Observer*, 128; see also 48–49.

22. Martin Jay, *Downcast Eyes: The Denigration of Vision in Twentieth-Century French Thought* (Berkeley: University of California Press, 1993), 132n181.

23. David Brewster, *The Stereoscope: Its History, Theory, and Construction* (London: John Murray, 1856), 53.

24. Crary, *Techniques of the Observer*, 122.

25. Allison, Wilcox, and Kazimi, "Perceptual Artefacts," 152.

26. Thomas Elsaesser and Malte Hagener, *Film Theory: An Introduction through the Senses* (New York: Routledge, 2010), 32.

27. Elsaesser and Hagener, *Film Theory*, 18.

28. See, for instance, Jen E. Boyle, *Anamorphosis in Early Modern Literature: Mediation and Affect* (Farnham: Ashgate, 2010); Stephen Greenblatt, *Renaissance Self-Fashioning: From More to Shakespeare* (Chicago: University of Chicago Press, 2005), 20–21.

29. Crary, *Techniques of the Observer*, 128.

30. This is precisely the appeal of those holograms witnessed in *Avatar, Iron Man 3*, and *Insurgent*, all of which, as chapters 3 and 4 showed, likewise explode screen-based interfaces into volumetric space while still retaining the social and technological functions associated with screens. 3D cinema is not navigable to the extent that these diegetic interfaces are shown to be, but it similarly enters our own perceptual space in a manner that seems irreconcilable with planar displays.

31. Philip Sandifer provides a helpful diagram of the intersection of the viewer's cone of vision with those portions of this vision in which the film takes place, in "Out of the Screen and into the Theater: 3-D Film as Demo," *Cinema Journal* 50, no. 3 (2011): 62–78, 67–68. Each of these zones offer perceptual quirks: elements in negative parallax, if they intersect with the edge of the frame, challenge binocular cues through what is often termed "edge violation," a problem solved through the use of "floating windows," or pseudoframes that exist in negative parallax space. See Barbara Flueckiger, "Aesthetics of Stereoscopic Cinema," *Projections* 6, no. 1 (2012): 101–22, 116–18. An in-depth discussion of the box-like shape of positive parallax space, and its own perceptual strangeness, will occur in chapter 8.

32. Yong Lui refers to this potential space as an "oval sphere," in *3D Cinematic Aesthetics and Storytelling* (New York: Palgrave, 2018).

33. Ron Burnett, "Transitions, Images, and Stereoscopic 3D Cinema," in *3D Cinema and Beyond*, ed. Dan Adler, Janine Marchessault, and Sanja Obradovic (Toronto: Public Books, 2013), 200–13, 206.

34. Stephen Prince, *Digital Visual Effects in Cinema: The Seduction of Reality* (New Brunswick, NJ: Rutgers University Press, 2012), 215–16, 209.

35. Sandifer, "Out of the Screen and Into the Theater," 68.

36. On novelty, see John Belton, "Digital 3D Cinema: Digital Cinema's Missing Novelty Phase," *Film History* 24, no. 2 (2012): 187–95; on destabilization, see Sandifer, "Out of the Screen and Into the Theater." The arguments of these scholars have been summarized in chapter 1.

37. Barbara Klinger, "Beyond Cheap Thrills: 3D Cinema Today, the Parallax Debates, and the 'Pop-Out,'" in *3D Cinema and Beyond*, ed. Dan Adler, Janine Marchessault, and Sanja Obradovic (Toronto: Public Books, 2013), 186–99, 197.

38. Kristen Whissel, "Parallax Effects: Epistemology, Affect, and Digital 3D Cinema," *Journal of Visual Culture* 15, no. 2 (2016): 233–49, 235.

39. Building on Panofsky's suggestion that some perspectival images seek to spill out in front of the frame, Ross proposes that, rather than a window metaphor, "in stereoscopic cinema it might be more apt to consider an open patio doors arrangement where plant fronds, leaves, and other objects trail through into our side of the frame" (*3D Cinema*, 112). See also Panofsky, *Perspective as Symbolic Form*, 56.

40. Alla Gadassik, "Anticipation of Contact: *Pina 3D* and Stereoscopic Cinematography," in *3D Cinema and Beyond*, ed. Dan Adler, Janine Marchessault, and Sanja Obradovic (Toronto: Public Books, 2013), 174–85, 178; Miriam Ross, *3D Cinema: Optical Illusions and Tactile Experiences* (New York: Palgrave Macmillan, 2015), 126. As Ross describes, this membrane creates a sense of shared space between viewer and film, bulging and receding according to dramatic and aesthetic requirements. This helpfully moves away from the concept of the screen

as something that is ruptured (or not) in 3D exhibition and rightly articulates 3D space as contoured and ever-present. To develop this idea, Ross evokes Giuliana Bruno's concept of the "field screen," a reading of the film image as a "habitable geographic space" (*3D Cinema*, 8). See Giuliana Bruno, *Atlas of Emotion: Journeys in Art, Architecture, and Film* (New York: Verso, 2002), 250.

41. See Deborah Thomas, *Reading Hollywood: Spaces and Meanings in American Film* (New York: Wallflower, 2001), chapter 3.

42. On this, see my "Variation within Stability: Digital 3D and Film Style," *Cinema Journal* 55, no. 1 (2015): 52–73.

43. Prince, *Digital Visual Effects in Cinema*, 208.

44. The privileging of the screen plane as the site of key attention is a technique that has become such a normalized aspect of digital 3D practice that depth values that might initially be arranged in alternative, less normalized ways are sometimes changed by editors and post-production personnel, who seek out a more safe and proven 3D aesthetic.

45. Commenting on the same phenomenon, Owen Weetch refers to it as "convergence racking," in *Expressive Spaces in Digital 3D Cinema* (Basingstoke: Palgrave, 2016), 89.

46. Cameron quoted in Ray Zone, *3-D Filmmakers: Conversations with Creators of Stereoscopic Motion Pictures* (Lanham, MD: Scarecrow, 2005), 143. Indeed, as we will see in chapter 8, Cameron and his crew's public emphasis on human physiology as a model for stereoscopic composition echoes proclamations made a century and a half earlier by David Brewster regarding the proper composition of stereocards. On this, see Robert J. Silverman, "The Stereoscope and Photographic Depiction in the 19th Century," *Technology and Culture* 34, no. 4 (1993): 729–56.

47. Prince, *Digital Visual Effects in Cinema*, 214.

48. David H. Fleming and William Brown, "A Skeuomorphic Cinema: Film Form, Content, and Criticism in the 'Post-Analogue' Era," *Fibreculture Journal* 24 (2015): http://twentyfour .fibreculturejournal.org/2015/06/04/fcj-176/ (accessed September 30, 2019).

49. See Lisa Purse, *Digital Imaging in Popular Cinema* (Edinburgh: Edinburgh University Press, 2013), 1–7; and Dan North, *Performing Illusions: Cinema, Special Effects, and the Virtual Actor* (London: Wallflower, 2008), 22. These artifacts also appear in video games such as *Battlefield 3* (2011) and *The Last of Us* (2013) and television programs such as *Supergirl* (2015–ongoing) and *The Expanse* (2015–ongoing).

50. Paul Becker, executive producer at conversion company Gener8, describes the employment of extreme negative parallax for lens "schmutz" in *300: Rise of an Empire* in exactly these terms: "Depth-wise we broke a lot of rules and placed lens schmutz far negative as though it landed on your glasses forcing you to look past it." Quoted in Ian Failes, "Inside the Battles of *300: Rise of an Empire*," fxguide, March 23, 2014, https://www.fxguide.com/featured/inside -the-battles-of-300-rise-of-an-empire/ (accessed September 30, 2019).

51. Miriam Ross explores stereoscopic flares in her blog post on "Star Trek Into Darkness," Cinema Lives Cinema Loves, May 10, 2013, https://miriamruthross.wordpress.com/2013/05/10 /star-trek-into-darkness/ (accessed September 30, 2019).

7. DISTORTION

1. Akira Mizuta Lippit, "Three Phantasies of Cinema—Reproduction, Mimesis, Annihilation," *Paragraph* 22, no. 3 (1999): 213–27, 221.

2. Sheldon Hall, "*Dial M for Murder*," *Film History* 26, no. 3 (2004): 243–55; William Paul, "Breaking the Fourth Wall: 'Belascoism,' Modernism and a 3-D *Kiss Me Kate*," *Film History* 16, no. 3 (2004): 229–42.

3. Lisa Purse, *Digital Imaging in Popular Cinema* (Edinburgh: Edinburgh University Press, 2013), 137–49; Scott Higgins, "3D in Depth: *Coraline, Hugo*, and a Sustainable Aesthetic," *Film History* 24, no. 2 (2012): 196–209, 206–7.

4. Caetlin Benson-Allott, "The *Chora* Line: RealD Incorporated," *South Atlantic Quarterly* 110, no. 3 (2011): 621–44; Miriam Ross, *3D Cinema: Optical Illusions and Tactile Experiences* (New York: Palgrave Macmillan, 2015); Owen Weetch, *Expressive Spaces in Digital 3D Cinema* (Basingstoke: Palgrave, 2016).

5. Michael Kerbel, "3-D or Not 3-D," *Film Comment* 16, no. 6 (1980): 11–20, 11.

6. Roger Ebert, "Why 3D Doesn't Work and Never Will. Case Closed," Roger Ebert's Journal, January 23, 2011, http://www.rogerebert.com/rogers-journal/why-3d-doesnt-work-and-never -will-case-closed (accessed September 30, 2019); Mark Kermode, *The Good, the Bad, and the Multiplex* (London: Random House, 2011).

7. On predigital misalignment, see Robert S Allison, Laurie M. Wilcox, and Ali Kazimi, "Perceptual Artefacts, Suspension of Disbelief, and Realism in Stereoscopic 3D Film," in *3D Cinema and Beyond*, ed. Dan Adler, Janine Marchessault, and Sanja Obradovic (Toronto: Public Books, 2013), 149–60, 150. On the absence of financial resources for image management, see Higgins, "3D in Depth," 199–200. As Matt Singer notes in a consumer guide, misalignment can also be the result of insufficiently maintained or supervised projection equipment, in "A Step-By-Step Consumer Guide to Good Theater Projection," Screen Crush, n.d., http://screencrush.com/consumer-guide-to-theater-projection/ (accessed September 30, 2019).

8. Jukka Häkkinen, Takashi Kawai, Jari Takatalo, Tuomas Leisti, Jenni Radun, Anni Hirsaho, and Göte Nyman, "Measuring Stereoscopic Image Quality Experience with Interpretation Based Quality Methodology," *Proceedings of SPIE* 6808 (2008): https://www.spiedigitallibrary .org/conference-proceedings-of-spie/6808/1/Measuring-stereoscopic-image-quality -experience-with-interpretation-based-quality-methodology/10.1117/12.760935.short?SSO=1 (accessed September 30, 2019).

9. Such bodily appeals might encourage us to associate cinematic 3D with the "fairground." Certainly, the medium's use in horror, exploitation, and pornographic films throughout its history underline this link with nonnarrative, bodily experiences.

10. Rod Bantjes, "Reading Stereoviews: The Aesthetics of Monstrous Space," *History of Photography* 39, no. 1 (2015): 33–55, 35.

11. John Plunkett, "Depth, Colour, Movement: Embodied Vision and the Stereoscope," in *Multimedia Histories: From the Magic Lantern to the Internet*, ed. James Lyons and John Plunkett (Exeter: Exeter University Press, 2007), 117–31, 119.

12. Colette Colligan, "Stereograph," *Victorian Review* 34, no. 1 (Spring 2008): 75–82, 78; see also Roland Barthes, "The Reality Effect," in *The Realist Novel*, ed. Dennis Walder (London: Routledge, 1996), 258–61.

13. Isobel Armstrong, *Victorian Glassworlds: Glass Culture and the Imagination, 1830–1880* (Oxford: Oxford University Press, 2008), 341, 339.

14. Jonathan Crary, *Techniques of the Observer* (Cambridge, MA: MIT Press, 1990), 122.

15. John Plunkett, "'Feeling Seeing': Touch, Vision and the Stereoscope," *History of Photography* 37, no. 4 (2013): 389–96, 396.

16. Aloïs Riegl, *Late Roman Art Industry*, trans. Rolf Winkes (Rome: Giorgio Bretschneider Editore, 1985).

17. Laura U. Marks, *The Skin of the Film* (Durham, NC: Duke University Press, 2000), 162.

18. David Trotter, "Stereoscopy: Modernism and the 'Haptic,'" *Critical Quarterly* 46, no. 4 (2004): 38–58, 48.

19. Crary, *Techniques of the Observer*, 123–24.

20. Crary, 125.

21. Crary, 125. Crary is building on the words of David Brewster, in *The Stereoscope: Its History, Theory, and Construction* (London: John Murray, 1856), 53.

22. Crary, *Techniques of the Observer*, 126.

23. Rosalind Krauss, "Photography's Discursive Spaces: Landscape/View," *Art Journal* 42, no. 4 (1982): 311–19, 314.

24. Oliver Wendell Holmes, "Sun-Painting and Sun-Sculpture: With a Stereoscopic Trip Across the Atlantic," *Atlantic Monthly*, July 1861, 13–29, 14–15, emphasis added. Available at http://www.gutenberg.org/cache/epub/11154/pg11154.html (accessed September 30, 2019).

25. Oliver Wendell Holmes, "The Stereoscope and the Stereograph," in *Classic Essays on Photography*, ed. Alan Trachtenberg (Stony Creek, CT: Leete's Island, 1980), 71–82, 77.

26. Jib Fowles, "Stereography and the Standardization of Vision," *Journal of American Culture* 17, no. 2 (1994): 89–93, 89.

27. Krauss, "Photography's Discursive Spaces," 314.

28. Bantjes, "Reading Stereoviews," 34.

29. Marks, *The Skin of the Film*, 162; Ross, *3D Cinema*, 24. 3D might allow for contrastingly more coherent compositional approaches than the intercultural haptic cinema Marks describes in her book, but it nonetheless overpowers and physiologically stimulates in similar ways.

30. Ross, *3D Cinema*, 20. Nanna Verhoeff also describes 3D films—and in particular *Cave of Forgotten Dreams* (2010)—as operating in a haptic visual mode, in "Surface Explorations: 3D Moving Images as Cartographies of Time," *Espacio, Tiempo Y Forma, Serie VII, Historia del Arte* 4 (2016): 71–91, 78–79.

31. André Bazin, "Will Cinema Scope Save the Film Industry?," in *Bazin at Work: Major Essays and Reviews from the Forties and Fifties*, ed. Bert Cardullo, trans. Alain Piette and Bert Cardullo (New York: Routledge, 1997), 77–92, 88.

32. Sergei Eisenstein, "Stereoscopic Films," in *Notes of a Film Director*, trans. X. Danko (London: Lawrence & Wishart, 1959), 129–37, 132.

33. Ivor Montagu, "The Third Dimension: The Future of Film?," in *The Cinema*, ed. Roger Manvell (New York: Arno, 1978), 132–39, 137.

34. Montagu, "The Third Dimension," 137.

35. Barbara Flueckiger, "Aesthetics of Stereoscopic Cinema," *Projections* 6, no. 1 (2012): 101–22, 106; Lance Duerfahrd, "For Your Glasses Only: *The Stewardesses* and Sex in Three Dimensions," in *3D Cinema and Beyond*, ed. Dan Adler, Janine Marchessault, and Sanja Obradovic (Toronto: Public Books, 2013), 161–71, 163. Duerfahrd's focus on a low-budget 3D pornographic feature (1969's *The Stewardesses*) leads him to directly contrast the amorphous visual oddities of this film with the "perfected digital image" of 3D cinema in the 2010s, but I propose that the strangeness of 3D's visual world he identifies remains latently in even the most high budget digital production (and, indeed, becomes overt in films like *Clash of the Titans*).

36. Benson-Allott, "The *Chora* Line," 623, 628.

37. Flueckiger explains something of the genesis of ghastliness, but does so with a visually normative agenda, articulating 3D's strangeness as a series of recurring "aesthetic problems" that the medium must "solve." Flueckiger, "Aesthetics of Stereoscopic Cinema," 105.

38. Bantjes, "Reading Stereoviews," 35.

39. Although the film is understood auteuristically, interviews with director of photography Fabrice Aragno highlight his own extensive involvement in planning, shooting, and editing some of the film's most notable 3D effects. See, for instance, Paul Dallas, "1+1=3 [interview with Fabrice Aragno]," *Film Comment* 50, no. 6 (2014), additional issue content available at http://www.filmcomment.com/article/fabrice-aragno-interview/ (accessed September 30, 2019).

40. When Kent Jones states, "I cannot give you an accurate assessment of the 'content' of *Adieu au langage*," he effectively speaks for many critics, in "Empire of Light: Three Highlights from Cannes Move in Poetic and Painterly Directions," *Film Comment* 50, no. 4 (2014): 52–54, 53.

41. Yaron Dahan, "Cinema's Zion: The Third Dimension," Mubi, June 9, 2015, https://mubi.com/notebook/posts/cinemas-zion-the-third-dimension (accessed September 30, 2019).

42. David Bordwell, "*Adieu au langage*: 2 + 2 X 3D," Observations on Film Art, September 7, 2014, http://www.davidbordwell.net/blog/2014/09/07/adieu-au-langage-2-2-x-3d/ (accessed September 30, 2019); see also David Bordwell and Kristin Thompson, "Bwana Beowulf," Observations on Film Art, December 7, 2007, http://www.davidbordwell.net/blog/2007/12/07/bwana-beowulf/ (accessed September 30, 2019).

43. Daniel Fairfax, "Montage in 3D Cinema: The Case of Jean-Luc Godard's *Adieu au langage*," in *Cinema Journal (Afterthoughts and Postscripts)* 54, no. 2 (2015): https://cmstudies.site-ym.com/?CJ_after542_fairfax (accessed September 30, 2019).

44. Miriam Ross, "Godard's Stereoscopic Illusions: Against a Total Cinema," *Screening the Past* 41 (2016): http://www.screeningthepast.com/2016/12/godards-stereoscopic-illusions-against-a-total-cinema (accessed September 30, 2019).

45. Andrew Utterson, "Goodbye to Cinema? Jean-Luc Godard's *Adieu au langage* (2014) as 3D Images at the Edge of History," *Studies in French Cinema* 19, no. 1 (2016): 69–84.

46. Andrew Utterson, "Practice Makes Imperfect: Technology and the Creative Imperfections of Jean-Luc Godard's Three-Dimensional (3D) Cinema," *Quarterly Review of Film and Video* 34, no. 3 (2017): 295–308, 295.

47. Amy Taubin, "Dog Days," *Film Comment* 50, no. 4 (2014): 48–51, 48; similar statements can be found in David Bordwell, "Say Hello to *Goodbye to Language*," Observations on Film Art, November 2, 2014, http://www.davidbordwell.net/blog/2014/11/02/say-hello-to-goodby-to-language/ (accessed September 30, 2019); and Fairfax, "Montage in 3D Cinema."

48. Florence Jacobowitz and Richard Lippe, "Godard's *Adieu au langage*," *CineAction* 96 (2015): 24–25, 24.

49. On this trait in other films by Godard, see Douglas Morrey, *Jean-Luc Godard* (Manchester: Manchester University Press, 2005), 25–28.

50. Bordwell, "Say Hello to *Goodbye to Language*." Such presumptions around normative 3D speak closely to this scholar's own (cognitive, narrative) preoccupations, but they are far from controversial, as we saw in chapter 4.

51. Bantjes, "Reading Stereoviews," 54; see also 45.

52. Similarly, shots filming the glass of a shower cubicle as it is covered with water, or looking through a car's windscreen as it is splattered with rain, feature divergent droplet patterns across left and right eyes, in marked contrast to the carefully aligned postproduction "schmutz" and artifacts explored in the previous chapter. Julian Murphet proposes that Godard must have sought out these "inevitable discrepancies between the distinct patterns of refracted light being focused by each of the two lenses," such are their abundance throughout the film, in "Godard's Stereopticon," *Screening the Past* 41 (2016): http://www.screeningthepast.com/2016/12/godards-stereopticon/#_ednref1 (accessed September 30, 2019).

53. Crary, *Techniques of the Observer*, 125–26.

54. Hito Steyerl, "In Defense of the Poor Image," *e-flux journal* 10 (2009): http://www.e-flux.com/journal/in-defense-of-the-poor-image/ (accessed September 30, 2019).

55. Fairfax, "Montage in 3D Cinema."

56. Dallas, "1+1=3."

57. Both brief clips focus on physical trauma visited on a female character (a vampire's immolation in *Fright Night*, a swimmer being skinned alive in *Piranha*), an emphasis that deserves further discussion for which there is unfortunately not room here.

58. Bryant Frazer, "Five Ways Jean-Luc Godard Breaks the 3D Rules in *Farewell to Language*," Studio Daily, October 3, 2014, http://www.studiodaily.com/2014/10/five-ways-jean-luc-godard-breaks-the-3d-rules-in-farewell-to-language/ (accessed September 30, 2019). The rigs used on the film (made by Aragno) placed each camera parallel to the other, rather than angling them toward one other so they converged on a particular depth plane in a given shot; see Fairfax, "Montage in 3D Cinema." Instead, decisions around convergence and the scale of depth and volume were left for the editing room—something Bordwell (in "Say Hello to *Goodbye to Language*") affirms is very much in line with Godard's existing reliance on postproduction.

59. Quoted in Fairfax, "Montage in 3D Cinema."

60. Nico Baumbach, "Starting Over," *Film Comment* 50, no. 6 (2014): 34–41, 37.

61. Miriam Ross, "*Goodbye to Language* 3D: Painful Sight," Cinema Lives Cinema Loves, August 6, 2014, https://miriamruthross.wordpress.com/2014/08/06/goodbye-to-language-3d-painful-sight/ (accessed September 30, 2019).

62. Bantjes, "Reading Stereoviews," 49.

63. Bantjes, 55.

64. Richard Corliss, "Box-Office Weekend: Cash of the *Titans*," *Time*, April 4, 2010, http://content.time.com/time/arts/article/0,8599,1977696,00.html (accessed September 30, 2019).

65. Daniel Engber, "Greek Tragedy: Why Is the 3-D So Bad in *Clash of the Titans*?," Slate, April 1, 2010, http://www.slate.com/articles/arts/culturebox/2010/04/greek_tragedy.html (accessed September 30, 2019).

66. Dana Stevens, "Half Mortal, Totally Stupid," Slate, April 1, 2010, http://www.slate.com/culture/2010/04/clash-of-the-titans-reviewed.html (accessed September 30, 2019).

67. Corliss, "Box-Office Weekend." See also Steve Persall's comment that the movie was "filmed with conventional 2-D cameras" and converted "into 3-D and higher ticket prices," in "*Clash of the Titans*: A Lame Remake in Lame 3-D," *Tampa Bay Times*, March 30, 2010, http://www.tampabay.com/features/movies/review-clash-of-the-titans-a-lame-remake-in-lame-3-d/1083873 (accessed April 18, 2018).

68. Mike Ryan, "Louis Leterrier: 'Now You See Me' Director on the Problems with *The Incredible Hulk* and *Clash of the Titans*," Huffington Post, May 28, 2013, http://www.huffingtonpost.com/2013/05/28/louis-leterrier-now-you-see-me_n_3333311.html (accessed September 30, 2019). As Mike Seymour describes in his article on conversion, "If *Clash of the Titans* taught the industry any overall lesson, it is that stereo conversion should not be a process 'tacked' on the end of a film's production," in "Art of Stereo Conversion: 2D to 3D—2012," fxguide, May 8, 2012, https://www.fxguide.com/featured/art-of-stereo-conversion-2d-to-3d-2012/ (accessed September 30, 2019). It should be noted that Prime Focus World, as already mentioned in these pages, continue to convert major blockbusters, finding greater success and critical prestige with the likes of *Gravity* and *Edge of Tomorrow*, among many others. A description of their conversion of *Clash of the Titans* can be found in Jody Duncan, "Gods and Monsters," *Cinefex* 122 (2010): 96–119. Somewhat unusually, they did not just create a seond-eye view to compliment the planar footage, but went about generating both left- and right-eye views: "We generally establish the original plate as the right eye, and then generate a new left eye,' said [Chris] Bond [president of Prime Focus at the time], 'but on this project we took another approach, which was to use the original photography as the center camera. So imagine there is a third eye between your two eyes. We do a right eye and a left eye, slightly offset from the position of that center eye or center camera. In the computer, [conversion software] View-D interpolates between those areas to fill in the blanks as it were. We did this process for all 1,900 shots in the movie." Duncan, "Gods and Monsters," 118–119.

69. Seymour, "Art of Stereo Conversion."

70. Crary, *Techniques of the Observer*, 125.
71. Bordwell, "*Adieu au langage.*"
72. Pam Cook, "Within and Without: The Great Gatsby's 3D Experience," Fashionintofilm, June 2, 2013, https://fashionintofilm.wordpress.com/2013/06/02/within-and-without-the -great-gatsbys-3d-experience/ (accessed September 30, 2019).
73. Crary, *Techniques of the Observer*, 125.
74. Ross, "*Goodbye to Language* 3D."
75. Jonathan Romney, "Film of the Week: Goodbye to Language," *Film Comment*, October 29, 2014, https://www.filmcomment.com/blog/film-of-the-week-goodbye-to-language/ (accessed September 30, 2019).
76. Nick Jones, "Variation within Stability: Digital 3D and Film Style," *Cinema Journal* 55, no. 1 (2015): 52–73, 71.

8. INTIMACY

1. Miriam Ross, *3D Cinema: Optical Illusions and Tactile Experiences* (New York: Palgrave Macmillan, 2015), 1.
2. Ross, *3D Cinema*, 2, emphasis added.
3. Stephen Prince, *Digital Visual Effects in Cinema: The Seduction of Reality* (New Brunswick, NJ: Rutgers University Press, 2012), 217–18.
4. Ron Burnett, "Transitions, Images, and Stereoscopic 3D Cinema," in *3D Cinema and Beyond*, ed. Dan Adler, Janine Marchessault, and Sanja Obradovic (Toronto: Public Books, 2013), 200–13, 203.
5. André Bazin, "*The House of Wax*: Scare Me . . . In Depth!," in *André Bazin's New Media*, ed. and trans. Dudley Andrew (Oakland: University of California Press, 2014), 251–53, 253, 251.
6. Quoted in Roger Ebert, "Why 3D Doesn't Work and Never Will. Case Closed," Roger Ebert's Journal, January 23, 2011, http://www.rogerebert.com/rogers-journal/why-3d-doesnt-work -and-never-will-case-closed (accessed September 30, 2019).
7. Quoted in Adam Chitwood, "Christopher Nolan Talks 3D, Why He Shoots IMAX His Approach to CGI, and Much More in Fascinating DGA Interview," Collider, April 13, 2012, http://collider.com/christopher-nolan-3d-imax-interview/ (accessed September 30, 2019).
8. Charles Wheatstone, *The Scientific Papers of Sir Charles Wheatstone* (London: Taylor & Francis, 1879), 225–26.
9. Robert J. Silverman, "The Stereoscope and Photographic Depiction in the Nineteenth Century," *Technology and Culture* 34, no. 4 (1993): 755–56.
10. Sheenagh Pietrobruno, "The Stereoscope and the Miniature," *Early Popular Visual Culture* 9, no. 3 (2011): 171–90, 171.
11. Oliver Wendell Holmes, "The Stereoscope and the Stereograph," in *Classic Essays on Photography*, ed. Alan Trachtenberg (Stony Creek, CT: Leete's Island, 1980), 71–82.
12. Holmes, "The Stereoscope and the Stereograph," 78. Wanting to justify this effect as an accurate reflection of embodied sight (in light with his positivist agenda), Holmes offers only insubstantial defences of such impressions of diminution. He argues that our awareness of the distance of certain objects can conceal how small they literally appear within our vision—a proximate tack may conceal an entire distant mountain, for instance. See also his comments on miniaturization in his "Sun-Painting and Sun-Sculpture: With a Stereoscopic Trip Across the Atlantic," *Atlantic Monthly*, July 1861, 13–29, http://www.gutenberg.org/cache /epub/11154/pg11154.html (accessed September 30, 2019).
13. Eadweard Muybridge, *Animals in Motion*, ed. Lewis S. Brown (New York: Dover, 1957), 14, emphasis added. It may be the case that Muybridge's reference to miniaturization—although

here made specifically in relation to stereoscopic presentation—pointed to a broader impression of smallness produced by these motion studies that also occurred when they were observed in a planar zoetrope or his later planar zoopraxinoscope. However, it is telling that he only refers directly to the miniaturizing effect in relation to stereoscopic presentation.

14. Brooke Belisle, "The Dimensional Image: Overlaps in Stereoscopic, Cinematic, and Digital Depth," *Film Criticism* 37, no. 3/1 (2013): 117–37, 122–26.

15. Silverman, "The Stereoscope and Photographic Depiction," 739.

16. Silverman, 742.

17. Jonathan Crary, *Techniques of the Observer* (Cambridge, MA: MIT Press, 1990), 24–125.

18. In his categorization of such stereocard scenes, Leon Gurevitch describes the prevalence of mammoth industrial objects and world wonders both natural ("mountains, valleys, volcanoes") and unnatural ("great cities, giant canals"), in "The Stereoscopic Attraction: Three-Dimensional Imaging and the Spectacular Paradigm 1850–2013," *Convergence* 19, no. 4 (2013): 396–405, 398.

19. F. Marion, *The Wonders of Optics*, trans. Charles W. Quin (London: Sampson Low, Son & Marston, 1868), 215.

20. Félix Drouin, *The Stereoscope and Stereoscopic Photography*, trans. Matthew Surface (London: Percy Lund, 1890), 109–10.

21. Changing the angles of convergence of the two cameras can produce related effects: the further away they converge (i.e., the more parallel they are), then the more perceptually close is that which is in front of the point of convergence; conversely, if converging at a tight angle, much of the stereoscopy of a scene recedes in positive parallax.

22. Those photographers that did use standard, human-centric interocular gaps for such distant views often included elements in the foreground in order to accentuate stereoscopic values. Holmes amusingly summarizes this tendency as a remarkable ability for the stereo-photographer, wherever they are, to find a clothesline and position it in the foreground of their scene, in "The Stereoscope and the Stereograph," 80. Looking forward to cinema, Ivor Montagu's account of his visit to the Moscow stereokino in the late 1940s suggests that many of the films showed there engaged in similar strategies, as he complains that "there was too much surrender to picture postcard sight-seeing with an obvious foreground foliage bordering the valley view." Ivor Montagu, "The Third Dimension: The Future of Film?," in *The Cinema*, ed. Roger Manvell (New York: Arno, 1978), 132–39, 139. This kind of "foliage" has a historical precursor in the use of *faux terrain* in the eighteenth- and nineteenth-century panorama, elements of constructed scenery to add depth impressions (and so further realism) to the highly detailed but planar (albeit curved) canvasses that were the main attraction of the display.

23. Pietrobruno, "The Stereoscope and the Miniature," 174; see also Hermann von Helmholtz, *Treatise on Physiological Optics*, vol. 3, ed. and trans. James P. C. Southall (Birmingham, AL: Leslie B. Adams, 1985), 312.

24. The series from which this Sphinx is taken is particularly telling, as it offers a tour of Egypt in which many of the scenes are rendered hyperstereoscopically, from palace interiors to gardens to mountainsides. This series is available in the Bill Douglas Cinema Museum, University of Exeter, items 48342–48346 inclusive.

25. Wheatstone, *Scientific Papers*, 271.

26. Susan Stewart, *On Longing: Narratives of the Miniature, the Gigantic, the Souvenir, the Collection* (Durham, NC: Duke University Press, 1993), 65.

27. Claude Lévi-Strauss, *The Savage Mind* (Letchworth: Garden City, 1966), 23. He goes on: "Being quantitatively diminished, [an object] seems to us qualitatively simplified. . . . And even if this is an illusion, the point of the procedure is to create or sustain the illusion, which

gratifies the intelligence and gives rise to a sense of pleasure which can already be called aesthetic on these grounds alone." (23–24).

28. Pietrobruno, "The Stereoscope and the Miniature," 178.

29. Pietrobruno, 188.

30. Silverman, "The Stereoscope and Photographic Depiction," 748; John Plunkett, "Depth, Colour, Movement: Embodied Vision and the Stereoscope," in *Multimedia Histories: From the Magic Lantern to the Internet*, ed. James Lyons and John Plunkett (Exeter: Exeter University Press, 2007), 117–31, 121.

31. Crary, *Techniques of the Observer*, 125.

32. Albert E. Osborne, "Remarkable Results from Stereographs," in *Italy Through the Stereoscope: Journeys in and About Italian Cities*, ed. James C. Egbert (New York: Underwood & Underwood, 1900), 571–89, 576.

33. David Trotter, "Stereoscopy: Modernism and the "Haptic,"' *Critical Quarterly* 46, no. 4 (2004): 38–58, 40.

34. Holmes, "The Stereoscope and the Stereograph," 75.

35. Nicholas P. Holmes and Charles Spence, "The Body Schema and the Multisensory Representation(s) of Peripersonal Space," *Cognitive Processing* 5, no. 2 (2004): 94–105.

36. Rosalind Krauss, "Photography's Discursive Spaces: Landscape/View," *Art Journal* 42, no. 4 (1982): 311–19, 314.

37. John Mack, *The Art of Small Things* (Cambridge, MA: Harvard University Press, 2007), 5.

38. Jib Fowles, "Stereography and the Standardization of Vision," *Journal of American Culture* 17, no. 2 (1994): 89–93, 91.

39. See Laura Forsberg, "Nature's Invisibilia: The Victorian Microscope and the Miniature Fairy," *Victorian Studies* 57, no. 4 (2015): 638–66; and Nick Jones, "The Expansive and Proximate Scales of Immersive Media," *International Journal on Stereo and Immersive Media* 2, no. 2 (2019): 36–49.

40. Crary, *Techniques of the Observer*, 133. Similarly, Victor Flores proposes that stereoscopy's intimacy "anticipates a phenomenon of personal media" that finds full expression in today's "small screens and headsets," but that suffered from cultural instability during the twentieth century thanks to its inappropriate use in mass audience contexts like cinematic exhibition. Victor Flores, "The Animation of the Photographic: Stereoscopy and Cinema. The Experiments of Aurélio da Paz," *Early Popular Visual Culture* 14, no. 1 (2016): 87–106, 103–4.

41. Scott Higgins, "3D in Depth: *Coraline, Hugo*, and a Sustainable Aesthetic," *Film History* 24, no. 2 (2012): 196–209, 200.

42. Barbara Flueckiger, "Aesthetics of Stereoscopic Cinema," *Projections* 6 no. 1 (2012): 101–22, 107.

43. This shot is a digital effect, and so the hyperstereo has been created through digitally rendering twinned images that have a wider interocular, but the same could have been achieved in both 3D conversion and in native shooting (depending on the capabilities of the 3D rig being used).

44. On the perceptual rescaling that occurs in moments of negative parallax, *House of Wax*'s street entertainer offers another useful example. His paddleballs may appear to bounce out of the screen and near to us, but they do not simply "emerge"; if they did, they would be perceptually several feet in size (depending on the size of the screen onto which they are being projected). Instead, they appear more like paddleballs—fist-sized, not basketball-sized. As they enter negative parallax, they simultaneously reduce in size thanks to their proximity. This may seem a minor detail, but it again highlights the way the stereo continuum operates in ways quite different from our embodied experience of space and vision, and how size is not a stable value.

45. David Bordwell, "Coraline, Cornered," Observations on Film Art, February 23, 2009, http://www.davidbordwell.net/blog/2009/02/23/coraline-cornered/ (accessed September 30, 2019).

46. Higgins, "3D in Depth," 207; Prince, *Digital Visual Effects in Cinema*, 215; Sarah Atkinson, "Stereoscopic-3D Storytelling—Rethinking the Conventions, Grammar, and Aesthetics of a New Medium," *Journal of Media Practice* 12, no. 2 (2011): 139–56, 149; Jesko Jockenhövel, "What Is It if It's Not Real? It's Genre—Early Color Film and Digital 3D," *Cinemascope* 7, no. 15 (2011): 1–14, 6–8.

47. Higgins, "3D in Depth," 207.

48. Higgins, 200.

49. On this scene, see both Ross, *3D in Depth*, 164; and Alla Gadassik, "Anticipation of Contact: *Pina 3D* and Stereoscopic Cinematography," in *3D Cinema and Beyond*, ed. Dan Adler, Janine Marchessault, and Sanja Obradovic (Toronto: Public Books, 2013), 174–85, 183.

50. Nicholas J. Wade, *Brewster and Wheatstone on Vision* (London: Academic Press, 1983), 221.

51. Brian Winston, *Technologies of Seeing: Photography, Cinematography, and Television* (London: BFI, 1996), 111.

52. Kristen Whissel, "Parallax Effects: Epistemology, Affect, and Digital 3D Cinema," *Journal of Visual Culture* 15, no. 2 (2016): 233–49, 244.

53. Trotter, "Stereoscopy," 51.

54. Colette Colligan, "Stereograph," *Victorian Review* 34, no. 1 (2008), 75–82, 77.

55. Lynda Nead, "STRIP," *Early Popular Visual Culture* 3, no. 2 (2005): 135–50, 138.

56. Nead, "STRIP."

57. On *The Stewardesses*, see R. M. Hayes, *3-D Movies: A History and Filmography of Stereoscopic Cinema* (Jefferson, NC: McFarland, 1989), 303; and Lance Duerfahrd, "For Your Glasses Only: *The Stewardesses* and Sex in Three Dimensions," in *3D Cinema and Beyond*, ed. Dan Adler, Janine Marchessault, and Sanja Obradovic (Toronto: Public Books, 2013), 161–71, 162. For an overview of the production of X-rated 3D features in the early 1970s, see Daniel L. Symmes, "3-D: Cinema's Slowest Revolution," *American Cinematographer* 55, no. 4 (1974), 406–7, 434, 456–57, 478–85, 482–83.

58. Noé offhandedly refers to it in one interview as "that funny shot with the penis coming," hinting at its—to him—lighthearted nature. Quoted in Amir Ganjavie, "Love's Astral Spy: An Interview with Gaspar Noé," Mubi, November 4, 2015, https://mubi.com/notebook/posts/love-s-astral-spy-an-interview-with-gasper-noe (accessed September 30, 2019). It should be noted that, even though this moment offers the pinnacle/nadir of the "comin-at-ya" 3D approach, the director's previous *Enter the Void*, a 2D production and release, featured a similar to-camera ejaculation (in another scene *Love* even reuses a CG shot of sexual penetration from this earlier film).

59. Colligan describes how such stereocards are "unconcerned with setting or props" and seem to offer bodies and bodily acts that are marked with "few indicators of social, economic, or moral status," in "Stereograph," 76. For her, these cards describe sex wholeheartedly and even pathologically, at the expense of all other visual material. However, even the tightly focused stereocard upon which Colligan focuses somehow manages to feature prominent mise-en-scène: diamond-patterned wallpaper on the left, and a phallic, highly sculpted part of the chair upon which one of the lovers sit.

60. Duerfahrd, "For Your Glasses Only," 168–69. Of note in relation to this film and its strange 3D effects is Harold L. Layer's description of portions of it as "semi-abstract," and as traces of "new constructed realities that exist only in the imagination of the stereo artist," in "Stereo Kinematics: The Merging of Time and Space in the Cinema," *American Cinematographer* 55, no. 4 (1974): 438–41, 439.

61. The film's visual language, for all that it echoes similar following shots from Noé's previous films *Enter the Void* and *Irreversible*, does not engage in the kinds of swooping, often woozy aerial explorations found in those other films. This is perhaps surprising, given the director's stated enjoyment of the use of 3D to create a "visual rollercoaster" effect in films like *Gravity*: see Matthew Barney and Gaspar Noé (with Sabine Russ), "Matthew Barney and Gaspar Noé," *BOMB* 127 (2014): https://bombmagazine.org/articles/matthew-barney-and-gaspar-noé-1/ (accessed September 30, 2019).

62. Quoted in Dave Calhoun, "Gaspar Noé on Shooting Real Sex (in 3D!) for New Movie *Love* [interview]," Timeout.com, November 17, 2015, http://www.timeout.com/london/film/gaspar-noe-on-shooting-real-sex-in-3d-for-new-movie-love (accessed September 30, 2019).

63. Colligan, "Stereograph," 78.

64. John Plunkett, "Depth, Colour, Movement: Embodied Vision and the Stereoscope," in *Multimedia Histories: From the Magic Lantern to the Internet*, ed. James Lyons and John Plunkett (Exeter: Exeter University Press, 2007): 117–31, 120.

65. Gavin Adams, "Duchamp's Erotic Stereoscopic Exercises," *Anais do Museu Paulista: História e Cultura Material* 23, no. 2 (2015): http://www.scielo.br/scielo.php?script=sci_arttext&pid=S0101-47142015000200165&lng=en&tlng=en (accessed September 30, 2019).

66. As Colligan outlines, this means that the stereoscope's relationship with pornography in the late nineteenth century offers more than just a trace of how the latter alights upon new media in its search for fresh avenues of dissemination, but is actually related to the latter's peculiar form of optics, in "Stereoscope," 76. On this relationship between pornography and new media, see Laurence O'Toole, *Pornocopia: Porn, Sex, Technology, and Desire* (London: Serpent's Tail, 1998), 274; and Linda Williams, *Screening Sex* (Durham, NC: Duke University Press, 2008), 375.

67. Williams, *Screening Sex*, 1–2.

68. Williams, 15–17.

69. Jay David Bolter and Richard Grusin, *Remediation: Understanding New Media* (Cambridge, MA: MIT Press, 2000), 37.

70. Winston, *Technologies of Seeing*, 111.

71. Noé himself points to this facet of 3D when asked why he used the format: "The use of three-dimensional images provides the impression of capturing a moment from the past.... Because the movie connects to the story of a lost love, I had the feeling that 3D would provide the audience with a much better sense of identification with the main character and his nostalgic state of mind." Quoted in Ganjavie, "Love's Astral Spy."

72. Quoted in Anon, "*Love* [Press Kit]," Wild Bunch International Sales, n.d., https://www.wildbunch.biz/movie/love/ (accessed September 30, 2019).

73. This link with history is further emphasised by the presence of the *Flesh for Frankenstein* poster in the background of the stereoviews.

74. Nead, "STRIP," 138.

75. The same effect—inserting diegetically taken 3D photographs as side-by-side pairs—is used in the 3D album film *One More Time with Feeling* (2016), which shares with *Love* stereographer and cinematographer Benoît Debie.

76. Quoted in "*Love* [Press Kit]."

77. While the mise-en-scène features numerous windows, these usually look across at other nearby buildings or down at construction sites.

78. Charles Baudelaire, "The Modern Public and Photography," in *Classic Essays on Photography*, ed. Alan Trachtenberg (New Haven, CT: Leete's Island, 1980), 83–90, 87.

79. Nead, "STRIP," 142.

80. See, for instance, one reviewer's droll complaint that the "copulation is filmed in 3-D, while the copulators are written in 1-D." David Lewis, "*Love*: One-Dimensional Characters Have Sex in 3-D," *San Francisco Chronicle*, November 5, 2015, http://www.sfgate.com/movies/article /Love-One-dimensional-characters-have-sex-6610750.php (accessed September 30, 2019).

CONCLUSION

1. Jonathan Crary, *Techniques of the Observer* (Cambridge, MA: MIT Press, 1990), 2.

2. Henri Lefebvre, *The Production of Space*, trans. Donald Nicholson-Smith (Oxford: Blackwell, 1991), 47–48.

3. On these examples, see Susan Sontag, *On Photography* (London: Penguin, 1979); and Erwin Panofsky, *Perspective as Symbolic Form*, trans. Christopher S. Wood (New York: Zone, 1991). Crary's *Techniques of the Observer* is of course also a key text in this regard, while Wolfgang Schivelbusch too offers a useful account of the ways in which the dissemination of railway travel and other industrial processes changed visual perception in *The Railway Journey: The Industrialization of Time and Space in the Nineteenth Century* (Oakland: University of California Press, 2014).

4. Lefebvre, *The Production of Space*, 25. Lefebvre famously asserts here that this "common-sense" Euclidean space was "shattered" in 1910 thanks to new representational systems and technologies. Nonetheless, he reminds us that a perspectival-based code of realism could not "disappear in a puff of smoke without leaving any trace in our consciousness, knowledge or educational methods"—and indeed he understands this model of space to remain as a crucial undergirding of abstract space in the twentieth century.

5. David Kirby, "The Future Is Now: Diegetic Prototypes and the Role of Popular Films in Generating Real-world Technological Development," *Social Studies of Science* 40, no. 1 (2010): 41–70.

6. This is true regardless of the provenance of the 3D: films might be native productions advertised as major stereoscopic productions (*Transformers: The Last Knight* [2017]); converted to 3D only for specific global territories (*RoboCop* and *Noah* [2014] and *Jason Bourne* [2016]); or conversions of what were previously not 3D films (*I, Robot* [2004; rereleased 2012] and *The Last Emperor* [1987; rereleased 2014]). But, in any case, a latent stereoscopic continuum is employed in the 3D version that makes it entirely distinctive.

7. Laura Burd Schiavo, "From Phantom Image to Perfect Vision: Physiological Optics, Commercial Photography, and the Popularization of the Stereoscope," in *New Media, 1740–1915*, ed. Lisa Gitelman and Geoffrey B. Pingree (Cambridge, MA: MIT Press, 2003), 113–138; Rod Bantjes, "Reading Stereoviews: The Aesthetics of Monstrous Space," *History of Photography* 39, no. 1 (2015): 33–55, 35.

8. Bantjes, "Reading Stereoviews," 35.

BIBLIOGRAPHY

2001: A Space Odyssey. MGM, 1968.

2012. Columbia Pictures, 2009.

300: Rise of an Empire. Warner Bros./Legendary Entertainment, 2014.

3x3D. Fundação Cidade de Guimarães, 2013.

The Abyss. Twentieth Century Fox, 1989.

Adams, Gavin. "Duchamp's Erotic Stereoscopic Exercises." *Anais do Museu Paulista: História e Cultura Material* 23, no. 2 (2015): https://www.scielo.br/scielo.php?script=sci_arttext&pid=S0101-47142015000200165 (accessed September 30, 2019).

Alberti, Leon Battista. *On Painting*. Translated by Cecil Grayson. London: Penguin, 1972.

Alice in Wonderland. Walt Disney Pictures, 2010.

Allen, Antoine. "The 'Three Black Teenagers' Search Shows It Is Society, Not Google, That is Racist." *Guardian*, June 10, 2016, https://www.theguardian.com/commentisfree/2016/jun/10/three-black-teenagers-google-racist-tweet (accessed September 30, 2019).

Allison, Robert S., Laurie M. Wilcox, and Ali Kazimi. "Perceptual Artefacts, Suspension of Disbelief, and Realism in Stereoscopic 3D Film." In *3D Cinema and Beyond*, edited by Dan Adler, Janine Marchessault, and Sanja Obradovic, 149–60. Toronto: Public Books, 2013.

The Amazing Spider-Man 2. Columbia Pictures, 2014.

Amityville 3D. De Laurentiis Entertainment Group, 1983.

Andrejevic, Mark. *iSpy: Surveillance and Power in the Interactive Era*. Lawrence: University of Kansas Press, 2007.

Anglin, Sallie. "Generative Motion: Queer Ecology and *Avatar*." *Journal of Popular Culture* 48, no. 2 (2015): 341–54.

Ant-Man. Marvel Studios, 2015.

Armstrong, Isobel. *Victorian Glassworlds: Glass Culture and the Imagination, 1830–1880*. Oxford: Oxford University Press, 2008.

Arnheim, Rudolf. *Film as Art*. Berkeley: University of California Press.

The Arrival of a Train (L'Arrivée d'un Train à La Ciotat). Lumière, 1896.

Asselin, Olivier, and Louis Auger Gosselin. "This Side of Paradise: Immersion and Emersion in S3D and AR." In *3D Cinema and Beyond*, edited by Dan Adler, Janine Marchessault, and Sanja Obradovic, 132–41. Toronto: Public Books, 2013.

Atkins, Barry. "Replicating the Blade Runner." In *The* Blade Runner *Experience: The Legacy of a Science Fiction Classic*, edited by Will Brooker, 79–91. New York: Wallflower, 2005.

Atkinson, Sarah. "Stereoscopic-3D Storytelling: Rethinking the Conventions, Grammar, and Aesthetics of a New Medium." *Journal of Media Practice* 12, no. 2 (2011): 139–56.

Audioshield. Dylan Fitterer, 2016.

Avatar. Twentieth Century Fox, 2009.

Avengers: Age of Ultron. Marvel Studios, 2015.

Bak, Meredith A. "Democracy and Discipline: Object Lessons and the Stereoscope in American Education, 1870–1920." *Early Popular Visual Culture* 10, no. 2 (2012): 147–67.

Bantjes, Rod. "Reading Stereoviews: The Aesthetics of Monstrous Space." *History of Photography* 39, no. 1 (2015): 33–55.

Barney, Matthew, and Gaspar Noé (with Sabine Russ). "Matthew Barney and Gaspar Noé." *BOMB* 127 (2014): https://bombmagazine.org/articles/matthew-barney-and-gaspar-noé-1/ (accessed September 30, 2019).

Barthes, Roland. "The Reality Effect." In *The Realist Novel*, edited by Dennis Walder, 258–61. London: Routledge, 1996.

Batman v Superman: Dawn of Justice. Warner Bros., 2016.

Baudelaire, Charles. "The Modern Public and Photography." In *Classic Essays on Photography*, edited by Alan Trachtenberg, 83–90. New Haven, CT: Leete's Island, 1980.

Baumbach, Nico. "Starting Over." *Film Comment* 50, no. 6 (2014): 34–41.

Bazin, André. "*The House of Wax*: Scare Me . . . In Depth!" In *André Bazin's New Media*, edited and translated by Dudley Andrew, 251–53. Berkeley: University of California Press, 2014.

——. "The Myth of Total Cinema." In *What Is Cinema?*, vol. 1, translated by Hugh Gray, 17–22. Berkeley: University of California Press, 2005.

——. "A New Stage in the Process: Math Equations for 3D." In *André Bazin's New Media*, edited and translated by Dudley Andrew, 235–42. Berkeley: University of California Press, 2014.

——. "The Ontology of the Photographic Image." In *What Is Cinema?*, vol. 1, translated by Hugh Gray, 9–16. Berkeley: University of California Press, 2005.

——. "The Return of *Metroscopix*." In *André Bazin's New Media*, edited and translated by Dudley Andrew, 248–50. Berkeley: University of California Press, 2014.

——. "Will Cinema Scope Save the Film Industry?" In *Bazin at Work: Major Essays and Reviews from the Forties and Fifties*, edited by Bert Cardullo and translated by Alain Piette and Bert Cardullo, 77–92. New York: Routledge, 1997.

Belisle, Brooke. "The Dimensional Image: Overlaps in Stereoscopic, Cinematic, and Digital Depth." *Film Criticism* 37, no. 3/1 (2013): 117–37.

——. "Immersion." In *Debugging Game History: A Critical Lexicon*, edited by Henry Lowood and Raiford Guins with A. C. Deger, 247–57. Cambridge, MA: MIT Press, 2016.

Beller, Jonathan. *The Cinematic Mode of Production: Attention Economy and the Society of the Spectacle*. Lebanon, NH: Dartmouth College Press, 2006.

Belton, John. "Digital 3D Cinema: Digital Cinema's Missing Novelty Phase." *Film History* 24, no. 2, (2012): 187–95.

Bennett, Bruce. "The Normativity of 3D: Cinematic Journeys, 'Imperial Visuality,' and Unchained Cameras." *Jump Cut* 55 (2013): http://ejumpcut.org/archive/jc55.2013/Bennett-3D/text.html (accessed September 30, 2019).

Benson-Allott, Caetlin. "The *Chora* Line: RealD Incorporated." *South Atlantic Quarterly* 110, no. 3 (2011): 621–44.

——. "Old Tropes in New Dimensions: Stereoscopy and Franchise Spectatorship." *Film Criticism* 37, no. 3, and 38, no. 1: (2013): 12–29.

Beowulf. Paramount Pictures, 2007.

Berger, John. *Ways of Seeing*. London: Penguin, 1972.

Berry, Chris, Janet Harbord, and Rachel Moore. "Introduction." In *Public Space, Media Space*, edited by Chris Berry, Janet Harbord, and Rachel Moore, 1–15. Basingstoke: Palgrave, 2013.

A Better Tomorrow. CJ Entertainment, 2010.

Billy Lynn's Long Halftime Walk. Sony Pictures Entertainment, 2016.

Birth of a Nation. David W. Griffith Corp., 1915.

Blade Runner. Warner Bros., 1982.

Blade Runner 2049. Sony Pictures, 2017.

Bogard, William. *The Simulation of Surveillance: Hypercontrol in Telematic Societies*. Cambridge: Cambridge University Press, 1996.

Bolter, Jay David, and Richard Grusin. *Remediation: Understanding New Media*. Cambridge, MA: MIT Press, 2000.

Bordwell, David. "*Adieu au langage*: 2 + 2 X 3D." Observations on Film Art, September 7, 2014, http://www.davidbordwell.net/blog/2014/09/07/adieu-au-langage-2-2-x-3d/ (accessed September 30, 2019).

——. "The Classical Hollywood Style, 1917–60." In *The Classical Hollywood Cinema: Film Style and Mode of Production to 1960*, by David Bordwell, Janet Staiger, and Kristin Thompson, 1–84. London: Routledge, 1985.

——. "Coraline, Cornered." Observations on Film Art, February 23, 2009, http://www.davidbordwell.net/blog/2009/02/23/coraline-cornered/ (accessed September 30, 2019).

——. "Say Hello to *Goodbye to Language*." Observations on Film Art, November 2, 2014, http://www.davidbordwell.net/blog/2014/11/02/say-hello-to-goodby-to-language/ (accessed September 30, 2019).

——, and Kristin Thompson. "Bwana Beowulf." Observations on Film Art, December 7, 2007, http://www.davidbordwell.net/blog/2007/12/07/bwana-beowulf/ (accessed September 30, 2019).

——, Kristin Thompson, and Janet Staiger. *The Classical Hollywood Cinema: Film Style and Mode of Production to 1960*. London: Routledge, 1985.

Bottomore, Steven. "The Panicking Audience?: Early Cinema and the 'Train Effect.'" *Historical Journal of Film, Radio, and Television* 19, no. 2 (1999): 177–216.

Boyle, Jen E. *Anamorphosis in Early Modern Literature: Mediation and Affect*. Farnham: Ashgate, 2010.

Breathless (À bout de souffle). Les Films Impéria, 1960.

Brewster, David. *The Stereoscope: Its History, Theory, and Construction*. London: John Murray, 1856.

Brown, Adam, and Tony Chalkley. "'Beautiful, Unethical, Dangerous': Screening Surveillance and Maintaining Insecurities." *Reconstruction* 12, no. 3 (2012): http://hdl.handle.net/10536/DRO/DU:30049443 (accessed September 30, 2019).

Brown, William. "*Avatar*: Stereoscopic Cinema, Gaseous Perception, and Darkness." *Animation* 7, no. 3 (2012): 259–71.

——. *Supercinema: Film-Philosophy for the Digital Age*. New York: Berghahn, 2013.

Bruno, Giuliana. *Atlas of Emotion: Journeys in Art, Architecture, and Film*. New York: Verso, 2002.

——. "Ramble City: Postmodernism and *Blade Runner*." *October* 41 (1987): 61–74.

Brzeski, Patrick. "3D *Jason Bourne* Causes Nausea, Protest in China." *Hollywood Reporter*, August 26, 2016, http://www.hollywoodreporter.com/news/3d-jason-bourne-causes-nausea-923098 (accessed September 30, 2019).

Bukatman, Scott. Blade Runner. London: BFI, 1997.

Burch, Noël. *Life to Those Shadows*. Edited and translated by Ben Brewster. London: BFI, 1990.

Burnett, Ron. "Transitions, Images, and Stereoscopic 3D Cinema." In *3D Cinema and Beyond*, edited by Dan Adler, Janine Marchessault, and Sanja Obradovic, 200–13. Toronto: Public Books, 2013.

Bwana Devil. Arch Oboler Productions, 1952.

Calhoun, Dave. "Gaspar Noé on Shooting Real Sex (in 3D!) for New Movie *Love* [interview]," *Timeout,* November 17, 2015, http://www.timeout.com/london/film/gaspar-noe-on-shooting-real-sex -in-3d-for-new-movie-love (accessed September 30, 2019).

Calvillo, Nerea, Orit Halpern, Jesse LeCavalier, and Wolfgang Pietsch. "Test Bed as Urban Epistemology." In *Smart Urbanism: Utopian Vision or False Dawn?,* edited by Simon Marvin, Andrés Luque-Ayala, and Colin McFarlane, 146–68. New York: Routledge, 2016.

Campkin, Ben, and Rebecca Ross. "Negotiating the City through Google Street View." In *Camera Constructs: Photography, Architecture, and the Modern City,* edited by Andrew Higgott and Timothy Wray, 147–57. Farnham: Ashgate, 2012.

"Capture and Publish Your Own Street View." Google Maps, n.d., https://www.google.co.uk/maps /streetview/trusted/ (accessed September 30, 2019).

Carter, Marcus, and Eduardo Velluso. "Some Places Should Be Off Limits for Games Such as Pokémon Go." The Conversation, July 12, 2016, https://theconversation.com/some-places-should-be -off-limits-for-games-such-as-pokemon-go-62341 (accessed September 30, 2019).

Cassirer, Ernst. *The Philosophy of Symbolic Forms,* vol.1: *Language.* Translated by Ralph Manheim. New Haven, CT: Yale University Press, 1955.

——. *The Philosophy of Symbolic Forms,* vol.2: *Mythical Thought.* Translated by Ralph Manheim. New Haven, CT: Yale University Press, 1955.

——. *The Philosophy of Symbolic Forms,* vol. 3: *The Phenomenology of Knowledge.* Translated by Ralph Mannheim. New Haven, CT: Yale University Press, 1965.

——. *The Philosophy of Symbolic Forms,* vol. 4: *Metaphysics of Symbolic Forms.* Edited by John Michael Krois and Donald Phillip Verene. Translated by John Michael Krois. New Haven, CT: Yale University Press, 1996.

Cave of Forgotten Dreams. IFC Films, 2010.

Cavell, Stanley. *The World Viewed: Reflections on the Ontology of Film.* 2nd ed. Cambridge, MA: Harvard University Press, 1979.

Chamayou, Grégoire. *Drone Theory.* Translated by Janet Lloyd. London: Penguin, 2015.

Chan, Melanie. *Virtual Reality: Representations in Contemporary Media.* New York: Bloomsbury, 2014.

Chateau, Dominique, and José Moure. "Introduction: Screen, a Concept in Progress." In *Screens: From Materiality to Spectatorship—A Historical and Theoretical Reassessment,* edited by Dominique Chateau and José Moure, 13–22. Amsterdam: Amsterdam University Press, 2016.

Chicken Little. Walt Disney Pictures, 2005.

Chitwood, Adam. "Christopher Nolan Talks 3D, Why He Shoots IMAX, His Approach to CGI, and Much More in Fascinating DGA Interview." Collider, April 13, 2012, http://collider.com /christopher-nolan-3d-imax-interview/ (accessed September 30, 2019).

Clarke, James. *The Cinema of James Cameron: Bodies in Heroic Motion.* New York: Wallflower, 2014.

Clash of the Titans. Warner Bros./Legendary Entertainment, 2010.

Clover, Joshua. "The Struggle for Space." *Film Quarterly* 63, no. 3 (2010): 6–7.

Colligan, Colette. "Stereograph." *Victorian Review* 34, no. 1 (2008): 75–82.

Cook, Pam. "Within and Without: *The Great Gatsby*'s 3D Experience." Fashionintofilm, June 2, 2013, https://fashionintofilm.wordpress.com/2013/06/02/within-and-without-the-great-gatsbys-3d -experience/ (accessed September 30, 2019).

Coraline. Laika Entertainment, 2009.

Corliss, Richard. "Box-Office Weekend: Cash of the *Titans.*" *Time,* April 4, 2010, http://content.time .com/time/arts/article/0,8599,1977696,00.html (accessed September 30, 2019).

Crandall, Jordan. "Operational Media." *CTheory* (2005): http://www.ctheory.net/articles.aspx?id=441 (accessed September 30, 2019).

Crary, Jonathan. *24/7: Late Capitalism and the Ends of Sleep*. New York: Verso, 2014.
——. *Suspensions of Perception: Attention, Spectacle, and Modern Culture*. Cambridge, MA: MIT Press, 1999.
——. *Techniques of the Observer*. Cambridge, MA: MIT Press, 1990.
Creature from the Black Lagoon. Universal International Pictures, 1954.
Crogan, Patrick. "The Nintendo Wii, Virtualisation, and Gestural Analogics." *Culture Machine* 11, no. 1 (2010): 82–101.
Cubitt, Sean. *The Cinema Effect*. Cambridge, MA: MIT Press, 2004.
——. *Finite Media: Environmental Implications of Digital Technologies*. Durham, NC: Duke University Press, 2017.
——. "Making Space." *Senses of Cinema* 57 (2010): http://sensesofcinema.com/2010/feature-articles/making-space/ (accessed September 30, 2019).
——. *The Practice of Light*. Cambridge, MA: MIT Press, 2014.
——. *Simulation and Social Theory*. London: SAGE, 2001.
Dahan, Yaron. "Cinema's Zion: The Third Dimension." Mubi, June 9, 2015, https://mubi.com/notebook/posts/cinemas-zion-the-third-dimension (accessed September 30, 2019).
Dallas, Paul. "1+1=3 [interview with Fabrice Aragno]." *Film Comment* 50, no. 6 (2014); additional issue content available at http://www.filmcomment.com/article/fabrice-aragno-interview/ (accessed September 30, 2019).
Damisch, Hubert. *The Origin of Perspective*. Translated by John Goodman. Cambridge, MA: MIT Press, 1995.
"Data Observatory." Imperial.ac.uk, n.d., https://www.imperial.ac.uk/data-science/about-the-institute/facilities/data-observatory-/ (accessed September 30, 2019).
Davies, Char. "Landscape, Earth, Body, Being, Space, and Time in the Immersive Virtual Environments *Osmose* and *Ephémère*." In *Women, Art, and Technology*, edited by Judy Malloy, 322–37. Cambridge, MA: MIT Press, 2003.
De Rosa, Miriam. "Poetics and Politics of the Trace: Notes on Surveillance Practices through Harun Farocki's Work." *NECSUS: European Journal of Media Studies* (2014): http://www.necsus-ejms.org/poetics-politics-trace-notes-surveillance-practices-harun-farockis-work/ (accessed September 30, 2019).
Déjà Vu. Buena Vista International, 2006.
Deleuze, Gilles. *Cinema 1: The Movement Image*. Translated by Hugh Tomlinson and Barbara Habberjam. London: Athlone, 1986.
——. "Postscript on the Societies of Control." *October* 59 (1992): 3–7.
Der Derian, James. "'Now We Are All Avatars.'" *Millennium: Journal of International Studies* 39, no. 1 (2010): 181–86.
——. *Virtuous War: Mapping the Military-Industrial-Media-Entertainment Network*. 2nd ed. New York: Routledge, 2009.
Derrida, Jacques. *Of Grammatology*. Translated by Gayatri Spivak. Baltimore: Johns Hopkins University Press, 1976.
Deutelbaum, Marshall. "Memory/Visual Design: The Remembered Sights of *Blade Runner*." *Literature/Film Quarterly* 17, no. 1 (1989): 66–72.
Dhingra, Philip. "Real 3D or Fake 3D." Real or Fake, n.d., https://www.realorfake3d.com (accessed September 30, 2019).
Dial M for Murder. Warner Bros., 1954.
Divergent. Summit Entertainment, 2014.
Doherty, Thomas. "3-D Is Comin' at Ya!" *Chronicle of Higher Education*, September 18, 2011, http://www.chronicle.com/article/3-D-Is-Comin-at-Ya-/128979 (accessed September 30, 2019).
Drive Angry. Summit Entertainment, 2011.

Drouin, Félix. *The Stereoscope and Stereoscopic Photography*. Translated by Matthew Surface. London: Percy Lund, 1890.

Duerfahrd, Lance. "For Your Glasses Only: *The Stewardesses* and Sex in Three Dimensions." In *3D Cinema and Beyond*, edited by Dan Adler, Janine Marchessault, and Sanja Obradovic, 161–71. Toronto: Public Books, 2013.

Duncan, Jody. "Gods and Monsters." *Cinefex* 122 (2010): 96–119.

Earle, Edward. "Interpretive Chronology—Stereos, American History and Popular Culture, 1850–1915." In *Points of View: The Stereograph in America—A Cultural History*, edited by Edward Earle, 23–87. New York: Visual Studies Workshop, 1979.

——. "The Stereograph in America: Pictorial Antecedents and Cultural Perspectives." In *Points of View: The Stereograph in America—A Cultural History*, edited by Edward Earle, 9–21. New York: Visual Studies Workshop, 1979.

Ebert, Roger. "Why 3D Doesn't Work and Never Will. Case Closed." Roger Ebert's Journal, January 23, 2011, http://www.rogerebert.com/rogers-journal/why-3d-doesnt-work-and-never-will-case-closed (accessed September 30, 2019).

——. "Why I Hate 3D Movies." *Newsweek*, May 10, 2010, http://europe.newsweek.com/roger-ebert-why-i-hate-3d-movies-70247 (accessed September 30, 2019).

Edge of Tomorrow. Warner Bros, 2014.

Edgerton, Samuel L. *The Mirror, the Window and the Telescope: How Renaissance Linear Perspective Changed Our Vision of the Universe*. Ithaca, NY: Cornell University Press, 2009.

Eisenstein, Sergei. "Stereoscopic Films." In *Notes of a Film Director*, translated by X. Danko, 129–37. London: Lawrence & Wishart, 1959.

Elsaesser, Thomas. "James Cameron's *Avatar*: Access for All." *New Review of Film and Television Studies* 9, no. 3 (2011): 247–64.

——. "Pushing the Contradictions of the Digital: 'Virtual Reality' and 'Interactive Narrative' as Oxymorons Between Narrative and Gaming." *New Review of Film and Television Studies* 12, no. 3 (2014): 295–311.

——. "The 'Return' of 3-D: On Some of the Logics and Genealogies of the Image in the Twenty-First Century." *Critical Inquiry* 39, no. 2 (2013): 217–46.

——, and Malte Hagener. *Film Theory: An Introduction through the Senses*. 2nd ed. New York: Routledge, 2015.

emart. "INSURGENT: Shatter Reality on the Oculus Rift!!!" YouTube.com, March 11, 2015, https://www.youtube.com/watch?v=8VuWRhGuJ7o&nohtml5=False (accessed Sep 30, 2019).

Engber, Daniel. "Greek Tragedy: Why Is the 3-D So Bad in *Clash of the Titans*?" Slate, April 1, 2010, http://www.slate.com/articles/arts/culturebox/2010/04/greek_tragedy.html (accessed September 30, 2019).

Enter the Void. Wild Bunch, 2009.

Enyedi, Delia. "Auteur 3D Filmmaking: From Hitchcock's Protrusion Technique to Godard's Total Immersion Aesthetic." *World Academy of Science, Engineering and Technology: International Journal of Innovative Research in Science and Engineering* 11, no. 3 (2017): 644–48.

Failes, Ian. "Inside the Battles of *300: Rise of an Empire*." fxguide, March 23, 2014, https://www.fxguide.com/featured/inside-the-battles-of-300-rise-of-an-empire/ (accessed September 30, 2019).

——. "*RoboCop* Redux: Inside the Film's Biggest Scenes." fxguide, February 13, 2014, http://www.fxguide.com/featured/robocop-redux-inside-the-films-biggest-scenes/ (accessed September 30, 2019).

Fairfax, Daniel. "Montage in 3D Cinema: The Case of Jean-Luc Godard's *Adieu au langage*." *Cinema Journal (Afterthoughts and Postscripts)* 54, no. 2 (2015): https://cmstudies.site-ym.com/?CJ_after542_fairfax (accessed September 30, 2019).

Fantastic Contraption. Northway Games/Radial Games, 2016.

Finding Dory. Pixar Animation Studios/Walt Disney Pictures, 2016.

Fleming, David H., and William Brown. "A Skeuomorphic Cinema: Film Form, Content, and Criticism in the 'Post-Analogue' Era." *Fibreculture Journal* 24 (2015): http://twentyfour .fibreculturejournal.org/2015/06/04/fcj-176/ (accessed September 30, 2019).

Flores, Victor. "The Animation of the Photographic: Stereoscopy and Cinema. The Experiments of Aurélio da Paz." *Early Popular Visual Culture* 14, no. 1 (2016): 87–106.

Flueckiger, Barbara. "Aesthetics of Stereoscopic Cinema." *Projections* 6, no. 1 (2012): 101–22.

Forsberg, Laura. "Nature's Invisibilia: The Victorian Microscope and the Miniature Fairy." *Victorian Studies* 57, no. 4 (2015): 638–66.

Foucault, Michel. *Discipline and Punish: The Birth of the Prison*. 2nd ed. Translated by Alan Sheridan. New York: Vintage, 1991.

Fowles, Jib. "Stereography and the Standardization of Vision." *Journal of American Culture* 17, no. 2 (1994): 89–93.

Frankenstein 3D (aka *Flesh for Frankenstein*). Compagnia Cinematografica Champion, 1973.

Frazer, Bryant. "Five Ways Jean-Luc Godard Breaks the 3D Rules in *Farewell to Language*." Studio Daily, October 3, 2014, http://www.studiodaily.com/2014/10/five-ways-jean-luc-godard-breaks -the-3d-rules-in-farewell-to-language/ (accessed September 30, 2019).

Freeland, Cynthia. "On Being Stereoblind in an Era of 3D Movies." *Essays in Philosophy* 13, no. 2 (2012): 550–76.

Friday the 13th Part III. Paramount Pictures, 1982.

Friedberg, Anne. *The Virtual Window: From Alberti to Microsoft*. Cambridge, MA: MIT Press, 2006.

Fright Night. DreamWorks, 2011.

Furmanek, Bob, and Greg Kintz. "An In-Depth Look at *Dial M for Murder*." 3-D Film Archive, n.d., http://www.3dfilmarchive.com/dial-m-blu-ray-review (accessed September 30, 2019).

Gadassik, Alla. "Anticipation of Contact: *Pina 3D* and Stereoscopic Cinematography." In *3D Cinema and Beyond*, edited by Dan Adler, Janine Marchessault, and Sanja Obradovic, 174–85. Toronto: Public Books, 2013.

Galloway, Alexander R. *The Interface Effect*. Cambridge: Polity, 2012.

Ganjavie, Amir. "Love's Astral Spy: An Interview with Gaspar Noé." Mubi, November 4, 2015, https:// mubi.com/notebook/posts/love-s-astral-spy-an-interview-with-gasper-noe (accessed September 30, 2019).

Gernsheim, Helmut, and Alison Gernsheim. *The History of Photography: From the Camera Obscura to the Beginning of the Modern Era*. London: Thames & Hudson, 1969.

Gibson, William. *Neuromancer*. London: HarperCollins, 1984.

Gombrich, E. H. *Art and Illusion: A Study in the Psychology of Pictorial Representation*. London: Phaidon, 1968.

——. *The Image and the Eye: Further Studies in the Psychology of Pictorial Representation*. London: Phaidon, 1982.

Gonzalez-Aguilera, Diego, and Javier Gomez-Lahoz. "Forensic Terrestrial Photogrammetry from a Single Image." *Journal of Forensic Sciences* 54, no. 6 (2009): 1376–87.

Goodbye to Language (*Adieu au langage*). Wild Bunch/Canal+, 2014.

"Google Tilt Brush: Impossible Now a Reality?" CNN Style, May 2016, http://edition.cnn.com/2016 /05/09/arts/google-tilt-brush/index.html?sr=fbCNN051016google-tilt-brush0210PMVODtop (accessed September 30, 2019).

Grabiner, Ellen. *I See You: The Shifting Paradigms of James Cameron's* Avatar. Jefferson, NC: McFarland, 2012.

Graham, Steven. "Geographies of Surveillant Simulation." In *Virtual Geographies: Bodies, Space, and Relations*, edited by Mike Crang, Phil Crang, and Jon May, 131–48. London: Routledge, 1999.

Grau, Oliver. *Virtual Art: From Illusion to Immersion*. Cambridge, MA: MIT Press, 2003.

Gravity. Warner Bros., 2013.

The Great Gatsby. Warner Bros., 2013.

The Green Hornet. Columbia Pictures, 2011.

Greenblatt, Stephen. *Renaissance Self-Fashioning: From More to Shakespeare*. Chicago: University of Chicago Press, 2005.

Groth, Helen. "Kaleidoscopic Vision and Literary Invention in an 'Age of Things': David Brewster, Don Juan, and 'A Lady's Kaleidoscope.'" *ELH* 74, no. 1 (2007): 217–37.

Grusin, Richard. "DVDs, Video Games, and the Cinema of Interactions." In *Multimedia Histories: From the Magic Lantern to the Internet*, edited by James Lyons and John Plunkett, 209–21. Exeter: Exeter University Press, 2007.

Guardians of the Galaxy, Vol. 2. Marvel Studios, 2017.

Gunning, Tom. "An Aesthetic of Astonishment." In *Viewing Positions: Ways of Seeing Film*, edited by Linda Williams, 114–33. New Brunswick, NJ: Rutgers University Press, 1995.

——. "Tracing the Individual Body: Photography, Detectives, and Early Cinema." In *Cinema and the Invention of Modern Life*, edited by Leo Charney and Vanessa R. Schwartz, 15–45. Berkeley: University of California Press, 1995.

Gurevitch, Leon. "The Birth of a Stereoscopic Nation: Hollywood, Digital Empire, and the Cybernetic Attraction." *Animation* 7, no. 3 (2012): 239–58.

——. "The Cinemas of Interactions: Cinematics and the 'Game Effect' in the Age of Digital Attractions." *Senses of Cinema* 57 (2010): http://sensesofcinema.com/2010/feature-articles/the-cinemas-of-interactions-cinematics-and-the-%E2%80%98game-effect%E2%80%99-in-the-age-of-digital-attractions/#b1 (accessed September 30, 2019).

——. "Computer Generated Animation as Product Design Engineered Culture, or Buzz Lightyear to the Sales Floor, to the Checkout and Beyond!" *Animation* 7, no. 2 (2012): 131–49.

——. "The Stereoscopic Attraction: Three-Dimensional Imaging and the Spectacular Paradigm, 1850–2013." *Convergence* 19, no. 4 (2013): 396–405.

——, and Miriam Ross. "Stereoscopic Media: Scholarship Beyond Booms and Busts." In *3D Cinema and Beyond*, edited by Dan Adler, Janine Marchessault, and Sanja Obradovic, 83–93. Toronto: Public Books, 2013.

Häkkinen, Jukka, Takashi Kawai, Jari Takatalo, Tuomas Leisti, Jenni Radun, Anni Hirsaho, and Göte Nyman. "Measuring Stereoscopic Image Quality Experience with Interpretation Based Quality Methodology." *Proceedings of SPIE* 68081B (2008): https://www.spiedigitallibrary.org/conference-proceedings-of-spie/6808/1/Measuring-stereoscopic-image-quality-experience-with-interpretation-based-quality-methodology/10.1117/12.760935.short?SSO=1 (accessed September 30, 2019).

Hall, Sheldon. "*Dial M for Murder*." *Film History* 26, no. 3 (2004): 243–55.

Halpern, Orit, Robert Mitchell, and Bernard Dionysius Geoghegan. "The Smartness Mandate: Notes toward a Critique." *Grey Room* 68 (2017): 106–29.

Hansen, Mark. *New Philosophy for New Media*. Cambridge, MA: MIT Press, 2006.

Haggerty, Kevin D., and Richard V. Ericson. "The Surveillant Assemblage." *British Journal of Sociology* 51, no. 4 (2000): 605–22.

——, and Richard V. Ericson. "The New Politics of Surveillance and Visibility." In *The New Politics of Surveillance and Visibility*, edited by Kevin D. Haggerty and Richard V. Ericson, 3–33. Toronto: University of Toronto Press, 2006.

Hawkins, Richard C. "3-D." *Quarterly of Film Radio and Television* 7, no. 4 (1953): 325–34.

Hayes, R. M. *3-D Movies: A History and Filmography of Stereoscopic Cinema*. Jefferson, NC: McFarland, 1989.

Heidegger, Martin. "The Origin of the Work of Art." In *Poetry, Language, Thought*, translated by Albert Hofstadter, 17–86. New York: Harper & Row, 2001.

——. "The Question Concerning Technology." In *The Question Concerning Technology and Other Essays*, translated by William Lovitt, 3–35. New York: Harper Perennial, 1977.

Helmholtz, Hermann von. *Treatise on Physiological Optics*. Vol. 3. Edited and translated by James P. C. Southall. Birmingham, AL: Leslie B. Adams, 1985.

Higgins, Scott. "3D in Depth: *Coraline, Hugo*, and a Sustainable Aesthetic." *Film History* 24, no. 2 (2012): 196–209.

Hillis, Ken. *Digital Sensations: Space, Identity, and Embodiment in Virtual Reality*. Minneapolis: University of Minnesota Press, 1999.

——, Michael Petit, and Kylie Jarrett. *Google and the Culture of Search*. New York: Routledge, 2013.

Hishack, Thomas. *The Oxford Companion to the American Musical: Theatre, Film, and Television*. Oxford: Oxford University Press, 2008.

Hoelzl, Ingrid, and Remi Marie. *Softimage: Towards a New Theory of the Digital Image*. Bristol: Intellect, 2015.

Holben, J. "Conquering New Worlds." *American Cinematographer* 91, no. 1 (2010): 32–47.

Holmes, Nicholas P., and Charles Spence. "The Body Schema and the Multisensory Representation(s) of Peripersonal Space." *Cognitive Processing* 5, no. 2 (2004): 94–105.

Holmes, Oliver Wendell. "The Stereoscope and the Stereograph." In *Classic Essays on Photography*, edited by Alan Trachtenberg, 71–82. Stony Creek, CT: Leete's Island, 1980.

——. "Sun-Painting and Sun-Sculpture: With a Stereoscopic Trip Across the Atlantic." *Atlantic Monthly*, July 1861, 13–29. Available at http://www.gutenberg.org/cache/epub/11154/pg11154.html (accessed September 30, 2019).

House of Wax. Warner Bros., 1953.

Hughes, Robert. *The Shock of the New*. London: Thames & Hudson, 1991.

Hugo. Paramount Pictures, 2011.

Huhtamo, Erkki. "The Four Practices? Challenges for an Archaeology of the Screen." In *Screens: From Materiality to Spectatorship—A Historical and Theoretical Reassessment*, edited by Dominique Chateau and José Moure, 116–24. Amsterdam: Amsterdam University Press, 2016.

The Huntsman: Winter's War. Universal Pictures, 2016.

I, Robot. Twentieth Century Fox, 2004.

Insurgent. Summit Entertainment, 2015.

Insurgent: Shatter Reality. Kite & Lightning, 2015.

Iron Man 3. Marvel Studios, 2013.

Irreversible. Canal+, 2002.

Ivins, William M., Jr. *On the Rationalization of Sight*. New York: Da Capo, 1973.

Jack the Giant Slayer. New Line Cinema/Legendary Entertainment, 2013.

Jacobowitz, Florence, and Richard Lippe. "Godard's *Adieu au langage*." *CineAction* 96 (2015): 24–25.

Jason Bourne. Universal Pictures, 2016.

Jaws 3-D. Universal Pictures, 1983.

Jay, Martin. *Downcast Eyes: The Denigration of Vision in Twentieth-Century French Thought*. Berkeley: University of California Press, 1993.

Jockenhövel, Jesko. "What Is It if It's Not Real? It's Genre—Early Color Film and Digital 3D." *Cinemascope* 7, no. 15 (2011): 1–14.

John Carter. Walt Disney Pictures, 2012.

Johnston, Keith M. "'Now Is the Time (To Put on Your Glasses)': 3-D Film Exhibition in Britain, 1951–55." *Film History* 23, no. 1 (2011): 93–103.

——. "Pop-up Footballers, Pop Concerts and Popular Films: The Past, Present, and Future of 3D TV." *Convergence* 18, no. 4 (2013): 438–45.

——. "A Technician's Dream? The Critical Reception of 3-D Films in Britain." *Historical Journal of Film, Radio and Television* 32, no. 2 (2012): 245–65.

Johnston, Sean F. "The Cultural Landscape of Three-Dimensional Imaging." In *Techniques and Principles in Three-Dimensional Imaging: An Introductory Approach*, edited by Martin Richardson, 212–32. Hershey, PA: Information Science Reference, 2014.

Jones, Kent. "Empire of Light: Three Highlights from Cannes Move in Poetic and Painterly Directions." *Film Comment* 50, no. 4 (2014): 52–54.

Jones, Nick. "Expanding the Esper: Virtualised Spaces of Surveillance in SF Film." *Science Fiction Film and Television* 9, no. 1 (2016): 1–23.

——. "The Expansive and Proximate Scales of Immersive Media." *International Journal on Stereo and Immersive Media* 2, no. 2 (2019): 36–49.

——. "Flexible Cities: Postindustrial Urban Space in *Inception*, *The Adjustment Bureau*, and *Doctor Strange*." In *The City in American Cinema: Post-Industrialism, Urban Culture, and Gentrification*, edited by Johan Andersson and Lawrence Webb, 223–50. New York: I. B. Tauris, 2019.

——. *Hollywood Action Films and Spatial Theory*. New York: Routledge, 2015.

——. "L'illusion partielle de la 3D: distorsions spatiales, stéréoscopie, et *Au Coeur de l'océan*." In *Stéréoscopie et Illusion*, edited by Miguel Almiron, Esther Jacopin and Giusy Pisano, translated by Frank Boulège, 213–27. Paris: Septentrion Universitary Press, 2018.

——. "Quantification and Substitution: The Abstract Space of Virtual Cinematography." *Animation* 8, no. 3 (2013): 253–66.

——. "'There Never Really Is a Stereoscopic Image': A Closer Look at 3-D Media." *New Review of Film and Television Studies* 13, no. 2 (2015): 170–88.

——. "This Is My World: Spatial Representation in the *Resident Evil* Films." *Continuum* 30, no. 4 (2016): 477–88.

——. "Variation within Stability: Digital 3D and Film Style." *Cinema Journal* 55, no. 1 (2015): 52–73.

Jurassic Park. Universal Pictures, 1993.

Kaplan, Caren. "Precision Targets: GPS and the Militarization of US Consumer Identity." *American Quarterly* 58, no. 3 (2006): 693–713.

Kemp, Martin. *Seen/Unseen: Art, Science, and Intuition from Leonardo to the Hubble Telescope*. Oxford: Oxford University Press, 2006.

Kerbel, Michael. "3-D or Not 3-D." *Film Comment* 16, no. 6 (1980): 11–20.

Kermode, Mark. *The Good, the Bad and the Multiplex*. London: Random House, 2011.

Kim, Jihoon. "Introduction: Three Dimensionality as Heuristic Device." *Convergence* 19, no. 4 (2013): 391–95.

Kirby, David. "The Future Is Now: Diegetic Prototypes and the Role of Popular Films in Generating Real-world Technological Development," *Social Studies of Science* 40, no. 1 (2010): 41–70.

Kiss Me Kate. MGM, 1953.

Kitchin, Rob, and Martin Dodge. *Code/Space: Software and Everyday Life*. Cambridge, MA: MIT Press, 2011.

Kittler, Friedrich. *Optical Media*. Translated by Anthony Enns. Malden, MA: Polity, 2010.

Klinger, Barbara. "Beyond Cheap Thrills: 3D Cinema Today, the Parallax Debates, and the 'Pop-Out.'" In *3D Cinema and Beyond*, edited by Dan Adler, Janine Marchessault, and Sanja Obradovic, 186–99. Toronto: Public Books, 2013.

——. "*Cave of Forgotten Dreams*: Meditations on 3D." *Film Quarterly* 65, no. 3 (2012): 38–43.

Kolb, William M. "Script to Screen: *Blade Runner* in Perspective." In *Retrofitting* Blade Runner: *Issues in Ridley Scott's* Blade Runner *and Philip K. Dick's* Do Androids Dream of Electric Sheep?, 2nd ed., edited by Judith B. Kerman, 132–53. Madison: University of Wisconsin Press, 1997.

Krauss, Rosalind. "Photography's Discursive Spaces: Landscape/View." *Art Journal* 42, no. 4 (1982): 311–19.

Kuhn, Annette, and Guy Westwell. *A Dictionary of Film Studies*. Oxford: Oxford University Press, 2012.

Lane, Anthony. "Third Way: The Rise of 3-D." *New Yorker*, March 8, 2010, http://www.newyorker.com/magazine/2010/03/08/third-way (accessed September 30, 2019).

The Last Emperor. Recorded Picture Company, 1987.

Latour, Bruno. "Visualization and Cognition: Thinking with Eyes and Hands." *Knowledge and Society: Studies in the Sociology of Culture Past and Present* 6 (1986): 1–40.

The Lawnmower Man. New Line Cinema, 1992.

Lawrence of Arabia. Columbia Pictures, 1962.

Layer, Harold L. "Stereo Kinematics: The Merging of Time and Space in the Cinema." *American Cinematographer* 55, no. 4 (1974): 438–41.

Lefebvre, Henri. *The Production of Space*. Translated by Donald Nicholson-Smith. Oxford: Blackwell, 1991.

The Legend of Tarzan. Warner Bros./Village Roadshow Pictures, 2016.

Lev, Peter. *History of the American Cinema*, vol. 7: *The Fifties: Transforming the Screen 1950–1959*. Edited by Charles Harpole. Berkeley: University of California Press, 2003.

Lévi-Strauss, Claude. *The Savage Mind*. Letchworth: Garden City, 1966.

Levoy, Marc, Ren Ng, Andrew Adams, Matthew Footer, and Mark Horowitz. "Light Field Microscopy." *ACM Transactions on Graphics* (Proceedings of SIGGRAPH) 25, no. 3 (2006): http://www.graphics.stanford.edu/papers/lfmicroscope/ (accessed September 30, 2019).

Lewis, David. "*Love*: One-Dimensional Characters Have Sex in 3-D." *San Francisco Chronicle*, November 5, 2015, http://www.sfgate.com/movies/article/Love-One-dimensional-characters-have-sex-6610750.php (accessed September 30, 2019).

Life of Pi. Twentieth Century Fox, 2012.

The Lion King. Walt Disney Pictures, 1994.

Lippit, Akira Mizuta. *Atomic Light (Shadow Optics)*. Minneapolis: University of Minnesota Press, 2005.

——. "Three Phantasies of Cinema—Reproduction, Mimesis, Annihilation." *Paragraph* 22, no. 3 (1999): 213–27.

Love. Wild Bunch, 2015.

"*Love* [Press Kit]." Wild Bunch International Sales, n.d., https://www.wildbunch.biz/movie/love/ (accessed September 30, 2019).

Lowensohn, Josh. "Google's Street View Now Lets You Step Back in Time." The Verge, April 23, 2014, http://www.theverge.com/2014/4/23/5640472/googles-street-view-now-lets-you-step-back-in-time (accessed September 30, 2019).

Lui, Yong. *3D Cinematic Aesthetics and Storytelling*. New York: Palgrave, 2018.

Mack, John. *The Art of Small Things*. Cambridge, MA: Harvard University Press, 2007.

Magerstädt, Sylvie. *Body, Soul, and Cyberspace in Contemporary Science Fiction Cinema: Virtual Worlds and Ethical Problems*. Basingstoke: Palgrave, 2014.

Malpas, Jeff. *Heidegger's Topology: Being, Place, World*. Cambridge, MA: MIT Press, 2006.

Maltby, Richard. *Hollywood Cinema*. 2nd ed. Malden, MA: Blackwell, 2003.

Man of Steel. Warner Bros./Legendary Entertainment, 2013.

Manovich, Lev. *The Language of New Media*. Cambridge, MA: MIT Press, 2001.

——. "The Mapping of Space: Perspective, Radar, and 3D Computer Graphics." Manovich.net., 1993, http://manovich.net/index.php/projects/article-1993 (accessed September 30, 2019).

Marion, F. *The Wonders of Optics*. Translated by Charles W. Quin. London: Sampson Low, Son & Marston, 1868.

Marks, Laura U. *The Skin of the Film*. Durham, NC: Duke University Press, 2000.

The Martian. Twentieth Century Fox, 2015.

The Matrix. Warner Bros., 1999.

Matsuda, Keiichi. "HYPER-REALITY." Vimeo.co.uk, May 16, 2016, https://vimeo.com/166807261 (accessed September 30, 2019).

McCarthy, Anna. *Ambient Television: Visual Culture and Public Space*. Durham, NC: Duke University Press, 2001.

McCarthy, Todd. "*Avatar* [review]." *Variety*, December 10, 2009, http://variety.com/2009/film /markets-festivals/avatar-2-1200477897/ (accessed September 30, 2019).

Mendiburu, Bernard. *3D Moviemaking. Stereoscopic Digital Cinema from Script to Screen*. Burlington, MA: Focal, 2009.

Minority Report. Twentieth Century Fox, 2002.

Mitchell, William J. *The Reconfigured Eye: Visual Truth in the Post-Photographic Era*. Cambridge, MA: MIT Press, 1994.

Montagu, Ivor. "The Third Dimension: The Future of Film?" In *The Cinema 1950*, edited by Roger Manvell, 132–39. New York: Arno, 1978.

Morrey, Douglas. *Jean-Luc Godard*. Manchester: Manchester University Press, 2005.

Morton, Emily. "Augmented Reality Property Searches – See it to Believe It!" Foxtons.co.uk, December 16, 2014, http://www.foxtons.co.uk/discover/2014/12/augmented-reality-property-searches -see-it-to-believe-it.html (accessed Sep 30, 2019).

Moulin Rouge! Twentieth Century Fox, 2001.

Moulton, Carter. "The Future Is a Fairground: Attraction and Absorption in 3D Cinema." *CineAction* 89 (2013): 4–13.

Murphet, Julian. "Godard's Stereopticon." *Screening the Past* 41 (2016): http://www.screeningthepast .com/2016/12/godards-stereopticon/#_ednref1 (accessed September 30, 2019).

Murray, Janet H. *Hamlet on the Holodeck: The Future of Narrative in Cyberspace*. New York: Free Press, 1997.

Muybridge, Eadweard. *Animals in Motion*. Edited by Lewis S. Brown. New York: Dover, 1957.

Naked Ambition 2. 852 Films, 2014.

Napoleon. Ciné France, 1927.

Nead, Lynda. "STRIP." *Early Popular Visual Culture* 3, no. 2 (2005): 135–50.

Need for Speed. Touchstone Pictures, 2014.

Neher, Allister. "How Perspective Could Be a Symbolic Form." *Journal of Aesthetics and Art Criticism* 63, no. 4 (2005): 359–73.

Ng, Jenna. "Seeing Movement: On Motion Capture Animation and James Cameron's *Avatar*." *Animation* 7, no. 3 (2012): 273–86.

Noah. Paramount Pictures, 2014.

Noble, Safiya Umoja. *Algorithms of Oppression: How Search Engines Reinforce Racism*. New York: New York University Press, 2018.

North, Dan. *Performing Illusions: Cinema, Special Effects and the Virtual Actor*. London: Wallflower, 2008.

Ogram, Geoff. "Analogue and Digital Stereo-Photography." In *Techniques and Principles in Three-Dimensional Imaging: An Introductory Approach*, edited by Martin Richardson, 59–86. Hershey, PA: Information Science Reference, 2014.

One More Time with Feeling. Iconoclast/JW Films/Pulse Films, 2016.

Osborne, Albert E. "Remarkable Results from Stereographs." In *Italy through the Stereoscope: Journeys in and about Italian Cities*, edited by James C. Egbert, 571–89. New York: Underwood & Underwood, 1900.

Osmose. Char Davies, 1995.

O'Toole, Laurence. *Pornocopia: Porn, Sex, Technology, and Desire*. London: Serpent's Tail, 1998.

Pacific Rim. Warner Bros./Legendary Entertainment, 2013.

Panofsky, Erwin. *Perspective as Symbolic Form.* Translated by Christopher S. Wood. New York: Zone, 1991.

Parikka, Jussi. *What Is Media Archaeology?* Cambridge: Polity, 2012.

Paul, William. "The Aesthetics of Emergence." *Film History* 15, no. 3 (1993): 321–55.

——. "Breaking the Fourth Wall: 'Belascoism,' Modernism and a 3-D *Kiss Me Kate.*" *Film History* 16, no. 3 (2004): 229–42.

Pennington, Adrian, and Carolyn Giardina. *Exploring 3D: The New Grammar of Stereoscopic Filmmaking.* New York: Focal, 2013.

Persall, Steve. "*Clash of the Titans* a Lame Remake in Lame 3-D." *Tampa Bay Times,* March 30, 2010, http://www.tampabay.com/features/movies/review-clash-of-the-titans-a-lame-remake-in-lame-3-d/1083873 (accessed September 30, 2019).

Person of Interest. Bad Robot, 2011–16.

Phillips, David. "Modern Vision [review of *Techniques of the Observer* by Jonathan Crary]." *Oxford Art Journal* 16, no. 1 (1993): 129–38.

Pietrobruno, Sheenagh. "The Stereoscope and the Miniature." *Early Popular Visual Culture* 9, no. 3 (2011): 171–90.

Pina. Neue Road Pictures, 2011.

Piranha. Dimension Films, 2011.

Plunkett, John. "Depth, Colour, Movement: Embodied Vision and the Stereoscope." In *Multimedia Histories: From the Magic Lantern to the Internet,* edited by James Lyons and John Plunkett, 117–31. Exeter: Exeter University Press, 2007.

——. "'Feeling Seeing': Touch, Vision and the Stereoscope." *History of Photography* 37, no. 4 (2013): 389–96.

Point Break. Alcon Entertainment, 2015.

The Polar Express. Castle Rock Entertainment/Warner Bros., 2004.

Prince, Stephen. *Digital Visual Effects in Cinema: The Seduction of Reality.* New Brunswick, NJ: Rutgers University Press, 2012.

——. "True Lies: Perceptual Realism, Digital Images, and Film Theory." *Film Quarterly* 49, no. 3 (1996): 27–37.

Prometheus. Twentieth Century Fox, 2012.

Purse, Lisa. *Digital Imaging in Popular Cinema.* Edinburgh: Edinburgh University Press, 2013.

Raley, Rita. "Dataveillance and Counterveillance." In *"Raw Data" Is an Oxymoron,* edited by Lisa Gitelman, 121–46. Cambridge, MA: MIT Press, 2013.

Ready Player One. Warner Bros., 2018.

Rheingold, Howard. *Virtual Reality.* New York: Touchstone, 1991.

Riegl, Aloïs. *Late Roman Art Industry.* Translated by Rolf Winkes. Rome: Giorgio Bretschneider Editore, 1985.

Robinson Crusoe. Goskino USSR, 1946.

RoboCop. Orion Pictures, 1987.

RoboCop. MGM/Columbia Pictures, 2014.

Rodowick, David. *The Virtual Life of Film.* Cambridge, MA: Harvard University Press, 2007.

Rogers, Ariel. *Cinematic Appeals.* New York: Columbia University Press, 2013.

Romney, Jonathan. "Film of the Week: *Goodbye to Language.*" *Film Comment,* October 29, 2014, https://www.filmcomment.com/blog/film-of-the-week-goodbye-to-language/ (accessed September 30, 2019).

Rosen, Philip. *Change Mummified: Cinema, Historicity, Theory.* Minneapolis: University of Minnesota Press, 2001.

Ross, Miriam. "The 3-D Aesthetic: *Avatar* and Hyperhaptic Visuality." *Screen* 53, no. 4 (2012): 381–97.

——. *3D Cinema: Optical Illusions and Tactile Experiences.* New York: Palgrave Macmillan, 2015.

——. "Godard's Stereoscopic Illusions: Against a Total Cinema." *Screening the Past* 41 (2016): http:// www.screeningthepast.com/2016/12/godards-stereoscopic-illusions-against-a-total-cinema (accessed September 30, 2019).

——. *"Goodbye to Language* 3D: Painful Sight." Cinema Lives Cinema Loves, August 6, 2014, https://miriamruthross.wordpress.com/2014/08/06/goodbye-to-language-3d-painful-sight/ (accessed September 30, 2019).

——. "Spectacular Dimensions: 3D Dance Films." *Senses of Cinema* 61 (2011): http://sensesofcinema .com/2011/feature-articles/spectacular-dimensions-3d-dance-films/ (accessed September 30, 2019).

——. *"Star Trek* Into Darkness." Cinema Lives Cinema Loves, May 10, 2013, https://miriamruthross .wordpress.com/2013/05/10/star-trek-into-darkness/ (accessed September 30, 2019).

——. "Stereoscopic Visuality: Where Is the Screen, Where Is the Film?" *Convergence* 19, no. 4 (2013): 406–14.

Ryan, Mike. "Louis Leterrier: *Now You See Me* Director on the Problems with *The Incredible Hulk* and *Clash of the Titans.*" Huffington Post, May 28, 2013, http://www.huffingtonpost.com/2013 /05/28/louis-leterrier-now-you-see-me_n_3333311.html (accessed September 30, 2019).

Sandifer, Philip. "Out of the Screen and into the Theater: 3-D Film as Demo." *Cinema Journal* 50, no. 3 (2011): 62–78.

Schiavo, Laura Burd. "From Phantom Image to Perfect Vision: Physiological Optics, Commercial Photography, and the Popularization of the Stereoscope." In *New Media, 1740–1915,* edited by Lisa Gitelman and Geoffrey B. Pingree, 113–38. Cambridge, MA: MIT Press, 2003.

Schivelbusch, Wolfgang. *The Railway Journey: The Industrialization of Time and Space in the Nineteenth Century.* Berkeley: University of California Press, 2014.

Schröter, Jens. *3D: History, Theory, and Aesthetics of the Transplane Image.* New York: Bloomsbury, 2014.

Sex and Zen: Extreme Ecstasy. China 3D Digital Entertainment, 2011.

Seymour, Mike. "Art of Stereo Conversion: 2D to 3D—2012." fxguide, May 8, 2012, https://www .fxguide.com/featured/art-of-stereo-conversion-2d-to-3d-2012/ (accessed September 30, 2019).

Silverman, Kaja. "Back to the Future." *Camera Obscura* 9, no. 3 (1991): 108–32.

Silverman, Robert J. "The Stereoscope and Photographic Depiction in the Nineteenth Century." *Technology and Culture* 34, no. 4 (1993): 729–56.

Singer, Matt. "A Step-by-Step Consumer Guide to Good Theater Projection." Screen Crush, n.d., http://screencrush.com/consumer-guide-to-theater-projection/ (accessed September 30, 2019).

Skidelsky, Edward. *Ernst Cassirer: The Last Philosopher of Culture.* Princeton, NJ: Princeton University Press, 2008.

Skyscraper. Legendary Entertainment, 2018.

Sobchack, Vivian. *Carnal Thoughts: Embodiment and Moving Image Culture.* Berkeley: University of California Press, 2004.

Sontag, Susan. *On Photography.* London: Penguin, 1979.

Source Code. Summit Entertainment, 2010.

"Sources of Photography." Google Maps, n.d., https://www.google.co.uk/streetview/explore/ (accessed September 30, 2019).

Spider-Man: Homecoming. Columbia Pictures, 2017.

Star Trek Into Darkness. Paramount Pictures, 2013.

Star Wars. Lucasfilm, 1977.

Star Wars: Episode I – The Phantom Menace. Lucasfilm, 1999.

Star Wars: Episode VIII–The Force Awakens. Lucasfilm/Walt Disney Pictures, 2015.

Stasukevich, Iain. "Adding a Third Dimension to *Hornet.*" *American Cinematographer,* February 2011, https://theasc.com/ac_magazine/February2011/GreenHornet/page3.html (accessed September 30, 2019).

Stevens, Dana. "Half Mortal, Totally Stupid." Slate, April 1, 2010, http://www.slate.com/culture/2010/04/clash-of-the-titans-reviewed.html (accessed September 30, 2019).

The Stewardesses. Louis K. Sher Productions, 1969.

Stewart, Garrett. *Closed Circuits: Screening Narrative Surveillance*. Chicago: University of Chicago Press, 2015.

Stewart, Susan. *On Longing: Narratives of the Miniature, the Gigantic, the Souvenir, the Collection*. Durham, NC: Duke University Press, 1993.

Steyerl, Hito. "In Defense of the Poor Image." *e-flux journal* 10 (2009): http://www.e-flux.com/journal/in-defense-of-the-poor-image/ (accessed September 30, 2019).

Strehlow, Anne. "Computer Scientists Create a 'Light Field Camera' That Banishes Fuzzy Photos." Stanford Report, November 3, 2005, http://news.stanford.edu/news/2005/november9/camera-110205.html (accessed September 30, 2019).

Symmes, Daniel L. "3-D: Cinema's Slowest Revolution." *American Cinematographer* 55, no. 4 (1974): 406–7, 434, 456–57, 478–85.

Szemeredy, Zsofia. "A Short Guide to Mirriad." *Mapping Contemporary Cinema* (2015): http://www.mcc.sllf.qmul.ac.uk/?p=1516 (accessed September 30, 2019).

Taubin, Amy. "Dog Days." *Film Comment* 50, no. 4 (2014): 48–51.

The Thirteenth Floor. Columbia Pictures, 1999.

Thomas, Alan. *The Expanding Eye: Photography and the Nineteenth-Century Mind*. London: Croom Helm, 1978.

Thomas, Deborah. *Reading Hollywood: Spaces and Meanings in American Film*. New York: Wallflower, 2001.

Thompson, Kristin. "Has 3-D Already Failed?" Observations on Film Art, August 28, 2009, http://www.davidbordwell.net/blog/2009/08/28/has-3-d-already-failed/ (accessed September 30, 2019).

——. "Has 3D Already Failed? The Sequel, Part One: RealDlighted." Observations on Film Art, January 20, 2011, http://www.davidbordwell.net/blog/2011/01/20/has-3d-already-failed-the-sequel-part-one-realdlighted/ (accessed September 30, 2019).

——. "Has 3D Already Failed? The Sequel, Part Two: RealDsgusted." Observations on Film Art, January 25, 2011, http://www.davidbordwell.net/blog/2011/01/25/has-3d-already-failed-the-sequel-part-2-realdsgusted/ (accessed September 30, 2019).

Thrift, Nigel. "Remembering the Technological Unconscious by Foregrounding Knowledges of Position." *Environment and Planning D: Society and Space* 22, no. 1 (2003): 175–90.

Tilt Brush. Google, 2016.

Titanic. Twentieth Century Fox/Paramount Pictures, 1997.

Top Gun. Paramount Pictures, 1986.

Transcendence. Alcon Entertainment, 2014.

Transformers: The Last Knight. Paramount Pictures, 2017.

TRON: Legacy. Walt Disney Pictures, 2010.

Trotter, David. "Stereoscopy: Modernism and the 'Haptic.'" *Critical Quarterly* 46, no. 4 (2004): 38–58.

Tryon, Chuck. "Digital 3D, Technological Auteurism, and the Rhetoric of Cinematic Revolution." In *Special Effects: New Histories/Theories/Contexts*, edited by Dan North, Bob Rehak, and Michael S. Duffy, 183–95. London: BFI, 2015.

Uricchio, William. "The Algorithmic Turn: Photosynth, Augmented Reality, and the Changing Implications of the Image." *Visual Studies* 26, no. 1 (2011): 25–35.

Utterson, Andrew. "Goodbye to Cinema? Jean-Luc Godard's *Adieu au langage* (2014) as 3D Images at the Edge of History." *Studies in French Cinema* (2016): 1–16, https://doi/full/10.1080/14715880.2016.1242045 (accessed September 30, 2019).

——. "Practice Makes Imperfect: Technology and the Creative Imperfections of Jean-Luc Godard's Three-Dimensional (3D) Cinema." *Quarterly Review of Film and Video* 34, no. 3 (2017): 295–308.

Väliaho, Pasi. *Biopolitical Screens: Image, Power, and the Neoliberal Brain*. Cambridge, MA: MIT Press, 2014.

——. "The Light of God: Notes on the Visual Economy of Drones." *Necsus* (December 4, 2014): http://www.necsus-ejms.org/light-god-notes-visual-economy-drones/ (accessed September 30, 2019).

Van Dijck, José. "Datafication, Dataism, and Dataveillance: Big Data Between Scientific Paradigm and Ideology." *Surveillance and Society* 12, no. 2 (2014): 197–208.

Verhoeff, Nanna. *Mobile Screens: The Visual Regime of Navigation*. Amsterdam: Amsterdam University Press, 2012.

——. "Screens in the City." In *Screens: From Materiality to Spectatorship—A Historical and Theoretical Reassessment*, edited by Dominique Chateau and José Moure, 125–39. Amsterdam: Amsterdam University Press, 2016.

——. "Surface Explorations: 3D Moving Images as Cartographies of Time." *Espacio, Tiempo Y Forma, Serie VII, Historia del Arte* 4 (2016): 71–91.

Virilio, Paul. *Open Sky*. Translated by Julie Rose. New York: Verso, 1997.

——. *The Vision Machine*. Translated by Julie Rose. Bloomington: Indiana University Press, 1994.

——. *War and Cinema: The Logistics of Perception*. Translated by Patrick Camiller. New York: Verso, 1989.

von Sychowski, Patrick. "RoboCop's 3D Success in China Spells Trouble for Imax." Celluloid Junkie, March 12, 2014, https://celluloidjunkie.com/2014/03/12/robocops-3d-success-china-spells -trouble-imax/ (accessed September 30, 2019).

Wade, Nicholas J. *Brewster and Wheatstone on Vision*. London: Academic Press, 1983.

Walters, Ben. "The Great Leap Forward." *Sight and Sound* 19, no. 3 (2009): 38–43.

Weetch, Owen. *Expressive Spaces in Digital 3D Cinema*. Basingstoke: Palgrave, 2016.

Wheatstone, Charles. *The Scientific Papers of Sir Charles Wheatstone*. London: Taylor & Francis, 1879.

Whissel, Kristen. "Parallax Effects: Epistemology, Affect, and Digital 3D Cinema." *Journal of Visual Culture* 15, no. 2 (2016): 233–49.

——. *Parallax Effects: Stereoscopic 3D Cinema and Media*. Forthcoming.

Williams, Linda. *Screening Sex*. Durham, NC: Duke University Press, 2008.

Winston, Brian. *Technologies of Seeing: Photography, Cinematography, and Television*. London: BFI, 1996.

The Wizard of Oz. MGM, 1939.

Wolf, Mark J. P. "Z-Axis Development in the Video Game." In *The Video Game Theory Reader 2*, edited by Bernard Perron and Mark J. P. Wolf, 151–68. New York: Routledge, 2009.

World War Z. Paramount Pictures, 2013.

Wreck-It Ralph. Walt Disney Pictures, 2012.

xXx: The Return of Xander Cage. RK Films, 2017.

Zimmer, Catherine. *Surveillance Cinema*. New York: New York University Press, 2015.

Zimmerman, Michael E. *Heidegger's Confrontation with Modernity: Technology, Politics, Art*. Bloomington: Indiana University Press, 1990.

Zone, Ray. *3-D Filmmakers: Conversations with Creators of Stereoscopic Motion Pictures*. Lanham, MD: Scarecrow, 2005.

——. *3-D Revolution*. Lexington: University of Kentucky Press, 2012.

——. *Stereoscopic Cinema and the Origins of 3-D Film 1838–1952*. Lexington, KY: University of Kentucky Press, 2007.

INDEX

FILM AND CULTURE

A series of Columbia University Press

Edited by John Belton